Sport and Exercise Psychology

The INSTANT NOTES series

Series Editor: B.D. Hames, School of Biochemistry and Molecular Biology, University of Leeds, Leeds, UK

Animal Biology 2nd edition
Ecology 2nd edition
Genetics 2nd edition
Microbiology 2nd edition
Chemistry for Biologists 2nd edition
Immunology 2nd edition
Biochemistry 2nd edition
Molecular Biology 2nd edition
Neuroscience
Developmental Biology
Plant Biology
Bioinformatics
Sport and Exercise Physiology

Chemistry series
Consulting Editor: Howard Stanbury

Organic Chemistry 2nd edition
Inorganic Chemistry 2nd edition
Physical Chemistry
Medicinal Chemistry
Analytical Chemistry

Psychology series
Sub-series Editor: Hugh Wagner, Dept of Psychology, University of Central Lancashire, Preston, UK

Psychology
Cognitive Psychology
Physiological Psychology
Sport and Exercise Psychology

Forthcoming titles
Sport and Exercise Biomechanics

Sport and Exercise Psychology

D. F. Shaw

Department of Psychology, University of Central Lancashire,
Preston, UK

T. Gorely

Department of Sport and Exercise Sciences,
Loughborough University, Loughborough, UK

and

R. M. Corban

Waikato Institute of Technology, Centre for Sport and Exercise,
Hamittan, New Zealand

 BIOS Scientific Publishers
Taylor & Francis Group

A CIP catalogue record for this book is available from the British Library.

ISBN 1 85996 2947

Garland Science/BIOS Scientific Publishers
4 Park Square, Milton Park,
Abingdon, Oxon OX14 4RN, UK and

270 Madison Avenue, New York,
NY 10016, USA
World Wide Web home page: www.garlandscience.com

Garland Science/BIOS Scientific Publishers is a member of the Taylor & Francis Group

Distributed in the USA by
Fulfilment Center
Taylor & Francis
10650 Toebben Drive
Independence, KY 41051, USA
Toll Free Tel.: +1 800 634 7064; E-mail: taylorandfrancis@thomsonlearning.com

Distributed in Canada by
Taylor & Francis
74 Rolark Drive
Scarborough, Ontario M1R 4G2, Canada
Toll Free Tel.: +1 877 226 2237; E-mail: tal_fran@istar.ca

Distributed in the rest of the world by
Thomson Publishing Services
Cheriton House
North Way
Andover, Hampshire SP10 5BE, UK
Tel.: +44 (0)1264 332424; E-mail: salesorder.tandf@thomsonpublishingservices.co.uk

Library of Congress Cataloging-in-Publication Data

Shaw, D. (Dave), 1947–
    Instant notes in sport and exercise psychology/D. Shaw, T. Gorley, and R. Corban.
        p. cm.
    Includes bibliographical references and index.
    ISBN 1-85996-294-7 (pbk.: alk. paper)
      1. Sports—Psychological aspects. 2. Exercise—Psychological aspects. I. Gorley, T. (Trish)
II. Corban, R. (Rod) III. Title.

    GV706.4.S52 2005
    796.01--dc22   2004017152

Production Editor: Andrew Watts
Typeset by Phoenix Photosetting, Chatham, Kent, UK
Printed by Biddles Ltd, Guildford, UK, www.biddles.co.uk

CONTENTS

ABBREVIATIONS

16PF	16 personality factor questionnaire
ACSI-28	athletic coping skills inventory
ADNFS	Allied Dunbar National Fitness Survey
CBT	cognitive behavioral therapy
CDSII	causal dimension scale II
CPGs	central pattern generators
CSAI-2	competitive state anxiety inventory 2
CSAQ	cognitive somatic anxiety questionnaire
EEG	electroencephalograph
EPI	Eysenck personality Inventory
FFM	five-factor model
GEQ	group environment questionnaire
GMP	generalized motor program
GSR	galvanic skin response
HBM	health belief model
IPA	interaction process analysis
IZOF	individual zone of optimal functioning
KP	knowledge of performance
KR	knowledge of results
LBS	leadership behavior in sport
LGN	lateral geniculate nucleus
LIM	lifespan interaction model
LPC	least preferred co-worker
LTM	long-term memory
MIQ	movement imagery questionnaire
MRF	mental readiness form
MSCI	multidimensional sports cohesiveness inventory
MST	mental skills training
nAch	need for achievement
NHM	national history model
PANAS	positive and negative affect scale
PMR	progressive muscle relaxation
PMT	protection motivation theory
POMS	profile of mood states
PSIS-5	psychological skills inventory for sports
PST	psychological skills training
PWB	psychological well-being
REM	rapid eye movement
RET	rational emotive therapy
SAI	state anxiety inventory
SAS	sport anxiety scale
SCAT	sports competitive anxiety test
SCI	stages of change instrument
SCQ	sports cohesiveness questionnaire
SCT	social cognitive theory
SEQ	self-efficacy questionnaire
SES	socio-economic status
SIQ	sports imagery questionnaire
SIT	stress inoculation training
SMYLOG	system for the multiple level observation of groups
SOQ	sports orientation questionnaire
SR	stimulus-response
SSCI	state sport confidence inventory
SSRI	specific serotonin re-uptake inhibitor
TAI	trait anxiety inventory
TAT	thematic apperception test
TDS	telic dominance scale
TEOSQ	task and ego orientation in sport questionnaire
TMAS	Taylor manifest anxiety scale
TOPS	test of performance strategies
TPB	theory of planned behavior
TRA	theory of reasoned action
TSCI	trait sport confidence inventory
TSM	telic state measure
TTM	transtheoretical model
VIE	valence instrumentality expectancy theory

PREFACE

The popularity of sport and exercise psychology as a subject of study continues to grow. It attracts those who want to work in the expanding sport, leisure and health industries, whether in relation to the performance enhancement of competitors at one end of the continuum or to promoting exercise and healthy lifestyles in the population generally. It also attracts those who simply want to study an interesting subject.

The primary aim of the book is to provide a study guide and revision aid for sport and exercise psychology. A secondary aim is to provide some of the crucial basic psychology that underpins sport and exercise psychology that is often missing in current texts. It is our view that before you can be a good sport and/or exercise psychologist you have to become a good psychologist. With this in mind we have made it possible for the reader to access the core psychology as well as the sport and exercise specific information they need.

As the popularity of sport and exercise psychology increases, so too does the number of introductory textbooks on the subject. *Instant Notes in Sports and Exercise Psychology* takes a different approach from most of these in that it is essentially a revision aid, rather than an elaborate textbook. We have extracted from the material generally covered in sport and exercise psychology courses, those facts and theories that are essential to the student facing examinations and tests. Similarly, our illustrations, rather than being colorful pictures or cartoons, are restricted to those that aid the understanding of the material, being mostly simple line drawings presented in a way that makes them easy for the student to reproduce in course assessment situations. While this book should help the student to pass exams, for those who wish to delve deeper, we have provided specific references throughout and a further reading list of key texts for each section.

The topics covered in the book have been selected on the basis of our knowledge of sport and exercise psychology syllabuses internationally, and on our experience of many years of teaching the subject in universities in the UK, Australia and New Zealand. The book is divided into 13 sections with a total of 66 topics. Each topic begins with a Key Notes panel containing concise summaries of the central points, which are expanded in the main text of the topic. To get the most from the book, readers should first learn the material in the main text of a topic, and then use the Key Notes as a rapid revision aid. Although each topic stands alone, it is the nature of sport and exercise psychology that topics are interrelated. To help the student see these interrelationships we have provided numerous cross-references between topics.

The sections have been grouped together under the four main themes of introductory issues, sport psychology, exercise psychology and interventions.

Introductory issues are dealt with in Section A, which covers the basic theoretical approaches and research methods used in both mainstream and sport and exercise psychology. The second theme is sport psychology, consisting of sections B through G. These are organized to move from the individual to the group level of analysis. Thus, section B focuses on cognitive processes in individuals, such as perception, attention, memory, imagery, motor control and learning. Section C looks at the motivation of the athlete and outlines cognitive evaluation theory, achievement goal theory, attribution theory, self-efficacy theory and goal setting. Section D concentrates on moods and emotions in sport with an emphasis on theories of the anxiety performance relationship. Section E describes the psychology of individual differences and in particular personality and sport. The final two sections of the sport psychology theme move attention from the individual level of analysis to relationships between people and groups. Section F deals with interpersonal processes and how we perceive others, influence others and are influenced by them. It covers social cognition, conformity and compliance, obedience to authority and interpersonal aggression. Section G looks at the psychology of groups including leadership, cohesiveness, social facilitation, social loafing, group decision-making and inter-group processes.

Sections H, I and J make up the exercise theme. Section H focuses on the psychological benefits of exercise, in terms of increased mental health and well-being, and also discusses some negative consequences of exercise such as exercise dependence. In section I the focus is on what determines and motivates participation in physical activity and exercise behavior. Section J covers the various theories and models of exercise behavior.

The fourth and final theme of the book is interventions. Here we move to a consideration of practical applications in sport and exercise psychology. In section K we discuss the consultancy process, including ethical issues, athlete assessment and communication and counseling skills. In section L the focus is on performance enhancement and practical techniques to help with issues of motivation, arousal, anxiety, concentration and confidence. Finally, section M deals with issues such as stress, coping, injury, burnout, overtraining and drugs.

A1 DEFINITIONS

Key Notes

Play	Play has been defined as 'behavior for the purpose of fun and enjoyment with no utilitarian or abstract goal in mind'. It has been suggested that play might serve a number of functions including allowing us to use up surplus energy, it lets us rehearse skills, it serves a recuperative function, and it helps us to reduce anxiety.
Game	A game is 'playful competition whose outcome is determined by physical skill, strategy or chance'. In play, rules are less prevalent than in games, but the major difference between them is that the latter involves competition.
Sport	Sport is institutionalized game. This institutionalization takes four forms. Firstly, sport is highly organized in terms of governing bodies, leagues, sponsors and managers. Secondly, it involves technological developments in equipment, clothing and facilities. Thirdly, it has a symbolic dimension in the form of ceremony, ritual, display and secrecy. Lastly, it has an educational aspect. Sport also involves a degree of physicality.
Exercise	Exercise is generally thought of as any form of physical activity carried out for the purpose of health or fitness. The main difference between sport and exercise is competition. Another difference is that exercise typically does not involve the same degree of institutionalization that characterizes sport.
Psychology	Psychology is the science of behavior. However, psychologists are also concerned to explore the inner world of people, i.e. mental phenomena. These inner aspects fall into two broad categories, thinking and feeling (known in psychology as the 'cognitive–affective' distinction). Thus, we can define psychology as the scientific study of thoughts, feelings and behavior.
Sport psychology and exercise psychology	With regard to defining sport psychology and exercise psychology we can take the line of least resistance and simply define them respectively as the scientific study of thoughts, feelings and behavior in relation to either the sporting or the exercise domain. The terms sport psychology and exercise psychology are often used to mean both the basic or pure study of sport (or exercise) psychology as an academic discipline, and the application of psychology to the physical domains of sport and exercise. The former endeavor is about the pure science of doing research, including theory building and conducting investigations. The second endeavor is concerned with applied issues.
Related topic	The scientific approach (A3)

Play The term **play** comes from 'plega', the Anglo Saxon for 'to guarantee, to stand up for, to risk for a purpose'. However, most writers have viewed play as a voluntary and deliberate stepping out of real life that is characterized by spontaneity, fun, pleasure and enjoyment. Further, play is seen as lacking structure and having no obvious purpose or external goal. As such it has been defined as 'behavior for the purpose of fun and enjoyment with no utilitarian or abstract goal in mind' (Vanderswaag, 1972). There are several theories that have offered explanations for why people play. The main ones have included the notion that play serves a relaxation/recuperative function, or that it allows us to use up surplus energy, or to practice or rehearse skills as youngsters that we will need for survival as adults. In addition it affords us an opportunity to reduce anxiety by letting us confront our fears in a safe environment.

Game

The term **game** has been defined as 'any form of playful competition whose outcome is determined by physical skill, strategy or chance' (Loy, 1968). In play, rules are less prevalent than in games, but the major difference between them is that the latter involves **competition**. For example, when we are playing at 'ping pong' we are happy to knock a table tennis ball back and forward for fun without caring about the score. This is play. When we begin to keep score and compete, play becomes game.

Sport

Sport takes another step away from play in that it is characterized by a high degree of **institutionalization.** This institutionalization has been said to take four main forms. Firstly, sport is highly organized in terms of governing bodies, leagues, sponsors and managers. Secondly, it involves technological developments in equipment, clothing and facilities. Thirdly, it has a symbolic dimension in the form of ceremony, ritual, display and secrecy. Lastly, it has an educational aspect as evidenced by the presence of coaches, trainers and manuals. In view of this, sport has been defined as institutionalized game. Working backwards this gives us sport as institutionalized competitive play involving physical skill, strategy and chance (Loy, 1968). Returning to the 'ping pong' example we might say that by institutionalizing the game of table tennis it becomes a sport.

One final feature of sport is its **physical dimension**. We tend only to consider activities as sport if they involve this. For example, few would consider spelling competitions or bridge matches as sport. However, it is not always easy to draw a firm distinction on physical grounds. Thus, you might be tempted to suggest that pool, or snooker, or darts, or even golf, is not really a sport because of the minimal fitness requirements they entail. You might feel fairly safe in arguing that chess is competitive play, but is not worthy of the title sport, since it has no physical dimension. However, even in chess top players are known to spend hours practicing the movement involved in taking an opponent's piece. (This is done as a psychological ploy to make it look as if the taken piece has been annihilated.) Clearly it is not as easy as it seems to draw lines of demarcation.

Exercise

Finally there is **exercise**, which is generally thought of as any form of physical activity carried out for the purpose of health or fitness. For example, jogging, having a workout on a rowing machine or a bicycle-ergometer, walking the dog and even taking the stairs rather than the lift could all be considered exercise.

While there is much overlap between sport and exercise, in that they both involve physical activity, there is at least one crucial difference between them, and that is competition. Exercisers don't win or lose. Another difference between sport and exercise is that exercise typically does not involve the same degree of institutionalization that characterizes sport. In general, most people who go jogging are simply exercising, rather than doing institutionalized competitive running, i.e. sport. Activities that are increasingly competitive and that involve greater institutionalization move themselves along the continuum from pure exercise to sport. Having said this, just as with the game–sport distinction, drawing hard-and-fast rules is not easy and there are activities that test these definitions. For example, ballroom dancing can be seen as a sport if it is done competitively but not if engaged in at the local dancehall purely for pleasure. Similarly, most aerobics classes are not competitive in a formal way, yet there are teams of exercisers who do compete with other teams.

Psychology

Psychology has been defined in different ways throughout its short history but is generally thought of as the science of behavior, or the science of mental life. These conceptions differ only in that the latter is broader and includes a greater range of interesting phenomena. Psychologists usually wish to investigate more than merely what people do, i.e. their overt behavior. They are also concerned to explore the inner world of people, i.e. mental phenomena.

These inner aspects fall into the two broad categories of **thinking** and **feeling.** This is known in psychology as the '**cognitive–affective**' distinction. It is probably important to understand and remember this basic distinction when you begin to study psychology because if you get it clear in your mind now, it will give you useful pigeonholes that will help you in your learning, and to avoid confusion later. Psychologists use the noun **affect** to refer to the world of **feelings**, **emotions** and **moods**. Thus we might say that something that makes us feel good has produced '**positive affect**'. Similarly, '**negative affect**' is simply negative mood or emotion. However, the verb 'to affect' is also used to refer to producing an effect on something, for example, 'losing the tennis match affected her chances of selection'. In contrast to the affective (emotional) component of mental life, the **cognitive** part relates to mental activities like perceiving, learning, remembering, believing, thinking and problem-solving. In simple terms the affective–cognitive distinction is between what we feel and what we think or believe. Given this we can define psychology as the scientific study of thoughts, feelings and behavior. One important feature of the definition of psychology used here is that it puts psychology firmly in the scientific camp. This simply means that it brings the methods of scientific enquiry to the study of people. Some from the traditional sciences (e.g. chemistry, physics) think that psychology is not really worthy of being called a science. We regard this issue as somewhat unimportant, yet take the view that psychology is a science because it employs the scientific method (see Topic A3).

Sport psychology and exercise psychology

With regard to defining sport psychology and exercise psychology we can take the line of least resistance and simply define them respectively as the scientific study of thoughts, feelings and behavior in relation to either the sporting or the exercise domain.

One final clarification is that when writers use the terms sport psychology and exercise psychology they sometimes use them to mean the basic or pure study of sport or exercise psychology as an academic discipline, and at other times to mean the application of psychology to the physical domains of sport and exercise. This is because sport and exercise psychology is actually two endeavors. The first, basic research, involves the work of gaining information about the role of mental factors in physical domains. It is about the **pure science** of doing research, including theory building and conducting investigations. For example, it might be about the nature of competitive anxiety and which theory most accurately explains its effects and so on. In contrast the second endeavor is concerned with **applied science**. For example, in the case of anxiety it might be about how to control anxiety levels in order to facilitate performance. In broad terms, given the centrality of competition to sport, the applied sport psychologist's aim is to help athletes to enhance their performance. For the applied exercise psychologist the focus is likely to be on helping people to lead physically and mentally healthy lives, and increasing participation in and enjoyment from physical activity.

It will help your understanding as you learn about sport and exercise psychology if you bear in mind this distinction between sport and exercise psychology as a pure science (Sections A–J) and what we refer to here as applied sport or applied exercise psychology (Sections K–M).

A2 PSYCHOLOGY AND COMMON SENSE

Key Notes

What does psychology consist of?	Psychology is made up of several sub-disciplines. Cognitive psychology deals with perception, attention, memory, thinking and language. Developmental psychology concerns itself with how people's behavior changes as they grow older. Individual differences are about how people differ in stable and consistent ways such as intelligence and personality. Psychopathology, or abnormal psychology, focuses on psychological dysfunctions, such as addiction, depression or schizophrenia. Physiological psychology links what we know about physiology to thinking, feeling and behaving. Social psychology concerns itself with the interactions between people.
Common sense	One criticism leveled at psychology is that it is 'just common sense'. However, there are problems with common sense as a source of psychological knowledge. Firstly, common sense is often contradictory. A second major problem with common sense is that it is often simply wrong. For example, in one of psychology's all time classic studies, Stanley Milgram discovered that people behave in a totally unexpected way. In his studies on obedience to authority, he found that participants obeyed an authority figure who told them to administer extremely high levels of electric shocks to other human beings.
Related topics	Conformity and compliance (F2)

What does psychology consist of?	We have defined psychology above, but now we need to spell out more about its actual subject matter. The parent discipline of psychology is made up of several sub-disciplines. **Cognitive psychology** deals with topics like perception, attention, memory, thinking and language. **Developmental psychology** concerns itself with how people's behavior changes over time from being newborn, through childhood and adolescence, adulthood and into old age. **Individual differences** or differential psychology are about how people differ from each other in stable and consistent ways, such as intelligence and personality. **Psychopathology,** or abnormal psychology, focuses on people's coping problems and psychological dysfunctions, such as addiction, depression or schizophrenia. **Physiological psychology** links what we know about the physiology of the nervous system, endocrine system, and other systems of the body, to thinking, feeling and behaving. Finally, **social psychology** shifts the focus of the other sub-disciplines from the study of the thoughts, feelings and behavior of individuals, to the interactions between them, for example, why we like and dislike others, or how we influence each other in social situations.

In contrast to mainstream psychology the focus of sport and exercise psychology has tended to be more narrowly drawn. This is because its practitioners have been interested in the direct relevance of psychology to and applications of psychology in the world of physical activity. So, for example, it has drawn from cognitive psychology in addressing issues like the use of vision in sport, skill development, mental imagery, selective attention and concentration. Developmental psychology has provided theories and research on the development of, for example, attitudes to sport and exercise, achievement motivation, motivational style, exercise adherence and moral reasoning. Differential psychology has been the source of work on the personality of athletes and exercisers. Abnormal psychology has helped in areas like counseling, for example, for drug problems or eating disorders in exercisers, and for injury rehabilitation. In sport it has helped our understanding of competitive anxiety and the effect of mood on performance. Social psychology has been particularly fruitful for sport psychologists. It has helped in the understanding of topics such as social facilitation, aggression, confidence, leadership and group cohesion.

Common sense   One criticism leveled at psychology is that it is 'just common sense'. It is easy to see why people might think this, because we are all psychologists up to a point. However, there are problems with common sense as a source of psychological knowledge. Firstly, common sense is often contradictory. Two people can have completely opposing views and insist their view is common sense. For example, one football manager might assume that the best way to motivate players at half time is to scream at them in the changing room, another might believe that common sense dictates a calm, encouraging voice. Folk wisdom is another source of common sense that can be contradictory. For example, 'birds of a feather flock together' and 'opposites attract' are not too helpful. Similarly, 'many hands make light work' and 'too many cooks spoil the broth' are apparently common sense when expressed in isolation but clearly offer different suggestions about effective teamwork. As we can see common sense is not particularly common!

A second major problem with common sense is that it is often simply wrong. The fact that many people believe something is no guarantee of its accuracy. Science is littered with examples of counter-intuitive findings, the view that the Earth is flat being one obvious example.

The world of sports too, has its examples. A simple analysis of the value of the sacrifice bunt in baseball, has shown that on average, the bunt option scored the equivalent of 142 fewer runs per thousand occurrences, than the non-bunt option. This was despite the deeply ingrained view of the top major league managers, that it was a useful tactic (Hooke, 1972). Similarly, the use of nose plasters, to help breathing during exertion, was seen by many competitors in professional sport, including Formula 1 racing drivers, as common sense. Again, this is despite the fact that it bestows absolutely no benefit in terms of oxygen uptake.

Another interesting sporting example of the failure of common sense occurs in relation to what we might expect athletes to feel about winning medals. It seems obvious that Olympic athletes who win silver medals will be happier than those who win bronze ones, yet this does not appear to be the case. Social psychological research into the issue of 'counterfactual thinking' has shown that in fact, bronze winning athletes tend to make downward comparisons to non-medal winners and feel relatively glad. In contrast, silver medal winners tend to make upward comparisons to gold winners and feel relatively disappointed (Medvec et al., 1995). Even the apparently non-contentious wisdom, that 'practice makes perfect', turns out to be wrong, since research shows that in fact 'practice makes permanent', in that if your practice includes inefficient or incorrect movements, these will become ingrained, and are not perfect at all.

Sometimes, the passing of time shows us how wrong common sense can be. It was not so long ago, that women were not allowed to run in marathons because it was obvious that the 'poor frail dears' would harm themselves. Try telling that to Liz McColgan or Paula Radcliffe! In a similar vein, one of us remembers hearing conversations in the 1970s at a time when only a handful of black players played professional soccer in England. In these conversations the common sense view was that black players would never make it at the professional level, because they were 'skilful but not tough enough'!

In relation to psychology, common sense has been shown to be completely wrong on numerous occasions. For example, in one of psychology's all time classic studies, Stanley Milgram discovered that people behave in a totally unexpected way (Milgram, 1963). In his studies on obedience to authority, he found that participants obeyed an authority figure who told them to administer extremely high levels of electric shocks to other human beings (see Topic F2). Despite all of this, some people do still think psychology is just common sense. Spare a thought for poor sport and exercise psychologists, who are in a no-win situation. On the one hand, if they discover something that fits an athlete's world-view they may be told their findings are obvious. On the other hand, if they discover something that is counter-intuitive, the athlete may well tell them that they are talking rubbish. One example of this is the issue of team cohesiveness. It seems common sense to assume that cohesive teams, where players get on well together, will perform better. However, studies of professional teams show little evidence of such a relationship (Carron et al., 2002). Of course, with hindsight and a bit more thought, we can see why there might be no relationship. Perhaps the players are all so involved with being friends that they do not take care of the business on the field. A little further reflection and we can think of cases of professional teams that have been very successful despite consisting of players who actively disliked each other.

One famous psychologist, Kurt Lewin, became so dismayed by the way that people tended to dismiss his findings as obvious that he played a little trick on them. Around the time of the Second World War Lewin was employed by the U.S. army to bring a psychological approach to understanding military efficiency. Every six months Lewin reported his findings to the generals and every six months they told him that they knew what he told them anyway because it was common sense. On one occasion he reported to the generals and they duly told him that everything they had told him was obvious. He then revealed that he had just reported exactly the opposite of what he had actually found over the past six months!

A3 THE SCIENTIFIC APPROACH

Key Notes

The scientific approach	A central position of academic psychology and this book is that the scientific approach offers a method of inquiry that provides better answers to questions about how the world is than any other. Science has been defined as 'understanding, prediction and control above the levels achieved by unaided common sense'. It employs systematic observation, description, precise measurement, replication and testability. It should be empirical in nature. Its findings should be verifiable, cumulative, public, parsimonious, and treated with skepticism. Philosophers of science have questioned traditional views of how science is conducted. Firstly, they have argued that the starting point for the scientific process cannot be unbiased observation, since it is impossible to start without assumptions. Secondly, they claim that falsifying theories rather than verifying them should be the task of the scientist.
Measurement issues	To be effective measurement typically needs to be reliable and valid. Reliability is the extent to which the same reading is obtained each time a variable is measured. Validity is the extent to which the measure actually measures what it claims to.
Causal vs correlational research	When we simply measure, rather than manipulate variables, and look for relationships between them, we are in the realm of correlational, as opposed to causal (experimental) research. One problem with correlational designs is that we cannot infer causality from them. To do this we need to conduct experiments. When two variables, A and B, are correlated, four possibilities exist: either A caused B; or B caused A; or causality is reciprocal, i.e. there is a circular relationship where A caused B and B caused A; or finally, a third variable C, caused both A and B. It is easy to fall into the trap of assuming that because one thing follows another, that it was caused by it. This fallacy is known as 'post hoc ergo propter hoc' (after the fact therefore caused by the fact).
Related topics	Research methods (A4) Mood and performance (D2) Theoretical perspectives (A7)

The scientific approach	People get information about the world from many different sources. For example, our elders provide us with information about others in the form of 'folk knowledge' or 'the wisdom of the ages'. One problem with much of this knowledge is that it lacks the advantages of scientific rigor and is often untestable. For example, belief in a God, or ghosts, or on a more down to earth note, that one will get a pension after a lifetime of contributions to a pension fund are not easy to verify. A central position of academic psychology and this book is that the scientific approach offers a method of inquiry that provides better answers to questions about how the world is than any other. Science has been defined

as, 'understanding, prediction and control above the levels achieved by unaided common sense'. It employs systematic observation, description, precise measurement, replication and testability. Its theories help to structure experience, and to serve a heuristic function, that is they stimulate and guide further investigation. Its findings should be verifiable, cumulative, public, and parsimonious, and treated with skepticism. Finally, and crucially, as stressed by Francis Bacon in his early writings on science, it should be empirical in nature, i.e. it should be based on evidence.

Traditional views of how science is carried out suggest that scientists begin with unbiased observations, which they use to create (or 'induce' in scientific language) a theory. From this theory, they deduce specific consequences (hypotheses), which they test empirically. Finally, on the basis of the results, the theory is supported, rejected, or amended.

However, philosophers of science have questioned this traditional picture. Karl Popper has argued that the starting point for the scientific process cannot be unbiased observation, since it is impossible to start without assumptions (Popper, 1959). The scientist brings with him or her, expectations about what might be found. We will see in Topic A7 that psychologists start with different assumptions about human behavior. An amusing example of preconceived notions occurred, when, on using an early microscope, the Marquis de Plantade reported seeing tiny human beings in human semen. It is not too difficult to see, that the sport psychologist may well begin the investigation of a topic such as confidence, or mental rehearsal, with assumptions about whether it is effective or not, and how it impacts on athletes.

Popper offered a second amendment to the traditional view of science, when he argued that falsifying theories rather than verifying them was the task of the scientist. This idea was based on the logic that any number of confirming instances of an event could never prove a theory, and that the demonstration of one valid disconfirming instance was enough to disprove it. This is exemplified in the well-known 'all swans are white argument' where endless observations of white swans cannot prove the theory, yet the discovery of one black swan can disprove it.

Measurement issues

In science it is very important to measure variables effectively. Effective measurement typically means two things. Firstly, measures need to be reliable and secondly they need to be valid. **Reliability** is the extent to which the same reading is obtained each time a variable is measured. For example, we know that a tape measure will give us the same answer each time we use it to find out the circumference of a particular cricket ball. If it did not it would not be a useful measure. Similarly, in psychology, when we want to measure dispositional variables (such as trait anxiety or intelligence) we need to be sure that each time we measure these variables we get the same value. Measures that are not reliable are of little use. However, reliability alone is not enough since measures also need to be valid. **Validity** is the extent to which the measure actually measures what it claims to. Using the tape measure example, we could attempt to assess intelligence by wrapping the measure round athletes' heads and declaring their IQ in inches. This clearly falls short of a useful measure of intelligence, since we know that head size is not an indicator of intelligence. The tape measure will give reliable scores showing the same answer on subsequent readings, however, it is not a valid measure because it does not measure what it claims to measure, i.e. intelligence. This leads to the question, how do we know when something does measure what it claims to? To use the intelligence example, how do we know head circumference does not validly measure intelligence. The answer is that we can compare people's head circumference scores with their scores on other tests of intelligence. Not surprisingly, when we do this, we see no correlation. This leaves the question, how do we know that the intelligence test we used measures intelligence validly? The answer is that when intelligence tests were first developed, researchers correlated test scores with variables that might be expected to relate to intelligence, such as educational attainment, occupational status, and earnings.

Causal vs correlational research

When we simply measure, rather than manipulate variables, and look for relationships between them, we are in the realm of **correlational**, as opposed to **causal**, research. Much research in psychology is of this type. This is largely to do with the relative ease of conducting such studies and the difficulty of doing experiments. Sport and exercise psychologists also make extensive use of correlational designs in their work. For example, most studies of the relationship between anxiety and performance are of this type. Similarly, studies into the nature of exercise adherence typically measure variables that are thought to predict exercise, and then look at the extent to which they relate to subsequent exercise behavior. While much useful information comes from this type of research the problem with correlational designs is that we cannot infer causality from them. To do this we need to conduct experiments (see Topic A4).

The extent to which two variables are related can be estimated statistically and expressed as a **correlation coefficient** (r) which can range from +1 through 0 to –1. Thus, a perfect relationship between two variables has a correlation coefficient of +1. For example, there is a perfect correlation between the length of a metal bar and its temperature. In psychology we seldom see perfect correlations. In general terms, a strong relationship might be say 0.8, a weak relationship might be 0.3, and when two variables are unrelated the correlation coefficient will be zero or close to it. Negative correlations occur when higher scores on one variable are associated with lower scores on another. For example, we might expect that amount of practice and number of errors made would relate negatively.

One very important distinction in psychology is that between a situation in which one variable is the cause of another, and that in which two variables are related but not causally. An often-made mistake is to assume that correlation implies causation. When two variables, A and B, are correlated, four possibilities exist: either A caused B; or B caused A; or causality is reciprocal, i.e. there is a circular relationship where A caused B and B caused A; or finally, a third variable C caused both A and B.

For example, if we know that there is a correlation between how long a basketball player's shorts are and how many points they score, we are faced with the following possibilities. It could be that the wearing of long shorts caused high scoring. It could be that the scoring of many points causes the player to wear longer shorts. A third possibility is that both of these are true. Finally, it could be that the link is correlational rather than causal, and that a third variable explains the high scoring and the wearing of long shorts, producing a spurious correlation between them. It is fairly obvious that there is little point in rushing out and buying longer shorts in the hope of improving your shooting averages. Equally, it is unlikely that scoring highly causes us to wear long shorts. What does make sense is that there is a third variable that causes both. The third variable in this case is height. Tall players play nearer the basket, and score more points. Tall players also have longer shorts.

While this all seems clear, there are many cases in sport and exercise psychology where it is easy to fall in to the trap of assuming that correlated variables are causally related. For example, suppose we do a study and find a strong correlation, say r = 0.8, between the confidence of world-ranked tennis players before a competition and how well they then perform in the competition. In other words we have shown that the players who were low in confidence had less success than the players who were high in confidence. We might be tempted to say, and many researchers unwisely have, that it is clear that being confident causes players to be successful. However, the correlation tells us only that they are related, but not necessarily in a causal way. Being confident might cause good performance, but it could just as easily be that playing well causes us to be confident. It could be that there is a reciprocal relationship, i.e. both of these are true. Finally, it could be that there is no causal link between confidence and performance and that the relationship is a spurious one resulting from a third variable such as skill level. It is likely that one's tennis ranking is the third variable in the spurious relationship, since players who are more highly ranked at the start of a tournament are likely to feel confident, and are also likely to perform better than more lowly rated players with lower rankings. But this is because they are more skilful not because of their confidence.

Similarly, many studies using the profile of mood states (POMS) have shown that positive mood and sporting performance are correlated. This has led some to conclude that being in a good mood makes us play better. However, it is at least just as likely that if we are good players we will play well and then as a result feel in a positive mood.

This is known as the **third variable problem**. It is easy to fall in to the trap of assuming that because one thing follows another, that it was caused by it. This is a common logical fallacy, known as '**post hoc ergo propter hoc**' (after the fact therefore caused by the fact) (see Topic D2).

A4 RESEARCH METHODS

Key Notes

Experiments	Experiments manipulate one variable (the independent variable) to see what effect this has on another (the dependent variable). Experiments should be internally and externally valid. To be internally valid, the true 'between-groups' experiment needs to consist of: random allocation to groups; pre-testing; administration of the treatment to the experimental group, but not the control group; and finally, post-testing of both groups. To increase external validity, researchers employ deception and conduct field experiments. Ethical issues must be considered when designing and carrying out experiments. The value of the true experiment is that it allows strong inferences about causality.
Single-subject, multiple baseline designs	The single-subject, multiple baseline design allows the benefits of experimental rigor with the possibility of gathering individualized data of a more detailed nature. It is particularly useful in applied research with top athletes, where large numbers of experimental participants are not available. The design typically involves the staggered introduction and withdrawal of the treatment to individual athletes over a set period, during which performance is repeatedly monitored. Evidence that the technique is effective would result if performance improves in each participant following the treatment, and declines again after its cessation.
Case studies and interviewing	Case studies involve an in-depth investigation of one individual. It is useful in sport research because it allows us to explore the psychology of elite athletes who can recount what it is to be in situations of extreme pressure. Case studies are more open to the possibility of subjectivity, but they are likely to uncover a much richer picture of events. Interviews are useful for exploring the athlete's perceptions in depth. They can also be helpful, when for practical or ethical reasons; experiments are difficult or unacceptable to do. Interviews can be structured, semi-structured or open-ended depending on the nature of the information required.
Observational techniques	Observational techniques basically involve monitoring and recording behavior. They are often used when we wish to gather data unobtrusively or when we are unable to conduct experiments or interview athletes. To guard against subjective bias, two or more observers are typically employed, and their inter-rater reliability is monitored. Without other evidence it is sometimes hard to correctly interpret observed behavior. As well as being useful in their own right they are often used in combination with other methods.
Related topics	The scientific approach (A3) Theoretical perspectives (A7)

Experiments The logic behind the experimental method is that we manipulate one variable (the **independent variable**) to see what effect this has on another (the **dependent variable**). We might, for instance, be interested in whether a new relaxation audiotape would be useful for athletes who under-perform because of anxiety. We could measure the performance of a group of athletes before listening to the tape and again after it and see if there had been any overall improvement. However, even if an improvement has occurred it would not be wise to conclude that the tape had been effective, because this type of simple experiment is flawed. In the language of experiments it suffers from a lack of internal validity. Threats to **internal validity** include, among other things, **history, maturation, testing,** and **selection**. **History** refers to the possibility that something else in the environment happens between trials. For example, the stadium sound system might play calming music between testing sessions decreasing arousal in athletes, which produces better performances that had nothing to do with the relaxation tape. **Maturation** refers to the problem that arises when participants themselves change in some way between sessions. This is not a big problem when time lapse between sessions is small, but in studies over longer periods of time, athletes may just have grown bigger or stronger between time 1 and 2. **Testing** is the term used to describe the possibility that the actual taking of the test at time 1 causes people to perform differently at time 2. This could be because people learn from the first session, or become more familiar with the task, or less anxious. In sports-related tasks it is often the case that performance is better at time 2 because of '**practice effects**'. Fortunately, these can be dealt with by including a control group that does not hear the relaxation tape. What this procedure does is to control for any factors other than the experimental variable that might operate between time 1 and 2, such as fatigue, or improvements over time, because we can assume that they would apply equally to both groups. It also deals with environmental problems such as presence of others, noise, weather, etc. The use of a control group ensures that history, maturation and testing will not threaten the internal validity of the experiment, however, even with a control group there may still be problems that stem from differences between the groups. **Selection** refers to the problem that the participants in each experimental group may not have been similar to start with. The control group might just be better at the task anyway. This problem can be dealt with by randomly allocating participants to each group.

Putting this all together, to be internally valid, **the true 'between-groups' experiment** needs to consist of the following stages: random allocation to groups; pre-testing; administration of the treatment to the experimental group, but not the control group; and finally, post-testing of both groups. The '**within-groups**' equivalent of this would involve giving the treatment to all participants, as well as having them act as their own controls when no treatment was given.

As well as being internally valid, experiments need to have **external or ecological validity**. This is the extent to which findings from an experiment can be generalized to the real world. An experiment to investigate the effect of crowd noise on soccer penalty kick performance, which has a few team-mates shouting at each other as they shoot, does not generalize to the real situation of taking a kick in a professional match with 10000 rival fans behind the goal. Similarly, we could employ an experiment to look at the effect of anxiety on the performance of a hockey penalty-shooting task, but we might not be able to simulate the anxiety that a player may feel in an Olympic final. Researchers need to take care to ensure there is a degree of realism between their laboratory settings and the real world. Another threat to external validity comes from the fact that people in experiments do not always behave 'normally'. One example of this was provided in an early experiment in industrial psychology, when researchers at the Hawthorne plant of a large electrical company varied the working conditions of a group of factory employees. The researchers found initially that if they increased factory lighting levels productivity rose, and that each time they increased the illumination, performance went up. Next, they gave people longer breaks and again found that each increase in break-time was accompanied by increases in productivity. None if this is too surprising. However, the researchers were surprised to find that when they reduced the illumination and break times to levels well below initial levels productivity reached an all time high. What was learned from this was that when people are made the centre of attention they sometimes perform in unpredictable ways. This is now well known in psychology as the **'Hawthorne effect'**. Another example of how external validity can be compromised in experiments is known as the problem of **demand characteristics**.

The term demand characteristics was coined by Martin Orne (1962) to describe the situation that people find themselves in when taking part in psychological experiments. Orne argued that the demands of the experiment overcome the natural behavior of participants, and that they operate to help the experimenter by being 'good participants' and by giving the experimenter the results they think are required.

He demonstrated that participants would behave in very compliant ways in the laboratory, which did not reflect how they would behave outside the experimental situation. For example, he asked participants to engage in a meaningless task, which involved repeated cycles of crossing out the letter 'e' every time it appeared on a sheet of Greek writing, and then cutting up their work, putting it in a wastepaper bin, and starting again with another sheet. Orne set people going at the start of the day, made an excuse to leave, and waited outside the door, to see how long it would take subjects to decide the task was meaningless, and leave. At the end of the day, he had to go back in and tell people to stop, and go home! Clearly, experimenters need to be aware of this kind of problem when designing and interpreting their studies.

One of the main ways to overcome demand characteristics, and participant expectations in general, is to employ **deception.** Researchers often try to hide the true purpose of an experiment by providing cover stories to participants to prevent them from guessing what is being studied. This is obviously done with due regard to appropriate ethical safeguards (see Topic K1). Another way to minimize the problems of external (ecological) validity is to take the research out to the real world and conduct field experiments. Apart from being more ecologically appropriate, field experiments benefit from the fact that participants are not generally aware that they have been experimented upon. One final word about experiments is that we need to take steps to ensure that when we do manipulate variables, we do so in an ethical way. For example, it would not be ethical to ask players to deliberately kick or punch other players to investigate the relationship between aggression and performance! Much time and effort now goes into ensuring that experiments follow detailed ethical guidelines.

Assuming internal and external validity, the value of the **true experiment** is that it allows us to make strong inferences about **causality**. In our earlier example, a true experiment would allow us to infer that the relaxation tape, and nothing else, had caused the improvement in performance.

Single-subject, multiple base-line designs

One approach to knowledge gathering that has been used recently in sport and exercise psychology is the **single-subject, multiple baseline design** (e.g. Landin & Hebert, 1999). One of its strengths is that it can combine aspects of a more detailed analysis with some of the benefits of experimental rigor. It is particularly useful in applied research with top athletes, where we are not able to have large numbers of participants in each of the conditions of an experiment. For example, with the single-subject multiple baseline design, an intervention such as using positive imagery, could be introduced over a 3-week period to each of the top three rowers in the country (*see Fig. 1*). The design is implemented by staggering the introduction of the treatment so that after a period of say 2 weeks of measuring baseline performance in all three rowers, rower A begins to use the imagery technique for 3 weeks. After this, rower B begins the use of the technique and rower A reverts to non-use of the positive imagery. After a further three weeks, rower B reverts to non-use of the technique and rower C begins the intervention, and so on. Strong evidence that the technique is effective would result if performance improves in each rower following the intervention, and declines again after its cessation. In this way the single-subject multiple baseline design goes some way to overcoming the problems of internal validity. For example, drop in performance following cessation deals with threats to internal validity. The value of this design is that it cleverly combines aspects of the traditional positivist approach (Topic A5), with a more individualized or ideographic one (Topic A7).

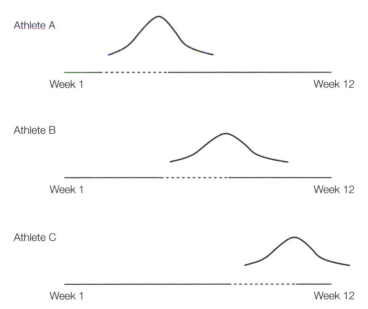

Athlete A

Week 1   Week 12

Athlete B

Week 1   Week 12

Athlete C

Week 1   Week 12

Fig. 1.   The typical single-subject multiple baseline design. In this example the length of the line might represent a 12-week-long investigation into the effectiveness of an imagery intervention. The main feature of this type of design is that the treatment is staggered. For each athlete the no-treatment period is represented by the solid line and the treatment period by the dashed line. The curved lines represent performance and in this example show strong evidence for the efficacy of the imagery intervention.

**Case studies
and interviewing**

Case studies involve an in-depth investigation of one individual. This will typically involve numerous occasions when the experiences of the participant are explored by open-ended interviewing techniques. While this approach loses the advantages of the experiment in terms of causal inferences it can provide much fruitful in-depth information. It is useful in sport research because it allows us to explore the psychology of elite athletes who can recount what it is to be in situations of extreme pressure. Clearly, in this rarefied company, experiments are not feasible, because we typically cannot have 60 such athletes to randomly allocate to an experimental and a control group! The problem with case studies is that they are more open to the possibility of subjectivity creeping in to our interpretations of the situation. On the other hand they are likely to uncover a much richer tapestry of what is going on than any experiment can. Again, we have the familiar trade off between depth and accuracy.

Interviews are used to gather information from groups as well as individuals. Often the practical or ethical problems associated with experiments make them difficult or unacceptable to do, and researchers use interviews to explore the things they are interested in. For example, much research has explored the antecedents and consequences of competitive anxiety as experienced by skilled athletes. This is typically done in unstructured or **open-ended interviews**, which allow athletes total freedom to structure their experiences in their own way as opposed to having to fit them in to a researcher's preconceived categories. Another approach to information gathering is the **structured interview**. As the name suggests structured interviews employ only preset questions, created by the researcher to fit the particular theory that he or she is testing. They are useful because they allow is to constrain the information elicited within the boundaries of interest for our research. However, they suffer from the problem that they restrict descriptions of experience. A compromise is the **semi-structured interview**, in which a set script is used, but researchers are more flexible and follow up deviations from it.

**Observational
techniques**

There are occasions when we are unable to conduct experiments or talk to athletes. There are times when we do not wish our presence to interfere with the behavior we are studying. In these circumstances researchers can employ **observational techniques**. For example, we might wish to investigate cohesion levels in a particular sports team. We could do this by observing behavior unobtrusively, and recording instances of the interactions between players, monitoring who talks to whom and how often. These observational data could be used to provide us with an index of social cohesion within the team.

To guard against subjective bias in observations, two or more observers are typically employed, and levels of inter-rater reliability are monitored statistically.

One problem with observational methods is the ethics of monitoring people without their consent. Another is that while we might generate objective data on exactly how often a particular event occurred, we run the risk of misinterpreting it. For example, when we observe a skier's hands to be shaking, prior to competing in the giant slalom, are we to assume this is an index of pre-competitive anxiety or simply that he or she is cold?

A5 THE QUALITATIVE–QUANTITATIVE ISSUE

Key Notes

The qualitative approach	Proponents of qualitative research are unhappy about the traditional approach of positivist science. They advocate a holistic approach in preference to reductionism, and a move from reliance on the experiment, to techniques such as action research, case studies, in-depth interviews, focus groups, participant observation, and discourse analysis. They also argue that positivism cannot reach the richness and depth of human experience and that what is needed is a shift in focus from research in the laboratory to research in the real world.
Quantitative vs qualitative debate	The qualitative–quantitative debate is one in which it is very easy for views to become polarized. The qualitative approach has the advantage that it provides a depth and richness of detailed information on the experience of the athlete. Furthermore, these experiences are expressed in categories that come from the athlete, rather than coming from the restricted options presented in the typical questionnaire. Another advantage claimed for the qualitative approach is that the distance that often exists between researcher and athlete is minimized. On the negative side, qualitative methods are said to increase the possibility that subjective bias might creep into the analysis. A second problem for qualitative methods is their reliance on the accounts of the participants. There is much evidence that suggests that people do not have access to, and are not always aware of, the factors which influence their thoughts, emotions and behavior.
Quantitative and qualitative research?	The two approaches have their pros and cons and the question of which is better, is one that must be considered in context. For applied work in the field, qualitative research characterized by richness and depth, in specific ecologically valid settings, would seem well suited. If the aim is to discover underlying processes and laws that govern behavior, then positivism has a great deal to offer. Another option is to use both. This might allow for a quantitative cross-checking of the more intuitive findings of qualitative analysis. Some researchers might argue against this eclectic approach, on the grounds that there is a fundamental incompatibility between the underpinning philosophies of the two approaches and that their ideas are mutually exclusive. Where the assumptions that drive the researcher are not incompatible, and where the finding will help to broaden a phenomenological understanding and deepen a positivist one, the use of both would seem fruitful.
Related topics	The scientific approach (A3) Theoretical perspectives (A7) Research methods (A4)

The qualitative approach

While it is widely held that there are many benefits to employing the scientific method, there have been some critics from within sociology and psychology who have argued that the particular brand of science that is generally employed, i.e. **positivism**, is too restrictive for the study of human behavior. They advocate a holistic approach in preference to reductionism, and a move from reliance on the experiment for data gathering. Proponents of **qualitative research** are unhappy about the traditional approach of positivist science, which takes a nomothetic, as opposed to an idiographic one. The **nomothetic approach** involves looking for general rules or laws (nomos being the Greek for law) that apply to all, rather than the **idiographic approach** which treats people as unique and is concerned with the behavior of the individual. The proponents of the qualitative approach also argue for a shift in focus from the laboratory to the real world.

Thus, the term qualitative research is a general one used to describe knowledge gathering, which employs methods that attempt to overcome the problems of adhering to a reductionist scientific model. These methods are wide ranging and include among other things, action research, participant observation, case studies, diary analysis, in-depth interviews, content analysis, and discourse analysis (which involve trying to tease out the meaning in people's accounts of their behavior). According to the phenomenologically oriented researcher, reductionist approaches may be sufficient to explain chemical reactions, but not human ones, and that to understand what it means for an individual to lose a gold medal by one hundredth of a second, we need more than an experiment. Positivism, it is argued, cannot reach the richness and depth of human experience.

Quantitative vs qualitative debate

The qualitative–quantitative debate is one in which it is very easy for views to become polarized. Proponents of the former believe that positivists engage in a shallow enterprise, employing an 'if it moves measure it' or, 'never mind the quality feel the width' approach. This has been cleverly parodied in the story of Karnap's drunk, in which the positivist approach is likened to the behavior of an inebriated man, who walks up his pathway to his house, away from the streetlight, into darkness by his front door. He fumbles with, and drops his door key. Realizing it is very dark where he is, he walks back down his garden path, and out to the street-lamp, to look for the key. The search is easier, more detailed, and more precise, under the streetlight but it is not going to produce the key. Stories on the other side of the divide are equally amusing. For example, one leading critic of positivist psychology, was reputed to have been so unhappy about numerical and statistical analyses, that he spent much of one summer unsuccessfully attempting to create a pagination system that would not require page numbers, for his forthcoming book!

The qualitative approach has the advantage that it provides a depth and richness of detailed information on the experience of the athlete. Furthermore, these experiences are expressed in categories that come from the athlete, rather than coming from the restricted options presented in the typical questionnaire. Another advantage claimed for the qualitative approach is that the distance that often exists between researcher and athlete is minimized. The focus is on real experiences of real events, rather than, as is often the case, on the behavior of handy students in experimental laboratories. Thus, it investigates real pressure, in a holistic, ecologically valid setting.

On the negative side, qualitative methods are said to increase the possibility that subjective bias might creep into the analysis. For example, the categorization stage of content analysis is clearly one in which a researcher with a phenomenological outlook could 'discover' what he or she expected to discover.

To be fair, it could be argued that the positivist puts the bias into categorization before data collection, for example, by creating rigid questionnaires that constrain answers. Qualitative researchers have taken steps to minimize these problems of bias, which include triangulation, thick description, reflexive journals, design checks, peer debriefing and audit checks.

A second problem for qualitative methods is their reliance on the accounts of the participants. While this is seen by the qualitative camp as a strength, for example, 'who knows better than the athlete?', it is viewed by the experimental psychologist as a source of enormous difficulty. This is because there is much evidence which suggests that people do not have access to, and are not always aware of, the factors which influence their thoughts, emotions and behavior. For example, they might rely on common sense to inform their judgments and as we saw in A2 this is problematic.

Quantitative and qualitative research?

As we might have guessed, the two approaches have their pros and cons and the question of which is better is one that must be considered in context. Specifically, we need to ask: better for what? If the answer to that question is for applied field research to assist athletes, then, given the fact that qualitative research is characterized by richness and depth, in specific ecologically valid settings, it would seem obvious that it is well suited to intervention. This is especially true if the particular qualitative method used employed some form of the action research spiral in which the stages of problem identification, trial solution, and evaluation were repeated. Action research refers to an approach to solving social problems that actively includes the problem holders in the social research process. The joint problem-solving nature of action research is also particularly important in intervention research. This is not just because of the likelihood of greater ownership, and commitment to any possible solution, but also because it is likely to lead to a wider, and better, solution search, by the research team. On the other hand, if the aim is to discover underlying processes and laws that govern behavior, thinking and affect, then positivism has a great deal to offer.

One other tempting option is to avoid choosing between approaches and to use both. This multi-method approach has been argued for and carried out, in the work of many sport and exercise psychologists in recent years (Johnson et al., 1999). One strength of a joint approach might be that it allows for a quantitative cross-checking of the more intuitive findings of qualitative analysis (it is not unheard of for people to swear by the efficacy of weird and wonderful remedies which are unlikely to have a real effect, such as faith healing).

However, some researchers might argue against this eclectic approach, on the grounds that there is a fundamental incompatibility between the underpinning philosophies of the two approaches and that their ideas are mutually exclusive. If you believe positivism is flawed because, for example, it puts the researcher in the power role, which alters the subject's behavior and so the findings are not worth having, there is little way forward for you than to take a more phenomenological stance on the data. Equally, the experimentalist might argue that since we can be sure people cannot accurately access their decision processes, there is little point in trusting their opinions, even if you are sure they were honestly held ones. Where the assumptions that drive the researcher are not incompatible, and where the finding will help to broaden a phenomenological understanding and deepen a positivist one, the use of both would seem fruitful.

A6 THE HISTORY OF PSYCHOLOGY

Key Notes

Psychology's beginnings	Scientific psychology began at the end of the 19th century and grew out of British empiricism and German physiology. At the beginning of the 20th century two major approaches, psychoanalysis and behaviorism emerged. Psychoanalytic theory was developed by Freud, and focused on the unconscious forces that drive behavior. It suffered from being counterintuitive and difficult to test and is no longer influential in psychology. Behaviorism was developed by J.B. Watson, who argued that psychology should only take observable behavior into account. In the 1950s and 1960s humanistic psychology emerged with its emphasis on people as higher beings with a desire for self-actualization; two of its most prominent figures being Abraham Maslow and Carl Rogers. The 1960s saw the beginning of cognitive psychology, in which people were viewed as complex processors of information who made active decisions based on their interpretations of situations. Cognitive psychology is the dominant approach used by most academic psychologists today.
History of sport and exercise psychology	Sport and exercise psychology's first experiment was carried out in the late 1890s by Norman Triplett on social facilitation. One of the first sport psychology laboratories was set up in 1925 by Coleman Roberts-Griffith, the 'father of sport psychology'. Early research focused on motor skills. Despite its early beginnings, sport psychology did not have much impact until the 1960s when there was some work on need for achievement theory. The 1970s saw the emergence of research on mental rehearsal, goal-setting, cohesiveness and leadership. In the 1980s research on confidence, anxiety, attribution theory, achievement goals and exercise began to flourish. Exercise psychology began to be influential in the mid 1980s. In part this was driven by the need to explain why around 50% of people who begin to exercise soon drop out. Dishman's 'Exercise Adherence', published in 1988, is a milestone marking the emergence of a wider interest in exercise psychology. The 1990s saw strong growth in the area.
Related topics	The scientific approach (A3) Theoretical perspectives (A7) Research methods (A4) The qualitative–quantitative issue (A5)

Psychology's beginnings

It is said that those ignorant of history are doomed to repeat its mistakes, and it is therefore important to have some idea about how we got to where we are in sport and exercise psychology. However, this is not a history book and therefore as a compromise we offer a very brief overview of psychology's past generally, and of its relevance to sport and exercise settings in particular.

Scientific psychology was born in the last quarter of the 19th century from a marriage between British empiricism and German physiology. **Empiricism** is the doctrine that knowledge comes from experience and observation, rather than being either inborn, or a product of rational thought. Empiricism was promoted initially by the philosopher John Locke, and built upon by David Hume. It was Locke who famously claimed that, at birth, the mind is a '**tabula rasa**' or blank slate, on which experience is written. Empiricist ideas, in combination with the sensory physiology of Helmholtz and Fechner's psychophysics, marked psychology's beginnings. Two schools of thought, structuralism and functionalism, marked this early stage in psychology's history. **Structuralism** as the name suggests, focused on the basic structure of the mind. It sought to do for psychology what physicists and chemists had done for the traditional sciences. Just as traditional science described the building blocks and structure of the physical world in terms of atoms, molecules and the chemical elements, so the structuralists employed the method of **introspection** to explore how basic sensations were combined to create complex perceptions. The method of introspection, developed by Wilhelm Wundt, involves looking inward to one's own mind and reporting on one's mental processes. It requires us to simultaneously experience the environment around us, and analyze and describe its effect on our perceptions. In this way it was assumed we could find out about the structure of the mind and how it worked. Although introspectionism was soon to be discredited for being unscientific, and subsequently ignored throughout most of the 20th century, it is interesting to see it making something of a comeback in the more qualitative approaches of some current psychologists.

In contrast to structuralism and as something of a reaction to it, **functionalism** focused on process, and what function or purpose behavior served. Functionalism was heavily influenced by Darwin's theory of evolution, which gave a central role to the functional significance of an animal's attributes or behaviors to its survival prospects. The main proponent of functionalism was William James who in 1890 published his classic book the 'Principles of Psychology'. At the beginning of the 20th century two major approaches to psychology blossomed and led to the demise of structuralism and introspectionism. The two schools were psychoanalytic psychology (or depth psychology) and behaviorism.

Psychoanalytic psychology (see Topic A7) was developed by Freud, and focused on the unconscious forces that drive behavior. It was always controversial in that it was counterintuitive and difficult to test. Although it still has its proponents it is not now a major part of either mainstream psychology or sport and exercise psychology.

The other major development in psychology that occurred in the early 20th century was **behaviorism** (see Topic A7), which was developed by J.B. Watson. A basic tenet of behaviorism is that in studying people it is only legitimate to take observable behavior into account. This disqualified mentalistic concepts like 'mind' and 'thinking' which were excluded because they could not be seen. What was appropriate, according to Watson, was the investigation of the link between a stimulus and the response to that stimulus (Watson, 1913).

Much of the 20th century was dominated by behaviorism, and to a lesser extent the psychoanalytic approach. However, in the 1950s and 1960s **humanistic psychology** emerged as a reaction to the prevailing mechanistic 'models of people' (see Topic A7). Here the emphasis was on people as higher beings, in comparison to other animals. The focus was also on human free will (rather than deterministic inevitability), human creativity, and the desire people have to achieve their potential (Maslow, 1954). Humanistic psychologists saw a more positive side to human nature than the somewhat negative one that psychoanalytic psychologists described (see Topic A7). In the 1960s a new set of assumptions about human behavior began to gain ground. These prompted the start of the '**cognitive revolution**'. At the time psychologists had begun to be unhappy about the current 'model of people' that prevailed. They felt it was too restrictive and could not account for the complexity of human activity (Neisser, 1976). **Cognitive psychology** saw people as complex processors of information, rather like computers. At the beginning of the 21st century cognitive psychology is still the dominant approach of most academic psychologists. However, recent trends in some quarters have included an interest in a more **qualitative** approach to finding out what makes people tick (see Topic A5). This means a move away from the use of experiments, and numerical data collection and analysis to gathering accounts and analyzing what people say (Hayes, 1997). This has been stimulated by a disappointment in some, that the precision of the experimental approach inevitably means a loss of depth and an inability to look at real world issues (i.e. it suffers from a lack of ecological validity (see Topic A4)). For example, if we want to know what effect confidence has on elite athletic performance we might be better served by asking top athletes about it, than by doing experiments on lesser athletes. (For obvious practical and ethical reasons we cannot expect top athletes to risk having their chances of winning being affected by participation in an experiment.)

A second trend in modern psychology has been the strengthening of the **biopsychological** perspective (Topic A7). This has been evident in a growth of evolutionary psychology and in neuropsychological research.

History of sport and exercise psychology

As far as sport and exercise psychology is concerned, despite the volume of research activity being relatively small in comparison to mainstream psychology, it has been represented from the beginning in the work of Triplett (1897) on social facilitation and Ringelmann (1913) on social loafing. In the late 1890s, Norman Triplett was interested in the observation that cyclists who rode together cycled faster than if they were alone. He knew this was not simply a slipstreaming effect because it happened even when riders rode side by side. Triplet decided to investigate this phenomenon, which he believed was due to 'psychogenic factors', in a systematic way by asking small boys to wind fishing reels either together or alone, using a specially devised rig which measured speed of winding. As we might expect, he found that winding was done faster in company than alone. This work prompted much investigation into the phenomenon we now call social facilitation covered in Topic G2. A second major milestone in the history of sport and exercise psychology occurred at the University of Illinois in 1925. It was here that **Coleman Roberts-Griffith** opened the first dedicated sport psychology laboratories. Roberts-Griffith, among other things, studied the nature of skill and its development, and the relationship between personality and sport. Laboratories had also been set up at much the same time in Berlin, by Sippel and by Schute, but it is Roberts-Griffith who is generally credited with being the 'father of sport psychology'. Despite having established laboratories in the 1920s, sport and exercise psychology remained a fairly restricted activity for the next 40 years, focusing largely but not entirely, on motor skills. However, the early 1960s saw work from mainstream psychology, on **need for achievement theory** (nAch), being picked up as potentially relevant by sport psychologists.

Psychologists interested in physical activity had also begun to make more use of behaviorist approaches to learning (Topic A7), in the form of **classical and instrumental conditioning** and had extended the research on social facilitation. However, it was not until the so-called cognitive revolution that sport and exercise psychologists began to invoke mental constructs in their work. Thus, in the 1970s we saw research on imagery, and in particular, on mental rehearsal (Topic B6). Another boost to sport and exercise psychology came from the findings of research into work motivation in the late 1970s. In particular, sport and exercise psychologists made extensive use of the goal-setting principles outlined in **Goal Setting Theory** by Edwin Locke (Latham & Locke, 1979). He also borrowed from research on cohesiveness and leadership because of their obvious relevance to teams.

During the 1980s work began on a widening sample of psychological areas, which related to sport, including confidence, anxiety, attribution theory, attentional focus and exercise. Confidence research was boosted by the seminal work of Albert Bandura (1977) on self-efficacy (see Topic C5). Anxiety was clearly another area that was closely tied to performance in sport, and researchers drew from work in educational psychology on test anxiety to inform their work on competitive anxiety. Studies of classroom achievement were also the inspiration for the particularly rich seam of research in sport psychology on achievement goals.

In relation to exercise psychology, although there had long been an interest in its effect on mental well being, it was not until the mid 1980s that it began to be more widely studied. One of the driving forces for this came from the need to explain why, at a time when the health benefits of exercise were becoming more apparent, it was found that typically around 50% of people who began to exercise quickly dropped out. Dishman's 'Exercise Adherence', published in 1988, can be seen as a milestone marking the emergence of a much wider interest in exercise psychology. The 1990s saw strong growth in the area, as indicated by the increase in the number of active researchers and the amount of published output. Indeed in the early 1990s the British Association of Sport Sciences changed its name to become the British Association of Sport and Exercise Sciences.

At the beginning of the new millennium sport and exercise psychology continues to flourish. We find ourselves with an increasing body of solid theory and empirical evidence in a wide range of areas, as reflected in the topics of this book.

On the applied side, more and more athletes, coaches, governing bodies and health professionals are turning to psychology for answers to a wide range of practical problems, including anxiety control, concentration, confidence and motivation (see Sections L and M). As a result, more and more people are being employed to deliver solutions to these problems. There can be little doubt that the first decade of the 21st century is an exciting time to be interested in the psychology of physical activity.

A7 THEORETICAL PERSPECTIVES

Key Notes

Perspectives in psychology	Unlike older sciences, where there is reasonable agreement on what constitutes the main theory in each area, psychology is characterized by several schools of thought or perspectives. Each perspective has its own set of assumptions about what people are like, i.e. it has its own implicit 'model of people'. While it might appear somewhat problematic for a science to have these differences of opinion, especially when some of these differences are mutually exclusive, it can be argued that this is not necessarily a bad thing. Perhaps multiple perspectives allow us a broader understanding of why people do the things they do, since each offers a complementary, rather than simply a competing view.
Biopsychological perspective	This perspective takes the view that the best way to explain human behavior is to investigate its biological basis. This includes the reductionist approach that focuses on the detailed psychophysiology of the nervous system, and the evolutionary psychology that has built upon the ideas of Charles Darwin. Biopsychology assumes that human behavior is best explained in the same terms as those used for lower animals. It also assumes a strong role for heredity and genetic influences on behavior. The biopsychological approach continues to grow in influence in psychology.
Psychoanalytic (depth) perspective	Psychoanalytic theory suggests that unconscious processes drive behavior. In Freud's view the mind consisted of three parts. The id was said to be impulsive, and selfish, consisting of two innate drives, sex and aggression. The superego, is the conscience, and it develops as we learn society's rules. The ego, concerns itself with the world as it is experienced. The mind is characterized by a constant conflict in which the ego tries to balance the demands of the id and the superego. The method favored by Freud for investigating the mind is 'free association'. Freud believed dreams reveal unconscious wishes. Freudian theory has been heavily criticized in scientific psychology, because the theory is not always testable. One idea that has endured is the notion of the defense mechanism.
Behaviorist perspective	Behaviorism was the brainchild of J.B. Watson who argued that to be truly scientific, psychologists should study overt behavior not thoughts or feelings (Watson, 1913). Watson asked what observable stimulus (S) could be associated with what observable response (R)? For behaviorism the environment determines behavior. Behaviorism is mechanistic. It denies free will and claims that we respond to the environment. Behaviorism is underpinned by Pavlov's work on the conditioned reflex, and by Skinner's ideas on operant conditioning and instrumental learning.
The humanistic perspective	The humanistic/phenomenological approach stresses the higher functions of humans. The founding father of humanistic psychology was Abraham Maslow, who suggested the need hierarchy theory of human motivation.

Self-actualization (the need to realize one's potential) is central to humanistic psychology as is the notion of free will. Humanistic psychology takes a phenomenological approach. Phenomenology is the belief that each person has their own view of the world around them, and that if we want to understand human action we have to find out what each individual's perspective is. Rather than doing experiments, the humanistic psychologist asks people why they did what they did. Humanistic psychology has had its biggest influence in counseling and psychotherapy.

| **The cognitive perspective** | Cognitive psychology sees human beings as complex, thinking beings who process and interpret information and make decisions about the situations they are in. Unlike behaviorism, cognitive psychology is willing to look inside the black box and deal in mental or abstract constructs, such as beliefs or feelings or memory stores. It differs from the humanistic perspective, in that it adopts a positivist approach, employs experiments and uses nomothetic as opposed to the ideographic methods. As such, cognitive psychology sees people as more like complex computers than environmental ping-pong balls. |

Related topic   Achievement goal theory (C3)

Perspectives in psychology

Unlike older sciences such as physics or chemistry, where there is reasonable agreement on what constitutes the main theory in each area, psychology is characterized by several schools of thought or **perspectives**. This is because psychology is still a relatively young science attempting to deal with differing views about the underlying causes of, and explanations for human action. Each perspective has its own set of assumptions about what people are like, i.e. it has its own implicit '**model of people**'. For example, perspectives differ on whether or not people have **free will**: whether or not they are basically selfish; whether or not they are similar to animals; whether or not behavior is influenced principally by nature or nurture, and so on. Proponents of one perspective rarely agree with those of different perspectives.

While it might appear somewhat problematic for a science to have these differences of opinion, especially when some of these differences are mutually exclusive, there are some who argue that this is not necessarily a bad thing. They suggest that multiple perspectives allow us a broader understanding of why people do the things they do, since each offers a complementary, rather than simply a competing view. The main perspectives in psychology is outlined below. Following this, the way each approach explains behavior will be illustrated by suggesting how it might account for the aggression of a soccer player who head-butts an opponent who has just tackled him. In this way you will be able to see how different perspectives have a different focus and offer different explanations for the same behavior.

Biopsychological perspective

As the name suggests this perspective takes the view that the best way to explain human behavior is to investigate its biological basis. This includes the **reductionist** approach (reductionism in this context is the belief that we can reduce behavior to its basic elements in neurochemistry) that focuses on the detailed psychophysiology of the nervous system, and the **evolutionary psychology** that has built upon the ideas of Charles Darwin. **Biopsychology** takes it as read that the best way to understand human behavior is to explain it in the same terms as those used for lower animals. For example, it would assume that the same basic mechanism would explain the memory or thought processes of both a human and a rabbit.

Biopsychology also assumes a strong role for heredity and genetic influences on behavior. The biopsychological approach has grown in popularity over the last decade as a result of several factors. Firstly, the measurement techniques that are now being employed in neuropsychological research have improved, and computers have made these measurements easier to obtain. The likelihood is that this will continue as more and more use is made of non-invasive brain-imaging techniques such as magnetic resonance imaging, and functional magnetic resonance imaging.

A second factor that has helped the growth in biopsychology has been a renewed interest in the application of **Darwinian** ideas to behavior, under the new label evolutionary psychology. This is probably due in part to a swing in the pendulum away from the environmental explanations for behavior that have dominated previous decades.

Finally, the increased success that has been achieved in recent years using pharmacological treatments for psychological problems has given extra credence to the biopsychological perspective. For example, specific serotonin re-uptake inhibitors (SSRIs) such as Prozac, have been hugely successful in alleviating problems as diverse as anxiety, obsessive compulsive disorder and depression.

How might the biopsychological perspective explain aggression? Consider the previously mentioned example of the soccer player who, following a tackle by an opponent, head-butts that opponent. The biopsychologist will undoubt-edly turn to Darwin's notion of **'survival of the fittest'** to argue that those humans who responded with aggression to the prehistoric environment were more likely to survive and pass on their aggressiveness trait to their offspring, while those humans who did not respond aggressively were less likely to survive. The biopsychologist will tend to stress the innate genetic basis of the aggressive behavior and the role of arousal in energizing responses that ignore learned restraints.

Psychoanalytic (depth) perspective

The main thrust of Freud's **psychoanalytic theory** (sometimes known as the depth approach) is that much of our behavior is driven by **unconscious processes**. Freud suggested that the mind was made up of three separate parts: the **id**, the **ego**, and the **superego**. The id was said to be impulsive, and selfish, consisting of two innate drives, namely sex and aggression that seek immediate gratification. The id operates on what Freud called the 'pleasure principle'. A second part of the mind according to Freud is the superego, which is said to develop as we learn and internalize society's rules about right and wrong. In common parlance this is the conscience. In Freud's view the superego is as unrealistic as the id, putting 'right' before everything, including even concern for self. In contrast the third part of the mind, the ego, is said to operate on the 'reality principle' and concerns itself with the world as it is experienced.

Putting this together, the mind is characterized by a constant conflict in which the ego tries to balance the demands of the id and the superego. For Freud most of what is going on for people is unconscious, with the conscious mind being just the tip of the iceberg. The mind in Freudian theory has been characterized amusingly, but not particularly sympathetically, as a dark cellar in which there is a constant battle between 'a spinster' and a 'sex-crazed monkey' being overseen by a 'nervous bank manager'. Freud argued that if we want to understand someone's behavior we will need to delve deep into their subconscious mind. The method favored by Freud for this is what he called '**free association**', which meant his clients lay on his couch and talked about whatever came to mind. The outpourings thus generated are then interpreted by the analyst who 'understands' their underlying 'real' significance. Another way to get at this inner life, according to Freud, is through analysis of dreams, which he said reflected unconscious wishes. Freudian theory has been the subject of much criticism within scientific psychology, not least because many of the central tenets of the theory are not testable. Modern psychology makes little use of psychoanalysis, and for most psychologists Freudian theory is largely of only historical value. There is no doubt that Freud came up with an elegant and complicated account of why people do the things they do even if we now seriously question its accuracy. However, he did make us aware that there is an unconscious aspect to mental life, even if he overstated the case. One interesting idea developed by Freud that has endured, despite mixed evidence, is the notion of the **defense mechanism**. Freud argued that the ego experiences threat – from the id, the superego and from reality itself – which it copes with by using 'defense mechanisms' such as denial, regression and projection. **Denial** occurs when the consequences of believing something bad are too traumatic for us to acknowledge to ourselves, so we push it into the subconscious mind. A sporting example might be when an athlete gets a career-ending injury that they cannot cope with, and they appear not to take on board the reality of the situation. **Regression** is said to occur when one's behavior is more in keeping with earlier stages of development, sometimes caused by frustration, for example, bursting into tears when trivial things go wrong. The argument is that by regressing we protect ourselves from having to face things in an adult way. **Projection** is said to occur when we defend the ego from the realization of something bad in us by suggesting that the bad thing is in others. For example, we might project our own selfish play on the sports field, by accusing a teammate of hogging the ball.

To explain the aggression of the head-butting soccer player, the psychoanalytic theorist, like the biopsychologist, is likely to invoke notions of **instinctual** aggression. However, for the psychoanalytically inclined psychologist, the aggression will be attributed to a build up of instinctual aggressive energy over time, that is released and thereby reduced, by the act of aggression.

Behaviorist perspective

Behaviorism was the brainchild of the American psychologist J.B. Watson who was convinced that to be truly scientific, psychologists should study only what could be seen, i.e. overt behavior and not internal events like thoughts or feelings, memories or ideas (Watson, 1913). Watson was unhappy with what he perceived to be the 'woolly' mentalistic concepts of previous approaches. For him the only legitimate object of study was overt behavior. Thus, to explain a person's response (R), or behavior, one needed to ask what stimulus (S) had caused it. Thus, behaviorism is also known as **stimulus–response** (S–R) psychology. Watson asked what observable stimulus could be associated with what observable response? In this way the mind was conceived of as a black box, the contents of which were not the legitimate concern of science. According to behaviorism the environment determines behavior, and to change behavior we need to change environments. This produces a very mechanistic view of people. It denies free will, and the possibility that we do things because we choose to. Rather its claim is that we do them because the environment made us. These ideas were underpinned by the Russian physiologist Ivan Pavlov's well-known 'salivating dogs' experiments. Pavlov showed how stimulus and response could be combined experimentally in the **conditioned reflex**. Pavlov gave us a basic building block of learning in the form of **classical conditioning**. This involves the association of a natural behavior such as salivating, with a new and initially neutral stimulus, for example, the sound of a bell. In a later development of behaviorism, Skinner promoted the idea of **operant conditioning** to explain **instrumental learning** in which rewards dictate what connections are made between stimulus and response (Skinner, 1938). The classic example of this was the way in which hungry rats learned to press a lever in a **Skinner Box**, to get the reward of a food pellet. Behaviorists have spent much time exploring the fine detail of rewards and punishments and the effect of various reinforcement schedules on behavior.

With regard to explaining aggression, the behaviorist might focus on the past reinforcement experiences of the aggressive athlete. For example, they would probably argue that the player who head-butts an opponent is likely to have been rewarded in the past for being aggressive. They might suggest that previous aggressiveness intimidated opponents and reduced opponent's determination to win, leading to positive outcomes for the aggressor. Similarly, the behaviorist might explain non-aggressive behavior in some players as being due to having learned that it led to negative consequences, especially if you were a small or weak player!

The humanistic perspective

The **humanistic** approach centers on the view that humans are special animals. The humanistic psychologist stresses those aspects of human thinking, emotion and behavior that make us different from other species. For example, they cite human intelligence, creativity and the ability to use complex language as evidence of the huge gap between us and the rest of the animal kingdom. They also point to the fact that we are the only beings who appear to exhibit **reflexivity**, e.g. we think about our own thinking.

The founding father of humanistic psychology was Abraham Maslow, who suggested that human needs could be viewed as a hierarchical pyramid, having basic needs at the bottom such as physiological needs for food and water, and needs for safety, up through love and esteem needs to **self-actualization** at the top (Maslow, 1954). It was the importance of this need for self-actualization, the need to realize one's potential or to make actual what is potential, that was central to humanistic psychology and much of what has been written under the humanistic banner has focused on self-actualization.

The humanistic perspective does not see human action as driven by hidden forces (psychoanalytic perspective) or past experiences (behaviorist perspective) but as something chosen on a rational basis. People have free will, decide what they want to do and given the chance, will display creativity and be motivated to achieve their potential whatever that might be. In humanistic psychology, personal growth is emphasized. In terms of finding why people do the things they do, humanistic psychology prefers to take a phenomenological approach. **Phenomenology** is the belief that each person has their own unique view of the world around them, and that if we want to understand human action we have to find out what each individual's perspective is. In practice this means that rather than doing experiments as the positivist would, the humanistic psychologist resorts to the obvious approach of asking people why they did what they did. This is because of what they see as the falseness of the experimental situation. They believe that experiments cannot access the richness of human experience and the diversity inherent in people. Thus, not only does the humanistic approach see humans as very different from other species, it also sees each person as unique, and not easily categorized in to pigeonholes. Not surprisingly, humanistic psychology has had its biggest influence in clinical settings in relation to counseling and psychotherapy. Another leading proponent of this humanistic approach was Carl Rogers, who is famous for his work helping people to reach their highest potential using a therapeutic technique called client-centered therapy (Rogers, 1951) (see Topic K5).

The phenomenologically oriented psychologist would possibly see the aggression of the soccer player as a failure to understanding that winning is not all important and that playing as well as you can is the essence of achieving. This echoes a distinction that is made later in terms of task and ego orientation in sport (see Topic C3). A humanistic interpretation of the head-butt situation might stress the meaning of the act of aggression for the aggressor. For example, the act of aggression might be one player's attempt to maintain a positive image of self, and might serve to say 'I am tough, I don't put up with that from anyone'.

The cognitive perspective

Cognitive psychology sees human beings in a much less passive light than behaviorism. It argues that people are not just pushed into a response by environmental events and stimuli, like some kind of table tennis ball, but rather are active in decision-making. It also argues that behaviorism's **stimulus–response chains** and **reinforcement schedules** cannot explain novel or creative behavior (Neisser, 1976). Like the humanistic perspective, it regards people as complex thinking beings who interpret the situations in which they find themselves. However, unlike the humanistic perspective, it is happy to adopt a **positivist approach**, employ experiments and use **nomothetic** as opposed to the **idiographic methods** (i.e. deal in the aggregate scores of groups as opposed to treating each individual as unique). Unlike behaviorism, cognitive psychology is willing to look inside the black box and deal in mental or abstract constructs, such as beliefs or feelings. One central construct employed in the cognitive approach is the **schema** (plural schemata) (see Topic F1). A schema is an organized mental framework that contains our personal knowledge about the world around us (including people, objects and events). Cognitive psychology is also willing to consider psychological structures like **memory stores** or **central executive processors**. As such, cognitive psychology sees people as more like complex computers than environmental ping-pong balls. This shift in perspective or '**cognitive revolution**' freed psychologists to investigate mental life more broadly and in a much less restricted way. As a result of this, we now have a very complex understanding of the intricacies of the processes involved in, for example, visual perception, memory systems, decision making, motor control and so on.

With regard to explaining our aggressive footballer's behavior, the cognitive theorist will focus on the way in which the situation was interpreted, rather than just on the reinforcement pattern that followed previous aggression. For example, classic research on aggression has shown that children imitated the aggressive actions of adults who modeled aggressive behavior. Thus, aggression occurred in the absence of reward, as a result of the children's cognitive interpretation of the situation.

Not much more will be said here about the cognitive perspective because it underpins much of what is now taught in mainstream and sport psychology. It is currently the most widely held perspective. However, as you will see as you read more widely, all of the above perspectives continue to contribute to some extent to our understanding of human behavior.

A summary of the different theoretical perspectives employed in psychology is given in Table 1.

Table 1.   The major perspectives in psychology

	Biopsychological	Psycho-analytic	Behaviorist	Cognitive	Humanistic/phenomenological
Major figures	Darwin	Freud	Watson Skinner Pavlov	Neiser Bandura	Maslow Rogers Kelly Harre
Originated period of major influence	1860s But recent resurgence	1890s Waned through 20th century	1913 Strong until the 1960s then waned but still widely held	Late 1960s Gradually superseded behaviorism Still strong	1950s But gentle resurgence as the qualitative approach since 1970s
Explanatory mechanisms and concepts	Natural selection Fitness Genes Competition Neurochemistry Neuroanatomy	Inter-psychic conflict Unconscious drives	Reinforcement Law of effect Stimulus–response bonds	Information processing Computer	Human potential Self-actualization Uniqueness
Motivated by	Instincts Survival	Instincts Sex Aggression	Rewards Punishment	Interpretations of situations Schemata	Need to self actualize
Preferred method	Observation Lesions Drug action	Case study Ideographic	Experiment Nomothetic	Experiment Nomothetic	Case study/discourse analysis Ideographic
Free will?	No	No?	No	Maybe	Yes
Role of learning	Low	Mixed	High	Mixed	High
Relative influence of personality and situation	Both?	Personality More	Situation More	Both	Personality more
Analogy employed	Clever animal	Reservoir of energy	Blank slate Automaton	Computer	Actualized being
People are active/passive	Passive	Passive	Passive	Active?	Active
Preferred method of therapy	Drugs	Analysis	Aversion therapy/conditioning	Cognitive behavioral therapy	Psychotherapy client-centered
Scientific standing	High	Low	High	High	Low

Please remember as you read the table that it paints a very general picture that would gain a measure of agreement on many issues from most psychologists, but would probably cause strong argument between some of them on others. Despite this it should help you to get a broad appreciation and understanding of the different biases that psychologists bring to the study of people. The table reiterates the point, made at the beginning of this topic, that unlike older sciences, where there is reasonable agreement on basic assumptions, psychology is characterized by several schools of thought or perspectives. This is because psychology is a fairly young science, still dealing with differing views about the underlying causes of and explanation for human action. This is not necessarily a bad thing. Indeed, it is the view of some that having a multiple perspective approach allows us a broader understanding of why people do the things they do, since each affords a complementary rather than simply a competing view. What has been said about psychology being a young science is even truer for sport and exercise psychology. For this reason the well-worn phrase 'more research is needed' is appropriate for many of the topics covered in this book.

B1 VISION

Key Notes

Vision in sport	It is clearly evident that in most sports there is a heavy reliance on visual input for successful performance. Thus it is important that the sport psychologist has at least a basic understanding of how the visual system works.
The eye	The retina of the eye contains two types of light sensitive cells called photoreceptors that are referred to as rods and cones. The majority of cones are located in the central area of the retina called the fovea, while rods dominate the peripheral regions of the retina. Rods and cones differ in their sensitivity to light and are responsible for different visual function. Rods operate at lower light levels and are achromatic (black and white) whereas cones operate at normal daylight levels and are involved in color vision.
The visual pathway	The optic nerve carries information away from the eye to the areas of the brain responsible for the processing of visual information. This information travels via the lateral geniculate nucleus to the visual cortex situated in the occipital area of the brain. From here information is sent to other areas of the brain for more detailed processing.
Visual abilities	Visual abilities can be assessed using a variety of tests. These tests are usually static tests of abilities that are assumed to be important for athletes such as visual acuity and depth perception. Central vision has the highest acuity and is thus ideally suited for performing tasks that need high resolution of the visual image, whereas peripheral vision is suited for rapidly identifying where objects are and how fast they are moving (or how fast the observer is moving). This information can then be used to initiate a response at the precise time to intercept an object.
Generalized visual skills in athletes	There is no evidence to suggest that athletes differ on tests of visual abilities. However, it is unclear whether tests of generalized visual abilities are adequate in investigating skill differences.
Related topics	Indirect and direct theories of Memory and decision making in motor control (B2) sport (B5)

Vision in sport

The eye is regarded as the most important source of sensory input, which is demonstrated by the fact that over 30% of the brain is dedicated to processing visual information. It is clearly evident that in most sports there is a heavy reliance on visual input for successful performance. For instance athletes are often required to perform in dynamic visual environments that are cluttered with information: athletes are required to pick up fast-moving and often changing images. Thus it is important that the sport psychologist has at least a basic understanding of how the visual system works.

The eye

The eye consists of two types of light-sensitive cells located on the **retina** called **photoreceptors** that are referred to as **rods** and **cones**. The majority of cones are located in the central area of the retina called the **fovea**, while rods dominate the **peripheral** (**extrafoveal**) regions of the retina. Both types of photoreceptor cells are connected to the optic nerve via a layer of **bipolar** cells and **ganglion** cells, with lateral connections being made through **amacrine** and **horizontal** cells. Light passes through the outer layer of the retina before reaching the photoreceptors from where image leaves the eye via the optic nerve.

Rods and cones differ in their sensitivity to light and are responsible for different aspects of visual function. Rods operate at lower light levels and are achromatic (black and white) whereas cones operate at normal daylight levels and are involved in color vision. They also differ in the distribution of projections to ganglion cells, with several rods projecting to one ganglion cell while the number of cone cells projecting to a single ganglion cell is much less, often being a one-to-one mapping. As a consequence of these differences cones have high **acuity** (the ability to see fine detail) but poor sensitivity, whereas rods have low acuity but high sensitivity.

The visual pathway

The optic nerve carries information away from the eye to the area of the brain responsible for the processing of visual information. Upon reaching the **optic chiasm** information from the **nasal** (inner) halves of each retina cross to the opposite cerebral hemisphere, while pathways from the **temporal** (outer) areas of the retina project to the equivalent hemisphere. It is important to remember that this cross over occurs for **right** and **left visual fields** and NOT for right and left eyes. From here information projects to an area of the thalamus called the **lateral geniculate nucleus** (LGN). The LGN is made up of several layers consisting of different types of neurons which are distinguished on the basis of their anatomy and function. These are called **magnocellular** and **parvocellular** cells, the former being more involved in the processing of moving stimuli and the perception of depth. These projections then continue to an area in the posterior region of the brain called the **occipital lobe** which, due to its visual function, is often referred to as the **visual** (or **striate**) **cortex**. Other (extrastriate) areas of the brain located in the temporal and parietal lobes then complete further processing of visual information.

Visual abilities

Visual acuity refers to an individual's ability to resolve fine detail in an image. Visual acuity is measured statically using standard eye charts. Obviously the importance of static visual acuity will depend upon the sport in question (e.g., being able to accurately identify a stationary target in sports such as golf and darts or taking a penalty in football requires good static acuity), although it is likely that **dynamic visual acuity** will be of more importance in most sports settings where the environment is continually changing. **Depth perception** is another important visual ability and is the ability of an observer to accurately judge the distance between themselves and another object as well as the ability to judge the comparative distance of two or more objects. An important source of depth information is obtained from the different views seen from each eye; this is referred to as **stereopsis**. However, it appears that stereopsis is only effective as a source of depth information for relatively close distances (approximately 1 meter). Thus many sports tasks may rely on other **monocular** (the view from one eye) sources of depth information.

Peripheral (or extrafoveal) **vision** is a term given to that part of the visual field that is away from the center of fixation. As already noted the physiological makeup of central and peripheral vision differ, reflecting their respective functions. As a consequence central vision is ideally suited for performing tasks that need high resolution of the visual image (e.g. target identification), whereas peripheral vision is suited for rapidly identifying where objects are and how fast they are moving (or how fast the observer is moving). This information can then be used to initiate a response at the precise time to intercept (hit, kick, catch) an object, an ability known as **coincidence timing**. Another visual skill involving perception of events in cluttered environments makes a distinction between **field dependence** and **field independence**. Also known as **perceptual style**, it is the ability to discriminate a target from its surround. Clearly, the ability to avoid distraction and rapidly locate key objects in complex environments is important in sport, and it is generally assumed that expert performers will be more field independent, as these individuals are usually able to ignore irrelevant stimuli and direct their attention to important information. However, there is very little empirical evidence to support this assumption.

Generalized visual skills in athletes

There is no evidence to suggest that athletes differ on tests of the visual abilities noted above. Even in tests of **visual reaction time** top athletes do not appear to perform better than control groups. However, it is unclear whether tests of generalized visual abilities are adequate in investigating skill differences (Abernethy & Wood, 2001). For example, since athletes usually perform under conditions that have temporal constraints and increased stress levels it would seem sensible to assess expert–novice differences under equivalent conditions. Until empirical research in this area addresses such issues the distinction between visual abilities in experts and novices will remain unclear. Moreover, the validity of the application of 'visual' training for athletes to improve visual performance also requires further empirical investigation.

B2 INDIRECT AND DIRECT THEORIES OF MOTOR CONTROL

Key Notes

Different theoretical perspectives	Theories of motor control can be generally identified as indirect or direct theories. Indirect theories borrow heavily from the area of cognitive psychology, whereas direct theories are based upon J.J. Gibson's ecological psychology.
Cognitive psychology and the motor program	Cognitive theories suggest that information from the environment is meaningless and needs to be processed by the brain via a series of hierarchical stages. These processes allow us to reconstruct internally the external world and make decisions regarding actions. The production of these actions relies on various motor programs consisting of sets of neural instructions that regulate movement in an open loop fashion.
Ecological psychology and perception-action coupling	According to ecological psychology the environment provides actors with a rich source of information for directly controlling their actions without the need of detailed analysis by the brain. This information comes from the structure of light information reflected off surfaces and objects. Organisms actively pick up this information as they move about their environments which in turn helps to guide further actions in a closed loop method of control, in this way there is coupling between perception and action.
Which theory?	It appears that a combination of both theories provides a more detailed understanding regarding the control of actions, although an ecological approach is perhaps more applicable to many sporting situations.
Relevance to sport psychology	An understanding of how athletes move within their particular sports should influence coaching practices in areas concerning motor skill development.

Related topics	Vision (B1)	Motor learning (B3)

Different theoretical perspectives

As sport psychologists are often interested in how individuals take in information from their environments and then perform related actions, psychological theories on the control of action should be central to any course on sport psychology. As a consequence sport psychologists, especially those interested in motor control, should be aware of the theoretical debate that has been developing in the area of **perception and action**.

Over the past 20 years or so there has been much debate within psychology regarding how organisms perceive their environment and then act upon those perceptions. This debate is centered on two different theoretical perspectives: **indirect theories** of perception, which are based upon a **cognitive** or **information-processing approach,** and **direct theories** of perception which are heavily influenced by **Gibson's ecological psychology** (Gibson, 1979).

Cognitive psychology and the motor program

Indirect theories suggest that information from the environment is meaningless and needs to be **processed** by the brain via a series of hierarchical stages. These processes that allow us to reconstruct internally the external world include such things as **memory** and **attention** and it is not until sense has been made of the environmental information that decisions can be made about the appropriate response. Central to these approaches is that representations of the external world must be constructed by the brain and compared to internal representations, which take the form of abstract rule-based symbols. In this respect humans can be likened to computers, in that computers also use a symbol-based system (combinations of zeros and ones) to represent external input (e.g., a keyboard).

A key concept for indirect approaches is that of the **motor program**. A motor program is essentially a set of neural instructions that regulate movements. These instructions may include information on the force, speed, timing and contractions of muscles, etc. Thus, once the process of perception has been completed and a subsequent decision made regarding the most appropriate action, a motor program then sends instructions to the relevant parts of the body (often referred to as **effectors)** to perform the desired action. For example, identifying a projectile as something to hit, catch or dodge would invoke a different set of instructions as to what parts of the body to move and when. Support for the idea of a central command center for movements comes from work with animals, which has demonstrated that stereotypical movements can be produced without perceptual input. In cats, for example, it has been shown that by changing the intensity of electrical stimulation to the spinal cord they can be made to walk and make transitions to trot and run. The discovery of these **central pattern generators** (CPGs) provides support for a central command center capable of controlling movement without perceptual feedback. One of the implications resulting from the motor program concept is that movements are executed in a ballistic fashion and are not subject to feedback, and thus operate as **open loop** control systems (see *Fig. 1*).

In its original form the motor program had many criticisms. Perhaps the biggest of these concerned storage. As the motor program is memory based and each movement requires its own specific motor program, even if they have the same goal (you would need one motor program for turning on a light switch with your right hand and another for performing the same action with your left hand or your nose, etc.), the demand on storage of these motor programs would exceed the capacity of our memory systems. Moreover, as the importance of perceptual information is neglected how do we generate new movements or change movements that are incorrect? Also, if you repeatedly perform a movement it is never exactly the same, an idea inconsistent with the motor program. Many of these problems were addressed by Schmidt's schema theory of motor control which introduced the notion of the **generalized motor program** (GMP) allowing the motor program to deal with the variability, flexibility and adaptability of human movements

Fig. 1. Schematic of an open loop control system.

(Schmidt, 1988). Rather than requiring a motor program for every single move-ment the generalized motor program controls a class of actions. What is stored in the generalized motor program relates to the timing and force of the movements, and when retrieved the GMPs are given movement-specific information. An exam-ple of how a GMP might work is given through the examination of a task that can be carried out by different parts of the body, such as writing your name. When you write your name with your preferred hand the direction of the strokes of the pen and the timing of the required movements are relatively consistent each time you perform this task. The same pattern of movements would also be observed if you were required to write your name with the pen in your mouth or with the pen held in your non-preferred hand: the instructions for the timing and pattern of the movement is the same for all methods of writing your name.

Ecological psychology and perception-action coupling

Perhaps one of the biggest differences between indirect theories and direct theo-ries of motor control concerns the link between perception and action. Indirect theories do not readily address this issue, concentrating on the processes that precede motor output; focusing on perception while ignoring action. Direct theories in contrast suggest that perception and the control of action are inextri-cably linked and that perceptual systems have evolved to allow us to interact with our environment. Thus, perception and action should not be studied in isolation. This is reflected in the different types of paradigms used to study perception. Indirect theorists tend to study perception using artificial lab-based tasks in isolation from action, whereas direct theorists tend to use tasks that have greater **ecological validity** with greater consideration of the required actions. Tasks that have greater ecological validity are those that reflect real-life tasks. For a sport psychologist interested in the control of catching, an ecologi-cally valid task would involve people catching or at least intercepting objects, whereas a task with low ecological validity might involve people pressing buttons on a keyboard in response to video images of objects coming towards them. Due to this lack of consideration of the close link between perception and action and the emphasis on top-down open loop control many theorists began to question information-processing approaches. Instead some individuals turned to the work of James Gibson, and in particular his work on ecological optics and the subsequent development of what he termed **ecological psychol-ogy** (Gibson, 1979).

Gibson rejected the **constructivist** view that the information on the retina had to be processed by the brain in order to make sense of the world. Rather, he suggested that information about an animal's environment was **specified** at the level of the retina. According to Gibson, animals pick up information from their environment as they move; this information comes from the patterns of light reflected from dif-ferent surfaces known as the **optic array.** This information changes constantly as we move through our environments, which Gibson referred to as **optic flow**. Optic flow provides information regarding interactions observers have with their envi-ronments. For example, as an observer approaches an object there is outflow: from the point of fixation, objects and surfaces in the environment move away from fix-ation (see *Fig. 2a*). In ecological terms outflow **specifies** approach, just as inflow specifies retreat (see *Fig. 2b*), a shift in the center of outflow from one object to the next specifies a change in direction, flow specifies locomotion and non-flow specifies no movement. Gibson emphasized the fact that by moving organisms actively pick up information about their environments through the resulting changes in the spatio-temporal nature of various **optic variables.** He also

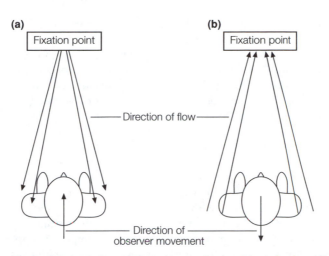

Fig. 2. The optic flow generated by an observer (a) moving forwards and (b) moving backwards.

suggested that the structure of the optic array contained information that did not change (even if the observer moved), which he termed **invariants**. By picking up these invariants organisms can directly gain information about their environments. An illustration of how such a mathematical concept can be used in perception is the **horizon ratio** which demonstrates that regardless of the distance from an observer, objects of the same height are cut by the horizon in the same ratio. Thus, the horizon ratio provides direct information with regard to the relative sizes of objects in an organism's environment.

Another idea central to ecological psychology is that of **affordances**. According to Gibson it is not objects themselves that are perceived but what objects afford (or offer) an observer: whether it can be stood on, jumped over, thrown, etc. These affordances are perceived directly without the need of further cognitive processing. A good example of what an object offers an actor is that of the handles of double doors that are common in the corridors of many public buildings, colleges and universities. These door handles come in two general forms: the U-shaped 'grab' handles which are grasped and then pulled (usually), and flat handles which the hand (or other part of the body) is placed against and pushed: The former handles afford pulling whilst the latter afford pushing. Commonly, even when the words 'push' are written above the U-shaped handles, people will pull the handle and fail to open the door successfully (much to their embarrassment).

The concept of affordances is crucial to Gibson's explanation of how actions are controlled, in that the perception of these affordances invites particular actions. For example, a ball in flight is not perceived in terms of its physical characteristics (color, size or even distance from the observer), but rather in terms of whether it can be kicked, hit, caught or dodged (Williams et al., 1999). Clearly though, what an object affords an observer/actor will depend upon their individual characteristics. For instance a soccer ball on a particular path may afford one player 'heading' while it may afford 'chesting' for a slightly taller player. This is an example of how affordances depend upon individual **biomechanical constraints**. Finally, implicit in Gibson's approach is that information is picked up by the observer moving around their environment, which in turn constrains or guides subsequent movements. This reciprocity between the actor and the environment is often referred to as **perception-action coupling**. Moreover, in this way the control of movement occurs in a **closed loop** (see *Fig. 3*) fashion in that actors receive constant feedback regarding their actions and accordingly make adjustments as they move.

One of the problems with Gibson's work is that it does not really address how actions are controlled in much detail: organisms pick up affordances and 'magically' act. Cognitive approaches would appear to provide a more complete description of the control of actions, for instance with the concept of the motor program in tandem with the perceptual processes that precede its execution. However, other approaches to the control of actions do suggest ways in which actions can be coordinated by directly interacting with the environment in ways that are consistent with an ecological approach. One such approach that has been used in conjunction with ecological views is that of the **dynamical systems theory** of control and coordination. Very simply, this approach suggests motor control is achieved through an interaction between the actor, their environment, and the associated biomechanical, environmental and physical constraints of this interaction. For example, how an athlete controls their actions will depend upon the interaction between the mechanics of the human body, the environment that they are required to perform in and what is physically possible. Another problem that faces an ecological approach is the identification of optic variables that are used in the perception action cycle. That is, can we identify quantifiable variables in the environment that can be coupled with particular actions? Indeed researchers have attempted to demonstrate how the timing of interceptive actions (e.g., hitting, jumping, kicking and catching) can be coupled to the optic variable **tau** (Savelsbergh and Bootsma, 1994). Several authors have shown that interceptive actions can be timed by using the rate of expansion of two image points on the retina: Tau.

Which theory?

There is no quick answer to this question and the debate is continuing. However it appears that a combination of the two approaches yields a more complete theory of how actions are controlled. For instance, it may be that cognitive (indirect) theories best describe those actions that are relatively slow and planned in advance which benefit from greater cognitive control, whereas ecological (direct) theories explain how (once initiated) these actions can be controlled on line, particularly in situations where there are tight spatio-temporal constraints such as those found in many sporting situations.

Relevance to sport psychology

It is often difficult for students to see the relevance to sport of much of the jargon-filled, esoteric discussion outlined above. However, if we know what information in the environment is important for controlling actions then

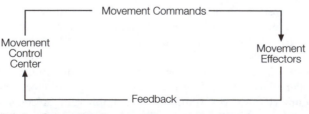

Fig. 3. Schematic of a closed loop control system.

coaches can point the athlete to these important sources. Also, further examination of how perception and action are linked may inform methods for teaching new skills and changing incorrect techniques. As a consequence, the motor control literature and research has direct implications and application for the learning and development of motor skills (Topic B5).

B3 MOTOR LEARNING

Key Notes

What is motor learning?

There are clear differences between the performance of experts and novices, although it is unclear whether differences in performance can be taken as a measure of learning. Thus an individual is said to have learned a skill if there is a change in the capability of performing that skill.

Closed skills vs open skills

Skills differ in nature and can be broadly defined as open or closed skills, which reflects whether the skill is performed in a changing or stable environment respectively.

Stages of learning

As a person learns a task they will pass through a series of stages marked by changes in their performance. These changes in performance will also be accompanied by changes in how the skill is carried out and controlled. Fitts and Posner's (1967) stages of motor learning model addresses the stages individuals pass through as they progress from novice to expert.

Practice

Practice is crucial in the learning of skill, although there are a number of things to consider when designing and structuring practice sessions. These may include varying practice conditions, the amount and length of practice and whether people practice the complete skill or separate components of the skill.

Feedback

Learning can only be achieved by receiving feedback on the production of a skill. There are many ways in which a learner (or expert) can receive information about performance. Individuals will receive perceptual and sensory feedback while performing the task. When this task-intrinsic feedback is inadequate or unavailable then learning may be facilitated by observing others or by receiving feedback from external sources such as instructions from coaches.

Related topics

Indirect and direct theories of
  motor control (B2)
Attention in sport (B4)

Memory and decision making in
  sport (B5)
Issues of concentration (L3)

What is motor learning?

In motor learning a distinction is often made between **performance** and **learning**. Performance is observable behavior, and refers to the execution of a skill at a specific time and place and learning can only be inferred from an individual's performance.

Usually there is an improvement in performance following practice and this performance change can be measured in a number of ways. But does this improvement in performance mean that learning has occurred? Consequently, it is useful to define learning in terms of the underlying **capability** for skilled performance developed during practice, with improved capability leading to improved performance (Schmidt, 1991). It is important to note that this defini-tion only refers to the potential for improved performance; whether or not there is an actual improvement will depend upon certain **performance variables,** which may include such things as fatigue, anxiety and motivation. Generally though, as an individual develops a skill we will observe an improvement in their performance, which will also be more **consistent** from one occasion to the next, and this improvement in performance will also **persist** over time. Perhaps the most important aspect for performance resulting from learning is an indi-vidual's ability to **adapt** their particular **motor skill** to cope with changing conditions. For example, a Goal Shoot or Goal Attack in netball should be able to adapt their shooting to different conditions: playing indoor or outdoor; play-ing against taller opposition than usual, using different types of balls, etc.

Closed vs open skills

When we talk about adaptability and motor skills it is also important to distin-guish between two general types of skill: **open skills** and **closed skills**. Open skills are those involving changing environments where the performer has to act according to these changes, for example catching, hitting or kicking balls in flight. Conversely, closed skills involve actions in stable environments where actors can respond when they like, for example hitting or kicking a stationary ball as in a golf swing or penalty in soccer, respectively.

Stages of learning

Clearly there are major changes in performance as individuals learn a motor skill, many of which can be easily observed when comparing the movements of novices and experts. For example, think back to when you were learning to ride a bicycle and how much effort was involved just to keep your balance, let alone ride in a straight line, compared to your present ability to ride a bike. Not only are there physical differences between experts and novices in how the skill is carried out, there are also differences in the types of information used and how it is used. For example, you will probably find it quite difficult to tell someone 'how' you maintain your balance while riding a bike, although when you were learning you almost certainly could. More specifically, when people learn a skill they tend to focus on individual components of the skill which allow them to adequately perform the required task. However, experts will most likely group these individual components together allowing them to perform the skill as well as they possibly can. This has many implications for sport psychologists and coaches. For example, the way beginners are given instructions will most likely differ from the way instructions are given to experts. Thus it is important that we have some understanding of the stages people pass through as they learn a new skill. Fitts and Posner's (1967) model of the stages of motor learning is perhaps regarded as the classical work in this area. They identified three stages along a continuum that individuals pass through as they develop from novice to expert (see *Fig. 1*).

In the first **cognitive stage** the control of the movements is very thought driven and focused on the very basic components of the skill: where/how do I hold this club/bat/racquet? What is the goal of this skill? At the same time the learner is also trying to integrate information and feedback given via instructions from coaches.

Fig. 1.   Fitts & Posners (1967). Model of the stages of motor learning.

This stage is indexed by large variability and errors in performance with the learner having little idea on how to correct these errors. In the second **associative stage** individuals learn to associate environmental information with the appropriate movements, as well as integrating smaller aspects of the skill with each other. For example, in the cognitive stage when learning to drive a car, the act of changing gear involves thinking about putting your foot on the clutch, releasing the other foot from the accelerator, moving the gear stick into the appropriate position, releasing the clutch while also depressing the accelerator, etc. In the associative stage all of these sub-components of changing gear are integrated into a larger skill component. Furthermore, this stage is accompanied by an increase in the consistency of performance as the learner begins to refine the skill. At the very end of the continuum and after many years of practice there is the **autonomous stage** where the skill has become automatic and occurs without the performer having to think about what they are doing. As a consequence of this automatic control individuals in this stage can often perform an additional task without a decrement in performance of either task. In general, performance in this stage is consistent, showing little variability from one time to the next, errors can be detected and appropriate changes instigated.

Practice

Of course most improvements in performance will result through practice. However will different types of practice be more appropriate to different skills (e.g., open vs closed skills)? There is a large amount of literature on this topic within the field of motor learning, and in particular on the importance of **variability**, **distribution**, and the merits of practicing the **whole skill** or smaller components (parts) of the skill. Varying practice conditions is thought to benefit the learner, and this appears to be consistent across many different theories of motor learning and motor control. Through varying practice conditions the learner can explore the relationship between the skill environment and their bodies. If you reconsider that adaptability is a consequence of learning then varying practice conditions will increase the likelihood that performance will be more adaptable under novel situations. There is a paradox however: variability in practice also results in an increase in performance error, although there is some evidence to suggest that greater performance error in the early stages of learning is beneficial to later performance. How the practice varies will depend upon the different types of skills. In closed skills, for example, such as taking a penalty kick in football, then it would be important to keep the **regulatory conditions** of the skill constant during practice. These would include things such as taking the penalty from the penalty spot, practicing with a regulation-size goal: keeping the things that are constant in the task constant during practice (although even top coaches seem to ignore this). In open skills, however, there would be greater variability in practice conditions reflecting the variability in requirements of the skill in question from one performance to the next.

The next question to consider is how much space to have between practice both within a session and between sessions, thus a distinction is often made between **massed** and **distributed practice**. Within a single training session this distinction will refer to whether there are rests in between drills or within a skills session, with a massed schedule having no, or very short, rests within a practice session, while a distributed schedule will have longer rest periods within the session. When this distinction is applied across sessions, massed schedules will have fewer and longer sessions compared to a distributed schedule, which will have the same amount of practice time but spread out across more, and thus shorter, sessions. Generally people learn better under these latter conditions, although within sessions the effectiveness of massed or distributed schedules will depend upon whether the skills are **continuous** or **discrete** in nature. Discrete skills are those that are simple unitary movements that have a clear beginning and ending like tossing a coin, whereas continuous skills usually require repetitive movements with a variety of possible beginning and end points. For continuous skills sessions that include longer rest periods tend to benefit the learner but for discrete tasks sessions using massed schedules are more beneficial.

Another important aspect of designing practice sessions is to decide whether to practice the whole skill or parts of the skill separately. Again this decision will rely on the nature of the skill in question and in particular upon the **complexity** and the **organization** of the skill. Complexity of skill refers to the number of components (e.g., number of body parts involved) and/or the processing demands involved. Triple jump would be an example of a skill with high complexity, whereas rifle shooting would be a skill with low complexity. Complexity is distinct from difficulty, as a skill can be low in complexity but still very difficult. The organization of a skill refers to the relationship between the different skill components. If the components of a skill are highly dependent on each other (as in the triple jump) then the skill has a high degree of organization. If on the other hand the components are relatively independent (such as different components in a dance or gymnastic routine) than the skill is low in organization. Generally, part practice is suited to complex skills low in organization, whereas whole practice is suited to skills low in complexity and high in organization.

It is clear that the manner in which practice sessions are designed should consider carefully the skill that is being learned and the environment in which it is performed. If the aim of practice is to achieve a **transfer of learning** to actual performance then it is important that both the **physical** and **skill** characteristics of the practice situation reflect the 'test' situation if the practice is going to lead to a **positive transfer** of learning.

Feedback

People learn through receiving instruction and feedback on their performance from a variety of sources. When learning a task individuals can receive feedback from watching other performers, which is known as **observational learning** or **modeling**, or they can receive **verbal feedback** from an external source. Information gained from an external source such as a coach is known as **augmented feedback**. A distinction is often made between two types of augmented feedback: **knowledge of results** (KR) and **knowledge of performance** (KP). Knowledge of results refers to the outcome of the performance (was I successful?), whereas knowledge of performance refers to information on how that outcome was achieved (this could include information on angles of joints, timing of movements, etc.). Augmented feedback appears to be most effective when individuals cannot easily interpret **task-intrinsic** feedback, which is sensory-perceptual feedback obtained as a consequence of the movement. Task-intrinsic feedback can be visual (e.g., seeing the path of a ball after striking it), proprioceptive (what the movement felt like) or auditory (e.g., the sound of ball hitting the bat or club). Augmented feedback is not just the domain of verbal instruction; it can be provided by examination of kinematic (movement) data, biofeedback and videotape. In terms of the type of feedback that promotes learning it would appear that **negative feedback** (feedback about errors) is the most effective for improving skill, although **positive feedback** (information regarding successful performance) is also important as it helps to keep the learner motivated.

B4 ATTENTION AND CONCENTRATION IN SPORT

Key Notes

Concentration and attention	Concentration can be viewed as focusing one's mental processes on internal (athletes may concentrate on bodily sensations of fatigue) or external events. Within the sport psychology literature the terms concentration and attention appear to be synonymous, although concentration is too general a term to describe the underlying psychological processes associated with attention.
What is attention?	Attention is the ability to direct one's mental processes to the task at hand, although there is some argument over whether attention is a conscious or subconscious act, and as a consequence there is no one agreed definition of what attention is. However attention can broadly be divided into two processes: focused attention and divided attention.
General theories of attention	Due to the limited capacity of the human information processor not all information can be effectively attended to at any one time. Thus filter theories of attention suggest that only relevant information is attended to whilst other irrelevant information is filtered out. Filter theories differ in at which point in the process this filtering occurs. Conversely, other theories address the limited capacity of the human information processor in terms of the limitations of processing resources. These theories propose that we can perform several tasks simultaneously, as long as the resource capacity limits of the system are not exceeded.
Selective vs divided attention	Selective attention refers to the ability to focus on one task while ignoring other tasks: in this way attentional focus has been likened to a spotlight. However there is some evidence that this spotlight analogy is flawed. Divided attention on the other hand refers to the ability to do two or more tasks simultaneously. The ability to successfully divide attention across tasks will depend upon such things as task difficulty, the similarity of the tasks and level of expertise.
Assessing attentional demands throughout a task	Research using dual task paradigms has suggested that attentional demands change throughout the task, which in turn may affect the ability to do several tasks at once.
Can skills become automatic?	As individuals become more practiced on a task these may become more automatic and thus place smaller demands on attentional resources enabling individuals to allocate attention to additional tasks.
Concentration in sport	Techniques to improve concentration in sport are in abundance, although the efficacy of these has not been assessed by empirical research.

Related topics	Motor learning (B3)	Issues of concentration (L3)
	Memory and decision making in	
	sport (B5)	

Concentration and attention

Concentration can be viewed as focusing one's mental processes on internal (athletes may concentrate on bodily sensations of fatigue) or external events. This implies that the focus of this concentration can change and/or exclude certain information while selecting to focus on relevant information. The ability to focus one's attention in sporting situations is perhaps one of the most important mental skills for successful performance, and the ability to concentrate at crucial moments is often used to differentiate successful from not successful athletes. For example, Graham Henry the former coach of the Welsh rugby team attributed some of the blame to the loss against South Africa in 1999 to a loss of concentration by his team as a result of a streaker. Furthermore, poor concentration may result in problems of **selective attention**: failing to differentiate between task-relevant and task-irrelevant information; directing attention to inappropriate information; or being unable to effectively switch attention between targets. Within sport psychology concentration and attention are often used synonymously, although concentration is perhaps too general a term to describe the underlying psychological processes associated with attention.

What is attention?

The study of attention has been one of the central areas in psychology and many of the most influential pioneers of psychology were interested in attentional processes. Unfortunately, despite having been at the center of psychological enquiry for over 100 years, a definition of what exactly attention is remains unclear. Early definitions refer to attention being a conscious process although, as you will see later in this topic and in topic B5, directing one's attention is not necessarily a conscious act and in sport we are often able to act without consciously directing our attention to producing that action. Also attention is not a single process but rather it is an organized set of procedures, and defining a set of procedures is inherently difficult. Thus the term attention is typically used to refer to different processes, although the relevant questions for sport psychologists include things such as: How much can we attend to at once (capacity)? Can we attend to more than one thing at any one moment (focused vs divided attention)? Do attentional requirements change as a result of expertise? Clearly these questions are relevant to performance in sport, and it is important that the reader is familiar with general theories of attention. As a consequence the next section provides a very brief and far from exhaustive introduction to the major types of attentional theories.

General theories of attention

Theories of attention are framed within a **human information-processing** approach as discussed in topic B2. One of the axioms of such an approach is that there is a **limited capacity** of resources available. In order to cope with this limited capacity there is a need for some sort of attentional mechanism to **filter** out unimportant information while selecting the most relevant information. For example, an equestrian in a three-day event has to be aware of the task at hand, which includes riding the horse and all of its complexities, remembering the course as well as considering performance in previous events. However, it may not be possible to attend to all of these things at any one time.

Theories differ in the location of this filter. For example, **early selection** models suggest that filtering of incoming information occurs early on in the process, whereas others have suggested that this filtering process is more flexible and can occur at a later stage of processing and as a consequence are often labeled as late selection models of attention. However, the relevance of these theories to sport is questionable. Accordingly, alternate theories that address the limited capacity of the human information processor in terms of the limitations of processing resources are more able to deal with attention allocation within a sports setting. These theories propose that we can perform several tasks simultaneously, as long as the resource capacity limits of the system are not exceeded. Like the earlier filter theories, opinion differs in where the resource limit exists. Perhaps the simplest example of these theories suggests that we have a **fixed attentional** capacity, and as long as attentional requirements do not exceed this capacity we are able to perform more than one task simultaneously. Alternatively, other theories suggest that rather than having a rigid fixed attentional capacity, this capacity can change according to the nature of the task. Although these approaches argue for a **flexible capacity** there is still an underlying assumption that there is a finite pool of attentional capacity. Kahneman's model of attention is an example of a flexible allocation model of attention (Kahneman, 1973). In Kahneman's model there are various conditions that affect the resources allocated to a task or tasks. One of the first components that impinges upon the allocation of resources is **arousal**. There is some evidence that if an individual is over-aroused then **attentional narrowing** may occur; that is, there is a reduction in attentional capacity. In addition there are certain conditions that will automatically grab one's attention, directly affecting attentional capacity. These are termed **enduring dispositions**, and may include such things as the novelty of the situation or the salience of the incoming information. Capacity is also affected by **momentary intentions** which can be self-directed or guided by external instructions (e.g., a coach may direct attention to a certain member of the opposition). In this way Kahneman's model is an extension of the over-simplified view presented by Easterbrook's cue utilization theory (1959), which suggests that arousal is the only thing that moderates an individual's attentional focus. Such approaches see attentional capacity as a uni-dimensional phenomenon, whereas **multiple resource models** of attention suggest that there are several attentional mechanisms each having their own limited capacity. According to this view resources for the processing of information are available from three sources: input and output sources (e.g., vision and limbs); stages of information processing (e.g., perception and memory); and the abstract codes for encoding information (e.g., language). Consequently, when two tasks performed simultaneously share common resources they will be performed less well than two tasks that compete for different resources. For example, it is more difficult to write and conduct a conversation simultaneously than to write and hum a tune simultaneously as the former requires access to the similar encoding information for language whereas the latter does not. Similarly in American football a quarterback would find it more difficult calling plays whilst listening to the coach's instructions, than to call plays and listen to the band simultaneously.

Selective vs divided attention

In the previous section two different approaches to the problem of capacity were introduced, one concerned with filtering non-important information and **selectively attending** to one source of information, the other suggesting that we can attend to several things at once dependent upon certain conditions. These two approaches are associated with the concept of **selective** (also referred to as **focused** attention) vs **divided** attention respectively. Furthermore, it would appear that focused attention is associated with closed skills whereas divided attention is associated with open skills. In terms of focused attention it has been suggested that attention is like the beam of a spotlight that can vary in size. This approach assumes that information falling outside of the attentional spotlight is not processed; thus we can only concentrate on one task at a time. However, within a sporting context there is anecdotal evidence suggesting that athletes can attend to information away from the line of gaze: looking out of the corner of one's eye. There is also empirical evidence that information falling outside of the attentional spotlight is processed. A distinction can be made between **overt** and **covert** orienting of attention with overt attention being associated with "conscious" focus of attention while covert attention is an **automatic** process, most likely associated with expectations (through experience) of what is likely to occur in particular locations. Clearly this may explain the ability of elite athletes to respond to changes in the environment even away from their focus of attention. Divided attention on the other hand suggests that we can attend to more than one task at once and our ability to do so will depend upon such things as task difficulty, the similarity of the tasks and expertise. As athletes are often required to attend to many things at once, especially when performing open skills, it is this latter aspect of attention that is perhaps of more importance to the sport psychologist. However, for actual performance, focused attention is most likely to be important when considering issues of concentration, which in turn will affect one's ability to efficiently divide attentional resources between tasks. Thus, it is clear that focused and divided attention are inextricably linked and although theories of divided attention may explain how athletes are able to perform several tasks at once, focused attention is essential to ensure that only important information is processed while other irrelevant information is ignored.

Assessing attentional demands throughout a task

It would appear that the attentional demands of a task change throughout the performance of a task. Thus, the ability to perform more than one task at once would also depend upon when the attentional load of any one particular task is at its greatest. A common paradigm (method) for examining attentional demands is known as the **dual task paradigm**. Within a dual task paradigm participants are required to perform two tasks at once, where the attentional demands of one of the tasks (the **primary task**) is assessed by its effect on the performance of the **secondary task**. When the attentional load of the primary task is minimal there will be little effect on performance of the secondary task. However, as the attentional load of the primary task increases then performance on the secondary task will be reduced.

Can skills become automatic?

As noted earlier attentional demands placed upon the system by any particular task will also depend upon the expertise of an individual, and evidence using dual task paradigms suggests that performance improves with practice. Additionally, comparisons of the ability of novices and experts within sport settings have shown that secondary task performance is superior in experts compared to novices (Abernethy, 2001). Results from such studies suggest that as skills become more **automatic** they can be performed with limited demands on the central processor, and without conscious control. As a consequence the execution of a skill that has become automatic will require less attention, enabling individuals to allocate more resources to any additional tasks. For an athlete this has the obvious advantage of freeing up attentional resources to focus on such things as the position of 'unmarked' team-mates, the location of the opposition or the state of play (increasing the ability to "read the game"). However, whether or not skills become entirely automatic is questionable. For instance, in dual task paradigms performance on the secondary task improves with practice of the primary task although it never reaches the same level as when the secondary task is carried out in isolation. Moreover, as noted above, some parts of a skill will require more attention than others so the whole task is unlikely to become truly automatic.

Concentration in sport

Given that concentration seems to be important to successful performance in sport, many aspects of mental skills training packages are aimed at improving concentration. Perhaps the most useful example of how the sport psychologist can help an athlete improve their concentration is through the use of an individualized **pre-performance routine**. A pre-performance routine consists of a set of mental activities carried out prior to performance with the goal of improving that performance. These mental activities can include such things as imagery, self-talk strategies, relaxation, thought stopping and the practicing of movements all of which are aimed at improving concentration and getting athletes to focus on the task at hand and while ignoring irrelevant information. However the effectiveness of techniques to improve concentration has not been subject to rigorous empirical investigation, although anecdotal evidence suggests that they may be beneficial.

B5 MEMORY AND DECISION MAKING IN SPORT

Key Notes

Experts vs novices	Expert athletes appear to have more time to carry out their respective skills than novices. These are not the result of differences in physical reaction times but most likely the result of experts being able to recognize particular scenes, thus enabling them to anticipate the likely outcomes.
Memory	Memory involves the processes of encoding, storage and retrieval of information and consists of three general components: the sensory register; short-term memory and long-term memory. It is the interaction between these three subcomponents and memory processes that affects memory performance.
Anticipation and decision making	Elite athletes do not possess better reaction times, but it is their ability to anticipate events that allows them to react quickly. Numerous studies have demonstrated that expert athletes require less time to make decisions than novices and that there are differences in their visual search strategies.
Knowing what vs knowing how	Within psychology a distinction is often made between two types of knowledge: knowing facts about objects and events that we can verbalize compared to knowing how to perform particular tasks without having conscious knowledge of how this is achieved. The latter type of knowledge is usually associated with expert performance of skills, thus it is assumed that experts will rely on this type of knowledge when performing their particular skill.
Related topics	Motor learning (B3) Attention and concentration in sport (B4)

Expert vs novices Generally, the skilled performer is characterized by descriptions such as someone who 'picks the right options', 'has all the time in the world' or 'reads the game well'. All of these descriptions imply that expert athletes are good at making the decisions within their respective sporting environment. Since there is no conclusive evidence that elite athletes are somehow different in terms of general reaction time or visual abilities, the ability to make speeded, accurate assessments and act accordingly is most likely central to an understanding of expert performance in sport. So, what is it about elite athletes that make them better decision makers than novices? Obviously there is no simple answer to this question and it will depend upon many things, including differences in **encoding**, **storage** and **retrieval** of information. Since differences in decision making clearly involve these memory processes, a brief introduction to the psychology of memory is warranted.

Memory

Within psychology theories of memory usually consider both the **structure** of memory and the **processes** involved. Traditionally memory has been viewed as broadly consisting of three different stores: **Sensory stores** that hold large amounts of information for very short periods of time (e.g., **iconic** and **echoic memory**, which are associated with the visual and auditory senses respectively); a **short-term** store (often referred to as **working memory**) which has a very limited capacity; and a **long-term** store which according to some has an unlimited capacity and can hold information for very long periods of time, it is probably associated with people's everyday definition of memory. These three stores work together in a serial fashion in the processes of **encoding, storage** and **retrieval** of information. Information comes in via sensory stores where only attended information is committed to short-term memory where there is an interaction with long-term storage mechanisms. It is this interaction that determines how effectively encoding, storage or retrieval occurs. Short-term memory has a limited capacity of about seven items, although this will depend upon how the items are organized or **chunked**. For example if I read out 12 numbers and asked you to recall them you could probably recall about seven of them (e.g., 3, 4, 5, 1, 6, 9, 7, 2, 8, 5, 3, 1), although if I read them out as three digit numbers representing hundreds (i.e., 345, 169, 728, 531) you could probably remember all of them. It has been suggested that the short-term store is made up of three components: the **central executive**, the **articulatory** or **phonological loop** and the **visuo-spatial sketch pad**. The latter two components act as slave systems for the central executive allowing it to deal with different types of information. The phonological loop is associated with language both spoken and read, whereas the visuo-spatial sketch pad is associated with spatial information. It is because of the amount of processing carried out within the short-term memory that it is often referred to as working memory. Through these components information is passed onto long-term memory (LTM), although how effective encoding, storage or retrieval is will depend upon the **depth of processing** the information receives.

Therefore one of the biggest constraints regarding encoding and retrieval would appear to be the limited capacity of working memory. Consequently, it is perhaps how experts are able to organize and attend to information that separates them from non-experts. There have been a number of classic studies showing that experts have a superior sport-specific knowledge base that enables them to encode and retrieve sport-specific information from memory more effectively than novices (Williams et al., 1999). Additionally, experts appear to use this superiority in memory to predict what is likely to happen in certain situations (Ward & Williams, 2003) and this ability seems to be central in making anticipatory decisions within a sporting context.

Anticipation and decision making

If one can identify organized patterns in the sporting display then this should help to make anticipatory decisions. Thus it is not better reaction times that allow the expert to react faster, it is their ability to anticipate events that allows them to respond quickly. One way to assess anticipation is to use a **temporal occlusion** paradigm. In these paradigms participants are shown films of a sporting scene that are stopped before completion of the scene (e.g., tennis serve, badminton serve, hockey flick, etc.) thus providing the viewer with varying amounts of advance information. The task is for the participant to predict the end result of the scene presented on the film (e.g., where the ball, shuttle, will end up). Numerous studies have shown that experts require less viewing of the scene than novices to make accurate judgments on the outcome in a variety of sports (e.g., Houlston & Lowes, 1993). Of course these studies do not inform us as to what it is the experts are looking at in these displays, but **event occlusion** paradigms do allow us to examine differences in the nature of the anticipatory cues by experts and novices. In this case participants are shown scenes that do not vary temporally but that occlude different parts of the display. For example in a tennis serve, one scene might prevent the viewer from seeing the server's arm and racquet, while another clip may prevent vision of the racquet only. These techniques have been criticized for their low ecological validity and the lack of contextual information they provide to participants (e.g., a fielder in cricket can use information regarding the type of bowler, state of the game, etc. to help them to anticipate the likely shot the batter may play) although despite these criticisms they still provide laboratory-based evidence that experts require less time to make their decisions and that they differ in visual search strategies.

Knowing what vs knowing how

If elite athletes have this superior knowledge enabling them to make anticipatory actions, how does it differ from the knowledge base of lesser athletes? Within psychology a distinction is often made between **procedural** and **declarative knowledge**. This distinction is also closely related to the distinction between **implicit** and **explicit memory**. There are subtle differences between these two distinctions although they basically represent similar views of memory. Declarative knowledge (explicit memory) represents what we know about the world and can verbalize (e.g., cricket bats are made of willow; the All Blacks are the best attacking rugby team in the world) whereas procedural knowledge (implicit memory) refers to one's knowledge of how we do things, but that we are not particularly aware of. This latter type of memory is usually associated with the ability to perform a skill. For example, most of us know how to ride a bike but would struggle to put this knowledge into words. There is some evidence that suggests that as we progress from novice to expert our knowledge about the skill relies more on procedural knowledge rather than declarative knowledge (Masters, 2000; McPherson and French, 1991). Furthermore, it appears that one of the reasons athletes may choke under pressure is that they revert back to a reliance on declarative knowledge in an attempt to gain conscious control of the skill. Consequently, as skills learnt implicitly are less likely to break down under stressful conditions then coaches should attempt to come up with **biomechanical analogies** (which encourage implicit learning) for teaching skills (Masters, 2000) or to focus on external sources of feedback in the learning process (Wulf et al., 2002).

B6 IMAGERY

Key Notes

What is imagery?	Imagery can be thought of as a conscious internal process that mimics real life experience in the physical absence of real life perceptual and sensory experience.
Imagery versus mental rehearsal	Mental rehearsal can be seen as a specific form of imagery and will most likely be used for training purposes, while emotional imagery will be useful during competition.
Imagery perspective and types of imagery	Images can be generated from an internal or external perspective, the latter resembling an image of watching your performance as a spectator. Also, images of the outcome of a skill can be used rather than the production of the skill itself. Recently a distinction has been made between imagery that is concerned with performance and/or mastery of a skill vs imagery concerned with the motivational aspects of a skill.
Does imagery work?	It appears that practicing through imagery is better than no practice at all, but is not as effective as physical practice. However, a combination of imagery and physical practice leads to an increase in performance. Additionally it appears that there are several factors that influence the effectiveness of imagery when used by athletes.
How does imagery work?	There are a number of theories attempting to explain the mechanisms through which imagery effects manifest themselves, these include theories based on physiological activity generated through imagery, cognitive consequences of the use of imagery or the potential for imagery to increase motivation or confidence.
Exercise and recovery from injury	Not much is known regarding the use of imagery within exercise, although it is attracting some interest from researchers. Also, it appears that imagery may be useful within an injury rehabilitation setting.
The use of imagery in sport	Imagery can be used in a variety of applied settings and for a variety of reasons. For example, it can be used in addition to physical practice to aid learning or it can be used to control anxiety, increase concentration and to boost confidence. However, one needs to consider the situation and the individual when deciding upon the most appropriate way to implement an imagery intervention.
Related topics	Motor learning (B3) Attention and concentration in sport (B4) Memory and decision making in sport (B5)	Issues of arousal and anxiety (L2) Issues of concentration (L3) Issues of confidence (L4)

What is imagery? Imagery can be thought of as a conscious internal process that mimics real life experience in the physical absence of real life perceptual and sensory experience (Richardson, 1969). For example, one can imagine smelling freshly cut grass in the middle of winter, seeing oneself perform a sporting task whilst sitting on a sofa or imagine feeling the consequences of a movement without actually performing that movement.

Imagery vs mental rehearsal Imagery can take many forms and within sport psychology it is often used in **mental rehearsal** (or mental practice). However imagery is a general process whilst mental rehearsal can be seen as a specific form of imagery. Mental rehearsal can also contain other sources of feedback: it is often not solely a form of imagery. For example a practice swing in golf may contain some aspect of imagery but it will also involve some sensory feedback through the physical practicing of the swing. As a consequence mental rehearsal will most likely be of use within training as an aid to improve the physical production of a skill. Other forms of imagery may be useful within a sporting setting to control emotions during competition.

Imagery perspective and types of imagery Perhaps the simplest distinction that can be made is between external vs internal imagery. That is, athletes can imagine watching themselves performing the task as an external observer or they can imagine themselves actually performing the task. These different types of **imagery perspectives** have been labeled **external** an **internal** respectively. Also individuals can generate images of performing the actual task, which may include the associated sensory input of the movements (imagine the act of putting in golf), or they can imagine the actual outcome of the movement (what happens to the ball **after** it has been struck). This latter example is often referred to as **outcome depiction** imagery. Research on outcome depiction imagery demonstrates two important points as to the nature of the effects of imagery. Firstly research has demonstrated the potential negative effects of imagery on performance. Specifically it appears that performance decrements are observed if participants are instructed to imagine unsuccessful outcomes. However, and perhaps more importantly, positive imagery does not necessarily lead to an increase in performance on tasks requiring a high skill factor: no amount of positive outcome imagery will turn a 28 handicap golfer into a scratch golfer. That is, on tasks where there is a performance ceiling effect imagery may not dramatically increase performance, although it may improve confidence or motivation to do the task.

Recently a distinction has been made by sport psychologists between five different types of imagery (Hall, 2001). **Cognitive general** refers to imagery concerned with an entire event or 'play' (e.g., a fullback in rugby may imagining themselves coming into the back line outside the center; contained within this image will be the positions of the defensive players and supporting players that they can potentially pass to). **Cognitive specific** (e.g., the fullback imagining the timing of their run and reception of the pass in the above move); **motivational general mastery** (e.g., imagining successful completion of the move); **motivational general arousal** (e.g., imagining the nervousness one might feel with regard to the execution of the move – 'what if I drop it?'); **motivational specific** which are images relating to successful outcome of the task (e.g., scoring a try, winning the game, etc.).

Does imagery work? In an examination of designs comparing the performance of imagery vs no imagery groups (excluding the issue of physical practice) Feltz and Landers (1983) suggested that imagery resulted in improved learning. Specifically, in their review of studies examining the relationship between imagery and performance they suggested that in general mentally practicing a task leads to a bigger improvement in task performance compared to no mental practice. Obviously common sense would dictate that even if mental practice does benefit the learning of a task, it would not be as effective as physical practice. Indeed, empirical data consistently shows that physical practice is better than mental practice alone. However, in general a combination of the two seems to be of more benefit than physical practice on its own.

Also, there appear to be several variables that moderate imagery effects, the most obvious being the nature of the task. For example it would appear that discrete tasks lend themselves more to the use of imagery than continuous tasks. Other variables that influence the use of and most suitable type of imagery are things such as skill level, gender, the intended goal of the imagery (e.g., motor skill improvement or anxiety reduction). Also it appears that athletes differ in their ability to use imagery. However with training it has been suggested that **imagery ability** as assessed by such things as the MIQ (**Movement Imagery Questionnaire**) or the SIQ (**Sports Imagery Questionnaire**) can improve.

How does imagery work?

Clearly any stimulation of muscles or neural connections involved in the production of a specific movement will be beneficial to improving performance, and there is some evidence suggesting that by imagining practicing a movement the equivalent neural and muscular substrates involved in the production of those movements are stimulated, albeit at a much lower level. This theory is often referred to as the **psychoneuromuscular explanation** of imagery effects. Another theory that has received some support is the **symbolic learning theory**. According to this approach, it is the opportunity to engage in the cognitive aspects of the sporting task through imagery that results in improved performance. Furthermore, mental practice through imagery allows for the movements to be represented in symbolic form with the consequence of creating a more detailed mental map of the skill in question, thus aiding future recall of the requirements of the movements involved. An alternative cognitive explanation of why imagery might aid learning is to do with the communication between action systems and language systems. That is, individuals are given verbal instructions on how to control actions and somehow must turn these into information the motor system can understand. It has been suggested that imagery may play a crucial role in translating verbal instruction into information that action systems can utilize. This view is termed the **dual coding approach**. Additionally it may well be that imagery allows for individuals to practice under conditions that recreate all aspects of actual performance. For example, if when imaging taking penalty shots in football the image contains aspects of the psychological and physiological responses associated with performing this task in a real world situation (increased arousal, tension and anxiety) then this will lead to better transfer of learning as discussed in Topic B3. This approach is often referred to as **bioinformational theory**. Also, imagery effects may be explained through motivational or confidence gains acquired that result from the use of imagery. The argument behind such a view is that by imaging success individuals increase their confidence to perform the task which in turn leads to an increase in their motivation. For example, it would appear within the sport domain that highly confident athletes tend to use **motivational images** compared to less confident athletes (Moritz et al., 1996). Moreover, as noted earlier it does appear that images can be distinctly motivational in nature.

All of the views presented have some face validity. However, no one theory appears to provide a comprehensive account as to why imagery may benefit an athlete's performance. Thus it is more than likely that combined they present a more complete explanation of why imagery may aid performance.

Exercise and recovery from injury

An examination of the use of imagery within exercise is a relatively new development but it does appear that people who exercise do use imagery, although the type of imagery is most likely to be of the motivational kind as outlined above. In addition it has also been suggested that imagery may be an effective tool in the recovery from injury. There are a number of areas where imagery may be a useful adjunct to traditional rehabilitation methods. For example, there is evidence that imagery has aided people's ability to cope with pain (Cupal & Brewer, 2001). Also, it can be used as a replacement for physical practice when an athlete is incapacitated or physically tired and may also increase adherence to the rehabilitation process by increasing confidence and motivation.

The use of imagery in sport

The prevalence of the use of imagery within sports by elite athletes is reported to be anywhere from 70 to 99%, and is an intervention commonly associated with sport psychology. Moreover, supporting the empirical work on the effectiveness of imagery as a tool to improve or change motor performance is the observation that mental packages for athletes will almost invariably include some imagery technique. It is clear that imagery can be used for a variety of reasons within a sports setting: to help the performer concentrate and focus, to reduce anxiety, to boost confidence, to aid practice or to 'ready' the appropriate cognitive mechanisms for action. But whatever the reason for its use its primary purpose is to improve an individual or individuals' motor performance. However, as noted earlier, not all people are good imagers, something that any sport psychologist should keep in mind when planning an imagery intervention.

C1 INTRODUCTION TO MOTIVATION

Key Notes

Instinct theory

Early attempts to explain motivation employed the concept of instincts based on the evolutionary ideas of Darwin. Over time, as vast lists of many thousands of basic instincts were produced, it became clear that instinct, as a concept, had lost explanatory power. Instinct cannot explain cultural differences in behavior and motivation. When its limitations became apparent, psychologists turned to drive reduction theory.

Drive reduction theory

In this basic theory of motivation a need is an internal state of deficit. This need initiates a drive, which is the state of being motivated to reduce the deficit. Drive persists until an effective response is made.

Homeostasis

Closely tied in with the drive reduction model is the notion of homeostasis. The most widely used analogy for homeostasis is the thermostat. Just as a thermostat tells a boiler when it should be on or off, based on a set temperature, so people are said to have a set level of physiological need, imbalance from which governs their drives.

Higher needs

While drive reduction provides a reasonable explanation for basic activities, it fails to be convincing for curiosity or self-actualization motives. Humans are motivated not just by the push of drives but also by the pull of incentives, such as winning medals.

Maslow's need hierarchy

Maslow suggested that human needs could be represented in the form of a pyramid. Basic needs, such as physiological needs for food and water and needs for safety, were located at the base of the pyramid. Less essential for survival, but important for psychological well-being, love and esteem needs were located further up the pyramid. Finally, the need for self-actualization, central to the humanistic perspective, was placed at the top. Self-actualization is the realization (or making actual) of one's potential. He also suggested that people prioritize the meeting of lower-order needs above higher ones. Despite problems, Maslow's theory continues to be popular because of its intuitive appeal.

Need for achievement theory (nAch)

Need for achievement is a function of approach tendency minus avoidance tendency, multiplied by the likelihood of success, and the value of a successful outcome to the individual. It predicts that individuals high in achievement needs will prefer tasks of intermediate difficulty, and that individuals low in achievement needs will prefer tasks that are either easy or hard. Research findings are not very supportive of the theory. The McClelland–Atkinson model has ceased to be widely used to explain achievement motivation.

Expectancy theories

Expectancy theories assume people are motivated by their expectations about the relationship between their actions and the outcomes of such actions. According to Vroom's Valence Instrumentality Expectancy theory (VIE), we will be motivated if: we value the outcome (valence), if we believe that our performance will be rewarded (instrumentality) and if we believe that if we put in the effort we will be able to perform well (expectancy).

Related topic   The scientific approach (A3)

Instinct theory   Motivation is about what energizes, directs and sustains actions. Early attempts by psychologists to explain motivation employed the concept of **instincts,** based on the evolutionary ideas of Darwin. In this view humans exhibit behavior that has evolved because of its survival value. For example, instinctual urges could explain aggressive behavior since aggressive organisms were more likely to survive to reproduce more offspring. In this way any behavior, like eating, drinking, washing or partying, could be explained as exhibiting the eating, drinking, washing or partying instinct. Pioneers in psychology such as William James and William McDougal began to lay down lists of basic instincts. However, by the 1920s some lists had grown to over 10 000 instincts! Clearly, when a concept becomes all embracing it loses explanatory power.

If the answer to the question 'Why does she like to paint?' or 'Why do they play sport?' is 'because its instinctual', then this does not advance understanding by much, even if true.

A second problem with instinct alone as a theory of motivation is that it cannot explain cultural differences in behavior and motivation. When the limitations of instinct theories became apparent, psychology turned to needs and drives, and proposed **drive reduction theory** to explain motivation.

Drive reduction theory   Drive reduction theory is another approach with a long history in psychology. It is based on the view that motivation occurs when there is a tension caused by a state of imbalance between the current physiological state of the organism and some normal or resting level. Some writers have use the terms need and drive interchangeably. Others have differentiated between them arguing that **need** is the internal state of deficit that initiates the **drive,** which is the state of being motivated to reduce the deficit. Thus, in this view the drive derives from the need, and persists until an effective response is made.

Homeostasis   Closely tied in with the drive reduction model is the notion of **homeostasis**. The most widely used analogy for homeostasis is the thermostat. Just as a thermostat tells a boiler when it should be on or off, based on a set temperature, so people are said to have a set level for each physiological need, any imbalances from which govern their drives. For example, if we engage in strenuous activity for some time without drinking, a tissue deficit will result. The homeostatic mechanism will register this deficit and produce a need signal, on the basis of which a drive (thirst) is created, which motivates us to search for a drink. Having drunk something, our tissue deficit is removed and the homeostatic regulator stops the need signal which removes the drive. Drinking too much also results in homeostatic regulation, except that in this case the tissue imbalance comes from overload rather than deficit.

Higher needs   While it is easy to see that drive reduction might provide a reasonable explanation for basic activities like eating, drinking and perhaps sexual behavior, it fails to be convincing for other human motives. For example, more complex needs such as curiosity needs, competence needs, and esteem needs cannot simply be based on physiological deficit and homeostasis. Humans do reach a point when they are sated with regard to eating but do not appear to do so in relation to needs for praise, or being cared for, or loved. Similarly, human motivation is not simply the result of the push of drives. Humans are motivated by the pull of **incentives**, such as anticipated rewards like money or winning medals in sport competition.

Maslow's need hierarchy

The founding father of humanistic psychology (Topic A3) was Abraham Maslow (1954), who offered a rather common sense theory of different types of motivation and the link between them. He suggested a **hierarchy of needs** and represented these needs in the form of a pyramid. Basic needs, such as physiological needs for food and water and needs for safety, were located at the base of the pyramid as essential to human existence. Less essential for survival but important for psychological well being, love and esteem needs were located further up the pyramid. Finally, the need for **self-actualization**, considered by Maslow and other humanistic psychologists as the sine qua non of the human condition was placed at the top. Self-actualization is the realization (or making actual) of one's potential. The other main claim of the theory is that people prioritize the meeting of lower-order needs above higher ones (*Fig. 1*). In simple terms this means that someone who is being chased by a bear is not likely to be concerned about self-esteem!

Maslow's theory continues to be popular and widely cited in general textbooks on human motivation. This is probably because of its simplicity and intuitive appeal. However, there are problems with the theory. Firstly, it was not based on a very solid empirical basis. Maslow derived his theory from interviews he conducted with a small number of women, when he was a young research assistant in his twenties. Secondly, there has actually been very little empirical work on its validity. Another issue is that it is selective in the motives it covers. For example, Maslow makes little reference to curiosity as a motive. Finally, it is easy to think of anecdotal examples that contradict its hierarchical premise. It is clear that on countless occasions, human beings have put higher-order needs, such as conquering a mountain, or crossing an ocean, above safety needs. Thus, some people are so driven by self-actualization that they take little

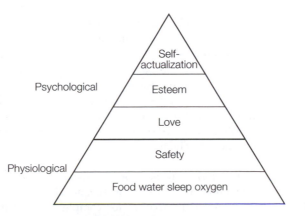

Fig. 1. Maslow's need hierarchy.

care of their lower-level needs. Another example of such behavior is the stereo-typical painter who wastes away in his garret to produce his masterpiece, while being unconcerned about basics like eating properly. Similarly, if humans satisfied lower needs in preference to higher ones, as Maslow suggests, we might expect athletes to stop running during marathons to deal with their tissue deficits, or for pain reduction reasons. As humans it appears we can choose to overlook basic needs when we want to meet higher ones.

Need for achievement theory (nAch)

One candidate that showed early promise as a theory of motivation that would be relevant to sport was McClelland and Atkinson's Need for Achievement Theory (1953). It grew out of the somewhat unlikely marriage of a Freudian underpinning, as evidenced by the use of projective measurement techniques, and the scientific respectability of a mathematical formulation.

The theory holds that people differ in the extent to which they desire achievement. The level of their desire is given by subtracting their motive to avoid failure (trait anxiety) from their motive for success, or approach tendency (**intrinsic motivation**). The resultant motivational tendency is then moderated by two situational variables, perceived probability of success, and the incentive value of success to the individual.

In summary, according to the theory, **need for achievement (nAch)** is a function of approach tendency minus avoidance tendency, times the likelihood of success, and the value of a successful outcome to the individual. The major prediction from the theory concerns choice of activity. Specifically, it is predicted that individuals high in achievement needs will prefer tasks of intermediate difficulty, and that individuals low in achievement needs will prefer tasks that are either easy or hard. The typical test of these ideas involves giving participants the choice, prior to each trial, of how far from a target they wish to perform an aiming task.

Research findings are not very supportive of the theory, since it is often found that all participants appear to prefer intermediate difficulty tasks! Also it becomes apparent that many people low on need for success, and high on fear of failure, nevertheless put themselves into achievement situations. Another problem was that it did not predict the achievement behavior of women. The notion of fear of success was introduced to deal with this; however, subsequent research has had little success in demonstrating a sex difference on fear of success scores. Another problem is that there is little supportive evidence that those with high nAch perform any better than those low in nAch, as one would expect. Finally, it should be said that problems with the measures used also cast some doubt on the theory. For example, motive for success is assessed by the Thematic Apperception Test (TAT), which is a **projective technique** that has been widely criticized on the grounds of low reliability. Further, the state anxiety measurement used in the early tests of the theory could be criticized in the light of more recent discoveries in sport and exercise regarding the multidimensional nature of competitive anxiety (see Topic D4). As a result of its many problems the McClelland–Atkinson model has ceased to be widely used to explain achievement motivation.

Expectancy theories

Need reduction theories are not particularly useful to explain other than basic drives. Consequently, the 1970s saw the development of more sophisticated theories that attempted to account for complex human motives. For example, organizational psychologists have developed cognitively oriented models to explain motivation in work settings (Porter & Lawler, 1968). Surprisingly, despite the fact that these potentially useful ideas have been around for over 30 years, sport and exercise psychologists have not paid much attention to them. The most widely publicized of these are the **expectancy theories**.

Expectancy theories assume that people are motivated by their expectations about the relationship between their actions and the outcomes of such actions. Specifically, they are motivated if they perceive that effort expended will lead to good performance, and that such performance will be rewarded appropriately. For example, in Vroom's (1964) **VIE approach**, valence (V) is the attractiveness of an outcome, instrumentality (I) is the relationship between performance and reward, and expectancy (E) is the subjective probability that effort will lead to performance. We can illustrate this with a concrete example. Think of the situation of first team selection. The theory says that to be motivated an athlete has to value the outcome of being selected (**valence**). They must believe that if they do perform at first team standard they will be selected (**instrumentality**). Finally, they must believe that if they practice, train hard, get sleep, don't drink too much and avoid junk food, they will be able to perform at first team standard (**expectancy**). Despite its value in organizational psychology and the world of work, expectancy theories have not been employed in sport psychology.

C2 Cognitive evaluation theory

Key Notes

Intrinsic vs extrinsic motivation	Intrinsic motivation refers to wanting to do something for its own sake, because it is, in and of itself, pleasurable or rewarding. There are three sub-divisions of intrinsic motivation: to know, to accomplish, and to experience. In contrast, extrinsic motivation refers to the desire to do things to gain external rewards. It involves doing something as a means to an end.
Cognitive evaluation theory	Cognitive evaluation theory proposes that intrinsic motivation is a function of people's perceptions of self-determination and competence. Rewards are said to contain both controlling and informational features. In general, the theory has been supported both in the laboratory and in ecologically valid settings.
The controlling aspect	A reward which is perceived to control behavior is predicted to reduce feelings of self-determination, and lead to a reduction in the desire to perform the behavior. Tests of the 'over-justification hypothesis' (so called because the reward is more than is necessary for a pleasurable activity) have shown the counter-intuitive finding that external rewards can undermine intrinsic motivation for activities that were initially seen as interesting.
The informational aspect	Rewards provide us with information about how we have performed. This affects our perceptions of competence, which in turn influence our level of intrinsic motivation. In particular, positive information about our competence (for instance, achieving a goal) will enhance our feeling of intrinsic motivation. In contrast, negative information about our competence (for instance, not achieving a goal) will result in low perceived competence, and low intrinsic motivation. Research has supported this aspect of the theory.
Related topic	Introduction to motivation (C1)

Intrinsic vs extrinsic motivation

One important distinction in this area is that between intrinsic and extrinsic motivation.

Intrinsic motivation refers to wanting to do something for its own sake because it is in itself pleasurable or rewarding. For example, most non-professional sport is carried out because it is fun or exciting. The pleasure is inherent in the activity and requires no tangible reward. Similarly, many people find drawing or painting intrinsically motivating. Some writers have sub-divided intrinsic motivation into intrinsic motivation to know, to accomplish, and to experience, i.e. a thirst for knowledge, a need to achieve and a need for pleasure.

In contrast, **extrinsic motivation** refers to the desire to do things to gain external rewards. This involves doing something as a means to an end other than for the activity itself. Typical examples of extrinsic rewards are material goods and money, or in the sporting arena, trophies and medals. Although not tangible, praise, recognition and approval are also considered to be extrinsic motivators. So, for example, being told by the coach that you are playing well, or being promoted to team captain, is likely to be a source of extrinsic motivation.

Cognitive evaluation theory

Cognitive evaluation theory (Deci, 1975; Deci & Ryan, 1985) proposes that intrinsic motivation is a function of people's perceptions of **self-determination** and **competence**. Thus, an athlete who feels she has had some choice in an activity is more likely to be intrinsically motivated, as is an athlete who perceives herself to be competent in the activity. The other main feature of the theory relates to rewards. A common sense assumption is that rewards will automatically motivate. However, the theory claims that rewards contain both **controlling** and **informational** features. A reward that is perceived to control behavior is predicted to reduce feelings of self-determination, and lead to a reduction in the desire to perform the behavior. Rewards which convey information suggesting increased self-competence will enhance intrinsic motivation, whereas rewards which convey information that suggests decreased self-competence will reduce it. The theory is represented in *Fig. 1*.

The controlling aspect

According to the theory, rewards consist of two main aspects: controlling and informational. An example of the controlling aspect is provided by the well-worn story of the old man who was being bothered by some noisy children, who were playing football outside his house. The old man had the wisdom to tell the children that he so much enjoyed them playing, that he would give them a dollar to come back and play the next day, which he did. After a day or two of paying a dollar, the old man said that he was short of money and could only pay 25 cents from now on. With a derisory look the kids refused to play, on the grounds that to stay, they needed more than 25 cents! In terms of the theory, the children had come to see the old man as controlling their behavior, which reduced their feeling of self-determination. This in turn reduced their intrinsic motivation to play outside his house.

When athletes feel 'controlled', the reason for their behavior resides outside themselves. This perceived 'locus of causality' determines whether intrinsic motivation will increase or decrease. An external locus of causality leads to feelings of low self-determination.

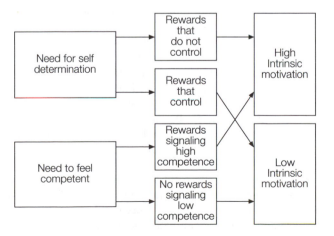

Fig. 1.   Cognitive evaluation theory.

Studies of the controlling aspect of the theory have tested the **over-justifica-tion hypothesis**, so called because the reward is more than is necessary for a pleasurable activity. Typically, these experiments involve manipulating extrinsic rewards in different experimental groups to see what this does to intrinsic motivation, as measured by the amount of subsequent free-choice behavior exhibited. The classic study was carried out by Lepper et al. (1973). They investigated children's intrinsic interest in a drawing and coloring-in activity, by randomly assigned children to one of three conditions. In one condition children had an expected reward (a good player award for completing the task). In a second condition children were given an unexpected reward (which was the same as in condition one except that it was unanticipated). Finally, in a control condition no reward was given to the children. Results revealed that children in the expected reward condition showed significantly less interest or time on task than the other two conditions. Interestingly, this not only supports the 'over-justification' hypothesis, but it is counter-intuitive, since it demonstrates that in some circumstances, by rewarding people we *reduce* their motivation. Specifically, it seems that external rewards can undermine intrinsic motivation for activities that were initially seen as interesting and enjoyable. According to the theory, this is because rewards that are contingent upon good performance signal to people that they are competent. However, rewards given regardless of performance are seen as controlling and result in diminished intrinsic motivation.

The informational aspect

The other aspect of rewards is the informational one. The theory says that rewards provide us with information about how we have performed, and that this information affects our perceptions of competence, which in turn influences our level of intrinsic motivation. In particular, positive information about our competence (for instance, achieving a goal) will enhance our feeling of intrinsic motivation. In contrast, negative information about our competence (for instance, not achieving a goal) will result in low perceived competence, and low intrinsic motivation.

The awarding of certificates of achievement to young athletes typifies the informational aspect of the theory. Here the gaining of the certificate provides children with information about their competence, which leads to enhanced motivation to achieve the next level of award. On the negative side, failure to gain the certificate can provide information that tells the child they are not competent, and can lead to loss of motivation.

To test this aspect of the theory, researchers have manipulated both type of feedback and perceptions of competence, and then measured subsequent free choice involvement in the task at hand. Again, results are supportive of the theory. For example, in one study, hockey players who had been given varying amounts of positive feedback were more intrinsically motivated than those who had been given none (Vallerand 1983). Another study demonstrated a linear relationship between intrinsic motivation and whether participants had received positive feedback, no feedback or negative feedback (Vallerand and Reid, 1984).

Increasing perceptions of competence has also been shown to raise levels of intrinsic motivation. For example, in one study two groups of basketball players matched on ability, competed in a shooting task. It was found that those players who perceived they were more successful in the competition recorded significantly higher intrinsic motivation scores than those who perceived themselves to have been less successful (McAuley & Tammin, 1989). Interestingly, the intrinsic motivation levels of actual 'winners and losers' did not differ, under-lining the fact that it is perceived outcome, rather than actual outcome, that influences subsequent motivation.

In general, the theory has been supported both in the laboratory and in ecologically valid settings. For example, it has been found that students with sports scholarships are less intrinsically motivated in their sports, than those without scholarships (Deci & Ryan 1980).

The theory offers two main approaches to increasing intrinsic motivation. Focusing on the self-determination issue, we could give players a say in the design and content of training sessions. For example, we might give players some choice about which practice drill to use next, or what type of defense to practice. Players could also be encouraged to set their own team and individual targets for training and matches. In terms of rewards, coaches could avoid anything that players might perceive as controlling, or they could let players have a say in the type of rewards that are given, for what and to whom. In short, strategies which empower players and encourage them to take ownership of their progress are likely to produce self-determining and thereby intrinsically motivated players.

Turning to the competence issue, intrinsic motivation could be increased by improving the quality of competence information available to athletes and by encouraging the use of self-referenced goals, so that all players can see progress and can experience competence development.

C3 ACHIEVEMENT GOAL THEORY

Key Notes

Achievement goal theory	The theory suggests that people have personality dispositions (task and ego orientations) in relation to achievement situations and that these orientations have an important influence on three things: our attitudes about achievement, our motivation in achievement settings and our actual achievement behavior. Much research has been carried out on achievement goals, and the theory has been supported in relation to its claims about orientation and attitude, and orientation and motivation. However, there is little evidence that orientation is correlated with performance.
Task-ego orientation	Task-orientation involves being motivated by a desire for mastery and doing as well as you are able to do. For the task-oriented individual, competence judgments are based on how well they did in relation to their previous performances, i.e. they are self-referenced. Ego-orientation involves being motivated to win or to out-perform others. Judgments of competence are based on how well one does in relation to others, i.e. they are other-referenced. These two orientations, task and ego, are conceived of as stable personality dispositions, or traits, along which different individuals vary.
Task-ego climate	Not only do people bring their achievement orientation with them to each competitive situation, but each situation has its own atmosphere, or task versus ego climate. Whether the climate is task or ego involving is largely determined by the behavior of coaches, managers and parents.
Task-ego involvement	The type of involvement (task or ego) that an athlete has at any given moment is their achievement goal state. This state is a function of the interaction between the goal orientation they bring to the competitive situation, and the goal climate in which they find themselves.
Related topic	Introduction to motivation (C1)

Achievement goal theory

Achievement goal theory has dominated the area of sport motivation over the last ten or so years. It was principally developed by Nichols (1984) to explain behavior in educational achievement situations such as tests and examinations. The theory was brought to the physical domain by Joan Duda, who has published extensively in the area (Duda 1987). The first part of the theory is that the two orientations are relatively stable dispositions, i.e. they are personality dimensions.

Before moving on to describe the theory further, it is important to make the point that this area has become unnecessarily complicated by the fact that different theorists have used different terms to describe the same basic concepts. Once you realize this, the literature that describes work in this area becomes much less confusing to read. The term that is now generally used is

achievement goal theory but you will also find it described as motivational orientation, achievement orientation, goal orientation and goal perspective theory. Another potential confusion comes from the fact that over the years, researchers have given task and ego-orientation different labels, such as, mastery versus ability orientation, or performance versus outcome orientation, and even learning versus performance goals. Fortunately, writers have begun to use the more common terms, task- and ego-orientation. Having clarified terms, we can now continue to outline achievement goal theory. In addition to suggesting that we have personality dispositions or orientations in relation to achievement situations, the theory claims that these orientations have an important influence on three things: our attitudes about achievement, our motivation in achievement settings and consequently, our actual achievement behavior.

With regard to attitudes, task-oriented athletes see the purpose of sport as being for enjoyment, and to offer mastery or personal growth opportunities. Ego-oriented athletes are more likely to think of sport as providing opportunities to favorably compare their performances with others. Task-oriented athletes also appear to hold more sporting attitudes with regard to fair play, and are less likely to endorse cheating and non-legitimate aggression than are ego-oriented athletes (Duda et al., 1991). Finally, in relation to attitudes, task-oriented athletes are more inclined to believe that effort is what leads to success, while ego-oriented athletes are more likely to assume that natural ability is the key.

In terms of motivational differences, the argument is that task-oriented athletes are more motivated and persist longer because of their belief that effort is worth expending, as opposed to the ego-oriented individual's belief that performance is a function of natural ability or talent, and that added effort will have little effect. Added to this is the likelihood that task-oriented athletes are more likely to feel competent following performance than ego-oriented athletes, because they assess success against their own standards, rather than on the vagaries of how closely matched to an opponent they might have happened to be. Finally, in relation to motivation, the theory claims that task-oriented athletes have higher levels of intrinsic motivation (Duda et al., 1995).

Turning to the relationship between orientation and performance, it is not surprising that given the above, proponents of achievement goal theory have argued that task-oriented athletes should out-perform ego-oriented ones. Although this does follow logically from the theory's claims about the higher levels of intrinsic motivation in task-oriented athletes, there are many people who question it (Hardy 1997). For example, it is hard to imagine that athletes at the top of professional sport, or their coaches, do not have strong win or ego-orientations. For some 'it is not just a matter of life or death, it is much more important than that' to quote Bill Shankly, the legendary Liverpool F.C. manager.

A second aspect of the theory in relation to sporting behavior is that the task-oriented athlete is more likely to choose a fairly challenging task, because it will give them feedback about their progress. In contrast, the ego-oriented athlete is more likely to choose to compete in a situation that is either easy (so that they can win and feel competent), or very difficult (so they can dismiss losing because they could not have been expected to win!).

Much research has been carried out on achievement goals, and the theory has been supported in many but not all areas. For example, the fact that task- and ego-orientation can be reliably and validly measured, provides some evidence that these two personality dispositions exist and are conceptually different.

In terms of the link between orientation and attitude, it has been shown that task-oriented athletes are more inclined to agree that hard work is important for success than ego-oriented ones. With regard to attitudes to cheating and legitimacy of action, again there is evidence that ego-oriented athletes are happier to endorse aggressive behavior and bend the rules than task-oriented ones.

The literature on orientation and its relationship to motivation also shows predicted patterns. For example, persistence has been shown to be greater in task-oriented athletes. Similarly, studies have shown a link between task orientation and higher levels of intrinsic motivation for various tasks.

Finally, in relation to the theory's somewhat controversial claim that orientation and achievement behavior are related (in particular that task-oriented athletes will out-perform ego-oriented ones), the situation is disappointing because not much research has been carried out. This is surprising given its practical implications. One or two studies have found mild support for the claim but as yet it is too early to pronounce on this issue. In terms of applying the theory there is typically little that can be done in terms of altering orientations. As personality dispositions, they are notoriously difficult to change. It is more fruitful to focus on the climate aspect and try to set up training environments that encourage task involvement. Such environments would stress mastery and improvement against ones own standards, as opposed to competition between athletes. In this way we may see long-term benefits to motivation. One crucial difference between the educational and the sporting situation is the importance of competition. In educational testing children are usually trying to perform well against a standard, as opposed to beating their classmates. While sport is not solely about competition it is a big part of it. Perhaps the theory does help us to understand aspects of motivation, but it may not be the whole story with regard to competitive situations, which are for many the essence of sport.

Task-ego orientation

The basic building blocks of **achievement goal theory** are the concepts task- and ego-orientation first outlined by Nichols (1984). **Task-orientation** involves being motivated by a desire for mastery and doing as well as you are able to do, matched against your own standards. The development of competence is crucial for the task-oriented individual whose competence judgments are based on how well they did measured against their previous performances or current ability level, i.e. they are **self-referenced**.

In contrast, **ego-orientation** involves being motivated to win or to out-perform others. Judgments of competence are based on how well one does in relation to others. Thus, in ego-orientated individuals, performance is **other-referenced**. These two orientations, task and ego, are conceived of as stable personality dispositions, or traits, along which different individuals vary. These dimensions are thought to be independent (orthogonal). Thus, athletes might be relatively high in both, low in both, or high in one and low in the other. Scales have been developed to measure these, the most widely used of these being the Task and Ego Orientation in Sport Questionnaire (TEOSQ) (Duda & Nichols, 1992).

Task-ego climate

It is important to be aware that not only do people bring their achievement orientation with them to each competitive situation, but also that the atmosphere of the session may have a task or ego climate. Whether the climate is task or ego involving is often determined by coaches, managers and parents. For example, a coach who sets up all drills to be competitive, with winners and losers, is creating an ego climate. The coach who avoids comparisons with other players and stresses personal growth is likely to create a task climate. Similarly, parents who ask their children returning home from training or practice sessions, 'Did you win?' are likely to be creating an ego involving climate. In contrast, parents who ask 'Did you learn anything?' or 'Did you have fun?' are helping to create a climate that is more task involving.

Task-ego involvement

From the above, we can see that the type of involvement (**task or ego involvement**) that an athlete has at any given moment, i.e. their achievement goal **state,** is a function of the interaction between the **goal orientation** they bring to the competitive situation and the **goal climate** in which they find themselves.

C4 ATTRIBUTION THEORY

Key Notes

Attributions

Attributions are the ordinary explanations people give for the events that happen in their daily lives. For example, if we think we have been deliberately fouled, we are more likely to respond with a negative reaction than if we attribute the foul to unintentional action by the other player.

Cognitive misers

When humans process information they tend to be 'cognitive misers'. They use heuristics, which are strategies that save processing time at the expense of thoroughness and often accuracy. For example, when people make attributions for failure they tend to blame the situation on others, rather than themselves. This tendency for self-serving attributions has a positive effect on motivation, because when we can avoid the blame for failure we can avoid its de-motivating effects.

Attribution theory

Weiner proposed that two dimensions, locus of control (internal–external), and stability, account for the lay explanations that people make for success and failure. Ability is seen as an internal stable attribution for outcome, while task difficulty is seen as an external and stable attribution. Effort and luck are classified as internal-unstable and external-unstable, respectively. The theory predicts that following success, stable and internal attributions will produce higher levels of motivation than unstable and external ones. Following failure, motivation is least damaged by attributions that are unstable and external as opposed to internal and stable. Research has generally supported Weiner's predictions.

Related topics   Introduction to motivation (C1)   Achievement goal theory (C3)

Attributions

Attributions are the ordinary explanations people give for the events that happen in their daily lives. For example, if we ask why Manchester United Football Club are so successful, we might be given the attribution by one person that they have bought their way to success, and by another that they have a good manager. If asked why someone fouled you on the playing field, you might attribute it to clumsiness or to 'dirty play'. Attributions are relevant to motivation because it is on the basis of our attributions that much of our behavior rests. For example, if we think we have been deliberately fouled, we are more likely to respond with a negative reaction than if we attribute the foul as unintentional.

Cognitive misers

We know from research on information processing that human beings tend to be '**cognitive misers**'. That is, they tend to take shortcuts to save time and effort in cognitive activity by not going systematically through all possible permutations in arriving at conclusions. They use **heuristics**, which are strategies that save processing time at the expense of thoroughness and often accuracy.

Stereotypes (see Topic F1) are one example of this where we use rough classification systems to help us to manage the vast number of types of people we might encounter and how we should respond to each. At a party, for example, our interactions with a man in a monk's habit might be quite different from those we might have with someone wearing a Hell's Angels jacket. In a similar way, we are biased in our assumptions when we make attributions.

It is well documented that when people make attributions for their own behavior, they tend to take the credit when things go well, and to blame others when they do not. In this way people protect their own egos and self-esteem. This inaccuracy is one of the most common mis-attributions people make and is known as the self-serving bias. The relevance of all this for motivation is that our tendency to have **self-serving attributions** has a positive effect on motivation, because we don't blame ourselves when things go wrong and we thus avoid the possible demoralizing and demotivating effects of defeat.

Attribution theory

Attribution theory attempts to account for the way in which people make attributions. The basic aspects of attribution theory were proposed in the 1940s by the Gestalt psychologist Fritz Heider. In fact there is not one attribution theory but several. However, from a sport and exercise perspective the most obviously useful, and certainly most studied, is Weiner's theory of attributions for achievement (Weiner, 1985). The theory originally proposed that two dimensions could account for the lay explanations that people made for success and failure in achievement situations. The first of these was **locus of control,** and the second **stability**, so that ability was seen as an internal stable attribution for outcome, while task difficulty was seen as an external and stable attribution. Effort and luck were classified as internal unstable, and external unstable, respectively (*Fig. 1*).

The theory has been extended with the introduction of three further dimensions: controllability, generality and intentionality, although there is some debate as to whether these extensions added much to the power of the theory. It is difficult, for example, to envisage an external controllable event, or an internal uncontrollable one. McAuley et al. (1992) have supported a four-dimensional model, with the development of the Causal Dimension Scale II (CDSII), the dimensions of which are locus of control, stability, external control and personal control. Further research with the CDSII will determine whether the newer dimensions prove to be as durable as the original ones. In addition to classifying attributions, Weiner specified the motivational implications of attributional processes. Not surprisingly, this aspect of the theory is of central interest for sport psychologists. *Figure 2* outlines the hypothesized links between sporting outcomes, attributions and subsequent motivation. The basic suggestion is that athletes who attribute stable and internal

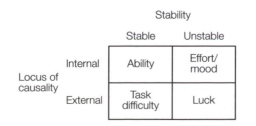

Fig. 1. Causal attributions.

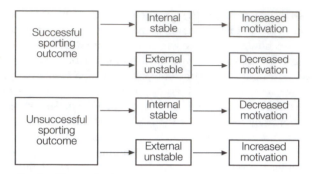

Fig. 2.   The motivational consequences of attributions.

causes to successful outcomes will be more likely to choose to participate again, to practice more, and as a result eventually play better than those who believe their success was unstable and externally caused.

Another less well-publicized aspect of Weiner's theory is the emotional consequences that are associated with different attributions. He argued that internal attributions for success will be associated with pride ('it was me') and external ones with gratitude ('I was lucky'). In the case of failure, internal attributions will be associated with shame, external ones with surprise and/or anger.

How well does the theory stand up to scrutiny? Surprisingly, there have been very few studies that directly test the link between attributions, motivation and performance. What has been done has generally supported Weiner's predictions. However, the research has been criticized for employing cross-sectional rather than more informative longitudinal designs. In terms of applying the theory, we should encourage players to see success in internal stable terms. For example, after a win, the coach could talk about the skill of our team, rather than the weaknesses of the opposition. It would also be important to avoid attributions for success that invoke luck, or that suggest good performance is unusual and is unlikely to be repeated. In contrast, after failure, coaches should encourage external and unstable attributions.

C5 CONFIDENCE

Key Notes

Confidence in sport and exercise	Psychologists make the distinction between trait and state confidence. Trait confidence is an enduring aspect of how we are generally. It is a personality dimension. Someone who is trait confident is confident across a wide range of situations. In contrast, state confidence relates to one's belief about a specific situation.
Self-efficacy theory	Self-efficacy is 'people's judgments of their capabilities to organize and execute courses of action required to attain designated types of performance'. It is synonymous with state confidence. The theory suggests that there are four main sources of self-efficacy: performance accomplishments, vicarious experience, verbal persuasion and our physiological state. Self-efficacy is said to affect task choice, effort and persistence. The theory has been supported in sports settings, but only in tasks that are predominantly effort based, as opposed to tasks requiring aiming or tracking skills. Collective self-efficacy is the efficacy of the group as a whole. Studies generally find that there is a relationship between collective self-efficacy and team performance.
Competence motivation	Harter's theory proposes that evolutionary processes have produced in humans an innate need to be competent, which motivates mastery attempts. Successful mastery attempts lead to satisfaction, increased perceived competence, higher levels of effectance motivation and more mastery attempts. In contrast, unsuccessful mastery attempts lead to dissatisfaction, lower perceived competence, lower levels of effectance motivation, and a reduction in mastery attempts.
Vealey's theory	Vealey proposes that athletes bring two personality dispositions, trait confidence and competitive orientation, to each sport situation. These two dispositions are said to interact to determine the level of state confidence of the competitor, which in turn determines the performance. Vealey suggests that performance-oriented (task-oriented) athletes should be more state confident than outcome-oriented (ego-oriented) ones. Despite being sport specific the theory has had little testing and remains unsupported.
Related topics	Achievement goal theory (C3) Issues of confidence (L4)

Confidence in sport and exercise

Confidence is seen by coaches, managers and athletes themselves as being absolutely crucial to motivation and peak performance. In fact it is a good example of when psychology could be accused of being 'just common sense'. However, psychology can add to common sense by discovering the limits of its effects, and by illuminating the processes involved. As we shall see, it may even show that common sense is not quite accurate and that there are times when confidence is of no benefit to athletic performance.

Before outlining the theories of confidence that sport psychology employs, it is important to make the distinction between trait and state confidence. As the name suggests, **trait confidence** is an enduring aspect of how we are generally, and as such it is a personality dimension. Someone who is trait confident is confident across a wide range of situations. In contrast, **state confidence** relates to one's belief about a specific situation. The state-confident tennis player may be sure he or she can serve an ace, yet be low in confidence about their skiing ability. While some work has been carried out on trait confidence the main focus in the area has been on state confidence.

A second important consideration is to remember the cognitive–affective distinction made in Topic A1. Cognition relates to thoughts and beliefs, while affect relates to feelings (emotions and moods). In everyday use people talk about feeling confident or being in a confident mood. However, this is to confuse beliefs with affect. Confidence is a belief not a feeling, i.e. it is cognitive not affective. We feel emotions and we feel 'in a mood' but we don't feel thoughts or beliefs. When we say 'I am confident I can shave a tenth of a second off my personal best today' we are saying we believe we have the capability to do what we claim.

Self-efficacy theory

The main theory that relates to confidence in sport is Bandura's theory of self-efficacy (Bandura, 1977, 1986). As a cognitive psychologist rather than a behaviorist, Bandura argues that it is not the stimulus or reward that drives our behavior, but rather our interpretation of it. He suggested that we would not be motivated to try something unless we believe we have a chance of succeeding. He showed for example, that people who were afraid of snakes were much more likely to be able to handle snakes after they had been made confident that they could do so. Bandura used the term **self-efficacy** for this state confidence and he defined it as 'people's judgments of their capabilities to organize and execute courses of action required to attain designated types of performance'.

Bandura's theory claims that there are four main sources of self-efficacy. The first and most powerful is previous **performance accomplishments**. Thus, if we have succeeded in a certain activity in the past, we are confident we can do it again. The second source of self-efficacy is **vicarious experience**, or modeling. This might be when we see others succeed and we think, 'If they can do it, I can too'. The third source of self-efficacy is **verbal persuasion**. An example of this is when our coach convinces us we can do something. Finally, and of least influence on self-efficacy, is our **physiological state**. Here the way we feel physiologically is an indication to us about how confident we are. For example, if we are aware of having butterflies in our stomach we may lose confidence. Over the years two further sources of self-efficacy have been added to the theory. Firstly, it is suggested that imaginal experiences can also affect self-efficacy levels, with images of positive outcomes leading to increased self-efficacy, and images of negative outcomes resulting in lower self-efficacy.

Secondly, it is argued that, just as our awareness of our physiological state can impact on self-efficacy, so our emotional states are a signal about our self-efficacy levels. For example, someone who is feeling depressed, or sad, prior to competition, might judge their self-efficacy to be low. A sports-specific approach to the antecedents of self-efficacy has been offered recently by Vealey (2001) who suggests that there are nine sources: mastery; demonstration of ability; physical and mental preparation; physical self-presentation; social support; coach's leadership; vicarious experience; environmental comfort and situation favorableness.

As well as describing the antecedents of self-efficacy, the theory also describes its consequences. Bandura states that expectations influence what we choose to attempt, i.e. task choice, how much effort we will expend, and how persistent we will be in the face of failure (*Fig. 1*). Much support for the theory has come from studies in a wide range of situations including health promotion, work and education.

Bandura's theory was quickly seized upon by sport psychologists and employed in the physical domain to explain the effects of confidence on performance. There have been hundreds of studies that have shown that confidence (self-efficacy) and sporting performance are correlated. However, the link should not be taken to mean there is a cause and effect relationship. As was pointed out in Topic A5, that would be to fall into the trap of believing in the logical fallacy '**post-hoc ergo propter-hoc**' (after the fact therefore caused by the fact). Because two things are correlated does not mean they are causally related. To be able to say that it was the confidence that caused performance (rather than for example, that being a good player makes us confident), we need to manipulate confidence experimentally. A small number of such experiments do show that when self-efficacy is manipulated, for example, by giving false feedback to participants, subsequent performance is affected. However, apart from being few in number, the experiments all appear to have been carried out on tasks that demand effort as opposed to accuracy. For example, participants in a muscular endurance task have been able to keep their leg extended longer following a positive manipulation of self-efficacy. Increasing confidence does appear to lead to more effort and persistence. However, it is difficult to see why the theory should apply in an aiming task like golf putting, since no amount of determination or effort is going to make a golfer instantly more accurate. The distinction being made here, which could loosely be termed the '**will versus skill distinction**' is between tasks where successful performance is more a product of effort or will, and those in which accuracy or aiming is the primary determinant of good performance. It should be said that the distinction between skill-based and effort-based tasks is not a perfect dichotomy. Most sporting tasks require both effort and skill. It is not being claimed that an effort-based task such as running a 5000-meter race does not require any skill, rather it is the relative contribution that is being alluded to. The suggestion is that trying hard is likely to have more effect on how well one performs in a distance event, than

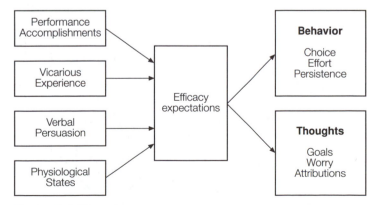

Fig. 1. Self-efficacy theory.

how well one performs in a basketball free-throw shooting competition. To date, none of the true experiments in the area has investigated accuracy or aiming performance. Bandura has claimed that self-efficacy will affect thoughts as well as effort. For example, low self-efficacy might lead to worry. However, again, true experiments that manipulate self-efficacy to determine its effect on worry and subsequent performance do not appear to have been carried out. Further research is needed before we can say that Bandura's theory applies to sports performance generally.

The idea that self-efficacy affects performance has been extended by those interested in group processes in sport and exercise. This has led to the notion of **collective self-efficacy,** which is the efficacy of the group as a whole. Studies generally find that there is a relationship between collective self-efficacy and team performance (George & Feltz, 1995; Feltz & Lirgg, 2001).

Competence motivation

A second approach to confidence that has been imported from mainstream psychology is the work on competence motivation by Susan Harter (1978). Harter's interest is in the development of competence in children, and she has proposed that humans have an innate need to be competent. This has clear links with evolutionary theory, so we might expect that those humans without such a need did not attempt to be competent, were less likely to excel, and had fewer resources when it came to competitive survival.

The theory proposes that our **innate need to be competent** motivates attempts to demonstrate competence in various activities. So the young child tries to walk and the older one might climb a tree. Harter argues that successful mastery attempts lead to positive affect (feelings of satisfaction), increased perceived competence, and higher levels of what Harter calls **effectance motivation**. High effectance motivation results in more mastery attempts. In contrast, unsuccessful mastery attempts lead to negative affect (feelings of dissatisfaction), lower perceived competence, lower levels of effectance motivation, and a reduction in mastery attempts. The theory neatly explains why people drop out of sport at an early stage if they do not experience success of some kind or another (*Fig. 2*).

Vealey's theory

Vealey has developed a sport-specific theory of confidence that combines trait and state sport confidence, while also including aspects of achievement goals

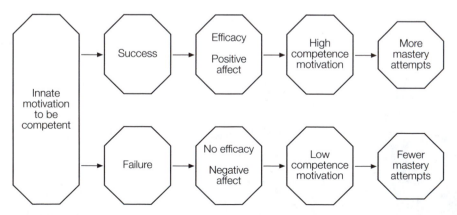

Fig. 2.   Competence motivation theory.

theory (Vealey 1986). Like Bandura, Vealey suggests that confidence is causally linked to performance. However, she also suggests that trait confidence will impact on state confidence in different ways depending on the athlete's competitive orientation. Thus, Vealey proposes that athletes bring two personality dispositions to any given objective sport situation. Firstly they bring a level of trait confidence, and secondly a competitive orientation. Their **competitive orientation** corresponds more or less to what was called achievement goal earlier in this section, when we considered task and ego orientation (Topic C3). Vealey prefers to use the terms performance (task) and outcome (ego) orientation.

These two dispositions are said to interact to determine the level of state confidence of the competitor, which in turn determines the performance. Vealey suggests that performance-oriented (task-oriented) athletes should be more state confident than outcome-oriented (ego-oriented) ones.

Although Vealey does not spell out the argument for why this might be so, it is presumably that for a task-oriented person, success is defined against their own standards, while for the ego-oriented athlete success means beating the other person. Thus, winning against others is much less in one's control than doing well against one's own standards, and consequently, the former situation should lead to higher levels of state anxiety.

On the positive side, Vealey's theory is sports specific and was created with competitive anxiety in mind. Unfortunately, it has seldom been empirically tested, and what little has been done has not been particularly supportive of the theory.

C6 GOAL-SETTING THEORY

Key Notes

Introduction to goal setting	Goal setting is central to motivation since we are motivated by the discrepancy between our goal or desired end state (what we want), and what we have now. Feedback tells us about the size of the discrepancy. Goal setting is the process of spelling out the aims and objectives that will be met by a set time, and at a set level.
Goal types	Three main types of goal have been identified. Process goals relate to how something will be carried out. For example, a golfer might have the process goal of keeping her head still throughout the swing. Outcome goals focus on the outcome of our actions, for example, to win a game or to make it to the semi-final stages of a competition. Performance goals specify a level of achievement against a measurable standard rather than against other competitors. For example, a player might aim to run 60 meters in 7 seconds.
Goal-setting theory	Locke's goal-setting theory was developed in industrial psychology. It claims that there is a linear relationship between goal difficulty and performance, so that as goals get more difficult, people perform better. The theory also claims that specific goals of sufficient difficulty produce higher levels of performance than no goals or 'do your best' goals. Since the theory was first proposed, hundreds of studies have demonstrated its validity.
Goal setting in sport and exercise	There is evidence that goal setting is effective in sport and exercise contexts, however its effect is less pronounced there than in the organizational context. This may be because athletes are more likely than industrial workers to be operating at, or close to, their performance ceiling. Another possibility is that athletes are more highly motivated to excel than industrial staff. Despite not being as powerful as it is in the occupational setting, goal setting is still a useful technique that is widely employed in sport and exercise psychology.
Related topic	Issues of motivation (L1)

Introduction to goal setting

Goal setting is central to motivation since we are motivated by the discrepancy between our goal or desired end state (what we want), and what we have now. Feedback tells us about the size of the discrepancy. Goal setting is the process of spelling out the aims and objectives that will be met by a set time, and at a set level.

One of the most widely cited examples of successful goal setting is that of John Naber, the American swimmer who wanted to win the Olympic 400-meter backstroke gold medal. In 1972 he was just under 4 seconds slower than the gold winning time, so he set himself the goal of being 4 seconds faster by the time of the 1976 Olympics. He broke his overall goal down into sub-goals of 1 second a year, and 0.08 seconds per month, and 0.02 seconds per week, which is about 4 milliseconds per training hour (about a fifth of the time it takes to blink). He said to himself, 'I can improve that much per training hour'. He did and won the gold in 1976!

Goal types

Three main types of goals have been identified. **Process goals** relate to how something will be carried out. For example, a golfer might have the process goal of keeping her head still throughout the swing. A rugby player might set the process goal of following through when he takes a kick. As the name suggests, **outcome goals** focus on the outcome of our actions. An example of an outcome goal is to win a game or to make it to the semi-final stages of a competition. **Performance goals** specify a level of achievement against a measurable standard rather than against other competitors. For example, a player might aim to have a 90% passing accuracy score or to run 60 meters in 7 seconds. It has been suggested that performance and process goals are 'better' than outcome goals on the grounds that the latter are not as much under our own control as performance or process goals (Duda, 1992, 1997). For example, our opponent may simply be vastly superior to us. Research into goal type has not supported the efficacy of one type over another. It is perhaps more appropriate to suggest that there are advantages and disadvantages to each. It may be that in some situations process goals are more appropriate, for example, when we are learning new skills, and that outcome or performance goals are more appropriate when we are competing. Some studies have shown that using a combination of different goal types is better than employing each alone.

Goal-setting theory

Goal-setting theory grew out of the work of Edwin Locke in the 1960s (Latham & Locke, 1979). Locke and his colleagues investigated how the setting of various targets for industrial workers affected their output. What they found, consistently, was that a goal-setting group out-performed a '**do your best**' group. The theory claims that there is a generally linear relationship between goal difficulty and performance, so that as goals get more difficult, people perform better. Secondly, the theory says that specific goals of sufficient difficulty produce higher levels of performance than no goals or 'do your best' goals. Thirdly, it is claimed that to be effective, goals need to be accepted by the performer, i.e. they should have 'ownership' of the goal, whether self-set, negotiated or assigned. Finally, the theory stresses that for goals to be effective, they need to be accompanied by feedback on performance. Since the theory was first proposed, hundreds of studies have confirmed its main claims and the effectiveness of goal setting. In particular, it has been shown that specific and sufficiently challenging goals are the key to increased performance.

Explanations for why goal setting is effective include that it directs attention, mobilizes effort, enhances persistence and leads to new strategies.

One aspect of goal setting that the original theory did not include, but that has been argued to be of relevance, is goal proximity. This refers to the closeness of the goal over time, and in particular, the distinction between short- and long-term goals. Many writers have suggested that the addition of short-term goals as opposed to long-term goals alone, improves the effectiveness of goal setting. As yet there is little evidence on this, but it seems reasonable to assume that it is worth including both, given that there is little cost to doing so.

Goal setting in sport and exercise

Having proved its worth in the organizational context, sports researchers began to investigate the effectiveness of goal setting in sport and exercise settings.

Here, the evidence has been less compelling. Goal setting does appear to work and is widely applied to athletic performance, however, research shows its effects to be less pronounced than in the organizational context. Meta-analyses (a way of combining the findings of many studies mathematically using a statistic known as the effect size), have shown it to have modest effect sizes of around 0.34, compared with effect sizes of from 0.42 to 0.8 for industrial studies. (Although there are no hard and fast rules the convention in meta-analysis is to consider effect sizes of less than 0.4 to be small, 0.4 to 0.8 to be moderate and above 0.8 to be large.) Several suggestions have been made to explain this discrepancy (Locke 1991). One argument is that athletes and exercise participants are more likely than workers to be operating at, or close to, their performance ceiling, leaving less scope for goal setting to have its effect. Another related claim is that people in sport and exercise contexts are more highly motivated to excel than industrial staff.

It could also be that there are methodological difficulties in the experimental research. For example, it has been suggested that athletes in the 'do your best' condition inadvertently subvert the experimental process by spontaneously setting their own goals. Another methodological problem is that sample sizes are smaller in sport-related research. This could be part of the reason why there have been more failures to demonstrate significant differences between goal-setting and 'do your best' groups.

Despite not being as powerful as it is in the occupational setting, goal setting is still a useful technique that is widely employed in both sport and exercise psychology. The principles of effective goal setting are outlined in Topic L1.

D1 DEFINITIONS

Key Notes

Affect	This is used as an umbrella term in psychology to cover all types of feelings including emotions and moods. It contrasts with cognition, which is used in a general way to refer to aspects of thinking.
Emotion	While in everyday language we tend to use the terms mood and emotion synonymously in psychology it is usual to think of them as different. The difference is not a precise one and there is a deal of overlap between them. However, emotion is used to describe a relatively specific, high-intensity, immediate, yet short-term reaction following the appraisal of an event or stimulus.
Mood	In contrast to an emotion a mood refers to a more diffuse feeling state that does not always have a clear trigger. A mood also tends to be more long lasting than an emotion. For example, we might just be fed up for no obvious reason and consequently, not want to go to the gym.
Arousal	Arousal is an alertness or activation level ranging from deep sleep to intense alertness. It has no affective component, i.e. it is neutral with regard to feelings, emotions or moods.
Anxiety	Anxiety is a negative emotion of apprehension and tension.
Stress	Stress is a process that involves one's perception of an imbalance between the demands of the environment and one's capabilities. The stress process may well result in anxiety, but it can also result in other emotions such as fear or curiosity. Anxiety is one possible product of the stress process.
Related topics	Mood and performance (D2) Stress and coping (M1) Anxiety: the basics (D3)

Affect

Affect is an umbrella term used in psychology to cover all types of feelings including **emotions** and **moods**. It contrasts with **cognition,** which is used to refer to aspects of thinking such as beliefs and thoughts. **Affect** is used at a very general level to describe good and bad experience (Vallerand & Blanchard, 2000). It has also been argued that affect is more primitive in nature, being experienced by lower species as well as humans. In contrast, emotions such as pride or revulsion and moods such as being fed up or enthusiastic are said only to be experienced by humans. Psychologists talk about positive and negative affect meaning positive and negative feelings. For example, they might say 'exercise led to a state of positive affect in aerobics class members'. Affect used in this way is a noun. It should not be confused with the verb to affect, which is entirely different and means to produce an effect on something, i.e. 'we affected people's perceptions of the tennis club'.

Emotion   While in everyday language we tend to use the terms **mood** and **emotion** synonymously, in psychology it is usual to think of them as different. The difference is not a precise one and there is overlap between them. However, emotion is used to describe a relatively specific, high-intensity, immediate yet short-term reaction following the appraisal of an event or stimulus. For example, the emotion of anger may follow having been badly fouled in a soccer match. If we believe the foul to be accidental we are less likely to feel the emotion of anger. The emotion is likely to dissipate as the game progresses, assuming no further provocation occurs.

Mood   In contrast to an emotion, a mood refers to a more general or diffuse feeling state that does not always have a clear trigger. Moods also tend to be more long lasting than emotions, but not enduring enough to be traits. Again, in contrast to emotions, moods tend to be more pervasive and about things in general, rather than specific incidents. For example, we might just be 'feeling down' for no obvious reason and consequently, not want to go to the gym.

Arousal   Unfortunately, in much of the literature **arousal** and **anxiety** are loosely employed to mean the same thing. However, arousal is more usefully viewed as an alertness or activation level, ranging from deep sleep at one extreme, to intense alertness at the other. As such arousal is an emotionally neutral concept, having no associated affective component, i.e. it is neutral with regard to feelings, emotions and moods. Sporting activities require a wide range of skills some of which are best performed at low levels of arousal for example, golf putting or pistol shooting. Other activities are probably performed more effectively when arousal is high, for example, weight lifting and pushing in a rugby scrum. One advantage of this distinction between arousal and anxiety is that it allows us to understand why an athlete can be 'pumped up', yet not anxious.

Anxiety   Anxiety has been a central concept for sport psychology and has received a huge amount of investigation because of its influence on performance. It is generally defined as a **negative emotion** characterized by feelings of apprehension and tension. Unlike arousal it is not emotionally neutral, but rather is at the unpleasant end of the affect continuum.

Stress   Another much used term in this area is **stress**, which some writers use synonymously with anxiety, but is defined here as a process that consists of people's perceptions of an imbalance between the demands of the environment and their capabilities. **The stress process** may well result in anxiety (but it can also result in other emotions, e.g. sadness, anger, depression). Anxiety is one possible product of the stress process. The stress process is discussed in Topic M1.

D2 MOOD AND PERFORMANCE

Key Notes

Mood measurement	Mood has been measured using paper and pencil tests in many ways. However, the most widely used method in the physical domain has been the Profile of Mood States (POMS). The POMS has six mood sub-scales: tension, depression, anger, vigor, fatigue and confusion. More recently, researchers have begun to use the Positive and Negative Affect Scale (PANAS), which consists of 20 items and is more evenly balanced between positive and negative moods.
The iceberg profile	In the early 1970s, William Morgan claimed that athletes with a particular profile, the iceberg profile, would out-perform those without it. The iceberg label comes from the way the profile looks when vigor is high and the other five negative mood scores are low. In more recent years it has become clear that performance can not be reliably predicted from a knowledge of the athlete's profile of mood states.
Mood and performance	Meta-analysis of the mood and performance literature shows that, overall there is an extremely small relationship between them. It also appears that mood profiles can distinguish athletes from non-athletes, but not skilled athletes from less-skilled ones. Finally, it appears that, to a modest extent mood profiles can distinguish between athletes of a similar standard.
Post hoc ergo propter hoc	On the basis of the above research some applied sport psychologists have engaged in mood manipulation to create iceberg profiles, in the hope that this will cause athletes to perform better. Unfortunately, the research into the POMS has been correlational not experimental in nature. To assume on the basis of this that the mood caused the performance is a logical fallacy known as post-hoc ergo propter-hoc, which means after the fact, therefore caused by the fact.
Related topic	Definitions (D1)

Mood measurement

Mood has been measured using paper and pencil tests in many ways. However, the most widely used method in the physical domain has been the **Profile of Mood States (POMS)** (McNair et al., 1992). The POMS is a 65 mood word inventory in which athletes are asked to say 'how they feel right now' in relation to each mood word. The words cluster into the following six mood sub-scales: tension, depression, anger, vigor, fatigue and confusion. The POMS was originally devised to measure the mood of clinical populations in mental institutions and its content reflects this with five of its sub-scales being negative and only one, vigor, being positive.

More recently, researchers in sport and exercise psychology have begun to use other mood scales (Crocker 1997), including the **Positive and Negative**

Affect Scale (PANAS) (Watson et al., 1988) which consists of 20 items and is more evenly balanced between positive and negative moods. The PANAS reflects current thinking on moods, which is that they can be represented in a two-dimensional way such that it is possible to be high (or low) in positive mood and high (or low) in negative mood. The theory suggests that moods can be represented in two-dimensional space around a circle (or circumplex) (Biddle, 2000) (see *Fig. 1*).

The iceberg profile

In the early 1970s, William Morgan published research on elite wrestlers and rowers in which he claimed that, using the POMS, he was able to predict with a high degree of accuracy which United States squad members would have been selected for the final US Olympic team. Specifically, he claimed that athletes with a particular profile, **the iceberg profile**, would outperform those without it. The iceberg label comes from the way the profile looks when vigor is high and the other five negative mood scores are low (see *Fig. 2*). He claimed that top athletes exhibit this profile and went as far as to label the POMS 'the test of champions'.

Given the known predictive power of psychometric tests, a claim like this, i.e. that a test will be able to discriminate at the extremes of a distribution, is not credible. Morgan seemed to be saying that the POMS could separate the 12 best wrestlers in the USA from the 12 next best. While it is not too hard to believe that the mood of an athlete will affect performance, it is hard to see how mood could provide this level of discriminatory power. On the basis of Morgan's work many people began to investigate the mood–performance relationship. Not surprisingly, they found that the predictive value of the POMS was much exaggerated. Looking back it appears that there had been some confusion over Morgan's claims and that there was ambiguity over his use of the terms 'unsuccessful' and 'non-athlete'. It has also been suggested that the statistical analysis

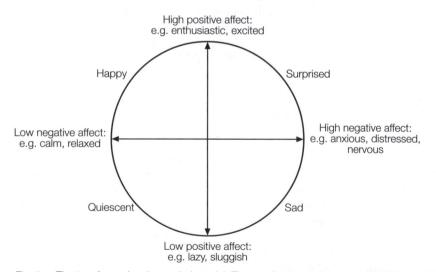

Fig. 1.   The two factor (or circumplex) model. The two factor model means that it is possible to be: high on both positive and negative affect, as in the case of someone who is surprised; low on both positive and negative affect, as in the case of someone who is quiescent; high on positive affect and low on negative affect, as in the case of someone who is happy; high on negative affect and low on positive affect, as in the case of someone who is sad.

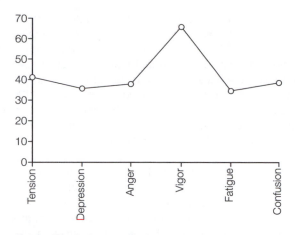

Fig. 2. The iceberg profile.

had been omitted in some reports of his findings and that differences between groups may not have been significant. One final reason why claims were over-stated is that there may have been a failure of researchers to go back to original sources (Renger, 1993).

While the POMS and its iceberg profile may not be able to predict perform-ance with as much accuracy as was once thought, there are still many studies that show that mood and performance are related.

Mood and performance

It seems reasonable to assume that mood will have an effect on performance. In simple terms, we would expect that if you are not in the mood to compete you are unlikely to do well. What is the scientific evidence? Traditional reviews of the literature provide a mixed picture. While there are many studies that have shown mood and performance to be related, there are also many studies in which this link has not materialized. The picture is clearer when we look at meta-analytic reviews. **Meta-analysis** is a procedure that compares the power of the effect of each study using a statistic known as **the effect size** (Glass, 1976). In this way we get an overall picture by combining studies arithmetically in a relatively objective way. Furthermore, meta-analysis allows us to look at sub-categories of interest. For example, we can see if the effect size is bigger for older as opposed to younger athletes or men as opposed to women. Meta-analysis of the mood and performance literature shows that overall there is an extremely small effect size of 0.15. However, meta-analysis allows us to ask more specific questions. In particular three main questions have been asked of the mood and performance relationship.

Firstly, can mood profiles distinguish athletes from non-athletes? Here the evidence is that athletes do have more iceberg profiles. This is not too surpris-ing because we know that physical activity affects mood in a positive way. Further it would not be surprising if depressed, tense, angry, tired, confused people do not want to exercise or play sport and thus self select away from these activities leaving happy, vigorous, people to participate.

A second question answered by meta-analysis is 'can mood profiles distin-guish skilled athletes from less skilled ones?'. Here the answer appears to be no. Athletes of different skill levels have similar profiles. Meta-analysis has shown that the difference in mean effect size for athletes of different ability levels is negligible. Thus, knowing mood profiles prior to competition does not allow us to predict who will perform well. Peter Terry, one of the most prominent researchers in the area, has argued that we should not expect POMS to predict performance differences in samples of different ability levels. This is because the performance of differently skilled athletes is more likely to be a function of their ability level, strength, fitness and experience than their mood. A poor runner in a good mood is still not going to outperform a good runner in a bad mood. In other words the effect of mood is likely to be swamped by other factors.

These considerations lead to the third question we can answer using meta-analysis, which is, 'can mood profiles distinguish between athletes of a similar standard?'. This is what Morgan appeared to have claimed in his 'Test of Champions'. The evidence from meta-analysis is mildly supportive, with reported effect sizes being in the mid 0.3s, which is small to modest as effect sizes go.

In defense of using mood to predict performance, researchers have argued that in addition to skill level, the relationship is masked by other moderator variables (Terry, 1995). For example, it is argued that because moods change, mood and performance will be related in short-duration events, but not over events of longer duration. A cricketer may be in a positive mood at the beginning of a test match but be in a negative mood by day two. Meta-analysis has supported this **moderator variable** argument, in that bigger-effect sizes have been demonstrated for open skills than for closed skills, in individual sports than team sports, and in shorter- than longer-duration sports. Another variable that affects the relationship is whether or not the performance is subjectively measured. Not surprisingly, subjective ratings of performance are more closely linked to previous mood. It also appears to be the case that effect sizes are bigger for performances that are self-referenced (for example, doing better than you did last time) as opposed to other referenced (based on outcomes, such as winning). Taken together it would appear that there is a moderate relationship between mood and performance in certain specific circumstances (Beedie et al., 2000).

Post hoc ergo propter hoc

At this point a word of caution is important. On the basis of the above research into POMS and performance, some applied sport psychologists have engaged in mood manipulation to create iceberg profiles, in the hope that this will cause athletes to perform better. Unfortunately, the research into the POMS has not been experimental in nature. Typically, in these studies mood was not manipulated. Rather, it was simply measured prior to performance and correlated with subsequent performance. To assume on the basis of this that the mood caused the performance is a logical fallacy known as 'post-hoc ergo propter-hoc', which means 'after the fact, therefore caused by the fact'. In everyday life we often use this way of thinking and it may well have survival value. Cave dwellers who assume that the stomach pain they experience following the eating of interesting looking, yet toxic, berries has nothing to do with the berries, are less likely to avoid them in the future and are less likely to survive. In sport we see this in the form of superstitions. Many athletes are notoriously superstitious about which sock they put on first, or about which place in the pre-game line up they occupy. They may do this because on a previous occasion doing whatever it was, was followed by a win. However, for scientists, this evidence is not acceptable because it rests on flawed logic. We saw in Topic A5 that when two variables are related it could be that either: A caused B; or B caused A; or there is a circular relationship where A caused B and B caused A; or finally, a third variable C caused both A and B, creating a **spurious correlation** between them. In this context we should ask whether a third variable might produce both a good mood and a good performance. Imagine a situation in which you are about to compete in a karate fight against someone you know you can beat (perhaps because each time you have fought previously you have won, or because you are of a higher karate grading than they are). If you were to complete a POMS questionnaire prior to competition, you would probably find you had an iceberg profile. In contrast, if your opponent completed the POMS, s/he might not be in a great mood nor show an iceberg profile because they anticipate defeat. Assuming the fight goes according to form, we would indeed find that mood and performance were related. Yet it was not the mood that caused the performance. Rather, a third variable, ability, caused both mood and performance. Although common sense suggests that mood should be causally implicated in sport performance, the fact is that as yet we just do not have the evidence to demonstrate it. What is needed is research in which mood is manipulated in a true experiment (with pre and post testing and a control group). Only when this kind of research has been done will we be able to be definitive about the causal role of mood in performance. The reason why this point is being labored here is that unfortunately all too often, in textbooks and research papers, some sport psychologists seem to assume that if a study shows that mood predicts performance, this means it caused it. A related misunderstanding occurs when authors of correlational research papers use titles such as 'the effect of x on y'. Again this is because 'effect' cannot be properly determined in non-experimental designs.

D3 ANXIETY: THE BASICS

Key Notes

Trait and state anxiety	As in the earlier section on confidence again it is important to make the trait–state distinction. Trait anxiety is a relatively enduring disposition that causes people at the high end of this continuum to view a wide range of non-dangerous circumstances as threatening. State anxiety is the negative emotion of apprehensiveness and tension experienced in threatening situations.
Cognitive and somatic anxiety	Cognitive anxiety is characterized by worrying thoughts and negative expectations, about performance, self-evaluation and the evaluations of others. Somatic anxiety relates to perceptions of our bodily state, such as awareness of a pounding heart or dry mouth.
Anxiety measurement	The most used method of measuring anxiety in sport is the self-report questionnaire, which has been employed to measure both trait and state anxiety. The most used measure of trait anxiety is the Sport Anxiety Scale (SAS). The most widely used measure of state anxiety is the CSAI-2.
Anxiety direction	Some researchers have claimed that anxiety has direction as well as intensity, leading to the somewhat strange notion of positive as well as negative anxiety. It is possible that the term directional anxiety is a misnomer and that the directional scale measures outcome expectations.
Drive theory	Drive theory predicts that at any given skill level, performance depends on arousal (or drive) in a simple linear way, such that the greater the arousal the better the performance. Drive theory does not explain the relationship between arousal and performance for the more complex tasks typical in sport.
'Inverted U' theory	The basic premise of 'inverted U' theory is that as arousal (drive) increases, so too does performance, but only up to an optimum point, after which increases in arousal result in reduced levels of performance. Although it has intuitive appeal, much research has shown that the predictions of the theory are not always confirmed, and it has largely been superseded by more complex approaches such as catastrophe theory (see Topic D5).
Related topics	Multidimensional anxiety theory (D4) Catastrophe theory (D5)

Trait and state anxiety

As in the earlier section on confidence again it is important to make the trait–state distinction. **Trait anxiety** is a relatively enduring disposition; i.e. it is a personality dimension that predisposes people at the high end of the continuum to view a wide range of non-dangerous circumstances as threatening. In contrast, **state anxiety** is the negative emotion of apprehensiveness and tension experienced in threatening situations. In the sporting domain much more research has been carried out on state anxiety than trait anxiety. This is probably because the performance enhancement applications that might come out of the study of sports anxiety are potentially much greater for state than trait anxiety. For example, even knowing that trait anxiety has a small inverse relationship with performance, it is not clear what we could or should do to enhance performance. Changing athletes' personalities is not really an option since there is much evidence from psychology that tells us that it is very difficult to do. In contrast, it is relatively easy to imagine ways in which we might be able to control state anxiety to improve performance. Indeed much of the focus of applied sport psychology does exactly this (see Topic L2).

Cognitive and somatic anxiety

Although initially conceptualized as a unitary construct it became clear from work in educational psychology that children about to sit tests suffered from two kinds of anxiety, namely worry and emotionality, which have more recently been labeled cognitive and somatic anxiety (Martens et al., 1990). **Cognitive anxiety** is characterized by worry and negative expectations, about performance, self-evaluation and evaluation by others. For example, young athletes might worry that they will perform poorly in front of their parents on school sports days, or the golf professional might start to think of how many thousands of pounds the next putt will cost if it is missed. **Somatic anxiety**, on the other hand relates to our perceptions of our bodily state, for example, when we are aware of having a pounding heart, clammy hands, trembling legs, butterflies in the stomach and a dry mouth. These two types of anxiety have been the focus of much research (see Topics D4, D5, D6, D7).

Anxiety measurement

The most obvious choice for the measurement of anxiety might seem to be **physiological indices** such as heart rate, blood pressure, electroencephalograph (EEG), galvanic skin response (GSR), and serum adrenaline (epinephrine) levels. While these provide a relatively objective measure, there are problems with their use. The major difficulty with them is that they measure arousal rather than anxiety. In other words they can give us an indication of the intensity of an emotion but cannot specify what that emotion is. For example, raised heart rate might signal high anxiety, but it could equally be caused by anger, lust, delight or excitement. Thus, physiological measures can indicate the strength of a reaction but not its focus. A second problem is that research has shown little correlation between the different indices; i.e. that there is no simple linear relationship between the various physiological measures. This leaves us in the awkward position that the relationships we discovered between arousal and performance will largely depend on the physiological measure used!

Behavioral measures have also been used, but only to a limited extent. Here psychologists observe activities, then rate anxiety on the basis of their observations. Again the drawback with this method is that confusion can arise when interpretations are in doubt. For example, a shivering swimmer may be either terrified, or just cold.

For the above reasons the most frequently used method of measuring anxiety is the **self-report questionnaire**. These psychometric tests have been employed to measure both trait and state anxiety. Looking first at trait measures, sport psychologists originally borrowed scales from general psychology e.g. the Taylor Manifest Anxiety scale (TMAS) and Spielberger's Trait Anxiety Inventory (TAI). The first sports specific scale to be developed was the uni-dimensional Sports Competitive Anxiety Test (SCAT). The realization that anxiety was a multidimensional construct led to the creation of the Cognitive Somatic Anxiety Questionnaire (CSAQ) and the sports-specific Sport Anxiety Scale (SAS). The SAS consists of three subscales of trait anxiety rather than the more usual two (cognitive and somatic). This is because it splits cognitive anxiety into two factors, worry and concentration disruption.

With regard to state measures of anxiety, again the first scale employed, Spielberger's State Anxiety Inventory (SAI) (Spielberger et al., 1970), was taken from general psychology. The first sport-specific scale used was the Competitive State Anxiety Inventory (CSAI). Following this, and reflecting the discovery of the multidimensional nature of anxiety, the **Competitive State Anxiety Inventory 2 (CSAI-2)** was developed (Martens et al., 1990). The CSAI-2 is by far the most widely used anxiety measure in sport. It is made up of three sub-scales, cognitive anxiety, somatic anxiety and self-confidence, each of which consists of nine items. Respondents are asked to say how they feel right now, on a four-point scale of 'not at all', 'somewhat', 'moderately' and 'very much so', in relation to cognitive items such as 'I am concerned about this competition', and somatic items such as 'my body feels tense'.

Brief three-item versions of the CSAI-2, have been developed for use in field settings, where time constraints prohibit the use of longer scales; the two most used of these being the mental readiness form (MRF) (Krane 1994) and the anxiety rating scale (ARS) (Cox et al., 1998). Being so short, they cannot have the same level of psychometric rigor that longer scales do. However, their convenience means they will probably continue to be used. Although much used, the CSAI-2 is not without its problems. For example, factor analytic studies do not always confirm the original factor structure claimed by its authors (Lane et al., 1999). It is also claimed that it is susceptible to **social desirability faking**. The suggestion being that rather than fill it out in a truthful way, athletes complete it in a way that shows them in a good light. For example, studies have shown that athletes who score highly on social desirability scales tend to under-report cognitive anxiety.

Anxiety direction   Based on the fact that many top athletes report that they welcome a fairly high level of anxiety prior to competition, it has been argued that a better understanding of the area results if, in addition to measuring the **intensity** of an athlete's anxiety, we also measured its **direction**; i.e. whether the anxiety that athletes feel is experienced as being facilitative or debilitative to subsequent performance. With this in mind a modified version of the CSAI-2 has been developed by adding what has become known as the directional scale (Jones et al., 1993). So, having rated the intensity of the anxiety on the standard four-point scale, athletes are then asked to rate on a seven-point scale how facilitative or debilitative they believe that level of intensity is likely to be for subsequent performance. Many studies now routinely include the directional scale to measure both the intensity and direction of competitive anxiety, and use the terms facilitative and debilitative anxiety. This approach has not gone uncriticized (Burton & Naylor, 1997). Unfortunately, on the basis of these developments some sport psychologists have concluded that anxiety is not just facilitative, but that it can be a positive as well as a negative emotion. However, since anxiety is defined as a negative emotion there can be no such thing as positive anxiety.

It is possible that anxiety has been confused with the consequences of anxiety. There is nothing inconsistent about a negative feeling leading to a positive outcome. For example, the worry that you might under-perform in a competition could motivate you to try harder or concentrate more, resulting in high levels of performance. The confusion is removed when we realize that the directional scale is not measuring anxiety at all, but rather the athlete's outcome expectancy, based on their anxiety. In support of this view is the fact that one of the main findings from the research on 'directional anxiety' is that it is a better predictor of performance than anxiety intensity. This is not surprising since there is bound to be a stronger link between our judgments of whether anxiety will help or hinder subsequent performance and the performance itself, than between the intensity of our anxiety and our performance.

Drive theory

The main reason for sport psychologists' interest in anxiety is its important role in competitive performance. Over the years our understanding of the relationship between anxiety and performance has developed greatly, and this is reflected in the ever more complex theories that have been used to explain it. Along with the 'inverted U' theory, Hull's **drive theory** was one of the early attempts, and it suggested that performance was a multiplicative function of **habit strength** and drive, represented mathematically by the equation $P = f (H \times D)$. Thus, the greater the habit strength, or how well learned the task was, and the more drive (arousal) the better the performance. The theory predicts that at any given skill level, performance depends on arousal in a simple linear way, such that the greater the arousal the better the performance (*Fig. 1*).

While early tests of drive theory were generally supportive they tended to be carried out using very simple tasks that were much less demanding than the tasks that sports performers typically perform. In subsequent research with more complex tasks it was found that only about 50% of studies provided supportive findings. As a result it was not long before drive theory was superseded.

'Inverted U' theory

Another early idea about the arousal–performance relationship was '**inverted U' theory.** Its basic premise was that as arousal (or drive) increases, so too does performance, but only up to an optimum point, after which increases in arousal result in reduced levels of performance (*Fig. 2*).

The theory has had lasting appeal and it is easy to see why, since it makes intuitive sense. If we are so low in arousal that we are very 'laid back' and lackadaisical we clearly won't perform as well as we potentially could. Equally, if we are highly aroused we might expect fine motor skills to suffer. Common sense thus demands optimal arousal for optimal performance.

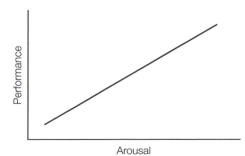

Fig. 1. The relationship between arousal and performance according to drive theory.

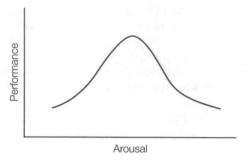

Fig. 2.   *The relationship between arousal and performance according to 'inverted U' theory.*

Another appealing aspect of the theory was that the curve could be shifted to account for different skill levels and different types of activity. So for example, optimal arousal level for beginners is predicted to be lower than for intermediate level players, which in turn is predicted to be lower than for highly skilled players (*Fig. 3*). Similarly, the theory predicts that optimal arousal for an activity requiring fine motor skills, such as golf putting, should be lower than for one involving strength, such as weight lifting (*Fig. 4*).

Unfortunately, the world is seldom this simple, and much research has shown that the predictions of the 'inverted U' theory are not always supported.

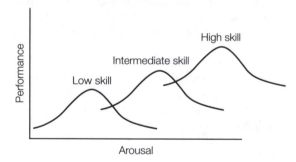

Fig. 3. *The relationship between the skill level of the athlete and optimal arousal level according to 'inverted U' theory.*

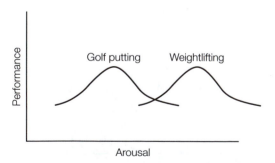

Fig. 4. *The relationship between activity type and optimal arousal level according to 'inverted U' theory.*

Additionally, the theory has been criticized for being impossible to falsify. This is because arousal levels are not measurable on an absolute scale. When a study to test the theory finds that increasing arousal is accompanied by an increase in performance, the theory can be said to be supported, but the same is true when increasing arousal accompanies decreased performance. Defenders of the theory simply need to assert that the arousal level may have been too low or too high when results do not fit the theory. Although useful for giving athletes and coaches a no nonsense, common sense way to think about the anxiety performance relationship, 'inverted U' theory has now been superseded by more complex approaches such as **catastrophe theory** (see D5) and **reversal theory** (see D6).

D4 MULTIDIMENSIONAL ANXIETY THEORY

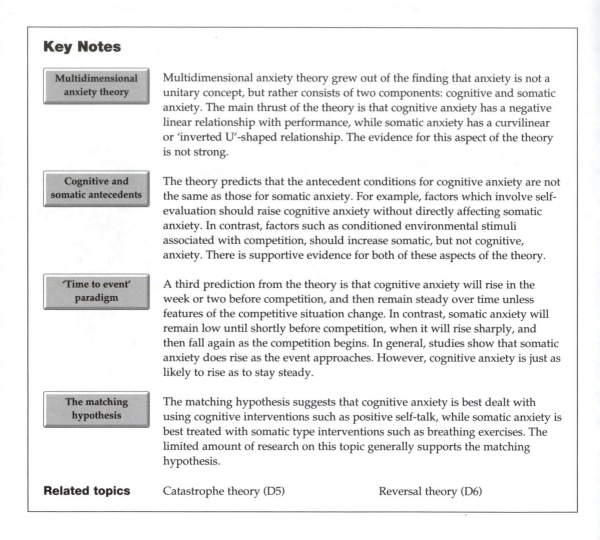

Key Notes

Multidimensional anxiety theory

Multidimensional anxiety theory grew out of the finding that anxiety is not a unitary concept, but rather consists of two components: cognitive and somatic anxiety. The main thrust of the theory is that cognitive anxiety has a negative linear relationship with performance, while somatic anxiety has a curvilinear or 'inverted U'-shaped relationship. The evidence for this aspect of the theory is not strong.

Cognitive and somatic antecedents

The theory predicts that the antecedent conditions for cognitive anxiety are not the same as those for somatic anxiety. For example, factors which involve self-evaluation should raise cognitive anxiety without directly affecting somatic anxiety. In contrast, factors such as conditioned environmental stimuli associated with competition, should increase somatic, but not cognitive, anxiety. There is supportive evidence for both of these aspects of the theory.

'Time to event' paradigm

A third prediction from the theory is that cognitive anxiety will rise in the week or two before competition, and then remain steady over time unless features of the competitive situation change. In contrast, somatic anxiety will remain low until shortly before competition, when it will rise sharply, and then fall again as the competition begins. In general, studies show that somatic anxiety does rise as the event approaches. However, cognitive anxiety is just as likely to rise as to stay steady.

The matching hypothesis

The matching hypothesis suggests that cognitive anxiety is best dealt with using cognitive interventions such as positive self-talk, while somatic anxiety is best treated with somatic type interventions such as breathing exercises. The limited amount of research on this topic generally supports the matching hypothesis.

Related topics   Catastrophe theory (D5)   Reversal theory (D6)

Multidimensional anxiety theory

The discovery that anxiety is not a unitary concept but made up of a cognitive and a somatic component (see Topic D3) meant that it was necessary to adapt existing theory, or to create new ways of thinking about the anxiety–perform-ance relationship. American sport psychologist Rainer Martens took up the challenge and developed **multidimensional anxiety theory** (Martens et al., 1990). The theory claims that the relationship between anxiety and performance takes a different form for the two types of anxiety. It was argued that cognitive anxiety would always be detrimental to performance, and that the relationship between cognitive anxiety and performance would be negative and linear. In contrast, the somatic component of anxiety was predicted to relate to perform-ance in a curvilinear way, taking the form of an 'inverted U' (*Fig. 1*).

Studies to investigate whether these two different forms of the relationship exist have produced a mixed picture. Strong support for the theory would be provided if both predictions were confirmed within the same study. This has occurred in only one or two cases (Burton, 1988). More often studies find support for either the cognitive prediction, or the somatic prediction, but not both. In direct contradiction to the theory, some research has demonstrated that cognitive anxiety is associated with improved performance. Still other studies show no clear relationship between anxiety and performance at all. Particularly damning for multidimensional anxiety theory is a recent meta-analysis of the relationship between CSAI-2 scores and performance which shows an almost negligible correlation between performance and both somatic and cognitive anxiety (Craft et al., 2003). Despite this patchy picture, multidimensional anxiety theory has moved our understanding forward. What it has not done is treat the two components interactively, as **catastrophe theory** does (see D5). A further problem is that it cannot account for the observation that sometimes in sport, rather than performance gently falling away as anxiety rises, it slumps dramatically. Again, this is something for which catastrophe theory does have an answer.

Cognitive and somatic antecedents

Another consequence of there being two types of anxiety is that they are likely to be influenced by different factors. Certain events may lead to cognitive, but not somatic anxiety, and vice versa. This constitutes the second part of multi-dimensional anxiety theory, namely that cognitive and somatic anxiety have different **antecedents**.

The logic of the argument is that cognitive anxiety relates to worry about not coming up to expectation, so that factors that involve self-evaluation should raise cognitive anxiety without directly affecting somatic anxiety. Similarly, because of its nature, the precursors of somatic anxiety are argued to be those features of the sporting environment that have become conditioned stimuli, associated with the competitive situation. For example, the sight of the doors of the sports hall, or the evocative smells and sounds of the locker room may well raise somatic anxiety, but they are less likely to affect cognitive anxiety. The evidence supports this aspect of multidimensional anxiety theory. The general picture is that the two types of anxiety do appear to have different antecedents. For example, it has been shown that perceived readiness, attitude to previous

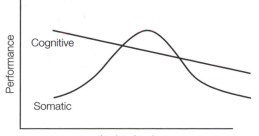

Fig. 1 The relationship between cognitive anxiety and performance, and somatic anxiety and performance, according to multidimensional anxiety theory.

performance, and position goal, all predict cognitive anxiety, but they are unrelated to somatic anxiety (Hanton & Jones, 1995).

'Time to event' paradigm

A third aspect of the theory relates to the different paths the two types of anxiety are said to take in the period of weeks and days before a competition. This is known as the **'time to event' paradigm** or **temporal patterning** hypothesis. In general, a paradigm is a particular approach or method of doing something. In this context, it is the method of focusing on the anxiety–performance relationship over time. Because of the nature of the two types of anxiety, predictions about their temporal patterning differ. Specifically, the suggestion is that cognitive anxiety, being related to perceived ability and performance expectancies, will rise in the week or two before competition and then remain steady over time, unless some feature of the competitive situation changes. For example, if you learned that your major rival was recovering from a bout of flu, this might reduce your cognitive anxiety. In contrast, it is predicted that somatic anxiety, being affected by the **conditioned stimuli** associated with the competitive situation, will remain low until shortly before competition, when it will rise sharply on arrival at the sporting venue, then fall again as the competition begins (see *Fig. 2*).

The evidence on the temporal patterning of multidimensional anxiety theory is equivocal (Cerin et al., 2000). Somatic anxiety does typically rise as the event approaches. However, it appears that cognitive anxiety is as likely to rise as stay steady.

The matching hypothesis

Finally, the practical implications of multidimensional anxiety theory led to **the matching hypothesis** (see Topic L2). The hypothesis suggests that since the two types of anxiety are caused by two different sets of antecedents, the intervention required to effectively reduce each will be different. In other words the intervention employed should match the type of anxiety being treated. If correct, the use of cognitive interventions such as positive **self-talk**, **thought stopping**, or **cognitive restructuring** should be more effective in reducing cognitive anxiety, while somatic-type interventions such as **progressive muscle relaxation** (PMR), breathing exercises, and other bodily relaxation techniques should be more effective for the reduction of somatic anxiety. While the amount of research into this question has been small, results suggest some support for the notion of the matching hypothesis (Maynard & Cotton 1993; Maynard et al., 1995).

Fig. 2.   The time to event predictions of multidimensional anxiety theory.

D5 CATASTROPHE THEORY

Key Notes

Introduction to catastrophe theory

Catastrophe theory provides a three-dimensional descriptive model of the relationship between cognitive anxiety, physiological arousal and performance. It considers the cognitive and somatic aspects of anxiety in an interactive way rather than simply by adding the effects of the two. It can account for sudden performance collapses such as 'choking' and why recovery from such collapse is difficult. Finally, it can account for the finding that cognitive anxiety is sometimes positively and sometimes negatively related to performance.

The catastrophe model

The central feature of the model is that it combines cognitive anxiety and physiological arousal in an interactive way. In particular it predicts quite different effects depending on whether cognitive anxiety is low or high. When cognitive anxiety is high, and arousal is rising, the theory predicts a sudden and catastrophic, as opposed to a smooth, decline in performance.

Predictions from catastrophe theory

There is an interactive relationship between cognitive anxiety and physiological arousal, such that when cognitive anxiety is high, there will be catastrophic effects on performance as physiological arousal reaches higher levels, whereas at low levels of cognitive anxiety there will be no such catastrophic effects. Under conditions of high cognitive anxiety, hysteresis will occur. Hysteresis describes the phenomenon that occurs when the measured values of one of two related variables takes a different value depending on whether the other variable is increasing or decreasing.

The status of catastrophe theory

Being relatively new, there are as yet only a handful of studies that have tested the theory. Research has found evidence to support the claim that there is an interactive link between cognitive anxiety and physiological arousal. There has also been support for the hysteresis-based predictions. Catastrophe theory does not concern itself with somatic anxiety directly, but instead focuses on physiological arousal.

Related topics

Multidimensional anxiety theory (D4)

Reversal theory (D6)

Introduction to catastrophe theory

Catastrophe theory was the brainchild of the French mathematician, Rene Thom, but was brought to prominence in the sport anxiety area by British sport psychologist Lew Hardy. It provides a three-dimensional descriptive model of the relationship between cognitive anxiety, physiological arousal and performance (Hardy & Parfitt, 1991). It has advanced our understanding of the anxiety–performance relationship because it is able to account for several things that previous theories cannot. In particular it considers the cognitive and somatic aspects of anxiety in an **interactive** way, rather than simply adding the effects of the two. It can also deal with the fact that in sport, players can suffer from 'choking', a sudden dramatic inability to 'get their game together'. One famous example of this occurred in the 1993 Wimbledon tennis final between Jana Novotna and Steffi Graf. Novotna appeared to be cruising and needed one more point in her service game to go 5–1 up in the final set. Going for broke on her second serve, she double-faulted and lost the game, and every remaining game, to throw away the championship. As this example shows, performance doesn't always just gently slip down some hypothetical curve, whether that be down the cognitive anxiety slope of multidimensional anxiety theory, or over the top of the 'inverted U' theory curve. In addition to accounting for catastrophic losses in performance the theory helps us to understand why recovery from a catastrophic drop in performance is likely to require more than simply reducing anxiety back to pre-catastrophic levels. Finally, the theory can explain why cognitive anxiety is sometimes positively related, and sometimes negatively related, to performance.

The catastrophe model

The model is a three-dimensional one, which can be understood by breaking it down into four constituent parts. Firstly, there is the situation of low physiological arousal (*Fig. 1*). Here, in contrast to multidimensional anxiety theory (Topic D4), cognitive anxiety is predicted to have a positive effect on performance. This can account for the finding that cognitive anxiety is not always detrimental to performance. Secondly, in the situation of high physiological arousal (*Fig. 2*) it is predicted that cognitive anxiety will have a negative effect on performance.

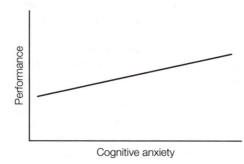

Fig. 1.   The relationship between cognitive anxiety and performance when physiological arousal is low.

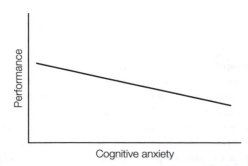

Fig. 2.   The relationship between cognitive anxiety and performance when physiological arousal is high.

The third constituent of the model relates to the situation of low cognitive anxiety, in which the arousal–performance relationship is said to take the shape of the 'inverted U' (*Fig. 3*). Finally, we have the situation of high cognitive anxiety. It is here that the theory departs significantly from previous theories, and where it gets its name, because it claims that when arousal rises above a certain level there will be a sudden discontinuity in the arousal–performance curve (*Fig. 4*) and that the athlete will suffer a catastrophic drop in performance.

Putting these four situations together it is possible to imagine the full catastrophe model in which performance level can be represented as a mountain surface (*Fig. 5*). Performance is represented on the vertical axis, physiological arousal rises from left to right, and cognitive anxiety rises from the back to the front of the page. When cognitive anxiety is low, at the back of *Figure 5*, performance takes the shape of a shallow 'inverted U'. As physiological arousal increases so too does performance until some optimum point is reached when performance begins to fall away again. In contrast, if we consider the case of high cognitive anxiety and move to the front of *Figure 5*, we see that increases in arousal lead to performance that follows the 'inverted U' profile until just over the optimum arousal level, and then drops off the edge of the performance surface. This catastrophic fall is where the theory gets its name. The model proposes that cognitive anxiety acts as a **splitting factor** which determines whether the effect of physiological arousal will be small and smooth, or large and catastrophic.

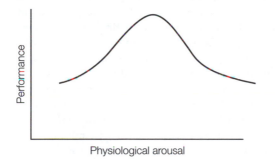

Fig. 3.   The relationship between physiological arousal and performance when cognitive anxiety is low.

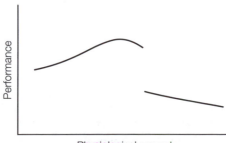

Fig. 4.   The relationship between physiological arousal and performance when cognitive anxiety is high.

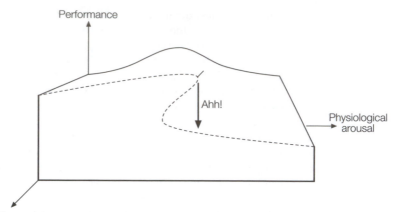

Fig. 5.   The complete catastrophe model: Performance is represented on the vertical axis, with increased physiological arousal represented by movement from left to right and increased cognitive anxiety from back to front of the page. When cognitive anxiety is low (at the back of the diagram) the performance takes the shape of an 'inverted U'. In the case of high cognitive anxiety (the front of the diagram) increases in arousal produce increases in performance, until there is a catastrophic drop off the edge of the performance surface.

Predictions from catastrophe theory

The main predictions from catastrophe theory are firstly, that when cognitive anxiety is high, there will be catastrophic effects on performance as physiological arousal reaches higher levels. Extending this slightly the theory predicts an interaction between cognitive anxiety and physiological arousal, so that performance should be bimodal (either high or low with not much in between) when cognitive anxiety is high, and uni-modal (consist of a full range of scores) when cognitive anxiety is low. Secondly, it is predicted that under conditions of high cognitive anxiety, **hysteresis** will occur. Hysteresis describes the phenomenon that occurs when the *measured values of one of two related variables* takes a different value depending on whether the other variable is increasing or decreasing. This is better understood by imagining a situation where we ask a golfer to run on a treadmill at low speed for a short period, so they have low physiological arousal, and then measure how well they perform in a golf putting task. We then ask them to do the treadmill running again at a slightly faster rate and again perform the putting task. We repeat this procedure for several more cycles, increasing the treadmill rate each time, thereby increasing their physiological arousal, until the golfer is close to their maximum work rate. Now we allow the golfer to rest and repeat the procedure, except that this time, they start with high treadmill rates and work down to low rates. Hysteresis is in evidence if the curve of measured putting performance follows a different path as physiological arousal rises, from the path that it takes as physiological arousal falls. This is illustrated in *Figure 6*.

The status of catastrophe theory

Catastrophe theory is a relatively recent addition to the literature and as such it has yet to be studied extensively. However, what research has been carried out has been very encouraging, if not totally supportive of all aspects of the theory. Research has shown the predicted interactive pattern with:

(1) low performance levels being observed when cognitive anxiety and physiological arousal were both high;

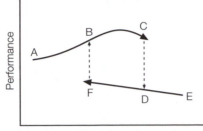

Fig. 6. The hysteresis effect. Catastrophe theory predicts hysteresis at high levels of cognitive anxiety, meaning that the performance pathway will be different depending on whether the athlete begins with a low physiological arousal and has it increased (path A, B, C, D, E), or with a high physiological arousal level that is gradually lowered (path E, D, F, B, A).

(2) high performance levels when cognitive anxiety was high and physiological arousal low;

(3) moderate levels of performance when cognitive anxiety and physiological arousal were low;

(4) moderate levels of performance when cognitive anxiety was low and physiological arousal was low.

Studies of the hysteresis hypothesis have also been supportive of this aspect of the theory. They have shown that when arousal is systematically raised the measured performance curve is consistently higher through the mid-range of arousal, before falling suddenly and catastrophically at higher arousal levels. When arousal starts high and is systematically lowered, performance starts low and stays low, only rising when very low levels of arousal are reached. This is exactly the hysteresis pattern. In contrast, when cognitive anxiety is low, as predicted, hysteresis does not occur (Hardy 1996).

Some critics of catastrophe theory claim that it is not a theory at all, but a model, because it does not explain why cognitive anxiety and physiological arousal affect performance. Rather it describes how they inter-relate. However, this is a criticism that can be applied to several theories in this area, including multidimensional anxiety theory. Secondly, it does not concern itself with somatic anxiety directly, but instead focuses on physiological arousal. Although these two variables may co-vary much of the time, there will be times when athletes are highly aroused, but not somatically anxious. For example, they may be angry, sad or excited (see D3). Indeed, reversal theory (see D6) rests on the argument that athletes can, and do, experience reversals in their emotional state from anxiety to excitement and vice versa, while remaining at a high arousal level. Hardy (1996) deliberately chose to include physiological arousal in preference to somatic anxiety, on the grounds that the former was likely to be more influential on performance. Future research could usefully test a version of the catastrophe model in which we manipulate somatic anxiety, rather than physiological arousal. One final practical problem for catastrophe theory is that it requires elaborate designs to test it, which may be part of the reason for the small number of studies that have so far investigated it.

D6 REVERSAL THEORY

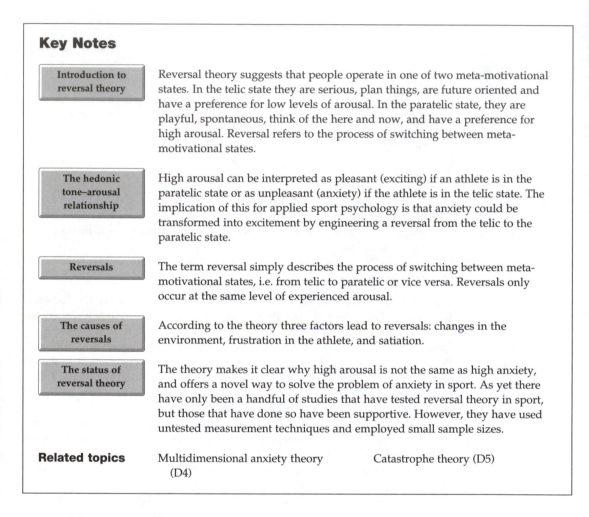

Key Notes

Introduction to reversal theory	Reversal theory suggests that people operate in one of two meta-motivational states. In the telic state they are serious, plan things, are future oriented and have a preference for low levels of arousal. In the paratelic state, they are playful, spontaneous, think of the here and now, and have a preference for high arousal. Reversal refers to the process of switching between meta-motivational states.
The hedonic tone–arousal relationship	High arousal can be interpreted as pleasant (exciting) if an athlete is in the paratelic state or as unpleasant (anxiety) if the athlete is in the telic state. The implication of this for applied sport psychology is that anxiety could be transformed into excitement by engineering a reversal from the telic to the paratelic state.
Reversals	The term reversal simply describes the process of switching between meta-motivational states, i.e. from telic to paratelic or vice versa. Reversals only occur at the same level of experienced arousal.
The causes of reversals	According to the theory three factors lead to reversals: changes in the environment, frustration in the athlete, and satiation.
The status of reversal theory	The theory makes it clear why high arousal is not the same as high anxiety, and offers a novel way to solve the problem of anxiety in sport. As yet there have only been a handful of studies that have tested reversal theory in sport, but those that have done so have been supportive. However, they have used untested measurement techniques and employed small sample sizes.
Related topics	Multidimensional anxiety theory (D4) Catastrophe theory (D5)

Introduction to reversal theory

Reversal theory was developed outside sport psychology by Michael Apter, but was brought to the attention of researchers interested in sport by John Kerr (Kerr, 1985). It provides a rather unusual approach to the anxiety–performance relationship in that its underlying philosophy is phenomenological rather than positivist (see Topics A5 & A7). Thus, instead of asserting that athletes have an 'objective', 'reality-based' or 'factual' view of a competitive situation it stresses the importance of their subjective interpretation of the situation. The theory proposes that there are four pairs of **meta-motivational states** in which we routinely operate (meta being the Greek for 'of a higher order'). They are termed meta-motivational rather than motivational states because they are reflexive, i.e. they are not the athlete's motivational state as such, but rather the athlete's interpretation of his or her motivational state.

It is the **telic–paratelic** pair that is most relevant in the context of anxiety. Someone in the **telic state** is serious, plans things, is future oriented and has a preference for low levels of arousal. In contrast the same person, when in the **paratelic state**, is playful, spontaneous and thinks of the here and now. Additionally, they have a preference for high arousal. A second important concept of the theory is **bi-stability**. The rather grand-sounding principle of bi-stability simply means we are always in one state or the other. Unlike a trait or personality dimension there are no shades of 'telicness' or 'paratelicness'. We are in one or the other state, a bit like a light switch that is off or on. Another basic concept employed by the theory is that of **hedonic tone**. Hedonic tone refers to the simple notion of subjectively experienced pleasure. Thus, high hedonic tone implies more experienced pleasure than low hedonic tone. The theory also postulates the notion of **reversals** from which it gets its name. A reversal refers to the process of switching between meta-motivational states. One final aspect of the theory is that of **meta-motivational dominance**, which means that although we switch between the telic and paratelic state, we do have a tendency to prefer one rather than the other.

The hedonic tone–arousal relationship

The theory states that athletes in the telic state (*Fig. 1*) have high levels of hedonic tone (pleasure) and feel relaxed when arousal is low. As experienced arousal increases, their level of hedonic tone (pleasure) falls, and at high levels of arousal, they feel anxiety. In contrast, athletes in the paratelic state (*Fig. 2*)

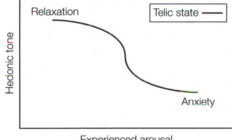

Fig. 1. The relationship between hedonic tone (pleasure) and experienced arousal for athletes in the telic state. Athletes in the telic state have high levels of hedonic tone (pleasure) and feel relaxed when arousal is low. As experienced arousal increases their level of hedonic tone (pleasure) falls and at high levels of arousal they feel anxiety.

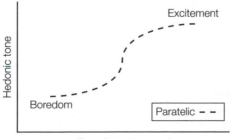

Fig. 2. The relationship between hedonic tone (pleasure) and experienced arousal for athletes in the paratelic state. Athletes in the paratelic state have low levels of hedonic tone (pleasure) and feel bored when arousal is low. As experienced arousal increases their level of hedonic tone (pleasure) increases and at high levels of arousal they feel excited.

have low levels of hedonic tone (pleasure), and feel bored when arousal is low. As experienced arousal increases, their level of hedonic tone (pleasure) increases, and at high levels of arousal, they feel excited.

Putting these together (*Fig. 3*), we see that high arousal can be interpreted as pleasant (exciting), or unpleasant (anxiety), and low arousal can be interpreted as pleasant (relaxing), or unpleasant (boring), depending on which meta-motivational state the athlete is experiencing. The practical implication of this is that by engineering a telic to paratelic reversal, at high arousal levels, anxiety can be turned into excitement. Similarly, a paratelic to the telic reversal at low arousal levels can turn boredom into relaxation.

Reversals

Two high-arousal examples should help to clarify the theory. Imagine playing in a competition, perhaps a golf tournament. For the first hole or two, you just go out to enjoy it. You don't expect to do well, knowing there are better players than you competing. You are in the paratelic state. You are under no pressure, but you start to play really great golf, and soon you are in the lead, and excited. However, it is not long before you begin to have future-oriented thoughts about the possibility that you can win. You become more serious, and reverse to the telic state, where enjoyment turns to anxiety.

An example of a telic to paratelic reversal might be, if you are competing in a martial arts competition and you are already in a fairly serious frame of mind because of the importance of the event. Your anxiety increases when you see your next opponent in the changing rooms, prior to competition, because s/he is huge, and fearsome in appearance. However, in the warm up period, and during the first few moments of competition, you realize that your opponent is actually very clumsy and uncoordinated. This may well result in a reversal to the more playful paratelic state, so that the competition is now experienced differently and you no longer feel anxiety or fear, but rather begin to enjoy a feeling of excitement about fighting well.

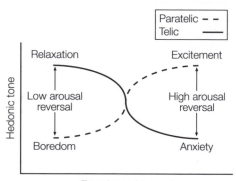

Fig. 3.   The relationship between hedonic tone (pleasure) and experienced arousal for both the telic and the paratelic state. Athletes in the telic state (represented by the solid line) have high levels of hedonic tone (pleasure) and feel relaxed when arousal is low. As experienced arousal increases their level of hedonic tone (pleasure) falls and at high levels of arousal they feel anxiety. Athletes in the paratelic state (represented by the broken line) have low levels of hedonic tone (pleasure) and feel bored when arousal is low. As experienced arousal increases their level of hedonic tone (pleasure) increases and at high levels of arousal they feel excited. Reversals occur at the same arousal level.

One final point about reversals is that they only occur at the same level of experienced arousal (see *Fig. 3*).

The causes of reversals

According to the theory three factors lead to reversals: **environmental contingency**, **frustration** and **satiation**. An example of an environmental event that might lead to a reversal, is a change in the weather. Motor racing drivers who love driving in wet conditions, may reverse from the telic to paratelic state following a downpour, with anxiety being replaced by excitement. The opposite might occur in rock climbers. Sudden rain, making the rock slippery, might lead to a reversal from the paratelic to the telic state with excitement being replaced by anxiety.

Frustration can also lead to reversals. For example, the frustration that results from bad refereeing could cause a reversal from the paratelic to the telic state. It is hard here not to think of the tennis player John McEnroe, who was infamous for reacting badly to umpiring decisions.

Finally, reversals can occur when satiation sets in. A paratelic to telic example of this might be when players start out in training sessions, just wanting to play scrimmage games, eventually becoming satiated, and then preferring to work on set pieces or training drills. Thus we see a reversal from the playful paratelic excitement of the scrimmage game, to the more serious telic anxiety about the team needing to do some hard practice.

The status of reversal theory

Two measures have been devised to support and test the theory. The **Telic Dominance Scale** (TDS) (Murgatroyd et al., 1978) measures people's typical or preferred style. The **Telic State Measure** (TSM) (Svebak & Murgatroyd, 1985) measures people's current meta-motivational state, and their tendency to stay in it. The TSM also asks for ratings of both felt and preferred arousal. **Tension stress** is defined as the discrepancy between felt and preferred arousal. The larger the discrepancy the more likely it is that low hedonic tone will follow.

As yet there have been only a handful of studies that have tested the theory in sport, but those that do so have found a measure of support (Kerr, 1999). For example, one unusual prediction from reversal theory is that paratelic-dominant people are less happy in the absence of moderate stressors in their lives, and there is some evidence for this. It has also been shown that paratelic-dominant players perform worse in a low-stress 'play for fun' situation than in a moderate-stress 'do your best' situation. In contrast, telic-dominant players perform better in a low-stress, 'play for fun' situation than in a moderate-stress 'do your best' one. Studies using the TSM have also supported the theory, showing an inverse relationship between tension stress and performance (Martin et al., 1987). Thus, in a high-arousal situation, people in the paratelic state out-performed those in the telic state. It has also been shown that athletes who are highly aroused perform better on a measure of explosive strength when they are in the paratelic state than the telic state (Perkins et al., 2001).

More empirical research is needed before we can be clearer about the value of the theory. However, it has the potential to provide a useful way of conceptualizing the anxiety–performance relationship. It has the advantage that it makes clear the distinction between arousal and anxiety, and in particular shows why high arousal is not the same as high anxiety. It also avoids over-emphasis on anxiety as the only relevant emotion which impacts on performance, focusing in addition on relaxation, excitement and boredom.

In terms of practical implications, the theory gives us a new set of interventions in addition to the more traditional arousal reduction techniques. For example, it offers the option, in anxiety-provoking situations, to engineer a reversal to excitement, or in situations of boredom, the option to engineer a reversal to relaxation. On the negative side, as with catastrophe theory, reversal theory is relatively new, and as yet has gone largely untested, particularly in sports settings. What little research has been carried out suffers from small sample sizes and employs measures that have yet to have their reliability or validity confirmed (see Topic A4). One final problem for reversal theory is that it employs a uni-dimensional conception of anxiety, without reference to its separate cognitive and somatic components.

D7 OTHER THEORIES

Key Notes

Individual zone of optimal functioning	Hanin conceived of the individual zone of optimal functioning (IZOF) as an 'inverted U', which is individualized, in the sense that it refers to the range of an individual athlete's arousal levels, when they are performing optimally. This range then constitutes their zone of optimal functioning. Research is mildly supportive of the theory in that a moderate effect size (0.44) was found between performances in and out of the zone.
Problems with IZOF research	There are several methodological problems with the research on IZOF. Hanin and others typically define the zone using retrospective recall measures, which raise the issue of the accuracy of recall. Another methodological problem is that the IZOF research relies heavily on self-reported performance. More research, measuring anxiety at the time rather than retrospectively, and that uses objective measures of performance, is needed before we can have too much faith in the value of IZOF.
Processing efficiency theory	Processing efficiency theory was devised by Eysenck and Calvo, to explain why anxiety does not always lead to attentional distraction and performance deficits in cognitive tasks. The theory distinguishes between performance effectiveness and processing efficiency. Tests of the theory do show that anxiety impairs processing efficiency more than performance effectiveness.
Applicability of processing efficiency theory	There may be problems with the relevance of the theory for the majority of sports activities. When cognitive psychologists talked about more effort, they were talking about allocating more processing resources to increase available working memory. In the sports domain, working memory is not something that is under continuous pressure.
Related topic	Anxiety: the basics (D3)

Individual zone of optimal functioning

The Russian sport psychologist Yuri Hanin first suggested the notion of the **individual zone of optimal functioning (IZOF)**. The idea has its origins in the 'inverted U' hypothesis in that it refers to the range of an athlete's optimal arousal in which peak performance occurs. While the 'inverted U' was said to be a general group-level phenomenon with, for example, an optimal arousal level for any given sport. Hanin conceived of the zone of optimal functioning as an individual phenomenon, with each athlete having their own IZOF (see *Fig. 1*) (Hanin, 2000). He developed the idea as a practical tool on the basis of his experience of working with elite athletes in the Soviet Union. He suggested that by monitoring an individual athlete's anxiety levels prior to several competitions, we could establish a range of levels around which good performance occurs. This range then constitutes their zone of optimal functioning. The job of the sport psychologist or athlete is then to monitor anxiety immediately prior to an event, and to regulate it so that it is within the appropriate range. In this way the athlete should be able to perform optimally. A recent development in the light of multidimensional anxiety theory, has been to include cognitive and somatic anxiety, and to consider what this means for zones of optimal function. To test the theory we need to measure an athlete's anxiety over a number of occasions to discover what level of anxiety is associated with their best performance. This range of anxiety scores, associated with playing well, is their zone. We can then look at how well they subsequently perform when in this anxiety zone, as opposed to outside it. A meta-analysis of the literature, looking at 19 studies between 1978 and 1997, was mildly supportive of the theory in that a moderate effect size (0.44) was found between performances in and out of the zone (Jokela & Hanin, 1999). However, even this modest support needs to be treated with some caution because there are some methodological problems in the research to date that need to be addressed.

Problems with IZOF research

One major issue here is the fact that Hanin and others typically define the anxiety zone by **retrospective recall** measures. Rather than measuring anxiety prior to performance at the time of the event, these techniques require athletes to think back over several days to remember their anxiety level immediately prior to performance. While this was done for good reason (it is less invasive and does not risk making athletes aware of their anxiety at a crucial time in a competition) it does lead to a serious possibility of bias. In the first place, it opens up the whole issue of the accuracy of recall. We may just not be good at recalling anxiety and it is also bound to be the case that some athletes will be better at it than others. There is empirical evidence of accuracy problems with retrospective recall and that these were worse for the CSAI-2 than the State Anxiety Inventory (Annesi 1997). Another possible source of bias is that our perception of our anxiety level 3 days earlier could easily be colored by the outcome of the competition.

Yet another methodological problem is that the IZOF research relies heavily on self-reported performance. This may well mean that participants' anxiety level contaminates their rated performance, i.e. 'I was more anxious than I like to be and it showed in my play'. One final problem is that in many of the IZOF studies, scores used to define the zone have then been re-used to support the hypothesis. This contamination artificially increases the likelihood of a relationship between IZOF and performance. More research, measuring anxiety at the time rather than retrospectively, and using objective measures of performance, is needed.

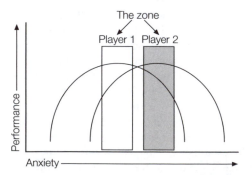

Fig. 1.   The zone of optimal functioning for two players.

Processing efficiency theory

Processing efficiency theory is another theory borrowed from mainstream psychology. It was devised by Eysenck and Calvo (1992) to explain why anxiety does not always lead to attentional distraction and performance deficits in cognitive tasks such as visual search and letter recognition. They argued that in addition to attentional disruption, worry serves a motivational function in that it increases mental effort. The theory distinguishes between **performance effectiveness**, which refers to the quality of the performance of the task, and **processing efficiency**, which refers to the relationship between the effectiveness of performance and the effort or processing resources invested in performance. In this way, worry can impair processing efficiency without affecting performance effectiveness. Thus, Eysenck and Calvo suggest that there is a self-regulatory control system in the central executive of working memory (see Topic B5) which monitors performance and in the face of poor performance, allocates additional resources (effort) or initiates different processing activities (strategies), to try to free up more working memory capacity. The theory is squarely aimed at cognitive processes and cognitive tasks. Tests of the theory have centered on the prediction that anxiety would be more detrimental to task performance in tasks that had high demand on the resources of working memory. Many studies, using a variety of cognitive tasks including anagrams, problem solving, digit span and letter recognition type attentional tasks, support the ideas of processing efficiency theory. They show that anxiety impairs processing efficiency more than performance effectiveness, and that the adverse effects of anxiety on task performance increase as the task demands more working memory capacity.

Sport psychologists had known for some time that anxiety does not always lead to performance deficits. With its emphasis on the allocation of extra effort in the face of worry, processing efficiency theory appeared to offer one explanation for why this might be so. It is not surprising then that the theory was imported into sport psychology.

Applicability of processing efficiency theory

Unfortunately, there may be problems with the relevance of the theory for the majority of sports activities. When cognitive psychologists talk about more effort, they are not talking about effort as an athlete understands it, i.e. being more determined, or increasing the work rate and trying harder. They mean allocating more processing resources to increase available working memory. In the sports domain, working memory is not something that is under continuous pressure. When we are going 'higher, further and faster', to quote the Olympic motto, **working memory** and its sub-systems of the phonological loop, the visio-spatial scratch pad and the central executive, are seldom busy. In most cases the demand is small because cognitive load is minimal. Even when it is not, the athlete usually has clear plans for each eventuality, or well-used tactics and previous experience of dealing with it. It is not being claimed that athletes never use working memory. Sport does sometimes require quick decision making and certain tasks require memory. However, in general, working memory is rarely involved and when it is, it is seldom under load. If you are sprinting, working memory is not an issue. If you are trying to putt a golf ball, again working memory is not involved. As such, it seems that sport psychologists may have made too much of a leap from cognitive gymnastics to physical ones, and overestimated the relevance of processing efficiency theory to explain aspects of the anxiety–performance relationship.

E1 INTRODUCTION TO INDIVIDUAL DIFFERENCES

Key Notes

Individual differences	Individual differences is the term used in psychology to describe the systematic way that people differ consistently from each other, and what effect these differences have on their behavior. The main individual differences that have been the focus of study in psychology are differences in cognitive ability, i.e. intelligence, and differences in character, i.e. personality.
Definitions	Personality is viewed in different ways by different theoretical perspectives in psychology. Those in the humanistic and psychoanalytic schools stress the uniqueness of the individual. The trait approach, favored by behaviorism and cognitive psychology stresses the range of difference expressed as a point along a continuum for each individual on each attribute. It is the trait approach that has been the most commonly used, both in mainstream and particularly so in sport psychology. Personality is defined here as the relatively stable set of internal traits that make one person's behavior consistent over time.
Trait–state distinction	Nowhere is this distinction more important than in relation to personality, because many sport psychologists appear to use the terms trait and state in a confusing way. In your reading in sport and exercise psychology, you may come across statements that talk about personality traits and 'personality states'. The term 'personality states' is highly misleading. Since psychologists agree that a state is something that is relatively short term, and a trait is relatively enduring, the term 'personality state' is a contradiction in terms.
Measurement	Personality traits are typically measured by paper and pencil inventories that have been constructed to be reliable, valid and standardized. The two most widely used inventories in sport psychology have been Cattell's 16 personality factors (16PF) and the Eysenck Personality Inventory (EPI). More recently, a newer inventory based on the five-factor model (FFM) has become popular.
Related topic	Personality and sport (E2)

Individual differences

Much of psychology is about how people think, feel and act generally. For example, we investigate how individuals as a whole manage to perceive depth, or how anxiety affects people's performance in general. However, it is also important to study the systematic ways that people differ consistently from each other, and what effect these differences have on their behavior. For example, if we want to be able to understand a young athlete's behavior at a post-match reception, it might help to know whether she is extraverted or introverted in terms of her personality. **Individual differences** is the term used in psychology to describe these enduring aspects of people.

The main individual differences that have been the focus of study in psychology are differences in cognitive ability, i.e. **intelligence,** and differences in character, i.e. **personality**. While in psychology generally, a vast amount of work has been carried out on the study of intelligence, surprisingly little has been done in the sport and exercise domain, and for this reason the focus here will be on personality. Before moving on to do this, it is interesting to note that what little work has been done on the intelligence of athletes tends to contradict the common stereotype of the brainless 'jock'. Comparisons of the IQ scores of athletes and the general population have favored the athletes. For example, one study of athletes and non-athletes at Oxford and Cambridge showed that athletes graduated with better degrees than their less-active counterparts. While this may not fit too well with our perceptions of some sports stars interviewed on television, or the fact that some scholarship students have trouble academically, we should remember that these top athletes do not constitute an unbiased sample. Self-selection both into and away from professional sport may explain the contradiction. For example, if an academic route out of poverty is not available to a young person, they may well be highly motivated to achieve in the sporting world. The opposite effect occurs when parents pressure clever and promising young athletes away from sport as a career, toward a more traditional profession, because of the uncertainty of making it to the top in sport.

When non-psychologists are asked to think about how psychology might be relevant to sport, it is often the **personality** of athletes that they first mention. The lay view appears to be that if we know people's personalities, that knowledge will be useful in sport. If pressed, however, they are not always sure how it might be so. One suggestion sometimes made is that knowing about the personality of the members of a large squad might help us with team selection. The idea here is that perhaps we could predict who will be better for the team, or which personality type would be more suited to what sport or exercise activity.

As we shall see (Topic E2), and surprisingly to the newcomer to sport psychology, there appears to be little evidence that particular personality profiles are associated with success in sport.

Definitions

Personality is defined in many ways by different theoretical perspectives or schools in psychology (Topic A7). These definitions are a testimony to the different approaches to personality that have been employed over the years. Those in the humanistic and psychoanalytic schools stress the uniqueness of the individual, but the **trait approach** favored by behaviorism and cognitive psychology stresses the range of difference, expressed as a point along a continuum, for each individual on each attribute. Thus, one athlete may be said to be a 16 on the extraversion–introversion dimension while another may be a 4. The trait approach has been the more commonly used, both in general and particularly so in sport psychology, and it will be the focus of the rest of the section. For our purposes, we shall define personality as the relatively stable set of internal traits that make one person's behavior consistent over time.

Although rarely used in sport psychology, one other approach to personality should be mentioned, and that is the type approach. In this view, all people can be pigeonholed into one of a limited set of types. Types differ from traits in that types are not possessed in degree: you are a particular type or you are not. In contrast, in the trait approach to personality, people are seen as being normally distributed along a number of dimensions.

Trait–state distinction

This distinction has already been made with reference to confidence (Topic C6) and anxiety (Topic D3), but nowhere is it more important than in relation to personality, because many sport psychologists appear to use the terms trait and state in a confusing way. In your reading in sport and exercise psychology, you may come across statements that talk about personality traits and 'personality states'. The term 'personality states' is misleading. Since psychologists agree that a **state** is something that is relatively short term, and a **trait** is relatively enduring, the term 'personality state' makes little sense. Despite this, even some of the best-known sport psychologists have perpetuated the confusion. To be fair this confusion is traceable back to Spielberger's original writings in general psychology on the State and Trait Anxiety Inventories (Spielberger et al., 1970) (see Topic D3).

Measurement

Personality traits are typically measured by paper and pencil inventories. (The term test is deliberately avoided, because it implies that there are right or wrong answers, which for personality there are not.) In the typical inventory, respondents are asked to say whether a series of statements applies to them or not. For example, they are asked to indicate true or false to statements like 'I find it easy to take control in many situations', or 'I don't like meeting new people'. These measures have been constructed carefully over time, bearing in mind the principles of reliability, validity and standardization. The basic assumption that underpins these inventories is that personality can be reduced to a small number of dimensions. These dimensions are derived from a statistical 'chunking' exercise, known as factor analysis. While trait theorists agree that this is a valid thing to do, they do not agree on how many factors best represent the structure of personality. The two most widely used inventories in sport psychology have been **Cattell's 16 personality factors** (16PF) and the **Eysenck Personality Inventory** (EPI). While Cattell favored 16 traits, Eysenck believed that just three were sufficient to explain personality (extraversion, neuroticism and psychoticism). In the last two decades a third approach known as the five-factor model (FFM) or the **big five** has become the most popular solution to the question of how many factors best describe personality (Costa & McCrae, 1992). The big five personality factors are: **openness** as opposed to conventionality; **conscientiousness** as opposed to spontaneousness; **extraversion** as opposed to introversion; **agreeableness** or tendermindedness as opposed to tough-mindedness; and **neuroticism** or anxiousness as opposed to stability (see *Table 1*). Despite its popularity in general psychology, there is almost no research in sport psychology that has employed the big five. This is probably because, as we shall see later, it is now clear that there does not appear to be a relationship between personality and athletic ability. Consequently, interest in such research has waned dramatically. Although most research employs inventories to measure the way in which people differ along a continuum, which can then be aggregated to give group scores (the nomothetic approach), there are other methods of personality measurement that focus more on the uniqueness of individuals (the idiographic approach). One of these that has much potential for working with athletes is **Kelly's repertory grid**. Here, rather than force athletes into predetermined trait descriptions, the repertory grid allows each athlete to construe personality in their own way. Kelly was the creator of **personal construct theory**, which is based on the premise that each of us has a unique view of the world that we see through the 'goggles' of our personal constructs (Kelly, 1955). Constructs are schemata (Topic A3) that are our own ways of seeing people and things around us that organize our world.

Table 1.   The personality dimensions of the big five

Factor	Typified by being	Opposite pole
Openness	Imaginative Love of variety Independent	Down to earth Love of routine Conforming
Conscientiousness	Organized Careful Disciplined	Disorganized Careless Undisciplined
Extraversion	Sociable Fun-loving Warm	Shy Serious Reserved
Agreeableness	Generous Trusting Helpful	Ruthless Suspicious Unhelpful
Neuroticism	Worried Insecure Self-pitying	Calm Secure Self-satisfied

E2 PERSONALITY AND SPORT

Key Notes

Personality and success in sport	The question of whether we can predict athletic performance from personality is known as the credulous–skeptical debate. The results of over a thousand studies have shown that personality traits, as measured by the EPI and the 16 PF, do not relate to sports performance in any meaningful or consistent way. The area is typified by hundreds of studies whose conclusions contradict each other. Even trait anxiety and trait confidence do not appear to help us predict performance in top athletes.
Personality and participation in sport	Do athletes and non-athletes differ in personality? Despite the fact that contradictory results are pervasive in this area there are one or two generalizations that do emerge. There is some evidence that athletes are more extraverted and more stable than non-athletes. There is also a weak link between sensation-seeking and participation in sports, particularly extreme sports.
The athletic personality	In its strongest form the notion of the athletic personality means that there is a specific set of personality traits that is unique to top athletes, is not present in lesser ones and is not present in other non-athletic groups. From what we have seen in the literature on personality and both success in sport, and participation in sport, it is clear that evidence for the existence of the athletic personality does not exist.
Related topics	Introduction to individual differences (E1) Problematic issues (E3)

Personality and success in sport

Although not a popular research area in recent years, more than a thousand studies have been conducted into the relationship between personality and sport since the 1960s. One of the main driving forces for all this research was the assumption that there was such a thing as 'the athletic personality', and that we could predict athletic performance from personality. This was important since it was assumed that knowing what the athletic personality was, we could use this in various ways to improve individual and team performance. Can we predict athletic performance from personality? If we compare the personalities of players in Super Bowl winning teams and those of less-successful teams, would we find more extraversion, or tendermindedness or spontaneousness in one group than the other? These issues are central to what became known as the **credulous–skeptical** debate. William Morgan was the champion of the credible side of the issue, arguing that knowing two athletes' personalities, we could predict who would be the better performer. The skeptical camp, championed by Rainer Martens, believed that this was not possible to do with any accuracy. The implications of these issues for practice are quite serious. For example, if the credulous side is correct, knowing what attributes the best athletes have, we could select young people with these attributes and focus training and coaching resources on them. The debate is a specific example of an issue in mainstream psychology that has been argued about throughout the history of personality research. The **person vs situation** debate is about the extent to which behavior is shaped by personality or by situation.

What has research into the relationship between personality and success in sport told us?

The simple answer is not much. Personality traits, as measured by the EPI and the 16 PF, do not relate to sports performance in any meaningful or consistent way. The area is typified by hundreds of studies whose conclusions contradict each other, with most of the main dimensions of personality having been linked to both good and poor performance somewhere in the literature. Even trait anxiety and trait confidence, two variables that we might expect to be important for athletes, do not appear to help us predict performance in top athletes. For example, it is not the case that trait anxious athletes perform any less well than those who are by nature relatively calm. More important is each athlete's level of state anxiety in any given competitive situation. Those trait anxious individuals who do succeed in sport at the top level have presumably learned how to work around their dispositional anxiety.

While there is no link between the main personality dimensions and performance, there have been some studies that show that specific non-central dimensions, such as perfectionism, pain tolerance and need for achievement are somewhat more prevalent in top-flight athletes.

Personality and participation in sport

As we have seen there is no evidence that there are clear and consistent personality differences between good and not-so-good athletes. A much weaker claim that has also been made is that there are differences in personality between athletes and non-athletes. Again, given the vast number of studies in the area, it is not surprising that all sorts of personality traits have been found to correlate with sports participation. However, there are just as many other studies that show those self same traits to be unrelated to sport participation! Despite the fact that contradictory results are pervasive in this area there are one or two generalizations that do emerge. For example, there is some evidence that athletes are more extraverted and more stable than non-athletes. Interestingly, this is reversed in long-distance runners who tend to be more introverted. This is neither too surprising nor particularly significant for practical purposes. We would hardly want to exclude people from distance running on the basis of a personality inventory. Rather we would encourage people of any personality type to do it if they wanted to. There is also some evidence of a link between measures of sensation-seeking and participation in sports, and in particular extreme sports. However, arguably the demonstration of these relationships is relatively trivial and does not provide much useful information. Having said that such differences exist it should also be said that they do not amount to anything that could be described as a consistent profile.

The athletic personality

Much of the impetus for the vast amount of research in this area has been to answer the question of whether there is such a thing as **the athletic personality** or not. In its strongest form the notion of the athletic personality means that there is a specific set of personality traits that is unique to top athletes, is not present in lesser ones and is not present in other non-athletic groups (such as top performers in other walks of life, for example, business, art or music). From what we have seen in the literature on personality and success in sport this notion is not sustainable.

It could be argued that the notion of the athletic personality should simply mean that athletes differ from non-athletes. However, to sustain the notion of the athletic personality we really need to have evidence of more than just a few general differences between athletes and non-athletes and a consistent general profile of what the athlete is like in terms of personality. No such evidence of a systematic set of traits has been demonstrated. The finding that, in general, athletes are more extraverted and less anxious than non-athletes is hardly sufficient evidence of the athletic personality, since these two traits may be characteristic of many groups of people, for example, rock musicians or police officers. Any newcomer to the study of sport and personality must surely be surprised and disappointed by the lack of solid evidence about the role of personality in sport. Even given the theoretical and methodological problems of many of the studies carried out in this area, it is fairly clear that there is no such thing as the athletic personality. Actually, when we stop and think about this, it is not really as surprising as it might at first seem. If we look at the great players in any sport we can see that huge differences in personality exist. For example, it is not hard to think of the very different types of people that make up national teams. Even at a lower level, the good players in your own team are probably not similar in personality. It is clear that in teams we see quiet, modest, open people, and loud, extraverted, conventional ones. Secondly, the reason someone excels in sport is a function of many factors. For example, natural ability, hand–eye coordination, reaction times, speed, skill, practice opportunities, motivation, experience, strength and fitness are all more likely candidates as better predictors of how well an athlete will perform than personality.

E3 PROBLEMATIC ISSUES

Key Notes

Direction of causality issues	The issue of why athletes appear to be more extraverted and less neurotic than non-athletes raises direction of causality issues. It could be that playing sport builds character. Not much research has been conducted but it tends to suggest, if anything, that young athletes become less altruistic as they play more competitive sport. On the other hand, it could be that the type of person we are determines whether we gravitate toward or away from sporting situations. This is known as the gravitational hypothesis. While the gravitational hypothesis makes intuitive sense, there is actually little evidence on the issue.
Theoretical issues	The biggest problem with the research into the relationship between personality and sport is that it has been atheoretical. Researchers have simply taken standard personality inventories, and administered them to handy groups of participants. Future personality research in sport must begin with personality theory and test hypotheses derived from it.
Methodological issues	Research has been dogged by methodological problems. Terms have been poorly defined, personality has often been measured in dubious or untested ways, and sample sizes have been very small.
Related topic	Personality and sport (E2)

Direction of causality issues

From the previous topic we have seen that while there is no such thing as the athletic personality, there does appear to be a link between personality and engaging in physical activity. In particular, it seems that sport and exercise participants tend to be more extraverted and less neurotic than non-partici-pants. This raises the question of why this might be so, and whether there is a causal relationship involved. For example, it could be that playing sport affects the development of personality. On the other hand, it could be that having a particular personality pushes us into physical activity. A third possibility is that both of the above are true, and causality is reciprocal. Finally, it may be that the relationship is merely correlational, and not causal at all.

Looking first at the possibility that sport participation causes changes in personality, it has often been claimed that sport is character building. For example, it has been said variously that it makes us tough, courageous, socially competent, and that it teaches us about fair-mindedness and sports-personship. Equally, there are those who argue that sport has a negative influence on personality development, and teaches us to become selfish and aggressive people who are egotistical, intolerant of out-groups, and overly competitive. Evidence from laboratory and field experiments shows that personality devel-opment in children might be affected by physical activity, and in particular that rather than making young people fairer, competition actually leads to reduced pro-social and altruistic behavior (Kleiber & Roberts, 1981). Typically, these studies show that younger children are fairer, but that slightly older ones have learned to be more concerned with winning and doing so at the expense of sports-personship. It does look then as if personality changes as a result of playing sport, but not in a character-building way! When it comes to the effect of sports participation on college-aged athletes, longitudinal studies over one to four years tend to show that 16PF scores are not affected. This suggests that, by young adulthood, personality is relatively set and that participation may only affect younger athletes.

The opposite explanation for why there is an association between personality and sports participation is that personality causes sport participation, i.e. that the type of person we are determines whether we gravitate toward or away from sporting situations. For this reason it is known as **the gravitational hypothesis**. For example, people who are extraverted might seek out sports situations because they like the higher levels of arousal that such situations bring, or for the company of others. Similarly, people who have an ability to tolerate pain might gravitate to those sports in which this trait is valuable, e.g. contact sports, wrestling, karate, rugby, etc. While the gravitational hypothesis makes intuitive sense, there is actually little evidence on the issue. What there is, suggests that people who engage in exciting sports are more extraverted than the normal population, and that people who engage in dangerous sports score higher in sensation-seeking scales.

One of the problems with this whole personality and sport area is that the practical problems of conducting longitudinal studies and experiments has meant we have only correlational evidence on which to base our theories.

Theoretical issues The biggest problem with the research into personality and sport is that it has been **atheoretical**. That is, there has typically been no theory underpinning each study. Researchers have simply taken standard personality inventories, and administered them to handy groups of participants, such as college teams or local sports clubs, and looked for correlations between personality trait scores and performance scores. Proper research requires a research hypothesis to be generated on the basis of a theory. The approach that has been taken in sport psychology has been called the blunderbuss approach, after the old-fashioned wide-barreled gun used to shoot game-birds. The wide barrel meant that as the lead shot came out of the gun, it sprayed out over a wide area making it easier to hit something. The similarity with personality research is that by firing off a 16PF or the EPI at lots of different athletic groups, sport psychologists were bound to hit something by chance, rather than by good aim. Consequently, this led to sporadic and contradictory findings. For example, one study found that basketball players were more depressed than swimmers, but swimmers were more neurotic than basketball players! Future personality research must begin with personality theory and test hypotheses derived from it.

Methodological issues In psychology 'methodological issues' refers to the technical merit of the way the research has been conducted. This includes, for example, whether research was designed properly for its purpose, whether variables were measured well, whether statistics were appropriate and whether sample sizes were adequate. Sport and personality research has been dogged by such methodological problems. For example, measurement has been problematic because researchers have used the same terms for variables that refer to quite different things. The term 'athlete' has meant anything from elite to recreational level, making comparisons unreliable. Similarly, the personality construct has been measured in a wide range of ways, some of which are dubious or untested in terms of reliability and validity. One final difficulty has been that sample sizes in studies have often been very small, making generalization a problem.

F1 SOCIAL COGNITION

Key Notes

Schemas	Schemas are mental frameworks used to interpret and organize experience. They consist of the attributes of concepts, and the links between these attributes. They are our personal 'mini-theories' about how the world is, and operates. There are five main types of social schemas: person schemas, role schemas, group schemas, self schemas, and event schemas. Schemas help us to manage our social world. When first being formed, schemas are relatively malleable. However, over time they become resistant to change.
Stereotypes	Stereotypes are widely shared group schemas. Stereotypes are often viewed in a negative way in psychology, as being too general to be useful. However, despite not always being accurate, they endure because they do serve the function of making the social world more understandable. The downside of stereotypes is when they are inaccurate and used in a negative way, in preference to direct evidence about individuals.
Attitudes	Attitudes are our evaluations of people, objects and events. As such, an attitude is the evaluative component of a schema. They are sometimes described as having three aspects, cognition, affect and behavioral intention; i.e. what we think or believe, what we feel and what we are inclined to do.
Attitude functions	Attitudes help us to structure our social world. They also serve an instrumental function, by helping us to get what we want. Attitudes can be value-expressive by letting people know what we believe. Finally, attitudes have been said to serve an 'ego defensive function', in that, by expressing a negative attitude about others, we deflect our negative feelings about ourselves on to others.
Attitude change	Dual process models of attitude change suggest that there are two routes to persuasion, the systematic (or central) route, and the heuristic (or peripheral) route. Which route we tend to use is determined by the importance of the issue to us, and how sure we are in our views.
Attitudes and behavior	There is actually very little relationship between how we evaluate something or someone, and what we do in relation to that thing or person. Consequently, psychologists have developed the Theory of Planned Behavior, and the Theory of Reasoned Action to explain this lack of a simple one-to-one correspondence between attitudes and behavior.
Attitude measurement	Attitudes are measured by questionnaires in which people are asked to indicate their views on a series of questions around any given issue. Several methods have been developed to measure attitudes, including Thurstone scaling, Osgood's Semantic Differential and Kelly's Repertory Grid. The simplest and most widely used method is the Likert Scale.

Prejudice and discrimination	The term prejudice is used in psychology to describe attitudes that are usually negative and are held about individuals, based on their out-group membership. As such prejudice is the affective part of a stereotype. In social psychology discrimination refers to negative behaviors that result when we act upon our prejudices.
Related topics	Attribution theory (C4) Cognitive-behavioral theories (J1) Inter-group processes (G9) Process models of exercise (J2)

Schemas

Social cognition is a general term that describes the way that we perceive, think about and organize our understanding of the social world around us. The term covers many aspects of social psychology including conceptions about self, others and social situations. Attribution processes dealt with in Topic C4 are also a form of social cognition.

Schemas are mental frameworks used to interpret and organize experience. They are cognitive structures that consist of the attributes of concepts, and the links between these attributes. In basic terms they are our personal 'mini-theories' about how the world is and operates. For example, we have all developed a schema for the concept 'golf ball', so that when we see an object that we have never seen before, we still have little trouble deciding whether it is a golf ball or not, based on its 'golf ball'-type attributes, or lack of them. Schemas are useful because they help us to make sense of the potentially overwhelming array of information coming in to the brain via the senses. The way we talk about rainbows provides a clear example of this. Most of us agree that there are seven colors in the rainbow, however; in fact the rainbow is made up of a continuous and infinite color spectrum. To 'see' it as seven colors is a convenient summary that makes the world more manageable. In addition to simplifying the world around us, schemas prepare us for the future. They allow us to anticipate what is likely, and to decide how to interact appropriately. In the golf ball example: to hit it with a golf club, if we decide it is a golf ball, and not to, if we decide it is an egg!

Similarly, we develop **social schemas** about the people and events around us. These give us a way of categorizing the social world into meaningful groupings, and allow us to interact appropriately. For example, we would probably behave in one way with a minister of the church and another way with a nightclub owner. Social psychologists have suggested that we use five main types of social schemas:

- **person schemas** are based on what we believe we know about particular individuals. For example, we have a schema about our coach, which includes our beliefs about the set of personality attributes he or she has;
- **role schemas** consist of our conceptions about sets of people based on the roles they fulfill, for example, politicians, psychology lecturers or coaches in general;
- **group schemas** are based around the ideas people have about different groups in society. These may be based on, for example, race, gender or religion;
- **self schemas**, not surprisingly, refer to our perceptions of ourselves;
- **event schemas** (or **scripts**) refer to our understanding of the rules that govern events. For example, we all have an event schema for what a team practice session, or a lecture should be like.

These schemas help us to manage our social world. They make the processing of social information faster, and they help us to encode new information and to retrieve information more effectively. In sport we often have to weigh up a social situation quickly. Did my opponent deliberately foul me? Is the referee unhappy with my comments? Do I need to calm my team-mate?

Because of the assumptions they contain, schemas help us to encode information quickly, affecting what we attend to, and what we store in memory. When we are told we are about to be introduced to a champion martial artist, we might notice how lean and fighting fit they look; with a jockey, we might be immediately aware of how short they are.

Schemas also affect how we respond to people and situations. We might be more careful not to upset the person introduced as the martial artist than the jockey. This is not to say that we are incapable of thinking more deeply and seeing past the schema, but that in many day-to-day situations we take the shortcut.

When first being formed, schemas are relatively malleable. However, over time they become more abstract, and their interconnecting attributes become more elaborately organized. As such, it is not surprising that they become resistant to change. In sport, we see the resistance to change of person schemas when coaches get a fixed impression of an athlete as lazy or uncoordinated, etc., and do not shift their opinion, even in the face of contradictory evidence (Fiske, 2004).

Stereotypes

Stereotypes are widely shared group schemas. For example, you might have a group schema about 'Scottish-ness' that includes the attributes 'careful with money', 'like whiskey', or 'have a dry sense of humor'. You might think football players are 'less than bright' or 'aggressive, macho bullies'. If this personal group schema of yours is widely shared by others, it becomes a stereotype about the 'Scots' or 'football players'.

Stereotypes are often viewed in a negative way in psychology, as being too general to be useful, biasing us into disliking others on the basis of non-relevant features, such as skin color or religion. However, despite not always being accurate, they endure because they do serve the function of making the social world more understandable and less chaotic. For example, when having tea with a minister of the church we know from our stereotype that it is probably unwise to tell a risqué joke, even if it turns out later that this particular clergyman curses and swears. The downside of stereotypes is when they are inaccurate and used in a negative way, in preference to direct and contradictory evidence about individuals. This happens in sport, for example, when we treat all rugby players as though they are aggressive thugs or all boxers as if they are lacking intelligence.

Similarly, stereotypes about racial groups are too general and too inaccurate to be helpful. As coaches and psychologists, we need to remember that even though there are cognitive processes operating in normal social interactions that take us away from the individualized approach, we should make special efforts to treat others as individuals. One example of treating individuals as stereotypes is in the case of the upper age limit rules imposed on referees by soccer's governing body F.I.F.A. These rules assume that when referees reach 45 years of age they are too old to be effective, regardless of how well they can do the job. This ageism is particularly problematic in the case of the Italian referee Pierluigi Collina, who is soon to be 45 yet is widely acknowledged as one of the best, if not the best, soccer referee in the world.

Attitudes   When psychologists first began to study attitudes they conceived of them in terms of affect; i.e. as evaluations. It later became popular to think of them as having a tripartite structure, meaning that they are made up of three things. These are **cognition**, **affect** and **behavioral intention**; i.e. what we think or believe, what we feel and what we are inclined to do. A concrete example will help. Take the case of a coach's attitude to junk food. She may think it is full of things that our bodies should have less of (her cognition). She may feel it is bad (her emotion), and she may be inclined to speak out about it to her athletes (behavioral intention). In contrast a young gymnast may have a quite different attitude to junk food. She may think it is tasty (cognition), she may feel good when she eats it (emotion), and she may plan to buy a burger on the way home after the training session (behavioral intention).

One major problem with the tripartite approach is that it assumes that attitudes are closely related to behavior, which is not always the case. Many of us have attitudes to, for example, exercising and eating healthily, that are not reflected in our behavior. Indeed one of the tasks of sport and exercise psychology is to increase the attitude–behavior consistency of the population, and how this is done is the subject of Topic J1. Because of this inconsistency, psychologists have moved back to the original and less-complicated view of attitudes, as a unitary concept that focuses on the evaluative dimension. Thus, attitudes are now usually defined simply as evaluations about people, objects and events (Baron & Byrne, 2003). As such, an attitude is the evaluative component of a schema. For example, your attitude to your coach is just one part of your person schema about your coach.

Attitude functions   Attitudes serve several functions. First, and most important, as one aspect of our schemas, attitudes serve a **knowledge function** by helping us to structure our social world and make it more manageable. Second, they serve an **instrumental function**, in that they can help us to get what we want. For example, when a child says to an adult as they pass a sports store, 'I like those football jerseys' he or she is probably really saying 'Please buy me one of those football jerseys.' Attitudes also have a **value-expressive function**. For example, when a player says 'I love playing against teams that are bigger than us', he or she may also be saying 'I am not the kind of person who is scared by anyone.' Attitudes have also been said to serve an **ego defensive function**. Here the argument is that by expressing a negative attitude about others, we reduce our own feelings of responsibility for negative consequences. For example, we might be quick to blame others for defensive mistakes when goals or points are scored against us.

Attitude change   Much of the work of the psychologist or coach involves trying to persuade athletes to change their attitudes. Exercise psychologists often want to convince people that they should exercise more, or stop smoking, while sport psychologists might want to persuade athletes that they should take training more seriously, or spend more time on mental preparation. Early approaches to understanding attitude change and persuasion looked at three sets of variables. These were the characteristics of the person who was doing the persuading, the content of the message, and the characteristics of the audience.

More recently, attention has focused on what are known as the **'dual process' models** of attitude change (*Fig. 1*). The essence of these models is that there are two routes to persuasion, referred to as the **central** (or **systematic**) **route**, and the **peripheral** (or **heuristic**) **route** (Petty & Cacciopo, 1986). Which route we

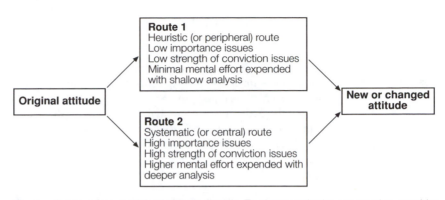

Fig. 1.   Dual process models of attitude change. To change attitudes, we need to consider factors like the importance of an issue for the target person, and their degree of certainty about it.

tend to use is determined by the importance of the issue to us, and how sure we are in our views. Thus, we are likely to process important issues, and issues we are unsure about, via the central or systematic route, expending more mental effort on them and analyzing things more deeply. For example, if we are trying to persuade a manager not to cram a player full of painkillers so that he can play with an injury, which is likely to have long-term health consequences, we need to use well-thought-through arguments that will survive systematic scrutiny. In contrast, if we feel confident about an issue, or it is about something of little consequence to us, we are likely to use less processing effort on it, taking the peripheral or heuristic route. For example, we might be persuaded to use a particular shampoo simply because a famous football star uses it. These dual process models suggest that, if we want to change attitudes, we should consider factors like the importance of an issue for the target person, and their degree of certainty about it.

Attitudes and behavior

One of the main reasons why psychologists were interested in attitudes from the earliest days of psychology was because they assumed that, by knowing someone's attitudes, we could predict their behavior. Surely, the argument goes, if I know you love French fries, I can predict you will eat lots of them, or if you dislike someone, you will avoid them. However, the attitude behavior link is another area where psychology proves to be more than common sense. Numerous studies have now shown that there is actually very little relationship between how we evaluate something or someone, and what we do in relation to that thing or person (Fiske, 2004). When we think a bit more deeply about this we can see why the two may not be related. I may love fries, but refuse to eat them because I want to lose weight or to avoid clogging up my arteries. An athlete may think that doing 3 hours of swim training before going to class every day is unpleasant, but do it nonetheless because of their desire to be the best swimmer they can be. Vast numbers of people join health clubs because of their attitude to keeping fit, yet all too easily stop exercising.

As a result of this lack of a simple one-to-one correspondence between attitudes and behavior, much effort has gone into the development of theories to better describe and explain these inconsistencies. These theories have then been used to inform interventions and policy aiming to increase exercise adherence and participation in sport. Among the theories are the Theory of Planned

Behavior, the Theory of Reasoned Action (see Topic J1) and the Trans-theoretical/ Stages of Change model (Topic J2).

Attitude measurement

Attitudes are measured by questionnaires in which people are asked to indicate their views on a series of questions around any given issue. Several methods have been developed to measure attitudes, including Thurstone scaling, Osgood's Semantic Differential and Kelly's Repertory Grid, however, the simplest and most widely used method is the Likert Scale. With the Likert Scale respondents are simply asked to evaluate an attitude object along a continuum. For example, the following question might be part of a typical attitude to health questionnaire.

How important do you think it is to avoid salt in your diet?				
Not at all important	Somewhat important	Important	Very important	Extremely important

Alternatively, the scale may only have end points to anchor it.

Eating fruit is pleasant
Strongly Agree _____ Strongly Disagree

Prejudice and discrimination

Taken literally, the word prejudice means to pre-judge. As has been said earlier, we pre-judge people and things using our schemas, because it is helpful to us to do so. However, the term prejudice is used in a more specific way in psychology, to describe attitudes that are usually negative and are held about individuals, based on their out-group membership. As such prejudice is the affective part of a stereotype. For example, if you were to dislike someone you have just met because they are Scottish, or because they are a football player, you are exhibiting prejudiced attitudes.

In everyday usage the terms prejudice and discrimination are often used interchangeably, however, in social psychology prejudice is reserved to describe (usually) negative attitudes, and discrimination to refer to (usually) negative behaviors that result when we act upon our prejudices. Thus, people may have prejudiced attitudes but not act upon them. For example, you might believe that boxing is a barbaric sport that should be banned, yet never actually do anything to further the cause of banning it, and you may know a boxer and be perfectly polite in their company.

This distinction between prejudice and discrimination can be useful in issues of equal opportunities in sport and exercise, where it is more likely that change will result from attempts to legislate against behavior, than against attitudes, i.e. it is much easier to control what people do, than what they think. However, this is not to imply we should not try to change prejudiced attitudes.

F2 CONFORMITY AND COMPLIANCE

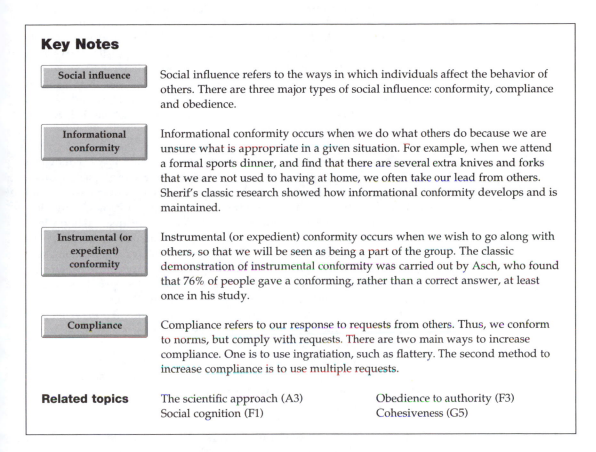

Key Notes

Social influence

Social influence refers to the ways in which individuals affect the behavior of others. There are three major types of social influence: conformity, compliance and obedience.

Informational conformity

Informational conformity occurs when we do what others do because we are unsure what is appropriate in a given situation. For example, when we attend a formal sports dinner, and find that there are several extra knives and forks that we are not used to having at home, we often take our lead from others. Sherif's classic research showed how informational conformity develops and is maintained.

Instrumental (or expedient) conformity

Instrumental (or expedient) conformity occurs when we wish to go along with others, so that we will be seen as being a part of the group. The classic demonstration of instrumental conformity was carried out by Asch, who found that 76% of people gave a conforming, rather than a correct answer, at least once in his study.

Compliance

Compliance refers to our response to requests from others. Thus, we conform to norms, but comply with requests. There are two main ways to increase compliance. One is to use ingratiation, such as flattery. The second method to increase compliance is to use multiple requests.

Related topics

The scientific approach (A3)
Social cognition (F1)

Obedience to authority (F3)
Cohesiveness (G5)

Social influence

In psychology social influence refers to the ways in which individuals affect the behavior of others. There are three major types of social influence: conformity, compliance and obedience. **Conformity** occurs when we allow our behavior to be affected by norms so that we respond in a similar way to others. The term **norms** is used to describe the sets of rules that groups deem appropriate, or not, in social situations. Norms can be formal or informal. Formal norms are written-down codes of conduct. For example, at Wimbledon, the All England Tennis Club requires players to conform to norms in the form of a dress code, by insisting that players play in white. Informal norms are about what groups believe is 'proper', or what 'ought' to be. For example, cricket players and basketball players think a little 'sledging' or 'trash talking' with opponents is acceptable, while golfers would not dream of it.

In the Tour de France and other cycle races, there is an informal norm that riders should not take advantage of competitors' misfortunes by attacking when their rival has had a puncture or crash. It is tempting to think of conforming behavior as something we do simply because it is sensible. However, we only have to look at norms about how long a player's shorts should be, to see that what is considered 'sensible' changes from generation to generation. Or consider how sensible it is to take a piece of cloth and wrap it tightly round one's neck all day as people do who wear ties to work. How sensible is it to try to walk around all day in a high-heeled shoe? If you really wanted to get sensibly from A to B, you would never totter along in a high-heel. Given this, why do we do these things? Conformity serves a very useful function for us, because it makes interaction with others more predictable. The number of ways people could interact is infinite. Norms constrain the number of possible ways to a more manageable set. For example, it helps to know that in Western society when you extend your hand to shake another's, they will put their hand in yours, and together you will waggle hands up and down. How confusing if other people were to react to your outstretched hand by scratching their ears or any of the infinite responses available!

Informational conformity

There are two main types of conformity. Informational conformity occurs when we are unsure what is appropriate in a given situation. For example, when we attend a formal sports dinner and find that there are several extra knives and forks laid out in front of us that we are not used to having at home. In this situation we wait to see which piece of cutlery others pick up first, taking a lead from others who know what to do. The classic research on conformity was carried out by Sherif in the 1930s. Sherif used an interesting phenomenon, known as the auto-kinetic effect, to demonstrate the development of conformity in groups (Sherif, 1936). The auto-kinetic effect occurs when people look at a fixed point source of light in a dark room for a short while and they begin to perceive the light as moving. Interestingly, each person sees the movement as being in a different direction, and for differing distances. Sherif asked small groups of people to say how the light moved. What was surprising was that despite the lack of movement and the individual nature of the experience, people soon began to agree on the light's 'movement'. This is an example of informational conformity; because we turn to the information others provide, to help us with our judgments.

Instrumental (or expedient) conformity

Instrumental (or expedient) conformity occurs when we wish to go along with others, to be seen as being part of the group. This might take the form of dressing in a similar way to each other, or sharing opinions about who the best professional athletes are in your sport.

Asch (1956) carried out the classic demonstration of instrumental conformity. He set up a situation where people were shown a card with a black line on it. They were then shown another card with three lines, A, B, C, and asked to say which of the lines was the same length as on the original card. The task is a simple one that people can get right every time. The twist introduced by Asch was to have five confederates give the wrong answer, before and in the presence of, the actual participant in the study. The question was how does the opinion of others influence what we say? So, as a participant in the study, you might think the correct answer is C, but if the five other people who you think are also participants in the study like you say B, do you say C, or go with the flow and say B?

What Asch found was that 76% of people gave the conforming, rather than correct answer, at least once in the study.

Much research since has shown that we do spend much of our time conforming to the norms of the groups we belong to. Research has also shown that various factors affect the levels of conformity we exhibit. For example, as you might imagine, more cohesive groups elicit higher levels of conformity from their members. Another interesting finding here is that gender and conformity do not relate in a stereotypical way. On the basis of early research, it used to be believed that women conformed more. However, more thoughtful work, focusing on the type of task involved in the early studies, showed that if the task was a 'male-stereotyped' task like automobile fault diagnosis, women conformed more, but, if the task was stereotypically female, then it was the male participants who conformed more. This makes sense if we are talking about informational conformity, where the task is less familiar to the members of the conforming gender. These findings remind us of the bias that researchers may bring to their work (Topic A3).

Compliance

In everyday usage conformity and compliance are more or less synonymous; however, psychologists see them as different. For psychologists, conformity describes behavior that is guided by norms. In contrast, compliance refers to our response to requests from others. Thus, we conform to norms, but comply with requests. For example, a player might be part of a team that believes in fair play, yet decide to make a dangerous tackle on an opponent, because his unscrupulous coach asked him to. In this case the player does not conform to the norms of the group, but does comply with the coach's unacceptable request.

Much research has tried to uncover the conditions under which compliance with requests can be increased. The evidence suggests that there are two main ways to increase levels of compliance. One is to use ingratiation, such as flattery. For example, a team-mate might say to you 'You are playing really well today – but could you get back on defense a bit more!'

The second method to increase compliance is to use multiple requests. For example, we might ask someone for a small favor, and then a bigger one. This is well known to salespeople as the '**foot in the door technique**'. A new team-mate might begin by asking you to let them stay at your place for a night, and then a day later, asks if they could stay for a week or two! In contrast to the small request – the large request approach, the '**door in the face**' technique starts with a big request, and follows with a more reasonable one. Your team-mate might ask you if you would let him or her borrow your car for a year, and on being politely told no, ask for it for a day. In this situation, we comply more readily with the second, much smaller request, if it follows a big request, than if it had been the only request. The evidence from many studies is that both techniques lead to higher levels of compliance than single request approaches (Baron & Byrne, 2003). These and other techniques should have practical value in terms of increasing the likelihood that someone will take up and/or adhere to exercise programs.

F3 OBEDIENCE TO AUTHORITY

Key Notes

Obedience	With compliance, we are doing what is asked; with obedience, we are doing what we are ordered to do. Conformity and obedience differ in that, with obedience we obey an order from above, but with conformity we conform to a norm.
Milgram's experiments	Milgram carried out psychology's most famous experiment by investigating how readily people would obey orders to harm others. He found that 65% of participants followed orders to give 450-volt shocks to others, suggesting human beings have the capacity to inflict suffering on others, because someone in authority tells them to.
The agentic state	Milgram argues that people operate in one of two states, the agentic state or the autonomous state. In the agentic state we act as agents of an organization, and for the sake of efficiency, switch off our conscience. In contrast, in the autonomous state we do consider the rights or wrongs of what we are doing.
Obedience in sport	Milgram's analysis of obedience situations is also applicable to sport. In sport we have agencies, value systems and people in power who might tell others to do unethical things in order to win.

Related topics	Conformity and compliance (F2)	Leadership (G4)
	Anti-social behavior (F5)	

Obedience

One final, but important type of social influence process is **obedience**. Compliance and obedience differ simply in that, with compliance, we are doing what is asked, whereas with obedience, we are doing what we are ordered to do. Conformity and obedience differ in that, with obedience, we obey an order but with conformity, we conform to a norm. In addition, with obedience, there is more of a vertical process, where people with higher rank or status or greater social power are telling others what to do. In the case of conformity, we change our behavior to align it with group or societal norms. This means that with conformity, there is less of an issue of inter-personal power, and the process is more horizontal. Thus, when the coach demands that we do a series of sprints, we obey the order from above. When we all buy the same sports shoe, the conformity pressure is at the same level, i.e. from our peers.

Milgram's experiments

It was on obedience that psychology's most famous experiment was undertaken (Milgram, 1963). Stanley Milgram was interested in the behavior of the Nazi guards who had obeyed orders and participated in submitting millions of people to Hitler's gas chambers. His experiment involved telling people to give electric shocks to others. Participants were under the impression that they were taking part in a study of the effect of punishment on learning. This required them to be a teacher, and another participant to be a learner, trying to learn lists of word pairs. An experimenter wearing a laboratory coat told participants to give ever-increasing electric shocks to the learner, each time they made a mistake. The question was, how far would the participant go in obeying the order to increase the shocks? What was surprising was how much obedience Milgram found. Sixty-five percent of participants went to the 450-volt level, and few stopped before 300 volts. Much research since his pioneering work has confirmed his counter-intuitive findings, and it does appear that otherwise ordinary, pleasant human beings, just like us, have the capacity to inflict suffering on others, simply because someone in authority tells us to do so.

The agentic state   To explain these shocking findings, Milgram suggested that people operate in one of two states, the **agentic state** or the **autonomous state** (Milgram, 1983). Normally, we are in the autonomous state and we consider the rights or wrongs of what we are doing. However, sometimes we shift to the agentic state, where we act as agents of an organization. Milgram argues that when we are operating in the agentic state, for the sake of system efficiency, the inhibitory mechanism that is our conscience has been switched off so that we no longer process the ethical issues associated with our actions. For example, armies might be less efficient if soldiers constantly questioned the ethical basis of every order given. They would also be less likely to commit atrocities.

In the experiment, there are three roles, the authority figure (the experimenter), the person who obeys (the teacher), and the person who suffers (the learner), and there is an ideology or value system that drives the organization or agency (see *Table 1*).

According to Milgram, the surprising levels of obedience shown in his experiments resulted because participants (the teachers) were willing to operate in the

Table 1.   *Milgram's research and its relevance for obedience in sport*

	Milgram's experiments	Nazi Germany	Sport and obedient coaches	Sport and obedient players
The agency	The scientific community	The Third Reich	The State	The team
The value system	Knowledge gathering	The master race	Communism	Win at all costs
The authority figure	The experimenter	Hitler. The concentration camp commanders who issue extermination orders	Politicians and through them the gymnastic governing body officials who tell coaches to give drugs to their girl gymnasts	The manager or coach who tells a player to injure an opponent
The person who obeys	The participant (teacher)	The camp guards who carry out the exterminations	Coaches who then promote drug use	The player who then deliberately injures an opponent
The person who suffers	The learner	The camp prisoners	Young gymnasts	An opponent

agentic state. This meant that they would do what they were told by the authority figure, for the sake of the agency, which in this case is the scientific community, whose value system or purpose includes the very reasonable one of pushing back the frontiers of knowledge (see *Fig. 1*). Milgram points out that in the Nazi extermination camps, there were again, the three roles and a driving ideology. Thus, we had the authority figures (the camp commanders) the people who obeyed (the guards), and the people who suffered (the prisoners). In this case however, the driving ideology was Hitler's desire to achieve the so-called 'purification' of the human race.

Obedience in sport

In a 'watered-down' way, Milgram's analysis of obedience situations is also applicable to sporting situations. In sport we have agencies, for example, one's team or club, and at international level, one's country. We also have value systems, i.e. winning (sometimes at all costs). We also have people in power who might tell others to do unethical things to opponents, in order to secure a win. Thus, Milgram's three roles could be filled by the authority figure, in the shape of the coach, the player who obeys the coach, and the person who suffers being the opponent (see *Table 1*). Unfortunately, it is not unheard of for coaches to tell players to deliberately inflict injuries on opponents. Milgram's analysis can also be applied further up the chain of command. For example, in the case of a team manager who orders the reluctant coach of a young gymnast to make sure that she takes drugs to keep her weight down. It is widely believed that in some countries, young gymnasts have had their health ruined in this way, without their being made aware of the consequences of the drugs, or in some cases by being given the drugs surreptitiously (see *Table 1*).

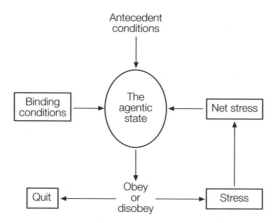

Fig. 1. The agentic state: Milgram's explanation for obedience. Antecedent conditions, such as the presence of an authority figure, switch us from being in the autonomous to the agentic state. In the agentic state we obey an authority figure and behave badly towards another person, which causes us some stress. We try to reduce the stress in various ways, for example, by ignoring or minimizing the suffering of the victim. Any remaining stress is balanced against the things that keep us in the obedience cycle, such as having agreed to take part in the experiment. We then continue to go round the obedience cycle. Disobedience only occurs when our net stress outweighs the binding conditions.

F4 PRO-SOCIAL BEHAVIOR

Key Notes

Altruism	Altruism is a sub-category of pro-social behavior defined as voluntary behavior carried out to benefit another, without anticipation of external reward, such as acts of bravery to save others. Why people would put themselves at risk for no reward has been explained in different ways by the different perspectives in psychology.
Bystander intervention	Bystander apathy is the term used to describe the lack of helping behavior often seen in emergencies. In contrast, bystander intervention describes helping behavior in such situations. Latané and Darley developed a five-stage cognitive model of apathy. First, witnesses have to notice the emergency. People cannot attend to everything around them, and sometimes we just do not see the emergency. Second, a bystander has to interpret it as an emergency. The bystander might think someone in the water is just waving, when in fact they are signaling for help. Third, the helper needs to assume responsibility. Some witnesses may think they do not need to help, because others will. Much research has confirmed the 'bystander effect' which is that when there are more witnesses to an emergency, less help is forthcoming. Fourth, witnesses have to decide whether they have the skills needed in the emergency. Finally, the bystander's analysis of cost and benefit comes into play. A bystander might weigh up the chance of a reward with the possibility of being harmed.
Negative State Relief Model	The Negative State Relief Model claims that pro-social behavior is motivated by a desire to reduce negative feelings, either pre-existing, or aroused by the victim's problem.
Moderator variables	How much help we give is influenced by many factors. We give more help to smartly dressed people, attractive people, and those we perceive to be similar to ourselves. Touch and mood have also been shown to influence pro-social behavior. Finally, if we have seen others helping in a previous incident we are much more likely to help in a subsequent one.

Related topics	Social cognition (F1)	Cohesiveness (G5)
	Anti-social behavior (F5)	Group decision-making (G6)

Altruism

Pro-social behavior is behavior that is carried out with the intention to help others. There are many reasons why we engage in pro-social behavior, some more obvious than others. For example, sometimes we do it to get something in return in a 'you scratch my back I'll scratch yours' way. Psychologists talk about this in terms of **social exchange theories** (Thibaut & Kelley, 1959). Sometimes we help others because we will be able to achieve something we could not do alone. Cooperating with others in sports teams is like this. On yet other occasions we are helpful to others because we are repaying a favor. This is known as restitution. In each of these cases it is fairly obvious why we help others, but sometimes we help others for no obvious reason, even when to do so could be very costly to ourselves. For example, in cases of emergency, some people behave altruistically, risking their own lives to rescue others in danger. A sporting example might be the single-handed ocean racer who gives up a chance to win a race and achieve fame and fortune, to turn back and help a competitor in trouble.

Altruism is a sub-category of pro-social behavior and is voluntary behavior carried out to benefit another, without anticipation of external reward.

Not surprisingly, explanations for why it occurs differ in different psychological perspectives (see Topic A7). In evolutionary terms the survival value of altruism is not immediately obvious, since a gene for altruism is less likely to be passed on by individuals who give away their scarce resources, or risk their lives to save others. To get round this problem evolutionary psychology argues that altruism benefits the species, rather than the individual. For example, by helping several of our kin to survive, even at the cost of our own lives, we may preserve more of our genes. Freudian psychologists might invoke the 'death wish' to explain heroic acts. Behaviorists stress the past history of reward and punishment for acting unselfishly, and point to occasions when people had been rewarded for small acts of bravery. As we shall see, cognitive psychologists invoke human decision-making and thinking to explain pro-social behavior of an altruistic nature. In humanistic psychology the explanation offered is that, in altruism, we see the nobility of humans, who must act in accordance with their higher values to achieve their potential and to do what is right.

Bystander intervention

Bystander apathy is the term used to describe the lack of helping behavior often seen in emergencies. In contrast, **bystander intervention** describes helping behavior in such situations. The study of helping behavior was given impetus by a notorious incident in the 1960s, in which a young woman called Kitty Genovese, was murdered in a New York suburb. What made this murder more shocking than most was the fact that, despite the murderer taking half an hour to commit the crime, and 38 people witnessing it, no one intervened to help the victim or phoned the police. How could this apparent lack of concern for another human being be explained? The press had their own view, namely that there was bystander apathy in people, and that they did not care for their fellow human beings, and that this was particularly true in the urban sprawl of the big city. Of course, as is often the case in psychology, human behavior proved to be governed by more complex processes than these pop theories from the media suggested. Two psychologists, Bib Latané and John Darley, were unconvinced by this newspaper explanation of apathy and preceded to develop a more cognitive approach to explain the problem (Latané & Darley, 1970). Their model offers a deeper understanding of the phenomenon, and paints a more sympathetic view of the unresponsive bystander. They suggested a five-stage process that people go through before helping. First, people need to notice the emergency. We know from cognitive psychology that people cannot take in everything in the perceptual world around them, and are constantly selecting aspects of the environment to attend to. Sometimes we just do not see the emergency. Think of times when you have been so engrossed in what you were doing you failed to notice someone else's plight. It is for this reason that pool attendants and life-guards are employed to focus only on watching us when we go swimming.

The second stage is, that having noticed the problem, a bystander has to interpret it as an emergency. This is not as unlikely as it seems. Emergencies, by their nature, are unusual. People go around in their own worlds trying to make sense of events, and the unusual explanation for events is not the one we come to first. The untrained bystander might think someone in the water is just waving, when in fact they are struggling to stay afloat and signaling for help!

Not surprisingly, studies in which the clarity of the emergency is manipulated show that the clearer the emergency, the more help is forthcoming.

The third hurdle that has to be overcome before help is given in emergencies is that the helper needs to assume responsibility. Again, at first sight it would seem obvious that anyone who noticed an incident and correctly identified it as an emergency would then give assistance. However, in the company of others, the issue of who should help arises. Some witnesses may take the view that they do not need to help, because others will, or that somehow, because they are not the only witness, that the responsibility to help is shared. Interestingly, this idea is counter-intuitive, since common sense dictates that if you are going to risk drowning you are best to do so in a crowded pool, on the assumption that the more bystanders, the more chance you will have of getting help. Much research has confirmed, however, that when there are more witnesses to an emergency, less help is forthcoming, and it takes longer to be given. For example, in one of their widely reported studies, Latané and Darley arranged for participants to be in a discussion with others, during which one of the others (a confederate) pretended to be having a seizure. By varying the number of witnesses to the emergency, they showed that as the number of witnesses rose, the time taken to give help rose significantly. This finding became known as the **'bystander effect'**.

The next stage in Latané and Darley's model involves witnesses having to decide whether they have the abilities needed in the emergency; for example, do they have the first aid skills, etc. If they can convince themselves they are not well equipped to help, they are less likely to do so. Taking the swimming example, the witness might decide that as a non-swimmer, there is nothing they can do to help. Again, studies which manipulate level of ability to help show that this is a factor in how much help is given.

Finally, Latané and Darley's cognitive model suggests that it is only after having hurdled the previous cognitive barriers that any bystander must decide whether to help or not. It is at this final hurdle that the bystander's analysis of cost and benefit will come in to play. For example, a bystander might weigh up the fact that they will get a reward with the possibility of becoming a target or being harmed. A fairly innocuous example of this from sport might be when your coach is screaming at one of your team-mates, and you decide not to speak out on their behalf for fear that you will be next or you will lose your place in the team. This aspect of the model has also been supported in various studies, one clever example of which was conducted by Batson. What he did was to manipulate the cost of helping, by telling some trainee priests that they had to hurry to get to a studio, where they had to give a practice sermon, and other trainee priests that they should not hurry, because there was plenty of time. Batson then arranged for a confederate to fall over, faking an emergency, in view of each priest on his way to the studio. The experimental prediction was that priests who were in a hurry would help less. This was exactly what he found. The sting in the tail for this study was that the sermon that the priests had to deliver was on the Good Samaritan! The five-stage model is represented in *Fig. 1*. Although bystander intervention is not as relevant to sport

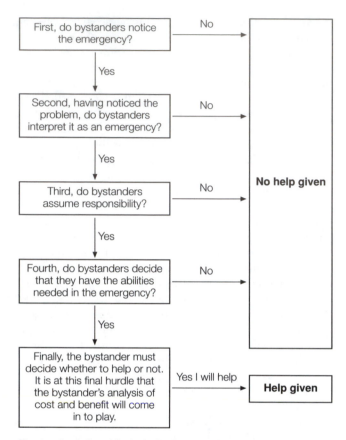

Fig. 1.   Latané and Darley's five-stage cognitive model of bystander intervention.

and exercise as other topics it has been an important area of mainstream psychology for some time, and it does demonstrate how the cognitive approach in psychology can be used to give a clear and more detailed understanding of people's behavior.

Negative State Relief Model

Latané and Darley's five-stage model helps us to understand why bystanders do not always help. However, it is also important to consider what explains why bystanders do help. After all, why would we help if we might get hurt, or suffer other unpleasant consequences? One widely held view is that we do it to avoid feeling bad (Cialdini et al., 1982). The Negative State Relief Model claims that pro-social behaviour is motivated by a desire to reduce negative feelings, either pre-existing, or aroused by the victim's problem. In particular, it suggests that help is given only if:

(1) the bystander experiences negative emotions;
(2) there is no other way to eliminate such feelings and;
(3) helping will eliminate them.

Moderator variables

Studies have shown that how much help we give is influenced by many factors.
    For example, research reveals that: smartly dressed people get more help than less well-dressed ones; attractive people get more help than less attractive

ones; and we give more help to people we perceive to be similar to ourselves (Baron & Byrne, 2003). Even touch has been shown to influence pro-social behavior. For example, studies have demonstrated that a fleeting touch, as brief as the contact that can occur when a librarian hands us back our library card, affects how helpful we are to others. In one study, experimenters deliberately left a coin in a phone booth and waited for people to take it. As they left the booth, participants were approached by a confederate, who asked them if they had found any money in the booth. The number of people owning up to having taken the coin was found to be dramatically higher if the confederate touched them on the arm as they asked the question! In another interesting study on the factors that affect helping, researchers manipulated the mood of students by giving out cookies, to some but not all, of the students in the university library (Isen & Levin, 1972). They then arranged for a confederate to wait outside the library and drop a pile of books just as students came out. The researchers recorded the amount of help given in this situation, and discovered that the students who had been given a cookie were much more likely to help!

One final important factor that affects how much helping behavior people exhibit is **modeling**. Studies show that if we have seen others helping in a previous incident we are much more likely to help in a subsequent one (Bryan & Test, 1967).

You may be wondering how all of this is relevant to sport and exercise. Although it is possible to think of sports examples of altruism, like the sailing example earlier, or of times when individuals make self-sacrifices for the greater good of the team, our answer is also a more general one. Athletes are people too, and by understanding why people behave the way they do, we get a better knowledge base and a better framework for understanding all sorts of behavior in the physical domain.

F5 ANTI-SOCIAL BEHAVIOR

Key Notes

Defining aggression	Any definition of aggression needs to exclude the delivery of noxious stimuli that are helpful, such as dental treatment, and include acts that intend to harm but do not deliver a noxious stimulus, such as when someone swings a punch but misses the target. Aggression is therefore defined here as any form of behavior directed to the goal of harming another being, who is motivated to avoid such treatment.
Instrumental vs hostile aggression	Instrumental aggression is that which serves a goal other than inflicting pain or suffering. In contrast, hostile aggression is associated with a desire to harm for its own sake. It is sometimes also called angry aggression. This distinction helps us to understand the causes of aggression.
Legitimate aggression	In some sports, physical aggression is actually necessary, or indeed the essence of the sport, such as punching an opponent in boxing or kicking an opponent in karate. In these cases, the reason for the aggression is legitimized by the rules of the sport, and bound up in the roles that combatants take.
Aggression as an instinct	One of the oldest ideas about aggression is that it is instinctive. This common sense view was given impetus by evolutionary theory. Another theory that relied on the notion of instinct was psychoanalytic theory. While there is much that appeals about the idea of aggression as an innate behavior, it is clear that instinct alone cannot explain aggression because there are huge differences in levels of aggression in different cultures.
Behaviorism and aggression	Behaviorist approaches to aggression argue that environmental and past experiences dictate aggressiveness. The frustration–aggression hypothesis claimed that all aggression was the result of frustration, and that all frustration causes aggression. We now know that these claims were too extreme. Instrumental aggression has little to do with frustration, and frustration can lead to problem-solving behavior, or to apathetic responses, as well as to aggression.
Cognitive approaches	One particularly influential cognitive approach to aggression was provided by Albert Bandura, who suggested that aggressiveness can result from social learning. In a classic study of children's aggression, he demonstrated the imitative learning of aggression in the absence of reward.
Self-theory and aggression	Self-theorists explain behavior in terms of the roles that people play, and the rules that govern these roles. They view aggressive behavior as a way for some people to gain self-respect and the respect of others, for example, by being aggressive in a street gang. This explanation has been used to account for the soccer hooliganism of fans in England and Europe.

Related topics	Theoretical perspectives (A7)	De-individuation (G7)
	Obedience to authority (F3)	Issues of arousal and anxiety (L2)
	Pro-social behavior (F4)	

Defining aggression

Although we tend to know what people mean by aggression, the term has not always been well defined in psychology and sport psychology. For example, people often confuse aggression and assertiveness when they talk about a player needing to show a bit more 'aggression'. A simple definition of aggression is 'the delivery of a noxious stimulus'. However, this is problematic because it does not cover some actions that we do consider to be aggression, but that do not actually harm someone. Consider the situation where one football player aims a punch at another, but misses the target, which most people would consider an aggressive act. A good definition would also need to exclude the delivery of noxious stimuli that are helpful. For example, the inflicting of pain that the fitness coach puts us through, or the pain that the dentist pulling a tooth causes, are surely better left out of any theory of aggression.

Another problem we have when trying to define aggression is that what is considered aggression is not entirely defined by the action. For example, the same action is sometimes interpreted by one victim as aggression, but not by another. This is particularly true in sport where, for example, a punch, which lands on the chin of a rugby player might be met with a shaking of the head to clear it, followed by carrying on with play. In contrast, a soccer player who receives the same strength of punch is more likely to fall, as if pole-axed, and remain on the ground to receive attention for several minutes. This is not actually to say that the average soccer player is any less tough than the rugby player, but that, cultural norms, and in sport, sub-cultural norms, dictate the seriousness of aggression, and the appropriate response to it.

To try to circumvent some of these problems, **aggression** is defined here as any form of behavior directed to the goal of harming another being, who is motivated to avoid such treatment (Baron & Byrne, 2003). This definition is more useful than the more simple definition because it removes some of the activities described earlier that serve to 'muddy the waters'.

Instrumental vs hostile aggression

A useful distinction made in the study of aggression is between instrumental aggression and hostile aggression. **Instrumental aggression** is that which serves a goal other than inflicting pain or suffering. One example of this comes from the classic cinema view of the Mafia hitman who is not angry, but just doing 'business'. We see this in football when a player deliberately attempts to injure the best player in the opposition team to increase his own team's chance of winning. **Hostile aggression** is associated with a desire to harm for its own sake. It is sometimes also called angry aggression. For example, a player may make a bad tackle on an opponent because the opponent has been taunting him throughout the game. This distinction helps us to understand the causes of aggression.

Legitimate aggression

Before moving on to consider theories of aggression, one final clarification needs to be made in relation to aggression in sport. In some sports, physical aggression is actually necessary, or indeed the essence of the sport, such as punching an opponent in boxing or kicking an opponent in karate. In these cases, the reason for the aggression is legitimized by the rules of the sport, and bound up in the roles that combatants take. As such, it presents psychologists with less of a puzzle. Of course it is not always easy to tell, in a boxing match, when aggression shifts from being instrumental (to knock-out or outscore the opponent) to hostile/angry aggression, going beyond the acceptable norms of the sport. This is one reason why we have referees in sport. However, when one boxer bites off a piece of another boxer's ear we can safely say, that a theory that goes beyond legitimate aggression is needed.

Aggression as an instinct

There are several different theories of why aggression occurs. Not surprisingly, the various perspectives in psychology (see Topic A7) have produced their own 'spin' on this. Aggression covers a huge range of different activities, and as such, almost certainly has multiple causes. Thus we should not be surprised if no one theory is enough to explain all types of aggression.

One of the oldest ideas is that we are instinctively aggressive. This common sense view was given impetus by evolutionary theory, where notions of survival of the fittest are central. It is easy to see how non-aggressive animals, within a species, might lose out in the battle for scarce resources, or access to mating partners. However, it should be said that convincing though evolutionary explanations are, they have been criticized on the grounds that they are justified by the selective picking of evidence that supports them, whilst ignoring possible counter arguments. For example, it could be argued that aggressive humans are less likely to survive and produce offspring than non-aggressive ones who do not get into fights. Similarly, it could be argued that it is not the aggressive warrior who goes off looking for a good war who will have more children, but the 'wimp' who stays at home with the women!

Another theory that relied on the notion of instinct was psychoanalytic theory. Freud initially argued that people were driven by **Eros**, the life or love instinct. However, having witnessed the widespread death and destruction of the First World War, he extended his theory to include **Thanatos**, the aggressive or 'death instinct'.

The theory employed the analogy of a reservoir that is continuously being topped up with instinctual aggressive energy. Freud suggested that the reservoir continues to fill up until the pressure is so great there is a sudden outpouring of aggression. Following an aggressive act, the reservoir of stored energy is back to a low level and further aggression is unlikely to occur until the reservoir fills up again. Freud also suggested that sport and exercise provided a socially acceptable way of releasing aggressive energy, i.e. that they were **cathartic**.

While there is much that appeals about the idea of aggression as an innately driven behavior, it is clear that instinct alone cannot explain aggression in humans. For example, if instinct alone explained aggression, we should find that levels of aggression are similar in different places and cultures. However, this is not the case, and if we look at murder rates around the world, we see that they are dramatically different in different countries. For example, a recent study revealed that, in Norway, there were 9 murders per million people, in the USA there were 99, and in Papua New Guinea there were 6,830! Differences as dramatic as these fit a cultural, rather than an instinctive explanation. We see similarly disparities in levels of aggression in the sporting context. For example, levels of soccer hooliganism differ widely across different countries.

Behaviorism and aggression

Behaviorist approaches to aggression argue that environmental and past experiences dictate aggressiveness. The first theory of aggression to stress the role of situational factors in the environment was the **frustration–aggression hypothesis**, which in its strongest form claimed that all aggression was the result of frustration (Dollard et al., 1939). Thus, if our goals were obstructed by environmental factors, this led to increased frustration and then aggression. Just as in psychoanalytic theory, there is the notion of a growing level of drive or frustration, however, in this case the cause of the drive was said to be environmental rather than internal.

While it is easy to see why the frustration–aggression hypothesis has appeal, it is also evident that it is too extreme to claim that all aggression is caused by frustration. For example, instrumental aggression has little to do with the blocking of one's goals, and everything to do with a cold decision to be aggressive to achieve a goal or purpose.

The frustration–aggression hypothesis also claimed the corollary that all frustration causes aggression. Again, examples that fit are easy to find. In a classic example of frustration leading to aggression, the Formula 1 racing driver Nelson Piquet jumped out of his car and kicked another driver who had just caused him to crash out, while leading in a crucial World Championship Grand Prix. However, not all responses to frustration are aggressive. For example, frustration sometimes leads to apathy, and sometimes it causes us to engage in problem-solving behavior. By invoking learning theory, behaviorism provides another obvious answer to the question of why people are aggressive. Here, the argument is that they have been rewarded for aggressiveness in the past, or punished for not being aggressive. Thus, bullies learn that there are benefits to aggression, and the bullied learn that there are costs to not fighting back. In sport, intimidating an opponent may well have brought rewards.

Cognitive approaches

Cognitive psychology views aggression as more than just being environmentally caused. It sees it as the result of an appraisal process in which the meaning of others' actions are interpreted, rather than immediately responded to. For example, when someone fouls us, we will probably react differently, depending upon whether we attribute his or her actions as being accidental or deliberate.

One particularly influential cognitive approach to aggression was provided by Albert Bandura, who suggested that aggressiveness can result from **social learning** (Bandura, 1977). By this he meant that we sometimes learn through more complex mechanisms than the simplistic stimulus response chain of Skinnerian learning theory. For example, he argued that people can engage in **modeled** behavior and vicarious learning, without tangible rewards. In a classic study, he allowed children to watch adults beating up toy blow-up plastic 'Bobo-dolls', of the kind that always return to an upright position if knocked over. Following this, the children were given a chance to play with the dolls. Not surprisingly they beat them up! This demonstrated the **imitative**, or social learning, of aggression in the absence of reward (Bandura et al., 1961). It is not hard to see how this might explain some aggression in youth sport.

Self-theory and aggression

Self-theory falls within the general domain of humanistic approaches to aggression. Self-theorists see behavior in terms of the **roles** that people play, and the **scripts or rules** that govern these roles. Aggressive behavior can be viewed in terms of the tough guy role as some people's way of gaining and maintaining self-respect and the respect of others. According to self-theory, we all strive to feel worthwhile, which we can do in many different ways. Some of us do well in education and go to college. Some of us succeed in the business world.

Others get their esteem from being good athletes, and so on. According to self-theorists, some aggressive behavior is enacted by people who have failed to gain respect in more conventional ways. They argue that there is respect to be gained from one's peers by, for example, being aggressive and brave in a street gang, or as a member of the Hell's Angels.

Exactly this explanation has also been used to account for much of the soccer hooliganism of fans in England and Europe. In fact, in his study of this phenomenon described in his book 'The Rules of Disorder', Peter Marsh shows how the behavior that the press calls 'mindless violence', is in fact highly ritualized, and rule-bound aggression (Marsh et al., 1978). This ritualized aggression affords a degree of respect to young people who have otherwise failed to negotiate the societal tests of worthiness. Thus, just as academic children have to face tests and examinations to prove their worth, Marsh sees aggressive situations at soccer matches as 'hazard sessions' that provide opportunities for fans to be brave or tough and gain respect from their peers. This same analysis can easily be applied to explain some of the on-field aggression often seen between players in sport.

G1 GROUPS AND TEAMS

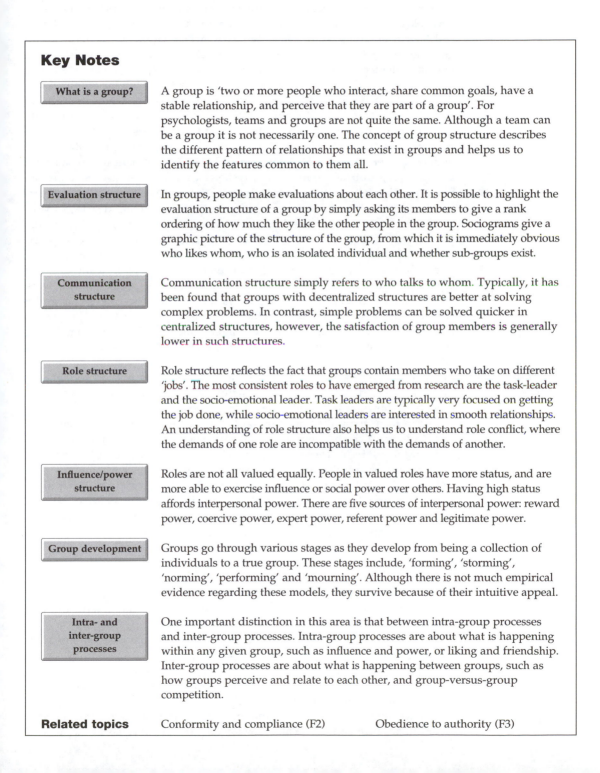

Key Notes

What is a group?

A group is 'two or more people who interact, share common goals, have a stable relationship, and perceive that they are part of a group'. For psychologists, teams and groups are not quite the same. Although a team can be a group it is not necessarily one. The concept of group structure describes the different pattern of relationships that exist in groups and helps us to identify the features common to them all.

Evaluation structure

In groups, people make evaluations about each other. It is possible to highlight the evaluation structure of a group by simply asking its members to give a rank ordering of how much they like the other people in the group. Sociograms give a graphic picture of the structure of the group, from which it is immediately obvious who likes whom, who is an isolated individual and whether sub-groups exist.

Communication structure

Communication structure simply refers to who talks to whom. Typically, it has been found that groups with decentralized structures are better at solving complex problems. In contrast, simple problems can be solved quicker in centralized structures, however, the satisfaction of group members is generally lower in such structures.

Role structure

Role structure reflects the fact that groups contain members who take on different 'jobs'. The most consistent roles to have emerged from research are the task-leader and the socio-emotional leader. Task leaders are typically very focused on getting the job done, while socio-emotional leaders are interested in smooth relationships. An understanding of role structure also helps us to understand role conflict, where the demands of one role are incompatible with the demands of another.

Influence/power structure

Roles are not all valued equally. People in valued roles have more status, and are more able to exercise influence or social power over others. Having high status affords interpersonal power. There are five sources of interpersonal power: reward power, coercive power, expert power, referent power and legitimate power.

Group development

Groups go through various stages as they develop from being a collection of individuals to a true group. These stages include, 'forming', 'storming', 'norming', 'performing' and 'mourning'. Although there is not much empirical evidence regarding these models, they survive because of their intuitive appeal.

Intra- and inter-group processes

One important distinction in this area is that between intra-group processes and inter-group processes. Intra-group processes are about what is happening within any given group, such as influence and power, or liking and friendship. Inter-group processes are about what is happening between groups, such as how groups perceive and relate to each other, and group-versus-group competition.

Related topics   Conformity and compliance (F2)   Obedience to authority (F3)

What is a group?   In contrast to its everyday usage, psychologists typically define groups more specifically as consisting of 'two or more people who interact, share common goals, have a stable relationship, and perceive that they are part of a group' (Paulus, 1989). Thus, people who are queuing for cup final tickets are not a psychological group. They do have a common purpose but do not all interact, and their relationship is not stable. Similarly, when we say 'by winning a fifth gold medal, she became a member of a very select group of Olympians' we are not using the term in the way psychologists use it. In sport, the term 'team' is typically used to describe a set of people who play for a club (or at representative level for a region, state or country). For psychologists, teams and groups are not quite the same. Although a team can be a group it is not necessarily one. For example, it is probably safe to say that a long-established pairing in badminton does constitute a psychological group. Similarly, a basketball team, with ten players may achieve 'groupness'. However, an American football team is just too big to be a group in the psychological sense, because there are too many people in it to allow for everyone to interact regularly. When players from different clubs first come together to represent their district, city or country, we are again probably talking about a team rather than a group. Indeed, the whole notion of team building testifies to the fact that some teams are not yet groups.

In everyday life we are surrounded by, and are members of, many different types of groups. For example, there are sports groups, study groups, work groups, family groups, friendship groups and so on. The concept of **group structure** describes the different patterns of relationships that exist in groups and helps us to identify the features common to them all. The four main dimensions of group structure are evaluation, communication, role and influence.

Evaluation structure   In groups, people make evaluations about each other. It is possible to highlight the evaluation structure of a group by simply asking its members to give a rank ordering of how much they like the other people in the group, or to choose the people in their group they like the most. It is possible to draw diagrams with lines to indicate choices between members. This technique is known as **sociometry** (Moreno, 1960). These sociograms give a graphic picture of the structure of the group, from which it is immediately obvious who likes whom, who is an isolated individual and whether sub-groups exist. We see in *Figure 1* that Ellen, Grace, Mari and Ruth make up a tight self-selecting subgroup, but that Julia is a bit of an isolated figure having not been chosen by anyone. Coaches and sport and exercise psychologists can use information on evaluation structure to monitor and improve relationships within groups and teams.

Communication structure   A second way to highlight what is going on in a group is to look at communication between members by monitoring who talks to whom. Again, it is possible to map this onto a diagram that throws the communication structure into relief.

It has been found that groups with decentralized communication structures are usually better at solving complex problems (*Fig. 2a*). In contrast simple problems can be solved quicker in centralized structures. However, in centralized structures the satisfaction of group members is generally lower, except for the person in the central position (*Fig. 2b*).

Another method for measuring communication structure is to focus on what is said rather than on who speaks to whom. Several systems have been devised

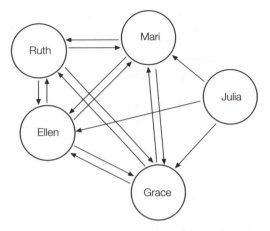

Fig. 1.   Sociogram of the evaluation structure of a five-person group each given three
friendship choices. Ellen, Grace, Mari and Ruth make up a tight self-selecting subgroup, but
Julia is a bit of an isolated figure having been chosen by none of the others.

to do this including Interaction Process Analysis (IPA) and the System for the
Multiple Level Observation of Groups (SYMLOG) (Bales & Cohen, 1979).

Role structure   Role structure reflects the fact that groups contain members who take on different
'jobs'. Research shows that roles become differentiated as the group develops. The
most consistent roles to have emerged from research are the **task-leader** and the
socio-emotional leader (McGrath & Altman, 1966). Task leaders are typically very
focused on getting the job done, even if it is sometimes at the expense of running
roughshod over the feelings of group members. In this situation the group will
benefit if it has a socio-emotional leader. Socio-emotional leaders are interested in
smooth relationships. They like to be in a happy group and are more aware of the
feelings of group members. They typically work to keep the atmosphere positive,
while the task leader is pushing on at all costs. Most groups have and need both
task and socio-emotional leadership. Research has also identified other roles in
groups. For example, commonly found roles include friend, fighter, thinker,

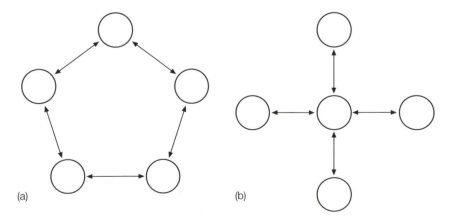

Fig. 2.   Communication structure. (a) Decentralized lines of communication in a five-person
group. (b) Centralized lines of communication in a five-person group.

comedian, commentator and deviant. With a moment's reflection about the sports and exercise groups that you belong to, you will probably be able to think of individuals who fit some of these roles. It should be pointed out however, that not every group will have someone in each one of these roles. More elaborate classification systems of 'group roles' have been developed within organizational settings. For example, Belbin's 'team roles' approach consists of nine roles that he argues are important if work groups are to function effectively. These roles fall into three categories. There are the action-based roles of shaper, implementer and completer-finisher, the person-oriented roles of co-ordinator, team-worker and resource investigator, and the thinking roles of plant, monitor-evaluator and specialist (Belbin, 2003). Although derived from industry and commerce, these team roles have relevance for the efficient running of sport and exercise clubs. An understanding of role structure also helps us to understand role conflict, where the demands of one role are incompatible with the demands of another. For example, role conflict might occur for the coach or teacher who teaches her own children, where the demands of being a good parent could easily conflict with those of being a good teacher or coach.

Influence/power structure

Although people in groups take on different roles, these roles are not all valued equally. People in valued roles have more status, and are more able to exercise influence or social power over others in the group. As groups develop, so does a 'pecking order' or dominance hierarchy. In sports teams status comes from several sources. It may be that the 'hard man/tough guy' is looked up to, or it may be the 'comedian', or the player with exceptional skill. Having high status affords a player interpersonal power. Studies of interpersonal power suggest that it is available to people who have something others want that they cannot gain by other means. For example, a lecturer has power over a student who wants the lecturer's knowledge, but the power base is reduced if the knowledge can be gained in the library (French & Raven, 1960).

There are, broadly speaking, five sources of interpersonal power:

- **Reward power** comes from being able to give someone something they want.
- **Coercive power** is the power we have when we can punish someone.
- **Expert power** comes from knowing things others need to know, as in the case of the coach.
- **Referent power** stems from identification with someone. If we admire someone, and they provide a model for us with regard to attitudes or values, we identify with that person and are influenced by them. Sponsors pay huge amounts of money to players like Michael Jordan or David Beckham, to endorse shoes or after-shave lotion, knowing that identification will lead to increased sales.
- **Legitimate power** is based on our acceptance of internalized norms or values. For example, most players accept that the captain is a legitimate authority for them. Age provides another example of these internalized norms where, other things being equal, older people tend to be accepted as legitimate authority figures for younger ones. This is why young bosses can meet resistance from staff who are older than them. Similarly, entrenched ideas about sexual inequality can lead to female bosses having problems with male employees. Karen Brady, the successful chairwoman of Birmingham City Football Club, has very effectively overcome both of these prejudices in the male-dominated world of professional soccer.

Group development

Groups go through various stages as they develop from being a collection of individuals to a true group. One often-cited description of such development was offered by Tuckman (1965) who suggested there were four stages in the process, 'forming', 'storming', 'norming' and 'performing'. In the 'forming' stage people are finding out about each other, goals are not clear and not much on-task work is done. 'Storming' occurs when group members vie for position, thrash out their initial differences and argue about what needs to be done and how. Again, productivity is typically low throughout this phase. In the 'norming' phase, members begin to agree more about who will take which different roles, and as a result the group starts to be more productive. Having established their norms and working practices, the group is then able to get on with 'performing'. It is in the 'performing' phase that the group comes together and sees itself as a group. By now members are committed to the goals of the group and to each other, and performance is generally at its highest. More recently, a fifth stage, 'mourning', has been added to Tuckman's classification in recognition of the fact that groups do not last forever and group members may experience a sense of loss.

Another classification scheme, focusing on the individual in the group rather than the group itself, describes the five phases of group membership as investigation, socialization, maintenance, re-socialization and remembrance.

Although there is not much empirical evidence regarding these models, they survive because of their intuitive appeal, and because they help us to understand what might be happening at any given time in the life of the group. For example, we should not be too concerned if, early on in the life of the group, there are clashes between individuals, because we know that later on, things will be ironed out. Sport and exercise practitioners can use their knowledge of group development processes to inform team-building practices.

Intra- and inter-group processes

One useful distinction in this area is that between **intra-group processes** and **inter-group processes**. Intra-group processes are about what is happening within any given group, e.g. influence and power, liking and friendship. Inter-group processes are about what is happening **between** groups, for example, how groups perceive and relate to each other, or in terms of rivalry and group-to-group competition. Intra-group processes are dealt with in Topics G2–8. Inter-group processes are dealt with in G9.

G2 SOCIAL FACILITATION

Key Notes

Mere exposure/drive theory	Social facilitation refers to the finding that performance is affected by the presence of others. In the mid 1960s, Zajonc proposed the first theory that attempted to explain why the presence of others was sometimes facilitative and sometimes disruptive. He argued that the presence of others raises arousal levels, which in turn causes an increase in the production of 'dominant responses'. He further suggested that, for simple tasks, dominant responses are appropriate and performance is enhanced. However, for more complex tasks, dominant responses are not sufficient and performance is impaired unless the task is well-learned.
Evaluation apprehension	Evaluation apprehension represents a more cognitive explanation for the debilitating effects of the presence of others, and is based on self-presentational concerns. Here, the idea is that we may become overly concerned with what others think of our performance, and this causes us to tighten up and play poorly, unless we are very skilled, in which case the effect is to facilitate performance. There is support for this view in studies that show that the presence of non-evaluating others does not disrupt performance.
Distraction–conflict theory	Another possible explanation for performance deficits in the presence of others is provided by distraction–conflict theory, which suggests that since people are hugely reinforcing for us, audiences create a powerful distraction that makes a conflicting demand on our attention to the task at hand.
Related topics	Social cognition (F1) Groups and teams (G1) Inter-group processes (G9)

Mere exposure/drive theory

Social facilitation refers to the finding that performance is affected by the presence of others. It was originally believed that this presence always led to improvements in performance, however, it is now clear that in some circumstances the presence of others can hinder it. The topic grew out of Triplett's finding, as long ago as 1897, that young boys could wind in fishing reels quicker in the presence of other boys than when alone (Triplett, 1897).

Many studies have now demonstrated facilitation effects across a wide range of tasks, in animals as diverse as cockroaches and horses, and of course in humans. One thing that has become apparent over the years, however, is that the presence of others is not always beneficial. Many studies have found it to be debilitating. Further, it appears that these debilitation effects are more likely when tasks are complex, or the participants are less skilful. For example, in one naturalistic study, researchers watched pool players of mixed ability, and secretly measured their performances (Michaels et al., 1982). They later returned and watched them again, this time making it obvious they were watching. As predicted, in the presence of an audience, the performance of the good players improved, and the performance of the poorer ones declined.

In the mid 1960s, Zajonc proposed the first theory that attempted to explain why the presence of others was sometimes facilitative and sometimes disruptive. As a behaviorist, he argued that the presence of others raises arousal levels, which in turn causes an increase in the production of well-learned or **'dominant responses'**. He further suggested that, for simple tasks, dominant responses are appropriate and performance is enhanced. However, for more complex tasks, dominant responses are not sufficient and performance is impaired (Zajonc, 1965). To take a sporting example, a novice tennis player may be at the stage where she is starting to be able to get her serve in 60% of the time when practicing alone. However, when others stop to watch her, she only gets 10% of her serves in. Zajonc argues that the presence of the audience increases her level of arousal or drive, which in turn, causes her to produce dominant responses, which, in the case of the novice, are not the necessary movements for serving well. In contrast, a skilled player would have appropriate service actions as her dominant responses, so that the presence of others would facilitate performance (see *Fig. 1*).

Support for the first link in the causal chain of this theory comes from studies that show that the introduction of audiences does increase sympathetic nervous system activation in experimental participants, as measured by palmar sweating. The second part of the theory has been supported in studies that involve a pre-training stage, during which participants develop well-learned or dominant responses. They are then tested in an audience and an alone condition. As predicted, in the audience condition there is an increase in dominant responses. Zajonc's theory was labeled drive theory, or the **mere presence theory**, because of its claim that the mere presence of others is enough to increase drive.

Evaluation apprehension

Evaluation apprehension represents a more cognitive explanation for the debilitating effects of the presence of others, and is based on self-presentational concerns. Here, the idea is that we may become overly concerned with what others think of our performance, and this causes us to tighten up and play poorly, unless we are very skilled, in which case the effect is to facilitate performance. Anyone who has just begun to play golf, and been faced with hitting their first drive from in front of the clubhouse, where the members are lined up and watching, will know how daunting that tee-shot can be. Top players who are more confident in their ability to send a great drive down the middle of the fairway do not feel this pressure, and may even benefit from a facilitation effect as they play to the crowd. There is support for this view in studies in which people carry out a task in one of three conditions: alone, in the

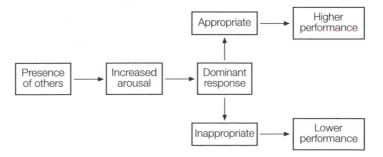

Fig. 1.   Zajonc's mere exposure theory.

presence of an audience, or in a third 'mere presence' condition, in which there is an audience, which is not able to evaluate the performance because its members are blindfolded! If drive theory is correct, the mere presence of others should lead to social facilitation/inhibition effects. In contrast, if evaluation apprehension is the explanation, then the effects should only be seen in the true audience condition. Typically in such studies, we find support for the evaluation apprehension idea, in that the mere presence and alone groups perform significantly better than the audience group (Cottrell et al., 1968). Evaluation apprehension is intuitively appealing as an explanation for these effects. However, there is one rather intriguing finding that argues against it. While it is generally wise to be skeptical when inferring things about complex human activities from studies of lower species, one somewhat amusing study merits a mention. Zajonc et al. (1969) trained cockroaches to learn two mazes, a very simple one and a slightly more complex one. In one condition they learned in the presence of other cockroaches, and in another, there was no 'audience' of cockroaches. The researchers found that in the simple maze the cockroaches learned faster in the presence of others. In contrast, in the complex maze they learned faster when there was no 'audience'. This pattern is exactly as predicted by the mere presence/drive theory. What makes this study interesting is that the facilitation effects can surely not be explained by evaluation apprehension, since it is hard to imagine the cockroaches worrying about what other cockroaches thought of them!

**Distraction–
conflict theory**

Another possible explanation for performance deficits in the presence of others is provided by distraction–conflict theory, which suggests that since people are hugely reinforcing for us, audiences create a powerful distraction that makes a conflicting demand on our attention to the task at hand (Sanders et al., 1978). Again this explanation has intuitive appeal. If it is correct, we should be able to demonstrate social facilitation effects even when a conflict is non-social. Research has indeed shown that mechanical distractions, such as flashing lights, do lead to poorer performance. One particularly clever study disentangled the theories, by asking participants to carry out tasks that required them to look carefully at a person on a TV screen. The clever part was that in one condition the audience person was the person on screen, and in another condition the person on screen and the audience person were different. In this way, the experiment involved the presence of another in both conditions but distraction in only one. As predicted by distraction–conflict theory, the performance only fell in the distraction condition, thus, mere presence was not enough to produce deficits in performance (Groff et al., 1983).

Bringing this all together, it appears that each theory may provide a part explanation for social facilitation effects. What this means in terms of the sport and exercise domain is that it offers practitioners alternative ways to minimize the negative consequences of the presence of others. For example, if distraction is the problem then concentration-type interventions might be useful (see Topic L3). If evaluation apprehension is at work then a technique like cognitive restructuring might be useful (see Topic L2).

G3 SOCIAL LOAFING

Key Notes

Process loss

Process loss refers to the finding that the effectiveness of groups is often less than the sum of the effectiveness of the individuals in the group working alone. Studies have shown that this is the result of 'social loafing' rather than being caused by coordination problems. Social loafing has been found to occur across a wide range of activities, both of a motor and cognitive nature.

Overcoming social loafing

There are three main ways in which social loafing can be reduced. Firstly, we can monitor individual performance. Secondly, we can manipulate commitment. Finally, social loafing can be minimized by providing comparative information on how other groups are doing, which suggests that competitive drive can overcome laziness. Since competition is central to sport, it may be that social loafing is less prevalent in sport groups.

Ecological validity

Ecological validity is the extent to which the findings from a laboratory study are applicable to the real world. Most of the research on social loafing has been carried out on laboratory groups rather than real sports groups. One suggestion is that what we see in laboratory groups is 'individual' rather than 'social' loafing because participants actually remain as individuals. Thus, we might expect that in real sport groups, athletes would demonstrate social *laboring* rather than loafing.

Related topics

Research methods (A4)   Social facilitation (G2)
Groups and teams (G1)

Process loss

Process loss in this context refers to the finding that the effectiveness of groups is often less than the sum of the effectiveness of the individuals in the group working alone. This is clearly an area of interest and potential concern for sports performance.

The effect was first discovered by Ringelmann, a German scientist working on the efficiency of agricultural workers and animals. In one study he found that when pulling on a rope against a spring balance, one person was able to exert a force of about 85 kilograms, however, seven people together could only exert an average force of about 65 kilograms, and 14 people exerted an average force of just over 61 kilograms (Ringelmann, 1913). More recent studies have supported Ringelmann's early findings, showing that as group size increases average group output diminishes. When the group grows to about six or seven members process loss tails off. Thus, with two people, performance drops to about 90% of the individual level, with three, to about 85% and with five or six, it is down around the 80% mark. Although tempting to assume that people become lazy in groups and that this is evidence of **'social loafing'**, alternatively it could be that process loss is the result of reduced efficiency due to coordination problems. Coordination problems can occur even when two people may be very highly motivated to perform a task, but fail to do so efficiently, because they do not link together well. For example, if two people were to simultaneously share the driving of a racing car with a manual gearshift, one shifting the gears, while the other depresses the clutch, they would probably not drive as efficiently as one person alone. Thus, process loss may have nothing to do with lack of effort or loafing. This issue has been investigated in clever tug-of-war studies, in which participants believed they were working with others, but were in fact pulling alone (Ingham et al., 1974). By employing confederates, who stand behind the unsuspecting participant and pretend to pull, these studies neatly separate coordination from motivation. Performance deficits do occur in such studies, suggesting that social loafing does exist, and is not simply, or even significantly, due to coordination problems (see Fig. 1). Social loafing also occurs in group tasks that require no coordination. For example, social loafing has been found in a study in which participants were required to cheer and clap as loudly as they could (Latané et al., 1979).

Social loafing has been found to occur across a wide range of activities, both of a motor and cognitive nature. One study has even suggested that it is evident in the song-writing work of John Lennon and Paul McCartney (Jackson & Padgett, 1982). The study compared the quality of earlier songs as measured by chart success, with later ones, and found the former to be of higher quality. This fits a social loafing explanation because the early Beatles songs were individually written, but jointly credited, while their later songs were written together. However, it should be noted that this study was not experimental in nature and there are other ways to explain any differences between early and later writing performance, such as limited creativity or changes in motivation.

In general, the evidence shows that we have a tendency to socially loaf when we perform in groups. Fortunately, as we see below, it is relatively easy to counteract this effect.

Overcoming social loafing

Social loafing could obviously be a problem in team sports and the question arises, can anything be done to reduce its effects? Fortunately the answer is yes. Firstly, we can monitor individual performance. In one study members of a university swimming team swam faster in team relay races if someone was monitoring and shouting out their individual leg times (Williams et al., 1989).

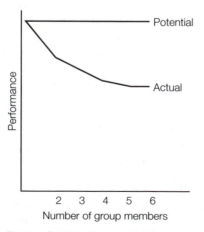

Fig. 1.   Social loafing in groups.

Secondly, we can manipulate commitment. For example, it has been shown that when a task is more attractive, social loafing is less evident. Finally, social loafing can be minimized by providing comparative information on how other groups are doing (Harkins & Szymanski, 1989). In other words, it looks as if competitive drive overcomes laziness. Since competition is central to sport, it may be that social loafing is less prevalent in sport groups.

Ecological validity   Ecological validity (Topic A4) is the extent to which the findings from a laboratory study are applicable to the real world. Most of the research on social loafing has been carried out on laboratory groups created specifically for each study. As such, they are not real groups but convenient aggregates of handy participants. We have seen that such studies demonstrate significant social loafing effects. However, it is reasonable to ask to what extent real groups, and in particular sports groups, will behave like laboratory groups. One suggestion is that what we see in laboratory groups is really 'individual' rather than 'social' loafing because participants actually remain as individuals in such gatherings of people. Thus, we might expect that in real sport groups, athletes would demonstrate social laboring rather than loafing. This suggests that perhaps coaches, managers and sport psychologists have less to fear from social loafing than they might imagine. In support of this view there is some evidence that when laboratory groups are given time to become real groups, levels of loafing drop (Holt, 1987). Although this suggests that findings from laboratory studies should be interpreted with caution, it is good news for those interested in helping to promote performance enhancement, since it again suggests that social loafing is not likely to affect real teams.

G4 LEADERSHIP

Key Notes

Trait vs situational approach	Early attempts to understand leadership suggested that leaders were those people who had the 'right stuff' in terms of personality traits. When studies were unable to identify what these traits were, researchers abandoned the trait approach for a situational one. In this view, the situation determines who will be a leader. Just as was the case for the trait approach, this view also came to be seen as somewhat simplistic and researchers began to take an interactionist approach, in which person and situation were said to act in conjunction.
The interactionist approach	In this view it is the combination of the traits a leader has, and the demands of the situation that together determine effective leadership. One example of such an approach is Fiedler's contingency theory. Fiedler focuses on task- versus person-centered styles of leadership as the trait dimension of interest and how favorable the leadership situation is as the situational variable.
Leadership in sport	The most influential theory of leadership in sport is that of Chelladurai, who proposed three sets of important antecedents to leader behavior: situational factors, leader characteristics and member characteristics. Next, he suggested three general categories of leader behavior: actual (what the coach does), preferred (what the athletes want the coach to do), and required (what the situation demands). Finally, he proposed that the congruence between these three categories of coach behaviors is the key to the outcome for athletes, in terms of performance and satisfaction.
Related topics	Obedience to authority (F3) Cohesiveness (G5) Groups and teams (G1)

Trait v situational approach

Early attempts to understand leadership took the **trait** approach, in what became known as the 'great man' theory of leadership. This simply suggested that leaders were those people who had the 'right stuff' in terms of personality traits or personal characteristics. Aligned with this view was the notion of the 'born leader', and that people either had these qualities or did not. However, when studies were unable to identify what these characteristics were, researchers abandoned the trait approach for a **situational** one. As the name suggests, this is the view that the situation determines who will lead, and that certain situations require certain qualities. One famous example of this is the way Winston Churchill emerged during World War II to provide great leadership in wartime Britain, having been relatively unsuccessful as a leader in peacetime. Just as was the case for the trait approach, this view also came to be seen as somewhat simplistic and researchers began to take an **interactionist** approach, in which person and situation were said to act in conjunction.

The interactionist approach

In this view it is the combination of the traits a leader has, and the demands of the situation that together determine effective leadership. One example of such an approach is **Fiedler's contingency theory** (1967). Fiedler focuses on task-versus person-centered styles of leadership as the trait dimension of interest. He measures this in a rather novel way by asking people how much they like the person they *dislike* most in the group! His measure is called the least preferred co-worker (LPC) scale. The logic behind this is that someone who is able to see some good in their least preferred co-worker, has a person-centered leadership style. The second main variable of the theory is how favorable the leadership situation is, in terms of three factors:

- how well liked they are;
- how difficult the task is;
- how powerful the leader is.

Taken together the trait and situation are said to predict how effective the leader will be. For example, task-centered leaders are predicted to be more effective in situations of low favorability, because direct approaches are needed without too much concern for the feelings of the group. Interestingly, the task leader is also said to be better in highly favorable situations because with power, and being liked, they again do not need to worry about people's feelings. In contrast, the person-centered leader prospers better when situation favorability is in the mid-range. This is because this type of leader is likely to get more from the group when power is low and the task is less clear. In general, research has supported Feidler's predictions.

Another influential contingency theory of leadership is **path goal theory** (House, 1971), which focuses on the needs of the subordinate rather than on the leader. It predicts that effective leadership is more likely when the leader's behavior helps subordinates to achieve their goals.

More recently, the **transformational approach** to leadership has emerged in organizational psychology (Northouse, 2001). Here the idea is that rather than trying to buy followers' compliance by exchanging rewards with them for their labor, as traditional approaches do, leaders should transform followers by getting them involved in the values of the organization. In this way, followers take ownership of the goals and problems of the group. In the transformational approach, leaders are interested in the personal and professional development of their staff, and help them to create opportunities to meet challenges. In addition, leaders have to be role models, having an optimistic but achievable vision for the group, and by doing themselves what they encourage others to do. They also need to help their team to see the intellectually stimulating aspects of the work of the group, and to see their own vision of the bigger picture. This transformational approach is one that fits well with the aims of people in sport, and contains much of what good coaches and captains already do.

Leadership in sport

In sport, captains and coaches predominantly occupy the leadership role, however, it is on coach behavior that most psychological research has focused.

For example, Chelladurai (1990) proposed three sets of important antecedents to leader behavior: situational factors, leader characteristics and member characteristics. Next, he suggested three general categories of leader behavior: actual (what the coach does), preferred (what the athletes want the coach to do), and required (what the situation demands). Finally, he proposed that the congruence between these three categories of coach behaviors is the key to the outcome for athletes, in terms of performance and satisfaction (see *Fig. 1*).

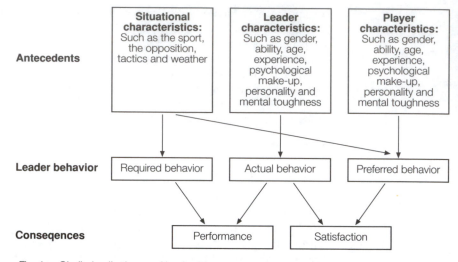

Fig. 1.   Chelladurai's theory of leadership.

In the first part of the model, which links antecedents to leader behavior, Chelladurai suggests that situational factors, such as the sport, the opposition, tactics and the weather are important, and that these influence, in particular, required and preferred behavior. Leader characteristics such as gender, ability, age, experience, psychological make-up, personality and mental toughness are said to affect actual behavior. Finally, player characteristics, again gender, ability, age, experience psychological make-up, personality and mental toughness are said to affect preferred behavior.

With regard to the second part of the model, where Chelladurai links leader behavior to consequences, he makes four claims:

(1) if the coach's actual behavior is what is required by the situation, and what players prefer, this should lead to good performance and high satisfaction in players;

(2) if the coach's actual behavior is incongruent with what is required, and with what players prefer, poor performance and low satisfaction should result;

(3) when actual coach behavior is congruent with what is required, but not with what players prefer, performance should be good, yet the players will be dissatisfied;

(4) when actual coach behavior is congruent with what players would prefer their coach to do, but not with required coach behavior, performance will be poor, but the players will be satisfied with the coach.

Although this second part of the model sounds complicated, it is actually a statement of four self-evident links, and is therefore not very helpful. For example, it tells us that if the coach does what is required, performance will be good. If the coach does what the team wants, they will be satisfied. Given this, it is not too surprising that support for the theory has been stronger in relation to this part of the theory.

One other sport-specific model should be mentioned, and that is Smoll and Smith's leadership behavior in sport (LBS) model (Smoll & Smith, 1989). Like Chelladurai, Smoll and Smith take a contingency approach, and their model consists of numerous hypothesized links between coach and athlete behavior.

However, they do differ in that the LBS model gives more emphasis to the perceptions of the coach and player. Smoll and Smith have summarized the evidence on their model as showing that coaches who:

- praise good performance and effort;
- encourage athletes who have underperformed;
- offer future-oriented technical feedback on negative performance;
- focus on personal improvement and having fun in preference to stressing winning;

produce athletes who perform consistently better, have better relations with team-mates, and enjoy their sport more.

G5 COHESIVENESS

Key Notes

What is cohesiveness?	Cohesiveness is 'a dynamic process which is reflected in the tendency for a group to stick together and remain united in the pursuit of its instrumental objectives and/or for the satisfaction of member affective needs'. It is now common in sport psychology to think of cohesiveness as consisting of both social cohesiveness and task cohesiveness. A team that is task cohesive shares goals and is well drilled. Players' activities are coordinated with each other, and each member knows their role in the overall strategy. In contrast, the socially cohesive group is one in which there are positive social interactions and players like each other.
Measurement of cohesiveness	Early measures tended to be unidimensional, and focused simply on social cohesiveness: the attractiveness of group members to each other. However, the trend in more recent years has been to develop multidimensional scales, measuring both task and social cohesiveness. The most used measure of cohesiveness in sport is the group environment questionnaire (GEQ). In addition to measuring social and task cohesiveness, the GEQ measures a second dimension of cohesiveness, which relates to the distinction between players' attraction to the group and their perception of the level of integration of the group as a whole.
Cohesiveness and performance	Despite there having been many studies on the relationship between cohesiveness and performance, the picture that emerges from them is not as clear as might be expected. Evidence suggests a stronger link between *task* cohesiveness and performance, than *social* cohesiveness and performance.
Problems in cohesiveness research	One fundamental problem in this area is that researchers have used the term cohesiveness in different ways. A second problem is the issue of causality. Studies on cohesiveness have almost exclusively been correlational in design from which it is not possible to assume a causal relationship. Thirdly, even if there is a causal link, it is possible, some would argue more likely, that the direction of causality is stronger from performance to cohesiveness.
Related topics	The scientific approach (A3) Groups and teams (G1) Conformity and compliance (F2) Leadership (G4)

What is cohesiveness?

In its everyday sense, cohesiveness is generally conceived of as being about how 'together' a group is. Here we shall use the definition given by Albert Carron and his colleagues, who have been the most prolific researchers in the area of sports cohesiveness. They define cohesiveness as 'a dynamic process which is reflected in the tendency for a group to stick together and remain united in the pursuit of its instrumental objectives and/or for the satisfaction of member affective needs' (Carron et al., 1998). As we see, the definition takes us a bit beyond common sense notions, which are usually restricted to the 'social' or interpersonal attraction aspect. It adds a 'task' dimension to cohesiveness in relation to an individual's perceptions of how well the group agrees about objectives and how to achieve them. It is now common in sport psychology to think of cohesiveness as consisting of these two aspects. A team that is task cohesive shares goals and is well drilled. Players' activities are coordinated with each other, and each member knows their role in the overall strategy. In contrast, the socially cohesive group is one in which there are positive social interactions and players like each other. The task–social distinction is clear to see when players play in representative games. A national team may well be task cohesive because its players have the experience and knowledge to know what to do in any given game situation, yet they may be playing with players who are their arch enemies in their domestic league, some of whom they might actively dislike. In other words they are far from socially cohesive. Even within domestic competition, there are many examples of teams that appear to be task cohesive, yet socially non-cohesive. For example, in basketball, the Los Angeles Lakers were able to remain task cohesive, and keep winning throughout a period of low social cohesiveness, when there was a great deal of animosity between their star players, Kobe Bryant and Shaquille O'Neal.

Measurement of cohesiveness

Several instruments have been developed over the years to measure cohesiveness, particularly in relation to occupational and sport psychology. Early measures tended to be unidimensional, and focused simply on social cohesiveness in terms of the attractiveness of group members to each other. For example, the first sport-specific cohesiveness scale, the sports cohesiveness questionnaire (SCQ), appeared in the early 1970s. However, the trend in more recent years has been to develop multidimensional scales, which measure both task and social cohesiveness. For example, the multidimensional sports cohesiveness inventory (MSCI) (Yukelson et al., 1984) appeared about a decade after the SCQ. About this time, Carron and his colleagues began to develop what has become the most used measure of cohesiveness in sport, the group environment questionnaire (GEQ). In addition to measuring social and task cohesiveness, the GEQ measures a second dimension of cohesiveness, which relates to the distinction between players' **attraction to the group** and their perception of the **level of integration of the group** as a whole (Carron et al., 1985).

Cohesiveness and performance

Coaches and managers expend much effort trying to ensure that their teams are cohesive. This is not just because they value friendship within teams for its own sake, but because they assume that it will result in better team performance. How warranted are these widely held assumptions? There have been many studies on the relationship between cohesiveness and performance, and several reviews of these. However, the picture that emerges from these is still not clear (Paskevich et al., 2001).

Even **meta-analytic** reviews (see Topic C6) have not clarified the issue entirely. For example, Mullen and Copper's meta-analysis concluded that overall there was a small positive correlation between cohesiveness and performance that was more to do with task than social cohesiveness (Mullen & Copper, 1994). In contrast Carron and his co-workers found moderate to large effect sizes of 0.7 for task cohesion and performance, and 0.61 for social cohesion and performance (Carron et al., 2002). This more positive picture is somewhat marred when level of competition is taken into consideration. They found that while effect sizes were medium to high at intramural (0.73), high school (0.77) and intercollegiate levels (0.81), the effect size for professional sports was a mere 0.19. Thus, surprising as it may seem, there is still not much compelling evidence that professional teams whose players get on well together out-perform teams whose players do not get on well together.

Although we might hope that a player would pass the ball to the best receiver and not the one who had annoyed them least recently, it may be that disharmony is more of a factor at lower levels. Presumably, at the professional level, players are more able to put the task before personal animosity toward team-mates.

Despite the lack of evidence of the value of cohesiveness to performance in professional sports, coaches at the highest level spend much time on team-building exercises. Indeed, a recent highly dubious example of such attempts to engender bonding in players was alleged to have occurred in the preparations of the South African Rugby Union team prior to the 2003 World Cup. According to media reports the squad was deprived of food and sleep, awoken by gunfire, and made to crawl naked across gravel. To add insult to injury, pictures of naked players appeared in the media. Fortunately, examples of such unethical team-building exercises are few and far between. It would be wrong to conclude, from what was said about the weak relationship between cohesion and performance in professional teams, that team building is a waste of time. Harmony is desirable in teams even if there is no effect on performance. To summarize, the correlation between cohesion and performance is probably stronger for task cohesion than social cohesion and is more evident in lower levels of competition.

Problems in cohesiveness research

One fundamental problem in this area is that researchers have used the term cohesiveness in different ways. It is not surprising then, to find inconsistent and contradictory results. A second problem is the issue of causality. Studies on cohesiveness have almost exclusively been correlational in design, and have typically involved simply measuring cohesiveness and then performance. From such studies it is not logically possible to assume a causal relationship. To do so would be to fall in to the 'post-hoc ergo propter-hoc' trap, described in Topic A3. Despite this, many sport psychologists have assumed that the demonstration of a correlation between cohesiveness and performance means that, by improving cohesiveness, performance improvements will follow. What this ignores is that it is also possible, some would argue much more likely, that even if there is a causal link, the direction of causality is from performance to cohesiveness. In other words that it is because our team keeps winning that we become socially cohesive (see *Fig. 1*). To be fair to researchers, correlational studies have dominated because it is not easy, for ethical and practical reasons, to conduct true experiments in which cohesiveness is manipulated. One compromise solution to this problem is to conduct longitudinal studies that measure both cohesiveness and performance on at least two occasions. Although still correlational in design, data can be scrutinized using a '**cross-lagged**' correlational analysis, from which a degree of causality can be inferred. The assumption behind this approach is that if cohesiveness is a cause of performance, we should find that cohesiveness at time one, correlates more highly with performance at time two, than performance at time one correlates with cohesiveness at time two. Although this is not a method that has been applied extensively in this area, when it has been used, the evidence is that the

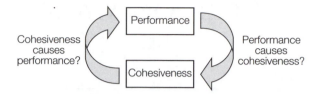

Fig. 1.   The question of causality. Even if there is a causal link between cohesiveness and performance the issue of direction of causality is still unresolved. It may be that when a team performs well this leads to an increased liking for team-mates rather than the liking of our team-mates causing an increase in team performance.

direction of causality is stronger from performance to cohesiveness, than cohesiveness to performance. For example, in one study of field hockey, early-season cohesiveness correlated more highly with late-season performance, than early-season performance correlated with late-season cohesiveness (Slater & Sewell, 1994). Further evidence on cross-lagged correlations comes from the two meta-analyses mentioned above. Mullen & Copper's (1994) data suggest that the more direct effect is from performance to cohesiveness than from cohesiveness to performance. In contrast, Carron et al. (2002) found similar effect sizes for cohesion to performance (0.57) and performance to cohesion (0.69). These not entirely consistent findings do appear to argue that in general the relationship is probably a circular one, where winning makes us more together and togetherness helps us perform well. Where they fail to agree is on the relative strength of the two alternative causal connections.

One final issue of concern for cohesiveness research is the appropriateness of the task–social distinction. While the task vs socio-emotional distinction is a well-known one in group dynamics, it may be that it is not appropriate for this area. In particular, it could be argued that task cohesiveness is not really cohesiveness at all, and that it is somewhat circular to define task cohesiveness in terms of how well coordinated the team are when it comes to getting things done. This might explain why the evidence for a task as opposed to a social cohesiveness–performance relationship has been more evident in the literature. Indeed, it could be argued that it would be a surprise given the way it is defined, if task cohesiveness and performance were not correlated.

Perhaps it would be better, conceptually, for researchers to return to a uni-dimensional view of cohesiveness, as social cohesiveness, with its essence being about the social relatedness of the players, rather than their level of task integration.

G6 GROUP DECISION MAKING

Key Notes

Groups vs individuals	The issue of whether groups are better decision makers than individuals is not a simple one, and depends on a number of factors, including the type of task involved. Groups typically perform better than individuals when tasks are divisible. Groups also have an advantage in problem-solving tasks because they are more likely to have someone in their midst who has an acceptable answer. Groups have the potential for building on group member's ideas, and error-trapping their mistakes. On the negative side, groups can suffer from process loss, arising from lack of coordination. They are also likely to be less efficient in terms of person-hours.
Polarization	Early research suggested that groups make riskier decisions than individuals. This became known as the 'risky-shift' phenomenon, however, subsequent research has shown that shifts to caution also occur. There is now much evidence that when people get together to discuss an issue polarization occurs, and they end up by settling on a position that is more extreme than the average position of group members, prior to discussion. There are three main theories that attempt to explain polarization: social comparison, informational influence and social identity theory.
Groupthink	Groupthink is defined as 'a premature concurrency-seeking tendency'. The major signs of groupthink are: an illusion of invulnerability; an unquestioning belief in the group's morality; a stereotyped view of out-groups; and an illusion of unanimity. Groupthink limits discussion by stifling criticism, dissent and the expression of alternative opinions. This results in poorer decisions. Groupthink can be avoided if groups value dissent rather than suppress it and ensure that leaders, and other powerful people, express their opinions after less-powerful ones. Groups should also: encourage discussion with experts outside the group; appoint a 'devil's advocate' whose job it is to disagree with everyone's views.

Related topics	Psychology and common sense (A2)	Cohesiveness (G5)
	Social cognition (F1)	Inter-group processes (G9)
	Conformity and compliance (F2)	

Groups vs individuals	In Topic A2 it was pointed out that the wisdom of the ages is not particularly helpful because it is often contradictory. For example, in relation to groups and how well they perform, are we to believe that two heads are better than one, or that too many cooks spoil the broth? Is it the case that groups make good decisions, or is it nearer the truth as has been amusingly suggested, 'a camel is a horse designed by a committee'? Not surprisingly, the answer is somewhat more complicated than a simple 'yes' or 'no', since it depends on a number of factors, including the type of task involved. For example, groups typically

perform better than individuals when tasks are divisible. Groups also have an advantage in problem-solving tasks because, statistically, they are more likely to have someone in their midst who has an acceptable answer. Another advantage for groups is that they have the potential for building on group member's ideas, and error-trapping member's mistakes. However, as we shall see when we discuss 'groupthink', groups do not always capitalize on these potential advantages. On the negative side, groups can suffer from process loss, arising from lack of coordination. They are also likely to be less efficient in terms of person-hours, however, depending on the importance of the decision, this may not be a problem. Clearly some of this research is less relevant for groups engaged in physical as opposed to cognitive tasks, however, sport and exercise groups do have to make decisions both on and off the field and an awareness of some of the advantages and disadvantages associated with group decision making will be helpful when they do.

Polarization

The question of whether or not decisions made by groups differ from those made by individuals, extends beyond the issue of the **quality** of decision-making. For example, early research suggested that groups make riskier decisions than individuals. This became known as the **'risky-shift'** phenomenon, and it raised concerns about the wisdom of letting groups decide on issues like going to war, or pushing the nuclear button. However, subsequent research has shown that shifts to caution also occur in groups. It was then realized that shifts to caution and to risk were opposite sides of the same coin, namely **polarization**. There is now much evidence that when people get together to discuss an issue, they end up by settling on a position that is more extreme than the average position of group members prior to discussion (Baron & Byrne, 2003). If on average, players are marginally in favor of going en-masse to tell the coach that training is boring, a discussion by players will strengthen that feeling. However, if the players are, on average, marginally opposed to confronting the coach, discussion will normally produce a more clear decision by players not to confront. In other words, groups decision making leads to polarization.

There are three main theories that attempt to explain polarization: social comparison, informational influence and social identity theory.

The **social comparison** explanation is driven by ego-enhancement or **self-presentational** considerations. There is lots of evidence that people tend to view themselves in a more positive light than average (Baron & Byrne, 2003). For example, we tend to think of ourselves as being a bit more ethical, less prejudiced, more attractive and more intelligent than average. In the polarization studies, when we do the task alone, we endorse a position that we think puts us on the positively valued end of the scale in terms of cultural values, and away from what we perceive to be the 'average' view. When we then join a group discussion on the issue, we then discover that others have also been more positive than we thought they would have been, and so, to again present ourselves as more positive than others, we move out to the extremes. In this view, polarization occurs as a result of our attempts, after social comparison, to maintain a positive impression of ourselves as a little better than others in terms of the values of our culture.

The **informational influence** explanation argues that polarization occurs for the simple reason that when people who are already committed to an opinion meet to discuss it they all express arguments to support that position, and thus the weight of argument influences the group's decision (Brown, 2000).

The **social identity** explanation rests on the idea that **self-identity** is made up of two parts, **personal identity** and **social identity**. The argument is that what group discussion does is to raise our awareness of our social identity, and diminish our awareness of our personal identity. This results in our focus changing from personal ideals to basing our judgments on what we think our group's view would be. As such, we are more influenced by our group's norms (Brown, 2000).

Studies to test these three explanations provide evidence that each appears to have some usefulness. It seems that sometimes group decisions become polarized because of social comparison, sometimes because of the weight of information, and sometimes as a result of shifts in the focus of identity. What the sport psychologist needs to be aware of is that polarization occurs, and that the more extreme decisions groups make are not always based on rational argument. Another source of less than optimal decision making is 'groupthink'.

Groupthink

Groupthink, a term coined by Irving Janis, is defined as 'a premature concurrency-seeking tendency' and 'a mode of thinking that people engage in when they are deeply involved in a cohesive in-group, when members' strivings for unanimity override their motivation to realistically appraise alternative courses of action' (Janis, 1982). Although this may seem like a bit of a mouthful, it simply means there are times when there is a tendency for groups to jump to conclusions, and not to fully discuss all the options.

As an example of this tendency, Janis points to political decision making on foreign policy by the Kennedy administration in the early 1960s. He compares the disastrous Bay of Pigs decision, with the very successful Cuban missile decision. He argues that, since it was more or less the same team of clever people who made both decisions, that groupthink must have been operating in the Bay of Pigs discussion. The relevance of this for sport is that it is possible that when team decisions are being made, groupthink could be operating. According to the theory, groupthink is more likely to occur when a group is cohesive, when it is insulated from outside information, and when it has a powerful leader who promotes his or her own preferred solutions. The signs of groupthink are:

- an illusion of invulnerability;
- an unquestioning belief in the group's morality;
- a stereotyped view of out-groups;
- direct pressure on dissenters;
- self-censorship;
- an illusion of unanimity;
- attempts to rationalize the group's opinion.

In terms of hard evidence, there have not been many studies that have tested the idea, however, what has been done is generally supportive. For example, when factual accounts of historic events have been analyzed, symptoms of groupthink have been more evident prior to bad decisions than good ones. What groupthink does is to limit the discussion by stifling criticism, dissent and the expression of alternative opinions. It also means that preferred solutions are not re-evaluated.

This is exacerbated by the failure of the group to seek information, either from within or from outside experts. Ultimately, this results in poorer decisions and poorer performance.

Sports groups are no less prone to groupthink than any others, so it is fortunate that there are steps that can be taken to avoid it. For example, groups should:

- value dissent rather than suppress it;
- ensure that leaders, and other powerful people, express their opinions after less-powerful group members, to reduce the likelihood that the less-powerful people self-censor themselves;
- set up wider subgroups to avoid insulation;
- encourage discussion with peers outside the committee or group;
- consult outside experts;
- appoint a 'devil's advocate' whose job it is to disagree with everyone's views;
- know their 'enemy' or opposition, so as not to underestimate them;
- hold 'residual doubt' sessions, where anyone can express any last worries they have about the group's decision.

G7 DE-INDIVIDUATION

Key Notes

De-individuation	De-individuation is a state that people are said to be in when they behave in impulsive anti-social ways, as a result of being immersed in the group. It is characterized by the presence of others, anonymity and a diffusion of responsibility. Zimbardo's classic study showed that 'de-individuated' students were twice as aggressive as individuated ones. Many studies since, including cross-cultural research, have produced similar results.
Social identity and de-individuation	Proponents of Social Identity Theory have stressed the inter-group aspect of crowd behavior, and see crowds as consisting of two groups, 'us' and 'them', as opposed to a collection of individuals. The social identity argument is that when de-individuated crowd behavior occurs, it is not caused by a loss of identity but a change in the focus of identity from personal identity to social identity. As such, behavior is less influenced by self-awareness of personal norms about right and wrong, and more by that part of self-awareness that relates to one's social identity and group, or crowd norms.
De-individuation in sport	The relevance of de-individuation for sport is that it helps us to understand why teams sometimes lapse into uncontrolled aggression or antisocial actions. It is easy to see how being in the midst of a soccer crowd, with a set of like-minded individuals, all wearing team colors, might make people feel anonymous, and free them up to engage in anti-social behavior. Similarly, we can see how being immersed in the crowd might lead to a focus on social identity, and being a good supporter or gang member, rather than being a responsible individual.
Related topics	Conformity and compliance (F2) Inter-group processes (G9) Anti-social behavior (F5)

De-individuation   In trying to explain the negative aspects of group behavior, such as crowd rioting, mob looting and so on, psychologists have come up with the notion of de-individuation (Zimbardo, 1969). This is a state that people are said to be in when they behave in impulsive anti-social ways as a result of being immersed in the group. Zimbardo defined **de-individuation** in terms of a loss of identity, accompanied by a lowering of inhibitions, resulting in the breaking of normative rules about acceptable behavior. He argued that when certain external conditions exist, such as the presence of others, **anonymity**, and a **diffusion of responsibility**, people become de-individuated. In this de-individuated state they are said to have low self-awareness, low restraint, low concern about social evaluation and a narrow focus of attention, all of which lead to behavior that is wild and impulsive. To test this idea, Zimbardo conducted now classic studies, in which women students in small groups were asked, on the pretext of investigating empathy, to give electric shocks to another woman (a confederate who did not actually receive shocks). In the '**individuated**' condition group members worked in normal lighting conditions, wore nametags and were dressed in their own clothes. In the 'de-individuated' condition the room was less well lit and participants wore standard laboratory coats, without nametags, and white hoods over their heads. What Zimbardo found was that participants in de-individuated groups were more aggressive, giving twice the length of shock of that given by individuated groups (Zimbardo, 1969). Many studies since have produced similar results, including cross-cultural research in which it has been shown that tribes that use face painting and masks when going to war, are more aggressive toward their enemies in terms of torture and mutilation of the dead (Watson, 1973).

In another famous study, the Stamford Prison experiment, Zimbardo created a situation where de-individuation was induced in 22 otherwise pleasant and law-abiding young men who were given the roles of prisoners and guards in a simulated prison. What Zimbardo found was that within a short period of time, the participants began to behave in extremely aggressive ways to each other. In fact, things got so bad that the study had to be terminated early. Interestingly, it has also been shown that sports teams that play in black uniforms are more aggressive and perhaps one reason for this might be that players feel de-individuated when dressed in black. There are certainly situations in sport where de-individuation might be expected. For example, American football helmets serve to give some anonymity to players, as do rugby scrums. Teams themselves afford opportunities for submersion and loss of individuality, which could lead to antisocial behavior if unchecked.

Although anonymity was originally central to the theory, more recently, attention has focused on the role of self-awareness. Research into self-awareness has highlighted two kinds of self-awareness, **private self-awareness**, which is about our awareness of our inner thoughts and feelings, and **public self-awareness**, which is about our awareness of how others see us. The argument is that there are two paths to unacceptable behavior. The first involves public self-awareness but not de-individuation. In this case people become less concerned about how they will be seen by others, because they realize that anonymity means that there is less likely to be a cost to behaving anti-socially. The second path does lead, via de-individuation, to a blocking of private self-awareness. This in turn results in behavior that is not in line with our normal beliefs and values. Again, experimental studies of private and public self-awareness and associated levels of de-individuation have supported this idea (Prentice-Dunn & Rogers, 1982).

Social identity and de-individuation

Proponents of Social Identity Theory (Topic G9) have suggested another approach that has shed light on de-individuation. This view stresses the intergroup aspect of crowd behavior and sees crowds as consisting of at least two groups, 'us' and 'them', as opposed to thinking of groups as a collection of individuals. The social identity argument is that when de-individuated crowd behavior occurs, it is not caused by a **loss** of identity but a **change** in the focus of identity from **personal identity** to **social identity**. As such, behavior is less influenced by self-awareness of personal norms about right and wrong, and more by that part of self-awareness that relates to one's social identity and group, or crowd norms (Reicher, 1984).

It should be said that de-individuation can lead to positive as well as negative behavior, because the theory suggests that we lose our inhibitions. Some inhibitions restrict positive actions, such as showing affection and warmth to others. For example, in one study participants were put in a room with strangers for an hour (Gergen et al., 1973). In the de-individuation condition they were in total darkness, and in the individuation condition they were in normal lighting. It turned out that in the normal situation people sat and chatted politely for the hour, but in the darkened room people quickly lost their inhibitions. For example, they soon began to talk intimately, 50% engaged in hugging, 90% admitted they deliberately touched each other, and 80% admitted they were sexually aroused!

Another example of de-individuation leading to positive outcomes comes from an interesting study in which participants were made to wear either a nurse's or a Ku Klux Klan uniform and were either individuated or de-individuated, with and without nametags, etc. (Johnson & Downing, 1979). The study found that the participants who were asked to wear the nurse's uniform gave lower shock levels in the de-individuated condition than the individuated one! This appears to conflict with previous findings; however, it can be explained by the Social Identity view, which argues that the shift from concern with personal identity to social identity, means that group norms become more important to participants than personal values. Thus, participants in the nurse's uniform who had undergone de-individuation, appear to have been moved to act in line with societal expectations about norms for nurses.

De-individuation in sport

The relevance of de-individuation for sport is that it helps us to understand one reason why teams sometimes lapse into uncontrolled aggression or anti-social actions. It is easy to see how being in the midst of a soccer crowd, with a set of like-minded individuals, all wearing team colors, might make people feel anonymous, and free them up to shout obscene chants about the opposition and referee, or to instigate violence against rival fans.

Similarly, we can see how being immersed in the crowd might lead to a focus on social identity, and being a good supporter or gang member, rather than being a responsible individual. Interestingly, in Britain there has always been a huge difference between the high levels of anti-social behavior in soccer fans, and its virtual non-existence in rugby fans. When soccer fans shift the focus of their identity from personal to social, they presumably concentrate on norms about aggressive responses to provocation. In contrast, the social identity and cultural norms of the rugby fan appear to lead them to engage in good-humored banter and civilized rivalry. Thus, de-individuation takes these two sets of fans through the same process but in different directions.

G8 HOME ADVANTAGE

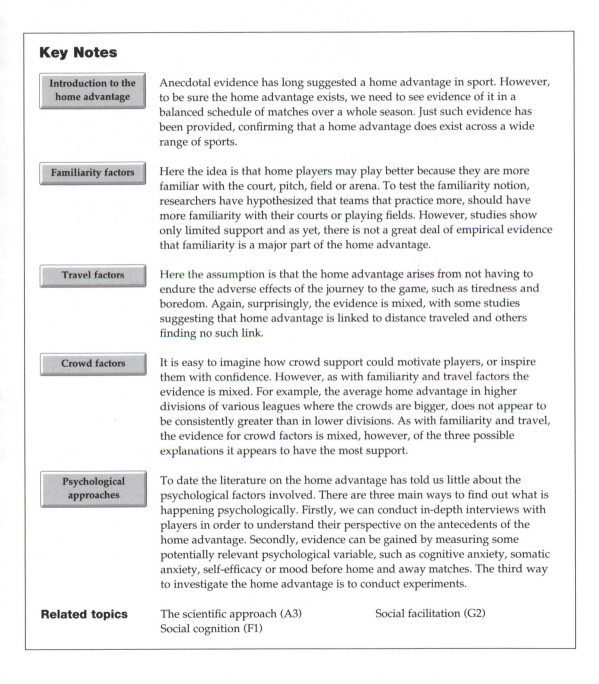

Key Notes

Introduction to the home advantage	Anecdotal evidence has long suggested a home advantage in sport. However, to be sure the home advantage exists, we need to see evidence of it in a balanced schedule of matches over a whole season. Just such evidence has been provided, confirming that a home advantage does exist across a wide range of sports.
Familiarity factors	Here the idea is that home players may play better because they are more familiar with the court, pitch, field or arena. To test the familiarity notion, researchers have hypothesized that teams that practice more, should have more familiarity with their courts or playing fields. However, studies show only limited support and as yet, there is not a great deal of empirical evidence that familiarity is a major part of the home advantage.
Travel factors	Here the assumption is that the home advantage arises from not having to endure the adverse effects of the journey to the game, such as tiredness and boredom. Again, surprisingly, the evidence is mixed, with some studies suggesting that home advantage is linked to distance traveled and others finding no such link.
Crowd factors	It is easy to imagine how crowd support could motivate players, or inspire them with confidence. However, as with familiarity and travel factors the evidence is mixed. For example, the average home advantage in higher divisions of various leagues where the crowds are bigger, does not appear to be consistently greater than in lower divisions. As with familiarity and travel, the evidence for crowd factors is mixed, however, of the three possible explanations it appears to have the most support.
Psychological approaches	To date the literature on the home advantage has told us little about the psychological factors involved. There are three main ways to find out what is happening psychologically. Firstly, we can conduct in-depth interviews with players in order to understand their perspective on the antecedents of the home advantage. Secondly, evidence can be gained by measuring some potentially relevant psychological variable, such as cognitive anxiety, somatic anxiety, self-efficacy or mood before home and away matches. The third way to investigate the home advantage is to conduct experiments.

Related topics	The scientific approach (A3)	Social facilitation (G2)
	Social cognition (F1)	

Introduction to the home advantage

Anecdotal evidence and basic statistics have long suggested a home advantage in sport. For example, in the Olympic Games, countries typically gain more medals when they are the host nation. The home nation is also over-represented among the winners of soccer's World Cup. The belief in the home advantage is even enshrined in many sports such as basketball's NBA, and Grid iron's NFL, where winning the division is rewarded with home fixtures in the play-offs.

However, to be sure the home advantage exists, we need to see evidence of it in a balanced schedule of matches over a whole season, in which every team plays every other team at home and away. Just such empirical evidence has been provided, confirming what most people in sport already 'knew', namely, that there is a home advantage (Courneya & Carron, 1992). Further, this home advantage has been shown to occur in a wide range of activities including football, soccer, baseball, swimming, basketball and cricket.

There are several obvious candidates as explanations for the home advantage. The three most cited of these are: **familiarity, travel factors** and **crowd factors**. One problem with researching in this area is that it is difficult to conduct experiments. We cannot manipulate crowd size, or ask some teams to take a 100-mile detour so that we can look in a controlled way at the effect of distance traveled on home advantage! Because of this, researchers have relied upon correlational designs, and in particular, have carried out **archival studies**. The archival method relies simply on looking back through sports archives for data on match scores.

Familiarity factors Here the idea is that home players may play better because they are more familiar with the court, pitch, field or arena. Familiarity can be as specific as knowing the dimensions of your field or the 'give' of your backboards. Familiarity, also refers to feeling at home in a place you understand and are comfortable with, where there are fewer uncertainties than in a strange or less familiar venue.

To test the familiarity notion, researchers have argued that teams that practice more should have more familiarity with their courts or playing fields, and that levels of home advantage should reflect this. Thus, we should find that professional sport exhibits greater home advantage than college sport, which in turn should exhibit greater home advantage than high-school sport. There is only partial support for this, in that some studies have shown high levels of home advantage in professional and college sport, and lower levels in high-school sport. Of course one confounding variable here is crowd size, which is bigger in professional and college sport than in high school. Others studies have found no difference between home advantage levels in professional and high-school sports (Agnew & Carron, 1994). Familiarity also predicts that teams playing on atypical fields should have greater home advantage levels. This hypothesis has been tested in a study on soccer, which looked at the home advantage of the teams that had the two biggest, and two smallest, fields in the English Football League (soccer). Contrary to the hypothesis, there was no difference between the combined home advantage of teams at these atypical grounds and the league average (Pollard, 1986). Similarly, we might expect that in baseball, where grounds vary to quite a large extent in dimension and visual layout, home advantage would be higher than, for example, in ice hockey, where rinks are arguably more similar. However, the evidence is that home advantage is greater in ice hockey. One recent study of 37 baseball, basketball and ice hockey teams that had moved to a new stadium has shown some support for familiarity as a factor. Controlling for crowd size and density (Pollard, 2002) found that the home advantage in the new and unfamiliar stadium was significantly lower than in it had been during the final season in the old one. In general, while it makes intuitive sense, there is only limited empirical evidence that familiarity is a major part of the home advantage (Nevill & Holder, 1999).

Travel factors

A second candidate to explain the home advantage is travel factors. Here the assumption is that the home advantage arises from not having to endure the adverse effects of the journey to the game, such as tiredness, or stiffness from being cramped in a bus or plane for hours. Travel might also induce boredom or frustration. Foreign travel may include additional difficulties such as stomach problems due to eating different foods, etc.

The simple way to test the travel factors explanation is to compare home advantage levels in teams traveling longer vs shorter distances. Again, surprisingly, the evidence is mixed, with some studies suggesting that home advantage is higher when away teams have traveled more than 200 miles, and others finding no difference over the same distance. For example, one study of college basketball showed a dramatic difference with a home advantage of 84% when opponents had traveled more than 200 miles and 58% when distance traveled was less than 200 miles (Snyder & Purdy, 1985). However, another study in professional soccer showed the same average home advantage percentage (63%) regardless of distance traveled by the away team (Pollard, 1986).

Finally, several studies, employing a statistical technique known as multiple regression, have shown that travel contributes only about 2% to variance in performance, making it relatively unimportant (Agnew et al., 1994).

Crowd factors

The most widely suggested explanation for the home advantage appears to be crowd factors. Certainly, we know from the research on social facilitation (Topic G2) that audiences can facilitate performance. It is also easy to see how crowd support could motivate players, or inspire them with confidence. However, as with familiarity and travel factors the evidence is mixed.

If crowds affect players positively, we might reasonably expect that the average home advantage in higher divisions of a league, where the crowds are bigger, would be higher than in lower divisions. However, this is not always what studies show. For example, in professional soccer, similar levels of home advantage have been found across divisions in which average crowd size differed dramatically (Pollard, 1986). One recent British study did find a decreasing linear trend in home advantage as crowd size diminished, but only by combining data from the quite different leagues of two different countries (England and Scotland). What did appear to be clear from this study however, was that there was a strong trend at the lower ends of the scale, indicating that crowd size may be important up to a certain figure, after which home advantage no longer increases, no matter how big the crowd is (Nevill et al., 1996).

One refinement of this approach is to argue that it is not the absolute size of the crowd that is crucial but rather its density. In other words, a small crowd in a small stadium might be just as uplifting as a big crowd in a big stadium. Two major studies have looked at this and have come down on opposite sides of the argument. In one density did appear to affect baseball home advantage (Schwartz & Barsky, 1977), however, even density differences of 70% to 20% were not linked to home advantage levels in the other study on soccer (Pollard, 1986).

Another argument that has been made is that if crowd noise spurs players on, then indoor sports and games played in domed stadiums should benefit more, because the roof keeps in the noise. Interestingly, this does appear to be the case, both when indoor versus outdoor sports, and when domed versus non-domed games are compared (Zeller & Jurkovac, 1988). Counter evidence about crowds and home advantage comes from Pollard's research (1986) in which it was found that baseball, with huge crowds, and English county cricket, with virtually no crowds, had similar levels of home advantage. Another recent field study found little support for the motivating influence of crowds. It employed simultaneous video analysis of crowd cheering and on-field performance in football (Strauss, 2002). Strauss found that good performance preceded cheering as opposed to following it. In other words, rather than affecting the play, spectators were reacting to the outcome of each down.

Another possibility in relation to crowds is that rather than affecting players they might influence referees and judges. There is some evidence that is the case, and it will be discussed under psychological approaches below.

Summarizing all of this, although crowd factors would seem to be implicated slightly more often in research than travel and familiarity, no one factor alone appears to be able to explain the home advantage. It is more likely that each may be a sufficient, but not a necessary condition, for it to occur (*Fig. 1*). The home advantage probably has multiple causes. To take the cricket example, we know that there is a home advantage in professional county-level cricket, despite negligible crowds. Yet cricket is a game in which knowing the wicket is very important. For example, being familiar with the slope of the Lords Cricket Ground almost certainly gives England's bowlers a distinct edge in test matches. Thus, familiarity rather than crowd factors is more likely as an explanation for the home advantage in cricket.

Psychological approaches

One problem with the literature on the home advantage to date is that it is almost exclusively archival in nature. It involves looking back at facts and figures from a variety of sources. As such, it tells us little about the psychology of the home advantage. To find out what is happening psychologically, we need to conduct studies that explore what is in the mind of the athlete. This can be done in three main ways. Firstly, we can conduct in-depth interviews with players in order to understand their perspective on the antecedents of the home advantage. Secondly, evidence can be gained by measuring some potentially

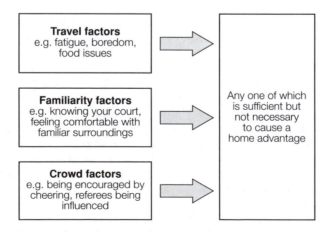

Fig. 1. The main factors thought to be sufficient but not necessary causes of the home advantage (travel, familiarity and crowds).

relevant psychological variable, such as cognitive anxiety, somatic anxiety, self-efficacy or mood. This could be done before home and away matches to see if levels of the chosen variable are related to venue. Surprisingly, such studies are only beginning to be carried out, and although it is too soon for a consistent picture to emerge, there is some evidence that cognitive anxiety levels are higher before away than before home matches, yet somatic anxiety levels do not differ. The third way to investigate the home advantage is to conduct experiments. Of course, it is not possible for the researcher to manipulate crowd size or distance traveled, but there are approaches that can be taken. For example, it has been suggested that crowds influence referees' decisions, and there is correlational evidence that this is the case. A study in basketball showed that referees called fewer fouls against star players when they were playing at home than when away. In contrast their treatment of non-stars was not influenced by venue (Lehman & Reifman, 1987). This backs up the claim often made by opposition basketball coaches that Michael Jordan benefited from this effect. In mitigation, it should be said that referees and umpires are under pressure from fans not to eject the star players that they have paid a lot of money to see. A clear example of this occurred in the case of John McEnroe who was famous, not just for being a great tennis player, but also for his angry outbursts at umpires. Under the rules, McEnroe could have been ejected from competitions on several occasions.

To look at the effect of crowd reaction on refereeing decisions experimentally, we could show soccer referees a video of various tackles in two conditions, one with loud crowd reaction to the tackle, and the other with low crowd reaction. In this way the referees would see the same set of fouls, but with different levels of crowd reaction. Referees could then be asked to rate the tackles on the extent to which they consider them to be fouls. In fact, just such studies have begun to be carried out, and initial findings do show that the louder the crowd reaction, the more likely referees are to award a foul (Nevill et al., 2002). Interestingly, the referees who participate in these sort of studies are often adamant that their decisions were totally unaffected by the levels of crowd noise.

G9 INTER-GROUP PROCESSES

Key Notes

The Robbers Cave study	Inter-group behavior is 'behavior which occurs between an individual (or individuals) belonging to one group and an individual (or individuals) belonging to another group, either or both acting in terms of their respective group membership'. The classic work on inter-group behavior was carried out by Sherif, on two groups of 12-year-old boys attending summer camp. In a group formation phase, each group engaged in typical camp activities like cooking, swimming and so on, unaware of the other group's existence. Over the course of a week, intra-group structure developed. In phase two of the study the boys met and competed with each other, which led to inter-group rivalry and conflict. Interactions became unpleasant and ethnocentrism developed. In phase three Sherif introduced super-ordinate goals, which reduced conflict and united the two groups.
Inter-group rivalry	It appears that the negative behavior exhibited in the study is not restricted to adolescent boys. Unfortunately, the evidence from many experiments, with both laboratory groups and real groups in field studies, shows that adults also demonstrate ethnocentrism and inter-group rivalry.
Functional theory	The functional theory of inter-group relations suggests that the nature of the relationship between groups is determined by the functional nature of goal activity, where incompatible goals and competition lead to conflict, with associated negative stereotypes and ethnocentrism, and where super-ordinate goals lead to harmony.
Social Identity Theory	The inadequacy of the functional theory of inter-group rivalry has been demonstrated by research which shows that mere categorization, in the absence of competition, is enough to induce inter-group bias. To explain inter-group rivalry, Tajfel developed Social Identity Theory, which is based on the assumption that human beings are motivated by a need for positive self-esteem. Further, he suggested that the self-concept (or self-identity) is made up of a personal and a social component. Our personal identity is based on, how clever or how attractive, etc., we think we are. Our social identity relates to how good we think the groups that we belong to are.

Related topics	Social cognition (F1)	Cohesiveness (G5)
	Anti-social behavior (F5)	Group decision-making (G6)
	Groups and teams (G1)	De-individuation (G7)
	Leadership (G4)	

The Robbers Cave study   Previous topics in this section have dealt with **intra-group processes**, in other words, about what is happening **within** any given group, such as, polarization, de-individuation, groupthink, social loafing, etc. In contrast, **inter-group**

processes focus on what is happening **between** groups. For example, how groups perceive and relate to each other, or in terms of inter-group competition and rivalry. Inter-group behavior has been defined as 'behavior which occurs between an individual (or individuals) belonging to one group and an individual (or individuals) belonging to another group, either or both acting in terms of their respective group membership (with its standards for loyalty, established views of the other group, goals, etc.)' (Sherif, 1976).

The classic work on inter-group behavior was carried out by Sherif, in what came to be known as the **Robbers Cave study**, after the name of the summer camp where the study was conducted (Sherif et al., 1961). It involved a group formation phase, a conflict phase and a conflict resolution phase. In the group formation phase, two sets of 12-year-old boys were separated into matched groups and allocated to separate cabins. For a week they engaged in typical camp activities like cooking, swimming and so on, each group being unaware of the other's existence. They named themselves the 'Rattlers' and the 'Eagles'. Over the course of the week, **intra-group structure** developed in terms of friendships, role relationships, status differences and leadership.

In phase two of the study, the two groups were introduced to each other, and conflict was introduced, in the form of competition. For example, a tug of war was organized between them. While some boys made initial attempts to exhibit sportsmanship, these did not last, and soon interactions became unpleasant. Following the tug of war, name-calling led to the 'Rattlers' burning the 'Eagle's' flag. Things escalated from there, with raids between cabins, involving the throwing of missiles and so on. In short, in this second phase of the study, the researchers observed the development of what has been called **ethnocentrism,** which is characterized by over-evaluation of one's in-group members and one's in-group products, and a tendency to devalue out-group members and out-group products. In a very brief space of time, the boys developed stereotypes of their own and the other group. Perceptions were prejudiced, and estimates of how brave, tough, or sneaky all of the campers were, could be predicted from group membership. Essentially, boys in the 'Rattlers' group saw all other 'Rattlers' in a favorable light, and all 'Eagles' in an unfavorable one, and vice versa. Group cohesiveness increased, as did hostility to out-group members. There was also an over-evaluation of in-group products, with boys believing that their group was better and did everything better, and there was a corresponding tendency to devalue the other group's efforts.

In phase three of the study, the conflict resolution phase, the researchers initially attempted to restore positive relationships between the groups by having the boys 'rub shoulders' and do things jointly. For example, they arranged for them to watch films and eat together. Unfortunately, this did not serve to diminish conflict; indeed it gave the boys a chance to throw food at each other! The researchers then decided to reduce conflict by creating super-ordinate goals. What this meant was that they set up false emergencies that could only be resolved if both groups worked together. For example, on a trip to the cinema they pretended that the camp truck had broken down, and that they would have to pull it to the top of a hill to bump start it. Symbolically, they used the tug of war rope to do this. Another ruse involved a fake emergency, in which the boys had to work together to form a water bucket chain, to bring water from the river to put out a fire. The researchers found that the introduction of these super-ordinate goals did serve to reduce conflict and unite the two groups.

Inter-group rivalry When these findings were first published it was argued that nasty, childish, inter-group behavior is what we might expect of schoolboys, but that adults would not behave in this way. Unfortunately, the evidence from many experiments, with both laboratory groups and real groups in field studies, shows that adults also demonstrate ethnocentrism and **inter-group rivalry**. Anyone who has much experience in sport will not find it too difficult to recognize how easily we fall into the trap of exhibiting ethnocentrism in competitive situations. For example, it occurs when we see our team as the better team, even when comprehensively beaten, or when we think of our team-mates as nicer, fairer, tougher, etc. Another symptom of out-group bias occurs when we are over-confident about our chances of winning and underestimate the opposition. We even see anecdotal evidence of this in the stereotypes we hold about people who play different sports from our own. For example, some rugby players see soccer players as 'wimps' who writhe in agony at the slightest contact. In return, there are soccer players who are willing to stereotype rugby players as 'thugs without skill'.

Functional theory One common-sense explanation for inter-group rivalry, suggests that the nature of the relationship between groups is a function of the interdependence between them. Thus, if there is positive interdependence (compatible goals and cooperation) the relationship will be positive. However, if there is negative interdependence (incompatible goals and competition) the relationship will be negative, with all the associated increased negative stereotypes and ethnocentrism. This straightforward explanation became known as the **functional theory** of inter-group processes because it claimed that social relations are determined by the functional nature of goal activity, where incompatible goals and competition lead to conflict, and super-ordinate goals lead to harmony.

This explains the way that allies who become competitors are quickly seen in a very different light. For example, during the Second World War, when the USA and Russia were allies against Germany, reports in the American media praised the brave heroism of the Russians who defended Stalingrad against dramatic odds. Not too much later, during the Cold War, this positive view of Russians changed, and they were quickly derided as 'Commies' and 'Reds'. Similarly, nowadays, with the reduced threat from the former Soviet Union, Western stereotypes about the Russian people have softened again.

You may have experienced much the same in sport if you have ever played in the same team as someone you had previously only played against, and viewed as a 'dirty' player. In this situation we often re-evaluate the player as hard but fair! While this paints a rather negative picture of how easy it is for people who are competing to perceive the world in terms of 'them' and 'us', there is evidence from research into Social Identity Theory that the picture is even more pessimistic than this, since it appears, as we shall see, that competition is not even necessary for ethnocentrism to develop.

Social Identity Theory In the early 1970s Henri Tajfel published the first of a series of experiments that demonstrated that out-group bias can occur even in the absence of competition (Tajfel et al., 1971). In the first part of these now classic studies, Tajfel divided people into 'minimal' groups on the basis of inconsequential differences, such as their preference for different styles of modern art (Paul Klee vs Vasili Kandinski), or even on something as arbitrary as the toss of a coin. The groups were minimal in the sense that members did not ever meet each other or members of the other group, they simply knew of their existence. Having been named as members of group x or y, participants were asked to allocate points to others participants, knowing only that they were in group x or y. What Tajfel found was that mere categorization was enough to induce inter-group rivalry and bias. In other words, the functional theory of rivalry is not adequate to explain inter-group bias, because bias can be shown to occur in the absence of competition.

To explain this, Tajfel developed **Social Identity Theory**, which is based on the assumption that human beings are motivated by a need for positive self-esteem (Tajfel & Turner, 1986). There is much evidence that we are prone to seeing ourselves in a favorable light. For example, as we have previously seen, we tend to think of ourselves as slightly more intelligent, slightly kinder and slightly more attractive than average, which by definition we cannot all be! There is even evidence from the work of Shelley Taylor that holding such 'positive illusions' is associated with positive mental health (Taylor, 1989).

Social identity theory suggests that the self-concept or self-identity is made up of both **personal** and **social** identity. Our **personal identity** is based on how clever, or how attractive, etc., we think we are. Our **social identity** relates to our group membership, and how good we think the groups are that we belong to. Given this, the theory proposes that inter-group rivalry is the result of our over-evaluating our group, and under-valuing other groups, because of our wish to see ourselves in a positive light. In other words, just as we often perceive ourselves in positively biased ways and have 'positive illusions' about our personal characteristics, we also appear to have biased perceptions about the groups we belong to, and see them in a favorable way to increase our self-esteem. Taking this a stage further, we can also increase our self-esteem by denigrating out-groups.

These two routes to high self-esteem, via personal and social identity are shown in *Fig. 1*. Social identity theory can explain the behavior of those sports fans who take the short and painless route to success, by supporting a successful team. In this way, they can feel good about themselves by being part of a winning team, and by denigrating poorer teams and their supporters. This might explain why successful soccer teams like Manchester United have fans from all over the world, and not just from Manchester. Interestingly, in support of this view, research has shown that people are more likely to wear their team's colors following a win, than following a loss.

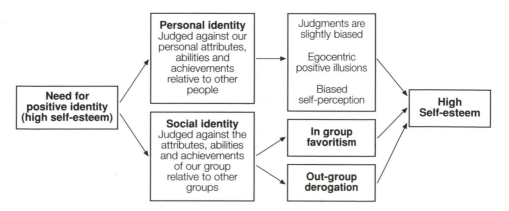

Fig. 1.   Two routes to self esteem: The personal identity route and the social identity route.

Support for Social Identity Theory has come from research that shows there is a direct link between level of self-esteem and the social categorization process. For example, one study repeated Tajfel's classic experiment, with three groups rather than just two (Oakes & Turner, 1980). Thus, it had a group categorized as a Klee group, a group categorized as a Kandinsky group, and a control group who simply sat and read newspapers. Self-esteem was measured in all three groups at the beginning and end of the experiment. It was found that the Klee and Kandinski group members had higher self-esteem after the categorization, whereas, the self-esteem of the control group remained unchanged. In other words, the simple process of categorization produced self-esteem rises in the groups that categorized, but not in the group that did not.

As sports enthusiasts, the importance of knowing about inter-group processes is that it alerts us to how easily the mere categorization of people into different groups can lead to a negative 'them and us' ethnocentric mentality. That this can happen in the absence of competition should make us even more conscious of its effects in sport, where competition will only serve to widen the divide between groups.

H1 PSYCHOLOGICAL WELL-BEING

Key Notes

Psychological well-being	Psychological well-being can be defined as a sense of satisfaction with life or degree of personal happiness. It is now seen as an important potential outcome from exercise participation. It is influenced by mood, affect, self-esteem, cognitive functioning, mental health disorders, and the potential negative influences of participating in an activity.
Physical activity, mood and affect	Participation in physical activity positively affects mood and affect. These positive effects are not automatic and will be influenced by perceived enjoyment, the mode of activity and training/practice factors. Several plausible biochemical, physiological, psychological and social mechanisms have been proposed to explain the exercise–mood relationship, but none have received a great deal of empirical support.
Physical activity and self-esteem	The effects of exercise on generalized self-esteem tend to be mixed. In the physical domain exercise participation can result in increases in physical self-worth and other physical self-perceptions such as body image. Feeling good about your physical self positively influences mental well-being. The mechanisms behind these changes are not clear.
Physical activity and cognitive functioning	Fit older adults perform better in cognitive performance tests especially those involving tasks that are attention demanding and rapid. The evidence for relationships between physical activity and academic performance in young people is equivocal.
Related topics	Definitions (D1) Negative outcomes (H3) Mental health (H2)

Psychological well-being

The benefits of exercise on physical health have received the most attention. However there is now widespread recognition of the importance of exercise to psychological well-being (PWB), a term used to describe a sense of satisfaction with life or degree of personal happiness. A range of topics are associated with PWB including mood and affect, self-esteem and cognitive functioning (this topic), mental health disorders such as anxiety and clinical depression (see Topic H2), and the potential negative influences of physical activity participation such as exercise dependence (see Topic H3).

Physical activity, mood and affect

Mood can be defined as the set of affective states experienced on a day-to-day basis that do not always have a clear trigger. By comparison **emotions** are specific feeling states that result from specific events or stimuli. **Affect** is a broader term covering all types of feelings including emotions and moods. The distinction between mood, emotion and affect in physical activity studies is often blurred and the terms, especially emotion and affect, are frequently used interchangeably (see Topic D1).

A comprehensive review by Biddle (2000) concluded that participation in physical activity is associated with positive mood and affect. This conclusion is considered robust because the evidence comes from a variety of sources and measurement approaches (e.g., different samples and assessment tools). Research using the Profile of Mood States (POMS, see Topic D2) shows that aerobic exercise has a small-to-moderate negative effect on tension, depression, fatigue and confusion. A small negative effect is seen for anger. Aerobic exercise has a small-to-moderate positive effect on vigor. A negative effect represents a reduction, and a positive effect an increase in a mood state. That is, the negative effect for tension demonstrates that aerobic exercise reduces tension in an individual.

There is evidence that personal exercise goals and group climate influence the exercise–affect relationship. Personal goals focused on personal improvement, effort and mastery (i.e., a task goal orientation, see Topic C3) have a moderate-to-high association with positive affect. A possible explanation for this is that a task goal orientation results in a greater sense of control. Likewise a group climate in exercise settings focused on personal improvement and effort (i.e., a task climate, see Topic C3) also has a moderate-to-high association with positive affect. For example, in an environment focused on individual effort and improvement participants report more satisfaction and less worry than in an environment focused on interpersonal comparison and normative standards. This effect may result from greater involvement in decision making, encouragement for personal improvement and effort, and the focus on learning new strategies.

Experimental trials support an improvement in psychological well-being immediately after participation in moderate exercise. However the relationship is less clear for participation in vigorous exercise, where a period of recovery may be required before people 'feel better'.

The positive mood benefits seen with exercise are not automatic. Bonnie Berger has proposed a taxonomy to help maximize the mood benefits from exercise. Three exercise considerations are thought important to maximizing positive effects:

(1) **Choosing an enjoyable activity** – individuals are more likely to experience positive mood changes if they are participating in an activity they like and enjoy. Enjoyment may also be influenced by activity factors such as exercise intensity, duration and frequency. It is important to remember that individual differences mean that the same activity may be experienced quite differently by different people. For example, one person may perceive an exercise class as really hard work and therefore not particularly enjoyable, another may also find it hard work but enjoy the challenge, and a third person may find it too easy and not enjoyable.

(2) **Mode of activity** – some types of activity may be more beneficial than others. Those that include abdominal, rhythmical breathing (e.g., swimming, jogging, yoga) may be more associated with positive effects. The absence of competition, or limited competition, may help create a task climate that reduces the chance of interpersonal comparison and the stress and anxiety that may be associated with it. A closed and predictable environment that does not require the close attention of the participant seems to be beneficial to mood (e.g., the environments provided by swimming lengths or jogging/walking). This may be because this sort of environment provides

opportunities for self-reflection. The final mode characteristic relates to activities that are repetitive and rhythmical (e.g., jogging/walking, swimming, dancing). Such activities provide greater opportunity for thinking, self-reflection, or maybe complete absence of thought.

(3) **Training or practice factors** – this relates to the frequency, duration and intensity of exercise. It is thought that participation a minimum or 2–3 times per week is needed to achieve a basic level of fitness. This will mean that the individual can exercise with less discomfort and is therefore more likely to enjoy the activity. As already mentioned, moderate-intensity exercise is thought to provide the most benefit in terms of mood changes. Finally, 20–30 minutes of exercise is associated with desirable mood changes.

Although physical activity is associated with positive mood and affect, it is illogical to expect that people will continue to feel better and better as they maintain an active lifestyle. Rather it is likely that regular exercise helps individuals manage the normal day-to-day fluctuations in mood, resulting in a mood profile that is more positive than that reported by inactive people. People with normal mood profiles will experience less exercise impact on mood than those who have abnormal profiles to start with (e.g., those who started out with higher levels of negative mood states such as anger and tension are likely to experience greater changes as a result of an exercise session than those who started out with lower levels of these mood states). It is not clear whether exercise has different impacts on the mood and affect of different population sub-groups (e.g., men vs women, different age groups, etc.).

Although plausible biochemical, physiological, psychological and social mechanisms have been proposed, how exercise improves mood and affect has not been clearly established and there is little evidence to support any one of these potential mechanisms. Possible biochemical or physiological mechanisms include the **thermogenic hypothesis**, the **endorphin hypothesis**, and the **monoamine hypothesis**. In the **thermogenic hypothesis** it is suggested that individuals feel better as a result of increases in core body temperature with exercise. However, the results examining this suggestion have been mixed, and there is little support for this as a valid explanation. The **endorphin hypothesis** has received much attention particularly in the lay population. It is based on the finding that the level of plasma endorphins (a natural opioid) increases during exercise and this results in the experience of a 'natural high'. However, there has been limited support for this hypothesis, perhaps due to the fact that the blood–brain barrier is relatively impermeable to changes in circulating endorphins. Therefore, changes in plasma endorphin levels would not alter mood as opioid activity in the brain would be largely unaltered. The **monoamine hypothesis** suggests that changes in neurotransmitter systems (e.g., serotonergic systems) underpin the exercise–mood relationship. Physical activity has been demonstrated to increase the production of serotonin in animals, resulting in heightened nervous system activity. This heightened activity is hypothesized to be associated with improvements in mood. In addition, exercise is associated with decreases in rapid eye movement (REM) sleep, which is linked with increases in the amount of serotonin available in the nervous system. Due to the extreme difficulties in measuring such changes in human beings most of the research on this hypothesis has been with rodents, and much more work is needed with human participants before conclusions can be drawn.

Alternatively, possible psychological mechanisms for positive changes in mood and affect as a result of exercise include the **distraction hypothesis** and the **mastery hypothesis**. In the **distraction hypothesis** it is proposed that participating in physical activity gives people a break from their daily hassles and stressors and provides an opportunity to relax and perhaps put things in perspective. This 'timeout' during exercise is hypothesized to enhance mood. This hypothesis has been tested in several studies and received some support. The **mastery hypothesis** is centered on the notion that gaining physical competence will result in positive feelings of achievement, self-efficacy and self-competence. While these feelings are related specifically to the exercise domain, it is hypothesized that they may generalize to other areas of life, resulting in an increase in PWB.

Proposed social mechanisms for the exercise–mood relationship center on the influence of being with friends while exercising. This time with friends may provide an opportunity to discuss worries/hassles, or may simply increase the amount of fun experienced while exercising.

It is possible that different mechanisms and combinations of mechanisms are more important at different times. For example, psychological mechanisms may be more important as individuals adopt exercise, and physiological mechanisms may be more important during the maintenance phase. The logic is that greater exposure to exercise results in physiological adaptation that in turn has greater influence on well-being.

Physical activity and self-esteem

Self-esteem is regarded as a key indicator of emotional stability and adjustment, and is regarded by many as the most important aspect of psychological well-being. In general terms it is a self-rating of 'how well I am doing' and refers to the value placed on aspects of the self. This evaluative component is what differentiates self-esteem from self-concept, which is simply a self-description.

Self-esteem is considered to be **multidimensional**, with people tending to have different perceptions of themselves in different life domains (e.g., as a student, as an athlete, as a family member, etc.). The overall or global self-esteem is most strongly influenced by the life domains the individual considers to be most important. Self-esteem is also thought to be **hierarchical**, that is, global self-esteem is underpinned by a sense of worth in general life domains such as the academic domain, social domain, and physical domain. Evaluations in each of these life domains result from perceptions in a number of sub-areas, for example, physical self-worth is influenced by perceptions of physical ability and physical appearance. Below these sub-areas are evaluations of specific situations or behaviors, for example, physical ability perceptions may be influenced by perceptions of ability in tennis vs track and field. It is hypothesized that perceptions lower down in the hierarchy will be more malleable and subject to change during interventions.

Because it is such a complex system of constructs, it is not surprising that the effects of exercise on generalized self-esteem tend to be mixed (see review by Fox, 2000). Indeed, these equivocal findings support the theoretical structure of self-esteem, which suggests that self-esteem is a stable construct influenced by a range of life events so a positive change in one domain (e.g., the physical) may not counterbalance negative influences from another domain. For example, Jane takes up exercise and feels better about her body as she loses weight and feels fitter, however, her job is not going well and she feels she has few friends. Because both her job and her social life are important to Jane the improvements in her physical self, while welcome, do not overcome the negative self-perception she has in these other domains, and her global self-esteem remains low.

In the physical domain exercise can be used as a medium to promote physical self-worth and other important physical self-perceptions such as body image. This improvement in physical self-esteem sometimes results in improved overall self-esteem. Feeling good about your physical self (physical self-worth) has been shown to positively influence mental well-being and therefore should be considered a valid end-point for exercise participation.

These exercise self-esteem effects can be experienced by all age groups and by both men and women. However, because research has mostly focused on children, adolescents and middle-aged adults the evidence is strongest in these groups. Those who start out with lower self-esteem are likely to show the greatest changes.

Different types of exercise have been shown to influence the exercise self-esteem relationship but the strongest evidence is for aerobic exercise and weight training. The effect of exercise frequency, intensity and duration has received limited attention. There is a higher chance of self-esteem change in programs lasting months rather than weeks. Changes in self-esteem do not appear to be linked to changes in fitness, suggesting that it is the perception of improvement that counts. When changes in self-esteem occur they have been shown to persist over time.

It is not clear how exercise produces positive changes in well-being via improved physical self-perceptions and sometimes self-esteem. It is likely that several possible mechanisms underpin these changes, some linked to body improvements (e.g., increases in fitness or weight loss), others to social factors (e.g., a sense of belonging) and others to the exercise setting (e.g., a sense of autonomy and personal control, leadership style). It is possible that some as yet undetermined psychophysiological mechanism underpins the changes.

Physical activity and cognitive functioning

As people age they experience a decrease in cognitive performance, which can have major consequences for older people (e.g., impacts the ability to drive and thus potentially independence, increases the risk of accident at home and work). Exercise has been suggested as a potential non-pharmacological intervention for counteracting this behavioral slowing. Boutcher (2000) reviewed work in the area and concluded that: (a) cross-sectional research shows that fit older adults perform better in cognitive tests than the less fit (i.e., when fit/active older adults were compared with unfit/inactive older adults, the active adults performed better in reaction time, math and acuity tasks), and (b) longitudinal studies show a small but significant increase in cognitive performance with increases in aerobic fitness in older adults (i.e., older adults who take up regular exercise and improve their fitness also show small positive changes in their cognitive performance). The relationship between fitness and cognitive performance is most obvious in tasks that are attention demanding and rapid (e.g., reaction-time tasks).

The mechanisms underpinning the effects of physical activity on cognitive functioning are unclear, and those that have been suggested (e.g., exercise participation offsets age-related declines in cerebral circulation, central nervous system function, or neural efficiency, or exercise results in greater health or motivation) have received little research support.

A more comprehensive review including research with a wider range of participants was provided by Etnier et al (1997). In this meta-analysis it was concluded that exercise has a small positive effect on cognitive functioning (i.e., exercise results in a small but significant improvement in cognition). The effects were stronger for chronic exercise compared with acute exercise. The strength of the relationship was influenced by the quality of the study with smaller effects (i.e., weaker effects) being found in the better-quality, more rigorous studies.

It has been claimed that physical activity helps children perform better academically. While a modest positive relationship has been observed between motor performance and intellectual performance in children, reviews of research in this area have generally concluded the evidence is equivocal. Where a positive relationship has been observed it is strongest in the early, pre-school years.

H2 MENTAL HEALTH

Key Notes

Mental health	A positive sense of well-being and personal satisfaction with self, life roles and relationships.
Physical activity, anxiety, and stress reactivity	Participation in physical activity positively affects state and trait anxiety, and reduces stress reactivity. Moderate intensity, aerobic and rhythmic activities are most strongly associated with reductions in anxiety. Physical activity produces comparable effects to non-medication treatments. Little is known about the exercise–anxiety relationship in young people.
Physical activity and clinical depression	There is evidence for a causal link between exercise and decreased clinical depression. Exercise is effective in the treatment of depression, usually as an adjunct to other treatment.
Limitations in research	Research is limited by poor study design, small sample sizes and problems with measurement of key constructs.
Possible mechanisms	Psychological, physiological, and neurobiological mechanisms have been proposed, but no single explanation is likely to be sufficient.
Related topics	Anxiety: the basics (D3) Psychological well-being (H1) Multi-dimensional anxiety theory Stress and coping (M1) (D4)

Mental health

Mental health can be defined as a positive sense of well-being and personal satisfaction with self, life roles and relationships. Mental health disorders such as anxiety and clinical depression affect millions of people worldwide and are associated with increased morbidity and costs to healthcare and industry. In addition, such disorders negatively affect the quality of life of individuals. Many mental health disorders are treated through counseling, drug therapy or both but there is increasing interest in the role of physical activity participation in improving or maintaining mental health.

Physical activity, anxiety and stress reactivity

Participation in physical activity may affect immediate anxiety levels (**state anxiety**), relatively stable anxiety characteristics of the individual (**trait anxiety**), or psychophysiological markers of anxiety such as blood pressure or heart rate (**stress reactivity**) (see Topics D3 and D4 for further definition of these terms). Research shows that physical activity results in a low-to-moderate reduction in anxiety (see review by Taylor, 2000).

Single exercise sessions result in short-term decreases in state anxiety and can reduce short-term stress reactivity. The greatest reductions in state anxiety appear to occur when the exercise is aerobic and rhythmic (e.g., walking, swimming). Moderate-intensity exercise appears to be most strongly associated with positive changes in anxiety, although more vigorous intensities have also been shown to reduce anxiety.

Studies in this area often employ a pre–post within-subjects design such as the one that follows:

- State anxiety is measured with a pencil and paper test.
- The participant then exercises for a given time (usually in the order of 20–45 minutes) at a pre-determined intensity.
- State anxiety is then re-measured immediately after the exercise ceases, and at regular intervals until the testing session concludes.

Regular participation in exercise has been shown to reduce trait anxiety in both males and females and in a range of other population sub-groups (e.g., active and inactive, anxious and non-anxious, healthy and unhealthy). The length of the training program influences the reduction in trait anxiety with at least 10 weeks being required for the greatest effects. The effects on trait anxiety appear independent of fitness changes suggesting that it is the participation in physical activity that is most important.

There is limited work comparing physical activity and other non-medication treatments, but these suggest comparable effects. For example, research comparing exercise to treatments such as meditation, biofeedback and quiet rest, reports a similar reduction in state anxiety across treatments. There is some evidence that the anxiety reducing effects from exercise last longer which could have important cost-effectiveness implications for treatment.

Most of the work on the exercise–anxiety relationship has been done with adults and there has been relatively little examination of physical activity effects on anxiety in children and young people. For example, in his review published in 2000 Taylor identified only one study published since 1988 that examined the anxiety–exercise relationship in people under 18. In this study Norris et al. (1992) compared four groups of 13–17-year-old healthy adolescents. The groups were:

(1) vigorous exercise;
(2) moderate exercise;
(3) flexibility;
(4) control.

Groups 1–3 participated in 25–30 minutes of exercise twice a week for 10 weeks. The vigorous exercise group showed a reduction in anxiety, from the start to the end of the program. This gap in our knowledge and understanding of the exercise–anxiety relationship in young people needs to be addressed as it has been estimated that about 10% of young people may suffer from mental health problems, including anxiety disorders.

Physical activity and clinical depression

Depression is one of the most common psychiatric conditions. Definitions range from episodes of the 'blues' (probably best labeled transitory negative affect, rather than depression, Topic H1) through to sustained periods of low mood and inability to find enjoyment (clinically defined depression).

Craft and Landers (1998) conducted a meta-analysis of the effect of exercise on clinically defined depression. They reported an overall effect size of –0.72, suggesting that those who exercised were less depressed than individuals who did not exercise. The relationship was not influenced by the mode of exercise (e.g., aerobic versus non-aerobic).

An extensive review by Mutrie (2000) examined a large body of research on the exercise–depression relationship and found:

- There is epidemiological evidence that physical activity participation is associated with a decreased risk of developing clinically defined depression. For example, in the Harvard Alumni study, Paffenbarger et al. (1994) showed that, compared to men who played sport for less than one hour a week, men who played for three or more hours a week at baseline had a 27% reduced risk of developing depression at follow-up 23–27 years later.
- There is no evidence that increasing physical activity increases the risk of depression.
- That, similar to Craft and Landers, both aerobic and non-aerobic (e.g., resistance training) exercise were effective in the treatment of moderate to severe depression, usually as an adjunct to other treatment.
- The effects of an exercise treatment are of the same magnitude as a variety of psychotherapeutic treatments.

Mutrie (2000) concluded that the evidence supports a **causal link** between exercise and decreased clinically defined depression. This conclusion was based on her interpretation that most of the criteria for causality outlined by Hill (1965) have been met. These eight criteria and the evidence in each one are outlined in *Table 1*. While

Table 1. Evidence for supporting a causal relationship between exercise and depression (summarised from Mutrie, 2000)

Criteria	Evidence
Strength of the association	This criterion has been demonstrated as epidemiological studies have shown a relative risk of 1.7 for inactive people developing depression at a later date
Consistency	Consistency has been demonstrated as similar findings have been reported across different countries, at different times and in different circumstances
Specificity (e.g., do other associations exist between the conditions and the disease?)	In exercise specificity does not exist, as depression is not the only condition linked to inactivity (e.g., inactivity is also linked to cardiovascular disease and all-cause mortality), and depression is not only influenced by inactivity (e.g., social factors may contribute to depression)
Temporal sequence (e.g. does inactivity precede depression?)	There is some evidence for temporal sequence as it has been shown that inactive individuals are more likely to develop depression at a later date
Dose–response curve	There is modest evidence for a dose–response curve as the least active have been shown to be at the most risk of depression. However there is little evidence to suggest that different doses of exercise (e.g., different intensities or modes) produce different psychological effects
Plausibility (e.g., is there a plausible explanation of the association?)	The mechanisms underlying the relationship between exercise and mental health are not known. However, several plausible explanations have been proposed. Further increases in biological knowledge and technology may help elucidate these mechanisms
Coherence (e.g., possible mechanisms should not conflict with the natural history and biology of mental illness)	The evidence for coherence is incomplete. One example of coherence would be the finding that more women than men report depression and women are less active than men
Experimental evidence (e.g., does manipulation of exercise result in changes in depression?)	There is experimental evidence as exercise programs have been associated with reductions in depression

further evidence is needed for some of the criteria Mutrie suggests that physical activity/exercise should be advocated in the treatment of depression. This will require health professionals working with depressed individuals to receive training on the anti-depressant effects of exercise.

Limitations in research

Much of the research on the effects of physical activity on anxiety and depression has been limited by poor study design, small sample sizes, and problems with measurement of key constructs. For example, studies have used a narrow age range, or they have relied on self-report of anxiety and depression rather than independent diagnosis of these conditions. However, the relative consistency of findings despite different protocols and measures increases confidence that the findings are real.

Possible mechanisms

The mechanisms by which physical activity improves anxiety and depression are not well established, however, several plausible mechanisms have been proposed. Many of these explanations for the improvements in mental health are the same as those proposed for improvements in psychological well-being (see Topic H1) and include the **distraction hypothesis, monoamine hypothesis, endorphin hypothesis, thermogenic hypothesis** and **muscle relaxation**. Few of these proposed mechanisms have been supported by randomized controlled trials. It is likely that a combination of psychological, physiological and neurobiological mechanisms are needed to adequately explain the effects of physical activity on mental health.

H3 NEGATIVE OUTCOMES

Key Notes

Exercise dependence	An abnormal reliance on physical activity, resulting in excessive exercise behavior that manifests in physiological and/or psychological symptoms. It is not the same as high commitment to exercise.
Primary exercise dependence	The dependence is associated only with excessive exercise behavior. The causes of exercise dependence are not clear and both psychological and physiological explanations have been proposed.
Secondary exercise dependence	This is when the exercise dependence is in association with eating disorders. Exercise is likely to be a symptom of an eating disorder rather than a cause. Highly committed exercisers and anorexics are psychologically different.
Exercise and eating disorders	There is evidence for a relationship between exercise and eating disorders in athletic populations, particularly in sports where weight maintenance is critical. The determinants of eating disorders in athletes are not well understood.
Related topics	Psychological well-being (H1) Mental health (H2)

Exercise dependence

The health benefits of regular participation in physical activity are widely accepted. However in a very *small* number of cases physical activity can lead to undesirable psychological outcomes. These negative consequences of physical activity can occur as exercise is adopted, or later once exercise has become a regular part of an individual's life. The effects may be acute and transient or chronic and persistent. Negative effects experienced during adoption of an exercise program are usually transient and may lead to dropout. For example, the novice exerciser may experience negative affect due to the intensity of the exercise participated in, or they may experience social physique anxiety if they perceive their appearance to be socially undesirable. Negative effects during maintenance are usually associated with attitudes towards physical activity and are therefore more likely to be persistent (e.g., exercise dependence).

Research into the negative consequences of physical activity participation has focused mostly on exercise dependence. **Exercise dependence** can be defined as an abnormal reliance on physical activity, resulting in excessive exercise behavior that manifests in physiological and/or psychological symptoms (e.g., tiredness, chronic injury, relationship problems, anxiety or depression). However, there is little consensus on the definition of exercise dependence within the literature. In addition, many definitions have relied on the presence of withdrawal symptoms, rather than the type, frequency and intensity of these symptoms. Defining exercise dependence in terms of withdrawal symptoms makes distinguishing exercise dependence from high exercise commitment difficult, as all committed exercisers will exhibit some withdrawal symptoms when unable to exercise. This variability in definition is reflected in problems when trying to measure exercise dependence with many instruments confusing dependence and commitment. Alongside this many of the measurement instruments used have poor validity. Although exercise dependence is the currently preferred term other terms that have been used are exercise addiction and obligatory exercise. As a result of these differences in terminology, definition and measurement it is difficult to reach conclusions about exercise dependence, its antecedents and consequences, and explanations for its existence (see review by Hausenblas & Symons Downs, 2002; and Szabo, 2000).

Exercise dependence is divided into two levels. **Primary exercise dependence** is where the dysfunction is associated only with exercise behavior. **Secondary exercise dependence** occurs when the exercise dependence is in association with eating disorders. In secondary exercise dependence the motivation for physical activity is control and manipulation of body composition.

Primary exercise dependence

Exercise dependence is not the same as commitment to exercise. The committed exerciser derives satisfaction, enjoyment and achievement from their participation and views exercise as an important, but not central, part of their life. In contrast to the exercise-dependent, the committed exerciser is not likely to allow exercise to interfere with their work performance, social relationships and other aspects of their lives. Exercise-dependent individuals may continue to exercise to avoid unpleasant withdrawal symptoms (negative reinforcements) and/or to continue to experience positive reinforcements such as 'runner's high'. Committed exercisers are unlikely to use negative reinforcement as a motivating factor. It is not clear from research when or why a previously 'healthy' exercise behavior becomes an 'unhealthy' exercise behavior.

According to Weinberg and Gould (2003) the main symptoms for exercise dependency are:

1. stereotyped pattern of exercise once or more a day;
2. giving priority to exercise over other activities (e.g., work or social life);
3. increased tolerance to the volume of exercise performed;
4. withdrawal symptoms when unable to exercise;
5. the withdrawal symptoms are relieved by going out and doing some exercise;
6. subjective awareness of a compulsion to exercise (i.e., the exercise dependent is often aware of the negative impact of their exercising but doesn't do anything about it as they believe that exercise adds something special to their lives);
7. quick return to the pattern of exercise and withdrawal symptoms after a period of abstinence.

Other characteristics of exercise dependency include a feeling of compulsion to exercise that overrides intrinsic reasons such as liking and enjoyment. For example, when asked why they exercise the exercise dependent is likely to answer that they 'have to' rather than 'its fun', or 'I enjoy it'. Exercise dependency may also be revealed in a continuation to exercise despite advice from doctors, friends or colleagues to stop or reduce the time spent exercising.

In their systematic review of primary exercise dependence Hausenblas and Symons Downs (2002) reported that research in this area has generally been approached in one of three ways:

1. comparing exercisers to patients with eating disorders;
2. comparing excessive and less-excessive exercisers;
3. comparing exercisers to non-exercisers.

Although a reasonable volume of research was identified (77 studies) Hausenblas and Symons Downs concluded that the findings should be interpreted with caution to avoid making unjustified claims and that no definitive statement could be made regarding exercise dependence. The basis of this warning was that along with the definition and measurement problems mentioned earlier there was a lack of experimental investigations, a failure to use appropriate control groups, and limited control for participant bias within the research to date.

The causes of exercise dependence are not clear. Both physiological and psychological explanations have been offered (Szabo, 2000). A popular explanation has been the **endorphin hypothesis**. In this explanation it is hypothesized that dependent individuals have become reliant on the endorphins (natural opiates) released in the brain during exercise that cause feelings of euphoria (the so called 'runner's high'). This explanation is not well supported (see Section H1 for an explanation of why the endorphin hypothesis has limited support). A second physiological explanation is the '**sympathetic arousal hypothesis**'. Szabo (2000) outlines how in this approach it is hypothesized that regular exercise results in decreased sympathetic arousal at rest, resulting in a lethargic state when exercise is withdrawn. The habituated exerciser must keep exercising to increase arousal levels. **Psychological explanations** include the use of exercise as a way of coping with psychological problems. As with those who use drugs or alcohol when distressed, some individuals may abuse their exercise such that a dependence develops. One of the problems with the research that has attempted to examine the causal mechanisms of exercise dependence is that it has been correlational. Hausenblas and Symons Downs recommend that longitudinal, ecological momentary assessments, qualitative and experimental studies are required to overcome this limitation and further our understanding.

Secondary exercise dependence

Secondary exercise dependence is common among individuals with eating disorders. In the case of secondary dependence excessive physical activity is used to maintain caloric control and facilitate weight loss. Generally, excessive physical activity is not a cause of psychological dysfunction, but rather a symptom of the latter.

There is insufficient evidence to support the argument that exercise is a contributing factor to eating disorders. Initially it was argued that highly committed exercisers and anorexics exhibited a strong psychological resemblance, this has now been discounted and the psychological characteristics of anorexics and highly committed exercisers have been shown to be significantly different.

Exercise and eating disorders

There is evidence for a relationship between exercise and eating disorders among high-level exercisers and professional athletes. Female athletes, and both males and females in sports where weight maintenance is critical (e.g., wrestling, gymnastics, diving) are at greater risk of developing eating disorders.

The determinants of eating disorders in athletes are not well understood. One model that attempts to explain this relationship is the psychosocial model for the development of eating disorders in female athletes (Williamson et al., 1995).

In this model it is suggested that a strong determinant of eating disorder symptoms is an over-concern with body size. This relationship is mediated by performance anxiety, negative self-appraisal of athletic achievement and being in an environment that creates a social pressure for thinness. This model has not received a great deal of research attention but would provide a good starting point in future studies examining the relationship between exercise and eating disorders.

I1 DETERMINANTS OF EXERCISE

Key Notes

Determinants of physical activity	Determinants are factors that show consistent/reproducible associations with exercise behavior that are potentially causal. Modifiable determinants are useful targets in interventions. Unmodifiable determinants identify target groups for interventions.
Determinants in adults	Positive associations (i.e., when levels of one get higher so do levels of the other) have been found for education, being male, socio-economic status, self-efficacy, perceived benefits, enjoyment, intention to exercise, self-motivation, perceived health/fitness, stages of change, processes of change, diet quality and adult activity history. Negative associations (i.e., when levels of one get higher levels of the other gets lower) have been found for age, ethnicity (non-Hispanic whites have higher levels), perceived barriers, perceived effort, intensity and climate/season.
Determinants in children and adolescents	In children positive associations have been found for having an overweight parent, being male, intentions to exercise, preferences for physical activity, healthy diet, previous physical activity, access to facilities and programs, and time spent outside. Negative associations have been found for perceived barriers. In adolescents, positive associations have been found for being male, ethnicity, achievement orientation, perceived competence, intention to be active, sensation seeking, previous activity, participation in community sports, parental support, sibling physical activity and opportunities to exercise. Negative associations have been found for age, depression and sedentary pursuits.
Related topics	Participation motivation (I2) Process models of exercise (J2) Cognitive-behavioral theories (J1) Ecological models (J3)

Determinants of physical activity

Early exercise motivation research was largely descriptive and atheoretical. Such research sought to identify the participation motives and determinants of physical activity. Participation motivation will be discussed in topic I2. Determinants research identifies factors that show consistent and reproducible associations with participation in physical activity (Buckworth & Dishman, 2002). Such determinants are potentially causal but the design of most determinants research (cross-sectional and correlational) does not allow causality to be established.

Determinants research has usually involved the comparison of exercisers and non-exercisers. The early determinants work was conducted largely with adult populations, although more recent work has examined the determinants in children and adolescents. Different determinants have been identified for these groups.

Determinants may be modifiable (e.g., enjoyment of exercise) or unmodifiable (e.g., age, gender). Identifying modifiable determinants is important as the logic of the determinants approach suggests that interventions that target change in modifiable determinants will be more successful in ultimately changing physical activity behavior. This has resource implications as activity promoters can target their resources at factors that are most likely to result in activity behavior change. Understanding unmodifiable determinants helps identify target groups (e.g., adolescent girls, older adults) of inactive people most in need of an intervention which again allows for more effective use of resources and time.

Although the early determinants work was largely descriptive, theories and models have also been applied in an attempt to uncover the consistent influences on physical activity behavior. These theories and models include the health belief model, the theory of planned behavior, social cognitive theory (see Topic J1), the transtheoretical model (see Topic J2) and ecological models (see Topic J3). The link between theories and determinants research is important because the identification of determinants can be used to inform and modify models and theories so that they better represent physical activity behavior. For example, a sense of having to exercise to please others has shown no consistent relationship to physical activity behavior. This finding has implications for theories such as the theory of planned behavior which includes subjective norms as a key variable (Buckworth & Dishman, 2002).

Determinants can be categorized under the following headings: demographic and biological factors, psychological, cognitive and emotional factors, behavioral attributes and skills, social and cultural factors, physical environment factors, and characteristics of the activity itself. No one factor or category of factors will explain exercise behavior. Rather the factors will interact within an individual, and across time and circumstances. This was recognized in early work, for example, the psychobiological model of adherence proposed by Dishman and Gettman (1980) postulated that both psychological and biological factors influenced participation.

Determinants in adults

Over 300 studies have been published on determinants in adults, and consistent associations have been found in each category of determinants (Trost et al., 2000). No one determinant or category explains most adult physical activity. The review by Trost et al. (2000) provides an overview of physical activity determinants in adults.

Age and gender are the two most consistent demographic and biological determinants of physical activity participation. Physical activity participation is consistently higher in men, and consistently higher in younger compared to older adults. Socio-economic status and education have also consistently been related to physical activity, with adults of higher social economic status or higher education being more likely to participate in physical activity. Being of non-white race or ethnicity is consistently associated with lower levels of physical activity. There is emerging evidence (Trost et al., 2002) that overweight and obesity influences physical activity behavior with those reporting high levels of physical activity being less likely to be classified as obese.

The most consistent psychological determinant of physical activity is self-efficacy (a person's confidence that they can be active on a regular basis). The more confident people feel the more likely they are to exercise. Barriers to physical activity (e.g., lack of time, too tired, bad weather, etc.) are also a consistent determinant with individuals who report fewer barriers being more likely to participate. While intentions to exercise are related to physical activity behavior, other components of the theory of planned behavior (e.g., attitudes, normative beliefs and perceived behavioral control) have received little or no support. Other important psychological determinants related to higher levels of participation include enjoyment of activity, an expectation of benefits, self-motivation, and stage of change. Knowledge of health and exercise and susceptibility to illness are consistently unrelated to physical activity.

Several consistent determinants within the behavioral category have been identified. Activity history during adulthood is positively associated with current physical activity behavior. That is, recent participation in activity is a strong predictor of your current participation. Adults with a better-quality diet are also more likely to participate in physical activity. Processes of change, which are cognitive and behavioral strategies that are used to modify thoughts and behaviors (see Topic J2) are also positively related to exercise participation. This demonstrates that individuals who actively engage in cognitive and behavioral exercise behavior change strategies are more likely to participate. Smoking and activity history during childhood and adolescence are not related to physical activity participation.

The most consistent determinant in the social and cultural area is social support from peers and family. Adults reporting greater social support are more likely to be active and reach recommended levels of physical activity participation. Support and encouragement from a physician is also related to greater physical activity participation.

Few physical environmental factors have been identified as determinants, although understanding these influences is now seen as a research imperative (see Topic J3). To date, the strongest evidence is for climate and seasonal effects on participation, with less activity occurring in winter. There is weaker evidence suggesting that exercise equipment in the home, access to facilities, satisfaction with facilities, perceived neighborhood safety, hilly terrain, seeing others being active, and enjoyable scenery are all related to greater physical activity participation.

The perceived effort of an activity and activity intensity are characteristics of the activity itself that are negatively associated with participation. That is, higher exercise intensities and greater perceived exertion are associated with lower participation.

Most determinants studies have examined determinants of vigorous exercise or total physical activity, therefore understanding of the determinants of moderate exercise (the current health message) is limited. In contrast to vigorous exercise, it has been shown that moderate-intensity exercise increases with age and women tend to do more than men. More research is required in this area. In addition, we need to know whether there are determinants for different types of activity (e.g., activity for transport, leisure time activity, occupational activity and incidental activity). It is important to understand this as it will help to more effectively design and target interventions in different contexts. More research is needed to provide an understanding of sub-group differences in determinants (e.g., cultural effects on determinants). Furthermore, longitudinal and intervention studies are needed to establish whether there are causal relationships between identified determinants and physical activity.

Determinants in children and adolescents

Significant determinants have been found in all categories for children (4–12 years) and adolescents (13–18 years). Determinants research with young people is complicated by the psychological, physical and social developmental changes that are occurring. The effects of these changes are not well understood. The review by Sallis et al. (2000) provides a comprehensive overview of physical activity determinants in young people.

Within children results for demographic and biological variables suggest a positive association between physical activity and being male and having an overweight parent. That is, if you are male or have an overweight parent you are more likely to participate in physical activity. Inconsistent findings have been reported for age and body weight/fatness. Socio-economic status (SES) and ethnicity appear unrelated to physical activity in this age group. For adolescents greater physical activity was found for boys compared to girls and non-Hispanic whites compared to all other ethnic groups. Less physical activity was associated with increasing age.

Psychological variables associated with physical activity in children include perceived barriers (negative, i.e., more perceived barriers is associated with less activity), intentions (positive, i.e., stronger intentions to be active are associated with greater activity) and preferences for physical activity (positive). For adolescents, achievement orientation, perceived competence, and intention to be active were positively associated, and depression negatively associated, with physical activity. It has been reported that activity may also be related to perceptions of enjoyment, self-efficacy, competence, control and autonomy, positive attitudes towards activity, and a perception of few barriers and many benefits. However, much of this research is cross-sectional using self-report measures of unknown validity.

Behavioral factors with a positive association with physical activity in children include healthy diet and previous physical activity. For adolescents, a positive association was found for sensation seeking, previous activity and participation in community sports. No consistent association was found between physical activity and sedentary behaviors in children (e.g., TV viewing), but time in sedentary pursuits in adolescents after school and at weekends was negatively related to physical activity.

No social variables were clearly associated with childhood physical activity (Sallis et al., 2000). For adolescents parental support was positively associated with activity. Sibling physical activity was consistently associated for adolescents whereas other social factors (e.g., peer modeling, perceived peer support) were not. Research using the theory of planned behavior (see Topic J1) has shown that subjective norms were a small but significant predictor of physical activity intentions. However, attitudes, perceived behavioral control, self-efficacy and past behavior were all stronger influences.

Some physical environment influences have been identified for young people. For children access to facilities and programs, as well as time spent outside, were consistently associated with greater physical activity. For adolescents, the general variable of 'opportunities to exercise' was associated with activity. Topic J3 explains why greater knowledge and understanding of environmental factors is now seen as important.

I2 PARTICIPATION MOTIVATION

Key Notes

Participation motivation	Participation motivation is a descriptive approach examining the reasons and barriers people give for starting, maintaining or quitting participation in physical activity.
Participation motivation in adults	There are five recurring motives: health and fitness, appearance improvement, enjoyment, social reasons and psychological benefits. Reasons commonly given for non-participation or dropping out are lack of time, lack of knowledge about fitness, lack of facilities and fatigue.
Participation motivation in children and adolescents	Five motives consistently emerge as important: fun and enjoyment, learning and improving skills, being with friends, success or challenge, and physical fitness and health. Common reasons given for ceasing participation or non-participation are conflicts of interest, lack of playing time, lack of fun, limited improvement in skills or no success, boredom, and injury.
Related topics	Psychological well-being (H1) Ecological models (J3) Determinants of exercise (I1)

Participation motivation

Determinants research (see Topic I1) identifies differences between those who exercise and those who do not. Participation motivation research addresses the question, why do people exercise? Typically it is a descriptive approach seeking self-reported reasons for starting, maintaining or quitting participation in physical activity. It also addresses the question of what prevents people from being more active. For the most part this research has relied on questionnaires and structured interview techniques. Participation motivation research is useful as a starting point for understanding motivation, but its descriptive, atheoretical approach limits its utility for a deeper understanding of motivation in physical activity settings. It has been a useful approach because it has helped provide the building blocks for more theoretical approaches to understanding behavior.

Most participation motivation research has been with children and young people and their involvement in organized youth sport. Participation motivation research with adults is more limited and tends to focus on health-related physical activity.

Participation motivation in adults

Reviews of the participation motivation literature for adults show that there are five recurring motives: health and fitness, appearance improvement, enjoyment, social reasons (such as being with friends or meeting new people) and psychological benefits (e.g., exercise makes me feel better). Appearance improvement sums up motives for weight loss and improved muscle tone. Physical appearance is important to both men and women; however, it seems to be somewhat more important for women. Health and fitness, or weight loss, are often the motives for beginning an exercise program, although they are seldom sufficient to maintain participation over a long period of time. Enjoyment of an activity is particularly important for maintenance of participation. Social reasons include being with friends and meeting new people. The psychological benefits that contribute to individuals reporting that exercise makes them feel better are described in Topic H1. Psychological benefits seem to be more important to older adults and women. Little is known about changes in motives across the adult years. Motives for participation identify potential selling points for physical activity and as such understanding changes in motives across the lifespan could be critical in attempts to prevent the age-related decline in physical activity participation. Within any group of exercisers there is likely to be a diverse range of motives, or reasons for being there, and exercise leaders need to be aware of these reasons so that they can try and structure the activity to meet as many needs as possible.

Four reasons are commonly given for either non-participation or dropping out of exercise programs: lack of time, lack of knowledge about fitness, lack of facilities and fatigue. Lack of time is the most frequent reason, although some have argued that it is more a matter of priorities than actual lack of time. Those with children are more likely to report a perceived lack of time, particularly among women. These findings highlight the importance of studying participation within a wider socio-cultural framework (e.g., using an ecological approach – see Topic J3).

In the Allied Dunbar National Fitness Survey (ADNFS; The Sports Council and Health Education Authority, 1992) conducted in the United Kingdom, barriers preventing adults from participating in more physical activity were categorized under five headings: physical, emotional, motivational, time and availability. Time barriers appeared to be most important for both men and women, but women were more likely to report emotional barriers such as I'm not the sporty type, or I'm too shy or embarrassed. Across the adult years physical barriers (e.g., I have an injury or disability that stops me, my health is not good enough) and emotional barriers increased, and time barriers (for those over 55 years) decreased. There is a need for more work identifying how barriers to exercise change across the lifespan, because as with understanding motives they identify selling points and targets for interventions.

Participation motivation in children and adolescents

A significant body of literature exists examining why young people take part in sport. Reviews of this work have highlighted diverse reasons for participation, although five consistently emerge as important: fun and enjoyment, learning and improving skills, being with friends, success or challenge, and physical fitness and health. There is some evidence to suggest that these motives are similar across activity settings and groups. More cross-national studies are required to examine cultural effects on participation motivation. The importance of these motives may change with age (e.g., success in competition may be more important in younger adolescents than older adolescents), however, the developmental influences on participation motivation are not well understood.

Frequently 'fun and enjoyment' is the most important reason and 'winning' the least important. Wankel and Kriesel (1985) examined what makes sport fun and enjoyable for young people and found that the process of sports activity (e.g., improving skills, performing skills, testing skills against others) was most important, factors related to the social aspect (e.g., being on a team, being with friends) were of moderate importance and outcome-related components (e.g., winning, pleasing others, gaining rewards) were least important. These results were consistent across the different age groups indicating that sources of enjoyment do not change significantly between the ages 7–14 years. Despite this general consistency in sources of enjoyment some age-related differences were reported with a decrease in the importance of pleasing others and using the skills of the game and an increase in the importance of excitement in the older age groups.

Among young people the most common reasons given for ceasing participation or non-participation are conflicts of interest, lack of playing time, lack of fun, limited improvement in skills or no success, boredom and injury. In sport settings dislike of the coach and competitive stress have also been reported as reasons for ceasing participation. Future research should draw the distinction between drop-out from one sport to go to another and drop-out from sport altogether.

There is less work done on the barriers to physical activity among young people. One qualitative research project (Mulvihill et al., 2000) has shown that many barriers emerge during the time of transition to secondary school. For example, greater embarrassment and self-consciousness concerning their bodies, especially for girls, and perceived time pressure from homework were barriers to physical activity. Coakley and White (1992) interviewed participants and non-participants in local sports initiatives. The decision to participate or not was influenced by perceptions of competence, external constraints (e.g., money), degree of support from significant others and past experiences (including physical education).

What is obvious from the descriptive participation motivation research is that adults and young people are motivated to participate in sport and physical activity for a variety of different reasons. Similar motives occur in both adults and young people but health concerns are more salient and learning and improving skills less salient in adults compared with young people. There is also evidence for changes in barriers to participation across the lifespan. Understanding changes in participation motivation across the lifespan is important in interventions to promote physical activity at different ages as it identifies potential selling points for the intervention.

J1 COGNITIVE-BEHAVIORAL THEORIES

Key Notes

Theories and models in exercise psychology	Models and theories attempt to structure what we know about the variables that affect exercise behavior and the processes that link them. Cognitive-behavioral models focus predominantly on social-psychological influences on exercise behavior. Process models examine the nature of behavior change and its influences. Ecological models give a prominent role to the influence of the environment on exercise behavior.
Social cognitive theory	Social cognitive theory proposes that self-efficacy, outcome expectations and self-evaluated dissatisfaction are important mediators of behavior and behavior change. Self-efficacy is the strongest and most consistent predictor of exercise behavior.
Theory of reasoned action/theory of planned behavior	These propose that behavior is best predicted by intention. Intention is predicted by attitudes towards the behavior and subjective norms and in the theory of planned behavior also by perceived behavioral control. The relationship between intention to exercise and actual exercise behavior is variable although in meta-analysis a large effect has been demonstrated. Attitudes and perceived behavioral control are the strongest predictors of exercise intention.
Health belief model	The health belief model proposes that health behavior is a function of the perceived threat of getting a disease, and a cost–benefit analysis of a particular behavior. Perceived threat is determined by perceived susceptibility and perceived seriousness of the disease. The likelihood of taking action will be influenced by cues to action and demographic, sociopsychological and structural variables. It has limited use in explaining exercise behavior.
Protection motivation theory	This proposes that motivation to undertake protective behavior is a function of: the severity of the threat, the perceived vulnerability to the threat, the ability to perform the necessary coping behavior, and the effectiveness of the behavior in reducing the threat. It has seldom been used in the exercise domain.
Related topics	Process models of exercise (J2) Ecological models (J3)

Theories and models in exercise psychology

Models and theories of exercise behavior are attempts to structure what we know about the variables that affect exercise behavior (e.g., determinants) and the processes that link them. Most theories in the exercise domain have been 'borrowed' from either general psychology or other health behaviors. Theories and models can be used to inform exercise interventions and are valuable tools in structuring the research process. Theories and models of exercise behavior can be loosely grouped into three categories:

1. **cognitive-behavioral models,** which focus predominantly on social-psychological influences on behavior (this topic);
2. **process models**, which look more closely at the nature of behavior change and its influences (see Topic J2); and
3. **ecological models**, which give a prominent role to the influence of the environment on exercise behavior (see Topic J3).

Social cognitive theory

Social cognitive theory (SCT; Bandura, 1986) is a general psychological theory that differs from other theories by the recognition of the reciprocal interaction between the person, the behavior and the environment (see *Fig. 1*). SCT is based on the idea that human behavior is guided by the ability to consider future consequences of a given behavior (outcome expectations) and the ability to form perceptions about one's own capabilities to perform a behavior (self-efficacy). Within SCT, self-efficacy, outcome expectations and self-evaluated dissatisfaction are assumed to be important mediators of behavior and behavior change (see *Fig. 2*).

Self-efficacy (Topic C5) is hypothesized to be the most important component, and it is assumed to influence choice, effort and persistence. It is proposed that self-efficacy can be altered through four mechanisms: performance accomplishments, vicarious experience, verbal persuasion and physiological states. Performance accomplishments are though to be the most powerful sources of self-efficacy as they are based on personal experiences of success and failure. Vicarious experience refers to the building of self-efficacy through imitation and modeling processes. Vicarious processes are likely to be strongest when the individual has similarities to the model. For example, an overweight middle-aged man may see other overweight middle-aged men out walking and as a consequence start to believe that he too could walk. The same man may not gain in self-efficacy by seeing young, super-fit men out running. Verbal and social persuasion such as encouragement or positive feedback is thought to be a relatively weak source of efficacy information. The final source of self-efficacy comes from judgments of physiological states. This may have particular relevance in helping people interpret the physiological changes

Fig. 1.   Reciprocal determinism.

Self-efficacy ⎤
Self-evaluated dissatisfaction ⎬ Exercise behavior
Outcome expectations ⎦

Fig. 2.   Social cognitive theory.

that occur with exercise (such as increased heart rate) in a positive or non-threatening way.

Outcome expectations are a person's expectation that a given behavior will lead to a given outcome. The difference between outcome expectations and self-efficacy is that a person may believe that a given behavior results in a desired outcome but not believe they can perform the given behavior. For example, Adam may believe that a daily walk will lead to weight loss but he may not have the belief that he can actually do a walk every day. Self-dissatisfaction reflects how an individual compares his or her performance or behavior to a standard and reacts with satisfaction or dissatisfaction. Dissatisfaction may lead to a change in behavior, whereas satisfaction with a behavior but a desire to avoid dissatisfaction in the future may lead to continuation of a behavior.

The majority of SCT and exercise research has focused on self-efficacy and ignored outcome expectations and dissatisfaction. Studies suggest that self-efficacy and dissatisfaction have an important role in exercise behavior. Self-efficacy is a consistent and strong predictor of exercise behavior and remains important even after previous experience is accounted for. Those with higher self-efficacy for exercise are more likely to both adopt exercise and maintain their participation. Self-evaluation and the resultant satisfaction or dissatisfaction appear to mediate exercise motivation, however this relationship may be confounded by previous exercise experience. The results for outcome expectation are equivocal possibly due to measurement issues. For behaviors where outcome is not closely linked to competence outcome expectation is hypothesized to make an independent contribution to motivation beyond that made by self-efficacy. The greatest amount of motivation for behavior change will arise in conditions of high self-efficacy, high outcome expectation and high dissatisfaction. That is, motivation to adopt regular exercise will be highest when, for example, Amy has a high confidence that she can exercise four times a week, has strong beliefs that this amount of exercise will lead to fitness changes, and she is dissatisfied with her current fitness levels.

Although the majority of research supports the utility of SCT components in predicting exercise behavior, a number of methodological concerns suggest the results should be viewed with caution. Most studies have used self-report physical activity which may be influenced by inaccurate recall or response bias. Research has been largely of a correlational design (e.g., compared different groups, say exercisers to non-exercisers) and therefore does not clarify cause and effect relationships. Prospective longitudinal studies are needed to help clarify causality. For example, a group of sedentary people could be monitored at regular intervals across a 2-year period. Changes in self-efficacy and exercise behavior in this period could then be examined to determine temporal relationships between the variables. Much of the research has considered the components of SCT in isolation meaning that the inter-relationships between them can not be clarified. It has been suggested that the components of SCT may be more or less important at different times of the exercise adoption–maintenance cycle and this should be considered when interpreting results.

The theory of reasoned action/theory of planned behavior

The theory of reasoned action (TRA; Fishbein & Ajzen, 1975) and the theory of planned behavior (TPB; Ajzen, 1991) are general models concerned with the relationships between attitudes and volitional behavior (see *Fig. 3*). Volitional behaviors are behaviors that an individual voluntarily participates in and the decision to participate is assumed to be under the control of the individual. The

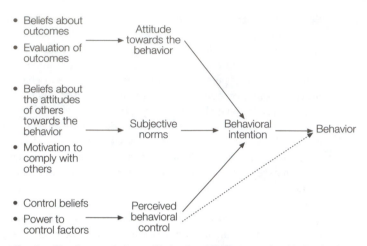

Fig. 3.   The theory of planned behavior. (Without perceived behavioral control, the schematic represents the theory of reasoned action.)

basic premise of the theories is that intention (the plan to carry out a behavior), is the most important determinant of behavior. In the TRA intention is hypothesized to be predicted from an individual's attitude toward the behavior and the individual's subjective norm for the behavior. Attitude is a function of an individual's beliefs that a behavior will lead to a certain outcome and an evaluation of whether these outcomes would be worthwhile. For example, Sam has a strong attitude towards working out in a gym because he believes that gym work will make him muscley and strong, and looking muscley and strong is important to Sam. Subjective norm is based on an individual's beliefs about significant others' opinions regarding the behavior and a motivation to comply with the expectations of others. For example, Hanza has a strong subjective norm for sport because she believes that her parents think she should play more sport and she very much wants to please her parents and meet their expectations.

The TRA was criticized for assuming that all behaviors were under the same degree of individual control. The TPB addresses this criticism and extends the TRA to also include perceived behavioral control, which reflects the extent to which individuals perceive they have control over external and internal factors that may interfere with performing a behavior. Perceived behavioral control is determined by a control belief (personal beliefs about resources and opportunities to perform a given behavior) and perceived power to control the factors that facilitate or inhibit behavior. Perceived behavioral control is thought to influence behavior directly and also indirectly through an influence on intentions.

For both the TRA and TPB the strength of the relationship between intention to exercise and actual exercise behavior is variable. In an attempt to synthesize these results Hausenblas et al. (1997) conducted a meta-analysis on the theories of reasoned action and planned behavior within the exercise domain. They found that intention had a large effect on exercise behavior. Attitudes have consistently emerged as the strongest predictor of exercise intention, and in the Hausenblas et al. meta-analysis it was concluded that attitude had a large effect on intention. The influence of subjective norm was much smaller, and only about half that of the effect for attitude.

The TPB has been shown to be superior to the TRA for predicting exercise intentions. Perceived behavioral control is strongly correlated to both sport and exercise behavior and intention (Hausenblas et al., 1997). These results show that the greater an individual's perceived control over physical activity participation, the stronger an individual's intention to participate in physical activity. The TPB offers more than TRA as it explains more variance in exercise intention, and accommodates previously identified barriers to exercise.

A major criticism of the TRA/TPB arises from studies that have shown that attitude, subjective norm and perceived behavioral control are not the only predictors of intention. For example, current behavior and prior experience both make a direct and independent contribution to the prediction of intention. In addition, intention is not the only determinant of exercise behavior (see Topic I1 for an overview of other determinants). From the methodological viewpoint much of the work has been correlational, and there have been problems in defining and measuring the perceived behavioral control variable.

The health belief model

The health belief model (HBM; Becker & Maiman, 1975) was initially devised to address the question of why people did not present for immunizations and medical screening tests. It is essentially an expectancy-value model (see Topic C1), that is, it assumes behavior is based on an expectation that a given behavior will lead to a particular outcome and the value attached to that particular outcome. The HBM assumes that health behavior is a function of the perceived threat of getting a disease, and a cost–benefit analysis of a particular behavior (see *Fig. 4*). Perceived threat is determined by two cognitive dimensions: perceived susceptibility to the disease (i.e., feelings of personal risk for getting a disease), and perceived seriousness of the disease (i.e., subjective assessment of the consequences of developing a particular disease). The more susceptible a person thinks they are and the more serious they perceive the consequences the more likely they are to take action. The cost–benefit analysis involves consideration of the perceived benefits and barriers of a health behavior. It is assumed that individuals will only take action if the benefits outweigh the costs. In addition it is hypothesized that the likelihood of taking action will be influenced by cues that prompt the individual to act (e.g., mass media campaigns) and by demographic (e.g., age, gender), socio-psychological (e.g., social class) and structural (e.g., knowledge) variables.

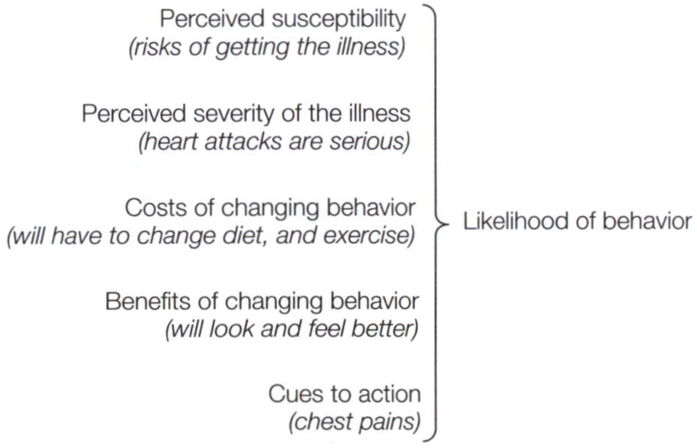

Perceived susceptibility
(risks of getting the illness)

Perceived severity of the illness
(heart attacks are serious)

Costs of changing behavior
(will have to change diet, and exercise) — Likelihood of behavior

Benefits of changing behavior
(will look and feel better)

Cues to action
(chest pains)

Fig. 4. The basic health belief model.

The HBM has been applied to a number of health behaviors including physical activity. A major review by Janz and Becker (1984) reported that (a) there was strong support for the model, (b) perceived barriers were the most powerful predictor, and (c) beliefs about susceptibility appear more important in preventive health behaviors. A more recent meta-analysis (Harrison et al., 1992) produced less positive results with only small effect sizes found. There has been limited use of the HBM in explaining and predicting exercise behavior and the results have not been as positive as for other health behaviors. The most consistent variable associated with exercise has been barriers to exercise.

Possible explanations for why the HBM has limited utility in the physical activity domain include: (a) it was developed to predict isolated illness-avoidance behaviors, but exercise is a complex behavior requiring on-going effort; (b) it ignores the possible non-health reasons for participating in some physical activity (see Topic I2); and (c) it emphasizes illness avoidance and may be less effective for those who view physical activity as a health-promotive behavior compared to those who see it as an illness-reducing behavior. Methodological issues may also have influenced results (e.g., the results may be influenced by the lack of standardized measures of physical activity, the failure to include all aspects of the model within a single study, and the common reliance on retrospective survey methods).

Protection motivation model

Protection motivation theory (PMT, Rogers, 1983) can be seen as a further development of the health belief model. It was initially devised to explain how people react to fear-inducing communications. Motivation to undertake protective behavior (e.g., exercise) is a function of: the severity of the threat, the perceived vulnerability to the threat, the ability to perform the necessary coping behavior, and the effectiveness of the behavior in reducing the threat.

There have been few studies which have directly tested PMT in the exercise domain. Generally this work has shown that self-efficacy is the most important component and is more important than health threats per se. A persuasive threat may increase intention to exercise but seems less effective in facilitating and maintaining behavior change.

J2 PROCESS MODELS OF EXERCISE

Key Notes

Process models of exercise	Process models of exercise focus on describing how individuals change their behavior. They are based on a hypothesis that behavior change is a dynamic process that occurs through a series of interrelated stages. Individuals may cycle through these stages as they attempt to change their behavior.
Transtheoretical model/stage of change model	This proposes five stages of readiness for exercise (ranging from not exercising and not thinking about it, to long-term regular exerciser). Movement through the stages is associated with differential levels or use of ten processes of change, self-efficacy and decisional balance.
A natural history model	This suggests three transition phases in exercise behavior: sedentary behavior to exercise adoption, exercise adoption to maintenance or dropout, and dropout to resumption of exercise. Determinants of exercise at each of these phases will be different.
A lifespan interaction model	This provides a global overview of exercise behaviors across the lifespan. It explains exercise behavior as the interrelationship between determinants, the activity itself, and characteristics of different population groups.
Related topics	Cognitive-behavioral theories (J1) Ecological models (J3)

Process models of exercise

Process models of exercise focus on describing how individuals change their behavior. This contrasts with theories such as social cognitive theory and the theory of planned behavior (see Topic J1) which are largely predictive models that have focused on identifying characteristics of those who exercise and those who do not. A process approach includes the information from these other models and theories, but uses the information to describe how people change.

A process approach hypothesizes that behavior change is a dynamic process that occurs through a series of interrelated steps or stages. Individuals may cycle through these stages with periods of progression and relapse as they attempt to change their behavior. It is recognized that different factors may be more or less influential at different times in the behavior change sequence. Inherent to a process approach is recognition that individuals will be at different levels of readiness to change and, as such, interventions should be tailored to the individual.

Transtheoretical model/stages of change model

The transtheoretical model (TTM; sometimes called the stages of change model; Prochaska & DiClemente, 1983) is the most widely used process model in exercise behavior (Prochaska & Marcus, 1994). It was initially developed to help explain change in addictive behaviors such as smoking. More recently it has been used to help explain change in a number of health behaviors including

physical activity. Five stages of exercise behavior are proposed: precontemplation (not participating in exercise and not thinking about starting, usually in the
next 6 months); contemplation (not participating in exercise but thinking about
starting); preparation (doing some exercise but below a criterion level); action
(started participating in exercise above a criterion level in the last 6 months);
and maintenance (participating above a criterion level for longer than 6
months).

Associated with movement through these stages are changes in three
constructs: processes of change, self-efficacy and decisional balance. The
processes of change are ten cognitive or behavioral strategies that individuals
may use to change thoughts, feelings and behaviors. *Table 1* provides a definition for each process of change. Studies have demonstrated that different
processes seem to be important at different stages of exercise behavior change,
with cognitive processes being used more in the early stages (e.g., contemplation) and behavioral processes being used more in the later stages (e.g., action).
However a recent meta-analysis (Marshall & Biddle, 2001) questions this finding and suggests that both cognitive and behavioral processes demonstrate
similar patterns of change across stages.

Self-efficacy is a person's belief that they can enact a specific behavior. Cross-
sectional research comparing self-efficacy between individuals in different
stages has shown a consistent positive relationship between self-efficacy and
stage of change (i.e., those in precontemplation have the lowest self-efficacy and
those in maintenance the highest). Decisional balance is based on a cost–benefit

Table 1.   Definitions of the ten processes of change (adapted from Marcus et al., 1992)

Process	Definition
Experiential	
Consciousness raising	Seeking new information, understanding and feedback about physical activity
Dramatic relief	Using affective experiences associated with change
Environmental re-evaluation	Consideration of how inactivity affects the social and physical environments
Self-re-evaluation	Emotional and cognitive reappraisal of values with respect to physical inactivity
Social liberation	Awareness, availability and acceptance of being physically active
Behavioral	
Self-liberation	Making a choice and commitment to change including the belief that one can change
Reinforcement management	Changing the contingencies that control or maintain an inactive lifestyle
Counterconditioning	Substitution of active behavior for inactive behavior
Stimulus control	Control of situations that trigger inactivity
Helping relationships	Trusting, accepting and utilizing support from others during attempts to change

analysis of a given behavior change. The assumption is that an individual will not change his/her behavior unless he/she perceives the benefits of change (pros) to outweigh the negatives (cons). Cross-sectional research comparing levels of pros and cons between individuals in different stages has generally shown that pros increase and cons decrease across the stages.

Intervention studies based on the TTM have worked from the premise that the differences between stages in the core constructs suggest that different interventions will be required at different stages and interventions will be most successful when they are matched to the individual's current stage. For example, if someone is in precontemplation, the primary aim of the intervention would be to increase the individual's awareness of the negative consequences of a sedentary lifestyle – you would not be presenting them with an exercise program. This might be done through media and individualized education packs promoting the pros of exercise. For someone in contemplation though the aim would be to increase awareness of the need to change and then work on developing a commitment to change. This might be achieved through work on increasing the individual's exercise self-efficacy (maybe through 'come and try' days), or by working through ways of overcoming barriers or the perceived negatives of exercise, while at the same time emphasizing the pros of exercise. Some efficacy for stage-matched exercise interventions has been demonstrated although there is a need for more work to test this premise adequately. For example, Marcus et al. (1998) in a randomized control trial compared the efficacy of a self-help intervention tailored to an individual's stage of change with a standard self-help intervention. A workplace sample was used. Across the 3-month study period those receiving the tailored intervention were more likely to show increases and less likely to show either no change or regression in stage of change for exercise. The change in stage was associated with changes in self-reported time spent in exercise.

A limitation of the TTM literature has been a strong reliance on cross-sectional research that means little is known about how these factors vary within an individual over time as they change their behavior. Where longitudinal studies have been conducted the results have generally supported the tenets of the TTM. Further limitations in the TTM literature include: (a) the processes of change construct has frequently not been included within a project; (b) self-efficacy, decisional balance and processes of change have been analyzed separately, meaning that relationships between them have not been examined; and (c) there are measurement issues with some of the constructs (e.g., stages of change, processes of change, and physical activity).

A natural history model

The natural history model of exercise (NHM; Sallis & Hovell, 1990) emerged out of a review of the determinants of exercise behavior. It is a process model that suggests three transition phases in exercise behavior: sedentary behavior to exercise adoption, exercise adoption to maintenance or drop-out, and drop-out to resumption of exercise. Most research on determinants has focused on exercise maintenance and dropout (see Topic I1) and little is known about the other phases, particularly the determinants of the resumption of exercise. Although it is expected that self-efficacy will be a strong influence at all phases, it is likely that the other determinants will be different for each phase.

Some limitations of the model include: (a) it assumes that exercise is a dichotomous rather than a continuous variable, but what defines an exerciser or a sedentary person is unclear; and (b) the model was designed for structured exercise and is therefore unlikely to be suitable for children whose activity tends to be unstructured and sporadic.

A lifespan interaction model

The lifespan interaction model (LIM; Dishman & Dunn, 1988, Dishman, 1990) provides a global overview of exercise behaviors across the lifespan. It provides a framework for understanding the complex, multifactorial nature of physical activity. It explains exercise behavior as the interrelationship between determinants, the activity itself, and characteristics of different population groups. Three broad categories of determinants are proposed: psychological, biobehavioral and social environmental. Characteristics of physical activity include such things as phase of involvement, type, frequency and intensity of activity and activity settings. The population subgroups highlight population groups that may have special characteristics that influence other factors in the model. The LIM rightly portrays exercise behavior as a complex phenomenon but the extent to which we can test such a complex model is debatable. Its strength lies in highlighting this complexity and warning against over-simplistic explanations of exercise behavior.

J3 ECOLOGICAL MODELS

Key Notes

Ecological models	These focus on people's interactions and relationships with their physical and social environment. Central to ecological models is the influence the physical environment has on behavior. Behavior is proposed to be influenced at five levels: intrapersonal, interpersonal, institutional, community and public policy.
Ecological models and exercise behavior	There are few studies that have examined the influence of the physical environment on physical activity behavior. Accessibility, opportunities and esthetics have a positive influence on physical activity. The research is limited by measurement difficulties, agglomeration of variables and a reliance on cross-sectional designs. Interventions based on environmental changes have shown some promise.
Related topics	Cognitive-behavioral theories (J1) Process models of exercise (J2)

Ecological models   Most theories employed within the exercise domain are focused on individually oriented psychological and social variables. These theories have been useful in identifying some of the factors that influence exercise behavior but have been able to explain only a small percentage of the variance in behavior. Ecological models, while not discounting psychological and social variables, move beyond these theories to explicitly suggest that multiple aspects of policy and the physical environment may influence exercise behavior. For example, the stairwells in many buildings are hard to find, poorly lit and sometimes locked, thus negating against stair use, while elevators and escalators are nicely lit and central to the building.

In biology, ecology is the study of the interrelations between organisms and their environments (Stokols, 1992). An ecological perspective in the behavioral sciences focuses on people's interactions and relationships with their physical and social environment (Sallis & Owen, 2002). The ecological approach essentially provides a framework for explaining behavior, rather than a series of specific constructs or variables. Other theories and models that have been used in the exercise domain (see Topics J1 & J2) can be incorporated within an ecological perspective as they may reflect intrapersonal and interpersonal influences on exercise behavior.

Ecological approaches to physical activity aim to provide an integrated account of the complex array of possible intrapersonal, interpersonal, cultural and physical environment determinants (see Topic I1). Central to ecological approaches is the influence the physical environment may have in behavior, giving rise to the notion of a 'behavior setting'. Behavior settings are the physical and social context in which behavior occurs. Some settings promote physical activity (e.g., parks, health clubs) and others discourage or prohibit physical activity (e.g., classrooms, offices). The influence of the physical environment may be passive through the design of the urban environment and buildings which influence incidental exercise, or active through the provision of opportunities to be active in accessible, safe, convenient and appealing environments.

Unique to ecological models is recognition of the multiple levels of influence on behavior. For example, McLeroy et al. (1998) suggested that behavior is influenced at five levels:

(1) Intrapersonal (e.g., psychological and biological variables and developmental history);
(2) Interpersonal (e.g., family, peers, and coworkers);
(3) Institutional (e.g., schools and worksites);
(4) Community (e.g., relationships between organizations and institutions within a local area); and
(5) Public policy (e.g., laws and policies of local and national governments).

Within ecological models it is suggested that these levels of influence are interdependent and therefore influence each other. Because of this multiple-level perspective ecologic approaches to behavior are inherently complex.

Ecological models and exercise behavior There are not many studies that examine the environmental influences on physical activity behavior. Accessibility of facilities, opportunities for activity, and the esthetic attributes of the environment have been shown to have significant positive associations with physical activity. Weather and perceived safety of the environment were found to be unassociated with physical activity. This research is limited by difficulties and inconsistencies in the measurement of environmental variables, the agglomeration of several variables into a single overall 'environmental' measure which may obscure important relationships, the use of different physical activity outcome variables and measures, and a reliance on cross-sectional correlational research.

Interventions based on environmental changes have shown some promise. Changing physical education programs consistently increases physical activity, at least during classes. Placing signs encouraging stair use over escalator use has been shown to increase stair use during the time the signs are up. Larger more complex interventions have shown that environmental and policy changes can result in increases in physical activity but these changes tend to be small and slow to occur. Methodological problems with these larger studies mean the results should be treated with caution.

Sallis and Owen (2002) identified several areas for future research including:

● continuing to identify environmental and policy correlates of physical activity behavior;
● development and refinement of measures to monitor changes in activity-related environmental and policy variables;
● conducting multi-level interventions based on critical intrapersonal, socio-cultural and environmental policy correlates. A high priority within this work will be to test the hypothesis that such multi-level interventions are more effective than single-level interventions.

Although the evidence base for the application of ecological models to physical activity is incomplete, Sallis and Owen believe it would be shortsighted not to encourage the development of health-promoting environments in the meantime.

K1 CONSULTANCY: BASIC ISSUES

Key Notes

The roles of the applied sport and exercise psychologist	In addition to being agents for change, applied sport and exercise psychologists may function as experts, counselors, detectives, toolmakers, colleagues, peacekeepers, sounding boards and teachers. Consultancy work falls into two major categories: educational and clinical. By far the larger of these is the educational one, which refers to all the ways in which psychologists help to educate and train sports participants. The clinical sport and exercise psychologist helps with the problems of the more troubled participant.
Consultancy styles	Consultancy styles can be characterized as falling on a continuum from directive, at one end, to shared problem solving at the other. One scheme suggests that there are four styles (tell, sell, ask, join) on a continuum. At one extreme there is the consultant who 'tells'. They take the expert role and assume they know what is best for the athlete. At the other end of the continuum is the 'join' style, the consultant and client engage in joint problem solving.
Ethical issues	The key ethical principles for a sport and exercise psychologist are that they should: deal with others with integrity and respect for their rights and dignity; be competent in what they do; obtain informed consent to carry out whatever intervention they intend to employ; maintain client confidentiality; maintain high standards of personal and professional conduct.

Related topics	Counseling skills (K5)	Issues of arousal and anxiety (L2)
	The consultancy process (K6)	Issues of concentration (L3)
	Issues of motivation (L1)	Issues of confidence (L4)

The roles of the applied sport and exercise psychologist

The previous Topics have focused on **basic** or **pure** sport and exercise psychology. The concern was to explain the why and how of psychology in exercise and sport. In contrast Topics K, L and M focus on the application of psychology to sport and exercise situations. So, for example, where earlier material concerned itself with the relationship between anxiety and performance, these sections describe what sport and exercise psychologists have done to help athletes to do what they do better; with more commitment and enjoyment; with less injury; or for better health outcomes. Applied psychologists carry out many different roles. In addition to being agents for change, they may function as experts, counselors, detectives, toolmakers, colleagues, peacekeepers, sounding boards and teachers. Within sport and exercise psychology, consultancy work falls into two major categories: **educational** and **clinical** (see *Fig. 1*). By far the larger of these is the educational one. Actually, the term educational is a little confusing, since educational psychology is generally thought of as a branch of developmental psychology that is concerned with factors affecting teaching and learning. However, the term has been used by sport and exercise psychologists to refer to all the ways in which they help to educate and

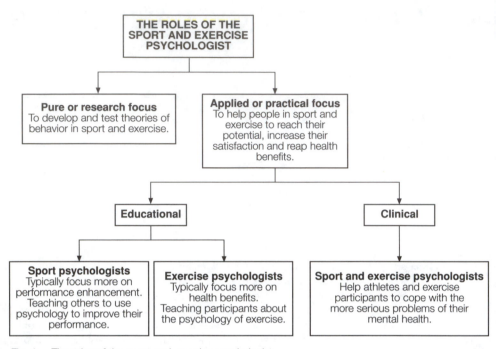

Fig. 1. The roles of the sport and exercise psychologist.

train athletes. **Applied sport psychologists** tend to focus on issues of **performance enhancement**. As the name suggests, performance enhancement in sport psychology involves strengthening athletes mentally, and helping them to overcome psychological barriers to optimal performance. However, before embarking along the enhancement route, we should satisfy ourselves that a psychological intervention is appropriate. Often, poor performance is more to do with lack of physiological fitness, or weak technique, than something psychological. In sport psychology, performance enhancement usually includes psychological skills training (PST) or mental skills training (MST), which refer to the implementation of an intervention that will include a commonly used set of techniques that are designed to help athletes to reach their potential. These techniques include, among other things: imagery use, attentional control, confidence building, anxiety control, relaxation and goal setting. While the list of such techniques is long, in practice most of the psychological factors that impact on individual performance can be described under the four main headings of motivational issues, issues of arousal and anxiety, concentration issues and confidence issues. The way that sport psychologists have tackled each of these will be outlined in Topic L.

From reading the literature on applied sport psychology, it would be easy to get the impression that the bulk of the psychologist's role is in delivering psychological/mental skills training. However, this would be inaccurate since it involves many more activities than this. For example, psychologists can help with issues such as lifestyle habits for health and fitness, working with injured athletes to increase adherence to rehabilitation programs, and to help athletes through this difficult time. The consultant sport psychologist might also get involved at the team level, by helping to increase cohesiveness through team building, or in relation to issues of leadership. Sometimes the role involves spending time in what might seem like fairly mundane activities, like just talking and hanging around. It is surprising how often well-known sport psychologists recount their experiences of carrying bags and fetching water. However, none of this is actually 'down' time. It all helps to create rapport, to be seen as 'one of the gang', to avoid being the 'boffin' with the clipboard, or the academic in the office. Sometimes the psychologist's contribution is to help athletes to deal with the routine problems of day-to-day living, and relationships with others. For those with the relevant knowledge, it may involve wider issues like helping sporting organizations think about effective communications or organizational change.

Another area of work often carried out is in coach education about psychological issues. It is not always possible for the psychologist to be with the team, and it may be that the coach can provide some psychological support if appropriately trained. This is actually a very useful way to get psychology into the sporting arena, and there are many benefits from having the coach and psychologist working together. Thus, mental skills training is one, but by no means the only, thing that the sport psychologist can offer. The sport psychologist should stress to clients that in sport psychology, there are no 'magic bullets', and that they should not expect instant results from interventions. Just as physical skills do not suddenly appear fully developed in players, the attainment of mental skills and mental toughness requires effort, commitment and practice.

The focus of the **applied exercise psychologist** has little to do with performance enhancement and is much more concerned with the health benefits of physical activity and a healthy lifestyle. This involves educating participants about the psychology of exercise, including issues such as the mental and physical benefits of exercise and problems of adherence to exercise programs. Exercise psychologists also have a role to play in applying theories of exercise behavior by helping with the implementation of schemes to increase people's motivation to begin exercising and having started, to persevere with it.

In relation to the **clinical** sport and exercise psychologist, this refers to the kind of work that is carried out by qualified clinical psychologists who attempt to deal with the problems of the more troubled athlete or exercise participant. After all, athletes and exercisers are people, and a small proportion of them will inevitably suffer from depression, schizophrenia, drug addiction and so on. Additionally, for some athletes at the top of their profession, fame and wealth can lead to extra psychological pressures that can result in a descent into deep psychological problems. Equally, for some, the very activity of exercising can bring with it the dangers of exercise addiction. Fortunately, this clinical role constitutes only a small proportion of sport and exercise consultancy work.

As we can see, the roles of the applied sport psychologist are varied and some aspects of the work are more appropriately dealt with by specially qualified clinical practitioners. It is important for professional and ethical reasons that we know our limitations and refer people on when these are reached.

Consultancy styles

Consultancy styles can be characterized as falling on a continuum from directive, at one end, to shared problem solving at the other. One scheme suggests that there are four styles (**tell, sell, ask, join**) on a continuum. At one extreme there is the consultant who 'tells'. They take the expert role and assume they know what is best for the athlete. This is a bit like the old medical model of helping where the doctor prescribes, and the patient is subservient and does what the doctor orders. In this approach, the power is firmly in the hands of the consultant. It has the merit of simplicity for the athlete, as they simply have to do what they are told, however, it is problematic in that it is likely to produce less commitment and ownership of the solution by the athlete. A slightly less directive approach is the **sell** style, where the consultant attempts to persuade and convince the athlete that what they are suggesting is best. Again, power is mostly in the hands of the consultant, but perhaps the athlete, having agreed, will be slightly more committed to trying the technique than with a telling consultancy style. A further move along the continuum takes us to the **ask** approach. Here the consultant not only gives their ideas but asks clients for theirs. However, having heard the athlete's ideas, the consultant still decides what is best for the athlete. The final style moves furthest away from the conventional medical approach, treating the client as an equal with valuable insights and wisdom. In the **join** style the consultant and client engage in **joint problem solving,** in a situation of mutual respect. One advantage of this approach is that it is likely to mean that the client is much more committed, and has more ownership of any agreed solution. Another advantage is that it is more likely to lead to better understanding of the finer points of the problem. After all, while the sport and exercise psychologist is more expert in relation to techniques than the athlete, the athlete is the world authority on their own problem, and often has better sport-specific knowledge than the sport psychologist.

It is fair to say that these days, the favored style of most consultants is at, or toward, the joint problem-solving end of the continuum, and there is empirical evidence that this approach is more successful, and is certainly preferred by athletes (Hardy & Parfitt, 1994). Having said this, there will be times when the consultant feels strongly enough to insist on simply telling an athlete what they think needs to be done. In other words, in practice some practitioners may well employ aspects of other styles.

The tell and the sell approaches have some advantages for the consultant, who retains power, status and perhaps the credit for the success of any intervention. In contrast, the consultant who employs the joining style may find they do not always get the credit for any successes. However, some see it as a sign of success if the athlete feels that they solved their own problem, signaling a positive movement in the athlete, from dependence to independence. Indeed some see the ideal consultancy as one which leads to the consultant's ultimate redundancy.

Ethical issues   Anyone who engages in consultancy work needs to operate in an ethical way. Guidelines on what this means for sport and exercise psychologists are available from a variety of sources. For example, the American Psychological Association and the American Association for the Advancement of Sport Psychology, the British Psychological Society and the British Association of Sport and Exercise Sciences, all have extensive and clearly stated codes of practice. The central issues of these guidelines are, not surprisingly, very similar and include the need to:

1. deal with others **with integrity and respect for their rights and dignity;**
2. be **competent** in what you do, ensuring that you do not overstep your ability or operate outside your knowledge base;
3. obtain **informed consent** to carry out whatever intervention you intend to employ;
4. maintain client **confidentiality;**
5. maintain high standards of **personal and professional conduct**.

K2 LISTENING SKILLS

Key Notes

Myths about listening

One common mistake people make is to think that listening is not very important, yet it constitutes about 40% of communication time. Another false assumption about listening is that it operates like a light switch. The final mistaken belief about listening is that it is something that people are either good or bad at. Listening is a skill that can be practiced and improved.

Benefits of active listening

Effective listening allows us to gather more accurate information, and consequently, to have better relationships with others. It helps us to avoid jumping to conclusions. It can raise the self-esteem of the speaker. It can be cathartic. Finally, it stops us from falling into the trap of talking too much.

Guidelines for effective listening

Effective listening requires us to minimize distractions and position ourselves so that we can attend. We should avoid hurried evaluations and remember that the content of the message is the focus of our interest, rather than the person sending it. We should select central ideas in what the speaker is saying. We also need to be aware of the emotional content in what is being said, as well as the bare facts. Finally, we should clarify any things in what we heard, that were not perfectly clear to us.

Related topics

Questioning (K3)	Counseling skills (K5)
Giving feedback (K4)	The consultancy process (K6)

Myths about listening

In addition to having skills and knowledge in relation to the area of sport and exercise psychology, the consultant must have social or interpersonal skills to be able to interact effectively with others. In particular, it is important to be able to communicate effectively with athletes, coaches and managers and, where necessary, to employ basic counseling skills. One important basic communication and counseling skill is listening. Several myths surround this skill. One common mistake people make is to think that listening is not very important or even worthy of attention at all. However, studies have shown that listening constitutes about 40% of our communication time. Another false assumption about listening is that it operates like a light switch, and that people are either listening or not. In fact, listening can be carried out at various different levels of effort. At one extreme, shallow or passive listening is typified by little effort, emotional detachment, and failure to analyze the meanings of what is said. On the other hand, **active listening** involves a conscious effort to see the other person's point of view (take the role of the other). Active listening involves avoiding distractions, paying attention to the other person's words and non-verbal behavior, and being empathetic, so that feelings as well as thoughts are detected.

The final mistaken belief about listening is that it is something that people are either good or bad at. In fact, listening is a skill and as such it can be practiced, and thereby improved.

Benefits of active listening

The value of effective listening is clear and includes the following benefits:

- We will gather more information, and the information we gather will be more accurate.
- We are likely to have better relationships with others: athletes, coaches and colleagues, who are more likely to feel we have their concerns at heart.
- It gives people a chance to talk about issues, which can have a cathartic effect, i.e. people can benefit from simply being listened to, and given the opportunity to talk through their problems. Sometimes people need the chance to get things out of their system, and to blow off steam, even if no solution is possible.
- It helps us to avoid jumping to conclusions based on insufficient evidence because we wait until we have heard the whole story.
- It can raise the self-esteem of the other person, because it makes them feel that we think they are worth listening to.
- By remembering to actively listen, we stop ourselves from falling into the trap of hogging the conversation and talking for the sake of hearing our own voice! Anytime we are talking, we are missing the chance to gather information and extensive information gathering is especially important in any counseling or problem-solving situation.

Guidelines for effective listening

There are some simple rules we can follow to increase our ability to listen.

(1) Minimize distractions. Some distractions are obvious ones like noise, telephone interruptions, other people's activities, etc. However, remember to avoid the less obvious distractions that arise from within yourself, such as allowing your attention to wander. The reason that attention can wander is that people talk at a rate of about 125 words/minute, whereas we can listen and deal with approximately 600 words/minute. The listener who fails to concentrate on listening tends to fill the extra capacity with non-relevant cognitions.

(2) Position yourself so that you can attend and be seen to be attending. Talking to someone who looks as if they are disinterested in what we have to say is not very rewarding, and can lead us to stop trying to explain our situation. It is important to look at the other person, and let them see that you are listening.

(3) Avoid hurried evaluations of what you hear. Before you jump in with what *you* think of the situation, wait until the speaker has finished and you have gathered as much information as possible. Only then should you consider offering your view.

(4) Remember that the content of the message is the focus of your interest, rather than the person sending it. A common error is to judge someone unfavorably early on in a conversation, and then only half listen to what they have to say.

(5) Select central ideas. Listening can be made more effective if central ideas can be selected from the mass of what the speaker is saying. In this way, the important themes can be concentrated on, and the peripheral issues can be avoided.

(6) Be aware of the emotional content. Good listening involves an awareness of the emotional content of what is being said, as well as the bare facts. Often, the way people feel is evident in their tone of voice, or facial expressions. Good listeners are alert to these cues.

(7) Clarify any doubts. Good listening involves clarifying things in what you heard, that were not perfectly clear to you. The cost of checking is cheap. The cost of misunderstanding could be extremely high.

K3 QUESTIONING

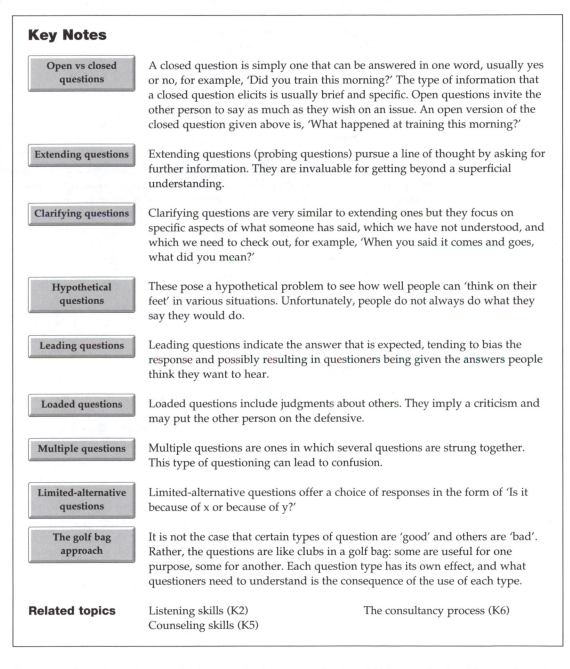

Key Notes

Open vs closed questions	A closed question is simply one that can be answered in one word, usually yes or no, for example, 'Did you train this morning?' The type of information that a closed question elicits is usually brief and specific. Open questions invite the other person to say as much as they wish on an issue. An open version of the closed question given above is, 'What happened at training this morning?'
Extending questions	Extending questions (probing questions) pursue a line of thought by asking for further information. They are invaluable for getting beyond a superficial understanding.
Clarifying questions	Clarifying questions are very similar to extending ones but they focus on specific aspects of what someone has said, which we have not understood, and which we need to check out, for example, 'When you said it comes and goes, what did you mean?'
Hypothetical questions	These pose a hypothetical problem to see how well people can 'think on their feet' in various situations. Unfortunately, people do not always do what they say they would do.
Leading questions	Leading questions indicate the answer that is expected, tending to bias the response and possibly resulting in questioners being given the answers people think they want to hear.
Loaded questions	Loaded questions include judgments about others. They imply a criticism and may put the other person on the defensive.
Multiple questions	Multiple questions are ones in which several questions are strung together. This type of questioning can lead to confusion.
Limited-alternative questions	Limited-alternative questions offer a choice of responses in the form of 'Is it because of x or because of y?'
The golf bag approach	It is not the case that certain types of question are 'good' and others are 'bad'. Rather, the questions are like clubs in a golf bag: some are useful for one purpose, some for another. Each question type has its own effect, and what questioners need to understand is the consequence of the use of each type.

Related topics   Listening skills (K2)   The consultancy process (K6)
Counseling skills (K5)

Open vs closed questions   A second important basic communication skill is questioning. Two main points need to be remembered in relation to this skill. First, there are several different question types and second, the question type used affects the kind of information elicited. Given the above, it is helpful to think of each question type as a different tool from a toolkit, or to use a sporting analogy, you could think of each question type as a different club in a golf bag. Just as the skilled golfer knows which club is best for each situation, so the skilled questioner knows which question type is most likely to elicit the type of information required.

Firstly, questions can be either open or closed. A closed question is simply one that can be answered in one word, usually yes or no. For example, 'Did you win?', 'Did you train this morning?', 'Has the pain returned?', 'Have you done any goal-setting today'?

The type of information that a closed question elicits is usually brief and specific. If all you need is a brief and specific answer, then this is the question type to use. Another feature of the closed question is that it is often easy to answer, and as such is useful at the beginning of a consultation, interview or conversation when the other person may need to be put at their ease.

Interviews can be thought of as 'conversations with a purpose'. It is sometimes claimed that closed questions are bad, and open questions are good, but our approach is to argue that when straight answers are needed, the closed question is the one to use. Another function of closed questioning is that it allows the questioner to be in control. Of course, if the aim of your conversation is to get lots of information, as it often is, then the closed question, unlike the open question will tend to be the less-effective tool. Asking too many closed questions in a row leads to a stilted conversation. This is quite a common problem for people who are inexperienced at interviewing or consulting with athletes.

Open questions invite the other person to say as much as they wish on an issue. This type of question allows them to focus on the things that they see as important. Open versions of the closed questions given above are, 'How did the game go?', 'What happened at training this morning?', 'Tell me about the pain?', 'How is the goal-setting working out?'

Extending questions

Extending questions (sometimes referred to as probing questions) pursue a line of thought by asking for further information, when you want to explore further in an area that has been raised, but not fully discussed. For example, 'You mentioned problems with the pre-shot routine. Could you tell me a little more about that?' This type of question is invaluable for getting beyond a superficial understanding, to a much broader and deeper one.

Clarifying questions

Clarifying questions are very similar to extending ones in that they also help us to arrive at a better, and more detailed understanding, of whatever is being discussed. They only differ from extending questions in that they focus on specific aspects of what someone has said, which we have not understood, and which we need to check out. For example, 'When you said it comes and goes, what did you mean?' or, 'I am not quite sure I understand you. Would you go over that again?' It seems obvious that it is important to be clear about the things people have already said, before moving on to other issues. Unfortunately, the evidence suggests that this is not always done. Again, clarifying questions are invaluable when detailed information is needed, but they are not too useful when we need to be brief and to the point. In much of the work of the sport and exercise psychologist the above questions are the tools to use.

The following questions fall into the less useful category for most consultancy work and it could be argued they are to be avoided. We simply suggest that they have uses but perhaps not for most sport and exercise consultancy situations.

Hypothetical questions

Hypothetical questions pose a hypothetical problem or situation, for example, 'What would you do if you were giving a talk and some players didn't listen?' This is a favorite of interview panel members. The claim is that the advantage of this question type is that it lets us discover how people 'think on their feet'. However, if you want to know how good a thinker someone is, you can use less subjective methods, such as reasoning tests. The problem with hypothetical questions is that what people say they would do, and what they would actually do, are not always the same.

Leading questions

Leading questions, as the name suggests, indicate the answer that is expected, and therefore tend to bias the response, for example, 'I assume that you think you should train twice as hard?' The problem here is that you are likely to be given the answers you want to hear, in which case you might as well question yourself! This might be acceptable if your purpose is interrogation, but is not likely to be as useful a strategy for sport and exercise psychologists.

Loaded questions

Loaded questions include judgments about others. They imply a criticism and may put the other person on the defensive, so that they cease to be as helpful as they might otherwise have been. For example, 'Why on earth did you stop following the mental skills training plan?' Again, the likelihood is that you would not find this form of question particularly useful in the sport and exercise psychology context. There may just be times however, when the coach or psychologist might want to achieve the goal of criticizing someone or letting them know they are unhappy with them, as well as finding out the answer to the question. However, this runs the risk of seeming to treat the athlete like a child.

Multiple questions

Multiple questions are ones in which several questions are strung together, for example, 'Are the problems different in competition, and do you like it any better?' This type of questioning can lead to confusion, and typically results in no answer, or an answer to one but not both parts of the question. The respondent who wants to avoid awkward questions (a politician perhaps?) will latch on to the least incriminating question, with relief. If your purpose is to confuse, you may want to use this approach, however, as with hypothetical, leading and loaded questions, multiple questions are not likely to be particularly useful in the consultancy context.

Limited-alternative questions

Limited-alternative questions offer a choice of responses in the form 'Is it because of x or because of y?' or 'What do you think is best a, b, c or d?' There are two problems here. First, a list of alternatives may be forgotten by the time the respondent begins to answer. Second, the actual answer may not be on your list, but for simplicity the respondent just gives you one of the alternatives you offer. Again, if forcing people into your categories is what you want to achieve, then this might be the question type to use.

The golf bag approach

The position we have taken is to stress that it is not the case that certain types of question are 'good' and others are 'bad'. Rather, the questions are like clubs in a golf bag: some are useful for one purpose, some for another (see *Fig. 1*). Each question type has its own effect, and what questioners need to understand is the consequence of the use of each type. Questioners need to ask themselves whether they want lots of information, or a few simple facts; whether they want to judge the respondent's intellect, scare them, trick them or probe deeper to understand what they really mean, and so on. Having said this, for those of us working in sport and exercise psychology, open, extending and clarifying questions will probably be more useful. Hypothetical, leading and loaded questions are likely to be less useful, and multiple and limited alternative questions are probably best avoided.

One final piece of advice we would offer is to not be afraid of the silences that might follow one of your questions. Although the silence may seem to last an eternity to you, short silences are not seen that way by the client who is busy thinking about how to answer. Avoid jumping in with a possible answer for the client or even with a second question. You will be surprised how much information will follow from allowing the client an opportunity to reflect.

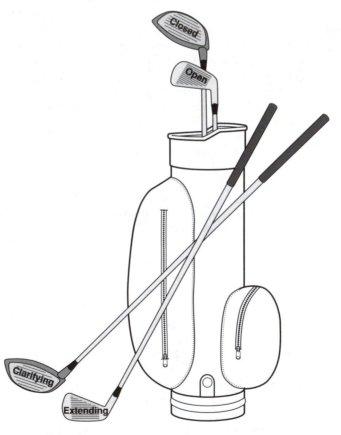

Fig. 1.   The golf bag approach to question types.

K4   GIVING FEEDBACK

Key Notes

Making feedback understandable	The single most common error made in giving feedback is failure to be specific. 'You are lazy' is not as informative as 'When the rest of the squad did extra sprints and then went to the weights room before lunch, you went back to your room'. Feedback may not be understood is if it contains too much information. The person giving the feedback should check that it has been understood.
Making feedback acceptable	To make feedback more acceptable, we can ask the other person if they want feedback. Secondly, feedback that describes rather than judges is likely to be more acceptable. Thirdly, feedback which is clear but offered in a non-strident manner is likely to be more acceptable. Fourthly, the amount of feedback should not be such that it overloads the receiver, especially if it is negative feedback. Timing can affect the acceptability of a piece of feedback.
Making feedback actionable	Feedback should be about something that the other person can act upon, otherwise there is little point in giving it. For example, to tell someone 'the problem with you is you are not tall enough' is not worth doing.
Related topics	Listening skills (K2) Counseling skills (K5) Questioning (K3) The consultancy process (K6)

Making feedback understandable

An absolutely crucial communication skill for any consultant is the ability to give others effective feedback. The main purpose of giving feedback is to help them to change their behavior. Achieving this can be done if we remember three main considerations:

(1) Can the receiver **understand** the feedback?
(2) Can the receiver **accept** the feedback?
(3) Can the receiver **act upon** the feedback?

In terms of making feedback understandable, the following needs to be borne in mind.

Probably the single most common error made in giving feedback is failure to be specific. A general comment is not enough to lead to understanding, e.g. 'You are lazy' is not as informative as 'When the rest of the squad did extra sprints and then went to the weights room before lunch, you went back to your room'.

A second reason why feedback may not be understood is if it contains too much information. This can overwhelm the receiver, both cognitively and emotionally, resulting in lack of understanding and resistance in terms of accepting what is said. In this case the receiver is likely to think 'I can't have been that bad, this person is too picky! I'll just ignore what they're saying'.

Since misunderstandings are very common in communicating with others, the person giving the feedback should check that it has been understood.

Making feedback acceptable

A major consideration in terms of giving feedback is its acceptability to the receiver. We may understand what has been said, but be emotionally resistant to it, or the way it has been said. To make feedback more acceptable, we can take the following steps. Firstly, we can ask the other person if they want feedback. A receiver is more likely to accept information that he or she has requested.

Secondly, feedback that describes rather than judges is likely to be more acceptable. By describing behavior and the effect of the behavior, rather than evaluating it, we are less likely to put others on the defensive. 'In team talks you're a loud-mouth' is less acceptable than 'You spoke much more than the rest of the team and I didn't get a chance to say what I wanted to'.

Thirdly, feedback which is clear but offered in a non-strident, tentative manner, and is open for discussion with the receiver, is likely to be more acceptable than that which is stated as hard fact and non-negotiable. You might begin with phrases such as 'I got the impression that....' or 'It seemed to me that....'.

Fourthly, the amount of feedback should not be such that it overloads the receiver, especially if it is negative feedback. If there are many problems with another person's behavior which require feedback, it is probably better to concentrate on one or two of the more important points, leaving others for another time.

Timing can affect the acceptability of a piece of feedback. Normally, feedback should be given as soon as possible after the behavior in question. Feedback that comes a long time after the actual event may well be seen by the receiver as unimportant, or they may react by thinking, why did you not tell me weeks ago when it happened! Although, in general, feedback is better soon after the event, there are circumstances when feedback may need to be delayed. One such occasion is when the receiver is too emotional to accept the feedback, e.g. when angry. Another occasion when feedback is best delayed is when there are others present. If we have hard things to say to an individual, we should be sensitive to the issue of privacy.

Finally, it is important to remember that feedback is designed to help others to change their behavior. As such, we should avoid the temptation to use a feedback session to 'let off steam by having a go at others', just to make ourselves feel better.

Making feedback actionable

Another major consideration for providing effective feedback is that it should be about something that the other person can act upon, otherwise there is little point in giving feedback. For example, to tell someone 'the problem with you is you are not tall enough' is not worth doing, unless you are suggesting they play a different sport or a different position. This consideration may extend to aspects of personality, which are notoriously difficult to change. For example, feedback to a very shy person such as 'you need to be more of an extrovert to make it in this team' may be difficult for them to act upon.

K5 COUNSELING SKILLS

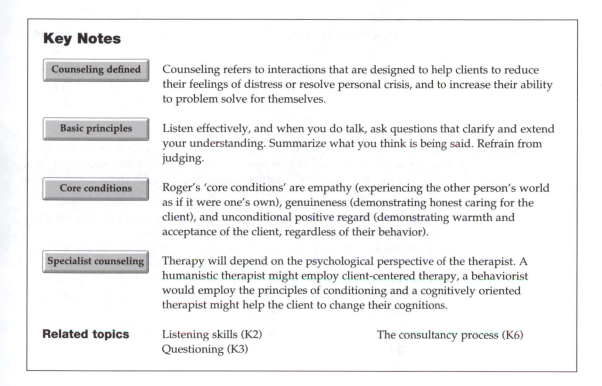

Key Notes

Counseling defined	Counseling refers to interactions that are designed to help clients to reduce their feelings of distress or resolve personal crisis, and to increase their ability to problem solve for themselves.
Basic principles	Listen effectively, and when you do talk, ask questions that clarify and extend your understanding. Summarize what you think is being said. Refrain from judging.
Core conditions	Roger's 'core conditions' are empathy (experiencing the other person's world as if it were one's own), genuineness (demonstrating honest caring for the client), and unconditional positive regard (demonstrating warmth and acceptance of the client, regardless of their behavior).
Specialist counseling	Therapy will depend on the psychological perspective of the therapist. A humanistic therapist might employ client-centered therapy, a behaviorist would employ the principles of conditioning and a cognitively oriented therapist might help the client to change their cognitions.

Related topics	Listening skills (K2)	The consultancy process (K6)
	Questioning (K3)	

Counseling defined

Some people might argue that any time a sport or exercise psychologist sits down to talk about helping an athlete or coach, in some way they are doing some counseling. We take the view, shared by for example the British Psychological Society, that counseling is a very specific term, and that it refers to 'interactions that are designed firstly, to help clients to reduce their feelings of **distress** or resolve **personal crisis**, and secondly, to increase their ability to problem solve for themselves'.

Sometimes sport psychologists are faced with situations where athletes have personal problems that require specialist counseling and/or clinical expertise. While some sport and exercise psychologists have such expertise, most do not and should refer clients on to those who do. Counseling is a highly skilled activity that should be carried out by people with extensive counseling training. Having said this, it is important that all sport and exercise psychologists have some awareness of the principles of good counseling practice, and a reasonable level of counseling skill available to them in their day-to-day interactions with clients, and for those difficult times when they might be faced with the initial need to 'fire-fight' when athletes first present with deeper personal problems.

Basic principles

In the event of such an occurrence it is useful to bear in mind a few basic counseling guidelines.

- The most important thing to do is to listen, and listen effectively, employing all the listening skills described in Topic K2.
- When you do talk, ask questions that clarify and extend your understanding (Topic K3). Remember to summarize with the athlete, what you think they are saying.
- Refrain from judging or evaluating the athlete, or their behavior.
- Avoid jumping to a solution for the problem, by giving advice, or by telling them what they 'should do'.

While all this may seem like stating the obvious, it is remarkable how often people fall into the trap of telling rather than listening, judging rather than being neutral, and suggesting what should be done to address the problem, none of which are helpful in such situations.

Core conditions   The strategy described above is often known as the client-centered approach, which was pioneered by the humanistic psychologist Carl Rogers (Rogers, 1951). Rogers suggested that effective counseling requires the following 'core conditions'.

- **Empathy**, described as the ability to experience **the other person's world** as if it were one's own, without ever losing that 'as if' quality.
- **Genuineness (or congruence)**, which refers to the ability to demonstrate **caring for the client, without playing a role** or being false.
- **Unconditional positive regard**, which refers to the ability to demonstrate **warmth** and **acceptance** of the client, which is not contingent upon their behavior, and is therefore non-judgmental.

Having dealt with the initial emotional state of the client, the consultant must decide whether the problem is one that they are competent to help with, or one that must be referred on to a specialist for some form of psychotherapy.

Specialist counseling   The form of any further treatment by a trained therapist would depend on the psychological perspective favored by that therapist. For example, a humanistic therapist might persist with Rogerian, client-centered therapy, as described above, whereas a therapist with behaviorist sympathies would employ the principles of conditioning in their treatments. In contrast, the cognitively oriented therapist might use cognitive behavioral therapy (CBT), or rational emotive therapy (RET), both of which involve getting the client to change their cognitions, i.e. see the world differently (Sherman, & Poczwardowski, 2000). For example, one approach to CBT is to help people to realize that they are susceptible to three basic errors of information processing.

- Catastrophizing: For example, taking the view that because you missed a penalty, that means you are a worthless person.
- Selective abstraction: For example, believing you played terribly because you dropped a catch, ignoring the fact that you bowled magnificently.
- Overgeneralization: For example, thinking 'I missed the tackle so I won't ever score again'.

K6 THE CONSULTANCY PROCESS

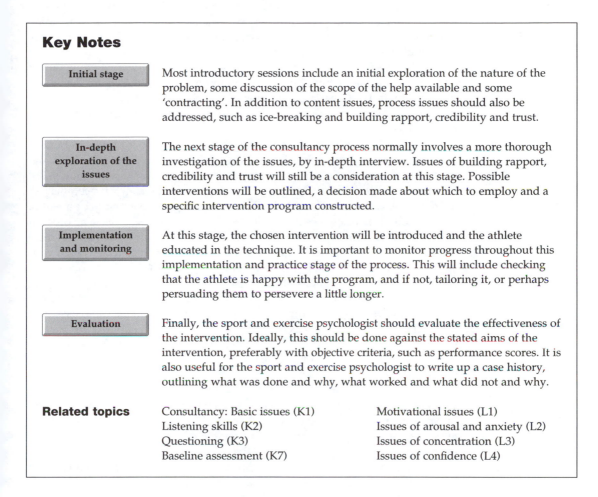

Key Notes

Initial stage

Most introductory sessions include an initial exploration of the nature of the problem, some discussion of the scope of the help available and some 'contracting'. In addition to content issues, process issues should also be addressed, such as ice-breaking and building rapport, credibility and trust.

In-depth exploration of the issues

The next stage of the consultancy process normally involves a more thorough investigation of the issues, by in-depth interview. Issues of building rapport, credibility and trust will still be a consideration at this stage. Possible interventions will be outlined, a decision made about which to employ and a specific intervention program constructed.

Implementation and monitoring

At this stage, the chosen intervention will be introduced and the athlete educated in the technique. It is important to monitor progress throughout this implementation and practice stage of the process. This will include checking that the athlete is happy with the program, and if not, tailoring it, or perhaps persuading them to persevere a little longer.

Evaluation

Finally, the sport and exercise psychologist should evaluate the effectiveness of the intervention. Ideally, this should be done against the stated aims of the intervention, preferably with objective criteria, such as performance scores. It is also useful for the sport and exercise psychologist to write up a case history, outlining what was done and why, what worked and what did not and why.

Related topics

Consultancy: Basic issues (K1)	Motivational issues (L1)
Listening skills (K2)	Issues of arousal and anxiety (L2)
Questioning (K3)	Issues of concentration (L3)
Baseline assessment (K7)	Issues of confidence (L4)

Initial stage

Although there are many different ways to carry out consultancy work in sport and exercise psychology, there are some fairly common stages that most consultancy activity involves (Poczwardowski et al., 1998). These will be outlined now with the emphasis, for the purpose of illustration, on how a sport psychologist might operate, however, the same stages and many of the issues are equally relevant to the work of the exercise psychologist. In any case, none of the following should be taken as the only way to do things. Circumstances will dictate what is or is not appropriate. What is offered here is meant to provide a general guide.

One of the first things that needs to be clarified in consultancy is the issue of who the client is. The answer to this might seem obvious, and it is in most cases, however, there are times when it is not, and the unresolved ambiguity can lead to ethical problems. For example, if a team manager employs you to help a player, do your allegiances lie with the player, the manager or the club?

Is the manager or club entitled to know what was said to you in confidence by the player? Ethical guidelines suggest you should not divulge confidential material. You should, therefore, make it clear right from the outset, that although the player is not paying the bill, you consider the player to be your client and as such you will not divulge any confidential information to others.

In consultancy work, most introductory sessions include an initial exploration of the nature of the problem, some discussion of the scope of the help available and some '**contracting**'. Contracting involves generally agreeing about what is expected of each party, in terms of what you, the consultant, can and cannot offer, and what you require by way of commitment from the client. For example, you might try to get a commitment from them that they will complete a reflective log or a diary, recording their efforts, successes, failures, feelings and performance?

In addition to such **content issues**, the consultant would typically attempt to deal with **process issues**, such as ice-breaking and building rapport, credibility and trust. Ice-breaking and establishing **rapport** require good communication skills. Consultants need to judge when they are being inappropriately over-familiar, or too distant. It can be useful to join in on some training sessions and to be a part of things, rather than being seen as 'a boffin' with a clipboard, who sits in an office. It has been said that, in a consultancy situation, that if you know the players' nickname for you, you are probably doing quite well. When you are unaware of your alias, they are probably talking behind your back; i.e. you are 'on the outside'. It can also be useful to communicate in the style the athletes use, as long as it is not seen as being contrived. Taking this 'joining in' idea one step further Bull (1997) has advocated the 'immersion approach' as useful for the sport psychologist working with teams. Here the idea is that the psychologist becomes one of the regular members of the coaching staff of the team rather than simply dropping in to do some consultancy sessions. Of course this is not something that all sport psychologists will have the time to do.

Credibility can come from several sources, for example, having some prowess oneself in a sport, or having coaching qualifications, or from having proven success in sport psychological service work. Word of mouth and the testimony of others can be an effective source of credibility. In a situation of low sporting credibility, perhaps for the newcomer to consultancy, the sport psychologist needs to work on small successes, and on building credibility as they go along. It might also help to remember that you don't have to be as good as Michael Jordan or Tiger Woods, to know when athletes have made a mistake, and what they could do to try to improve things!

In addition to the issue of the credibility of the consultant, lack of credibility can derive from the athlete's beliefs about the value of psychology in their sport. This can be made worse when psychologists are brought in by coaches or managers, rather than at the request of the athlete. It is important to be sensitive to an athlete's skepticism about psychological interventions by not attempting to force compliance. It is much wiser to continue to work with the athletes who are open to psychological methods, and hope that success will persuade the skeptical to come around.

Trust is something that can take time to develop, but is helped by ensuring that you do what you say you will do. For example, you could demonstrate your commitment to confidentiality by letting players see you keeping, even routine, non-sensitive information confidential. Trust can also be developed by being clear about what you think you can offer as a consultant, and by ensuring you do not promise what you cannot deliver. No one trusts the salesman who promises the earth. Particularly useful for the beginning sport psychologist, is to realize that, somewhat ironically, trust can come from being honest about what you do not know. It is therefore wise to remind clients, that just as improvement in physical skills require effort and perseverance, the same is true for the implementation of psychological interventions. Athletes need to understand that there are no 'magic bullets'.

One important decision for the consultant to make by the end of the first meeting, is whether they are confident that there is something they can offer the client. For example, it may well be that the problem is not a psychological one, in which case the consultant might refer the athlete to some other specialist. Alternatively, the consultant might have to persuade the athlete that the problem has, or needs, no solution.

In-depth exploration of the issues

The next stage of the consultancy process normally involves a more thorough investigation of the issues raised at the first stage, to help ensure any intervention takes the appropriate direction. This is typically done by in-depth interview. It is here that basic communication skills are paramount. Information gathering requires a good questioning technique, as well as active listening (see Topics K2 and K3). Questions should be open and probing, to ensure as much relevant information as possible is gained. In addition to exploring the problem in depth, the consultant may also wish to carry out some form of baseline assessment (Topic K7). This consists of quantifying attitudes, motivation, mental skills, etc., so that strengths and weaknesses can be highlighted, targets set and changes monitored. More will be said about this below.

This second stage of the consultancy process typically involves the sport psychologist and athlete focusing on those areas of greatest importance or concern, and discussing what they would like to achieve. Next, they will discuss some possible interventions, and select one or more to employ. Finally, they will construct a program, specific to the individual (or team). For example, if concentration is the issue for a golfer, the preferred solution might be to develop a pre-shot routine (Topic L3). If confidence is an issue, training in the development and use of a positive affirmation or 'Wow' list might be provided (Topic L4). If motivation to exercise is the problem, goal setting might be suggested (Topic L1). By the end of the session the psychologist and athlete will have set out their aims for the intervention. These will be used later, at the evaluation stage, as a basis for assessing the efficacy of the consultancy. In terms of process, as opposed to content, the sport psychologist is still building rapport, credibility and trust in this second stage.

Implementation and monitoring

The third stage in the consultancy process is where the chosen intervention would be introduced systematically. This would involve a period of training, during which the athlete is educated about and taught how to use the technique. For example, if relaxation was the agreed intervention, the athlete might be taught the basics of a full version of progressive muscle relaxation, and also taught about breathing and relaxation. Next, the procedure would be refined to produce a much shorter version of the relaxation technique, which could be used in competition. All the way through implementing and practicing the program, it is important to monitor progress. This will include checking that the athlete is happy with the program, and if not, tailoring it, or perhaps persuading them to persevere a little longer.

Evaluation   Finally, the sport psychologist should evaluate the effectiveness of the intervention in some way. The idea here is that rather than assume or hope things have improved, to make some kind of assessment of the worth of the work done, in terms of the extent to which the problem has been solved or performance has improved.

The best way to do this is to evaluate progress against the stated aims of the intervention, as derived at the end of the exploration stage. This can be done against objective criteria, such as performance scores or fitness levels. Alternatively, it can be done on the basis of ratings of intervention effectiveness, or satisfaction, by the athlete or coach. It is also useful for the sport and exercise psychologist to write up a case history, outlining what was done and why, what worked and what did not and why. This kind of reflective practice is invaluable for the ongoing development and improvement of consultancy skills and delivery (Anderson et al., 2002).

K7 BASELINE ASSESSMENT

Key Notes

Interviewing	Interviewing is one way to make a baseline psychological assessment. Interviewers should remember to engage in active listening. Questions should be open and probing and consultants should remember to seek clarification of issues. One simple tool often used in interviews is to carry out a pros and cons analysis.
Psychometric tests	A second source of baseline information comes from psychometric tests, which measure mental constructs. Sport-specific tests can measure confidence, anxiety, motivation, imagery ability and concentration. There is debate in applied sport and exercise psychology, about the value of psychometric tests. While some see the tests as very useful, others never use them.
Performance profiling	A third way to derive a baseline assessment is performance profiling. One recent approach to profiling has been offered by Butler who has drawn from the phenomenological approach of George Kelly's personal construct theory (Kelly, 1955). The assumption of this approach is that we get a better picture of where a performer is if we do not impose our preconceived notions upon them, but rather encourage them to think of the attributes (constructs) that they believe are crucial in their sport. Having selected a set of attributes, they then rate themselves on each. To help them to think about their constructs, we might suggest they consider the qualities of the very top performers in their sport. When mapped out graphically, this information shows where improvement is needed. This method of profiling emphasizes the athlete's perspective and increases ownership and commitment to the intervention.
Related topics	The scientific approach (A3) Listening skills (K2) Social cognition (F1) Questioning (K3) Introduction to individual differences (E1)

Interviewing

Baseline assessment involves gauging the athlete or exercise participant's current position in terms, not only of physical performance levels or fitness, but also a wide range of psychological attributes such as imagery ability, concentration, confidence, anxiety, motivation, personality traits, moods and so on. It is carried out to measure 'where we are now', so we can set goals for 'where we want to be', and to allow us to check our progress toward such goals. There are several ways to obtain baseline information and the sport and exercise psychologist will usually triangulate or combine information from different methods.

One relatively obvious way to find out about where participants stand in relation to some of these attributes is to interview them and ask them. Again, the interviewer should remember the basics of effective communication in such interviews, by asking open and probing questions, and by seeking clarification of issues. They should also remember to listen actively rather than passively. One tool often used in interviews is a variation on what is sometimes known as the critical incidents technique. This sounds rather grand but simply involves asking about the critical incidents that are relevant to the situation. For example, the psychologist might ask about two things that are going well and two that are not. A similar approach is to do a pros and cons (or advantages–disadvantages) analysis of the situation.

Psychometric tests

A second way to get baseline information is from psychometric tests. Psychometric tests measure mental constructs such as intellectual ability, aptitude, attitude, mood, emotion and personality. They are typically paper and pencil tests that have been constructed with due concern for reliability and validity (Topic A3). A number of such tests have been specifically designed for use in sport and exercise psychology. As their names suggest, the trait sport confidence inventory (TSCI) and state sport confidence inventory (SSCI) measure trait, and state confidence respectively (Vealey, 1986). There are also several tests of state and trait anxiety in sport. The most widely used of these is the competitive state anxiety inventory (CSAI-2) (Martens et al., 1990). Scales such as the sports orientation questionnaire (SOQ) (Gill & Deeter, 1988) and the task and ego orientation in sport questionnaire (TEOSQ) (Duda, 1989) have been devised to measure motivational orientation. Several general psychological skills inventories in sport measure things like imagery ability, concentration, confidence, motivation, anxiety, and so on. Prominent among these is the psychological skills inventory for sports (PSIS-5) (Mahoney et al., 1987), the athletic coping skills inventory (ACSI-28) (Smith et al., 1995) and the test of performance strategies (TOPS) (Thomas et al., 1999). In the exercise domain the consultant might use scales to get baseline information on participants' current exercise status or on their self-efficacy, such as the stages of change instrument (SCI) or the self-efficacy questionaire (SEQ) (Marcus et al., 1992).

It should be said that there is considerable debate in the literature of applied sport and exercise psychology about the relative worth of psychometric tests. While some see the tests as very useful, others never use them. Their supporters see them as central to the baseline assessment process and for monitoring progress. Some argue that they can be helpful to bolster an image of the expert with sophisticated tools. Some consultants merely use them as a prop, to give them something to talk about with the client.

Some prominent applied sport psychologists make no use of them at all, arguing that they have little relevance for the complex problems of the athlete, and further, that athletes often see them as irrelevant and a waste of time (Bull, 1997).

Performance profiling

Another way to get baseline information is to carry out some sort of performance profiling, which, in its most general form, usually involves representing aspects of performance in a graphical way. However, recently, the term has been used by Richard Butler to describe a particular approach to analyzing the factors that athletes themselves see as important to performance (Butler, 1996). The method is loosely based on the phenomenological approach of George Kelly (Kelly, 1955), who proposed personal construct theory (see Topic E1). The basis of the theory is that each of us views people in very different ways, and that no single classificatory system is rich enough to capture each individual's way of seeing others. Kelly talks about seeing the world 'through the goggles of our constructs'. Constructs are the sets of schemas (see Topic F1) that we use to understand the world. In terms of personality, it might be that intelligence is what one person might use as a major construct to judge others. Another person might think first in terms of honesty or generosity, and so on. In order to find out the central concepts that individuals use, Kelly devised the Repertory Grid (rep-grid) method. This involves asking respondents to list a group of people: perhaps best friend, mother, brother, sister, teacher, coach, etc., and then, in sets of three, to say how two people are similar and one different. For example, you might say my mother and best friend are generous, but my teacher is mean, or my sister and coach are cheerful but my brother is grumpy. In this way, the constructs that are important to you, your personal constructs, become apparent, i.e. generosity/meanness and cheerfulness/grumpiness. Although Butler does not use the rep-grid method to carry out sports perform-ance profiling, he does employ the personal view part of Kelly's theory. His belief is that we get a better picture of where a performer is, in terms of their profile of abilities and characteristics, if we do not impose our preconceived notions upon them.

In practice, this means giving the athlete a sheet of paper with concentric circles and several radiating lines on it that resemble a dartboard (see *Fig. 1*). Next, we encourage the athlete to think of the attributes (constructs) that he or she believes are crucial to high performance in their sport and to enter these on the outermost edge of the concentric circles. We also explain that there are no right or wrong answers and that it is just a way of finding out what they think is important. It may help at this stage to give some examples, and to explain that the exercise could help to direct their training effort. To help them to think about their constructs, you might suggest they consider the qualities of the very

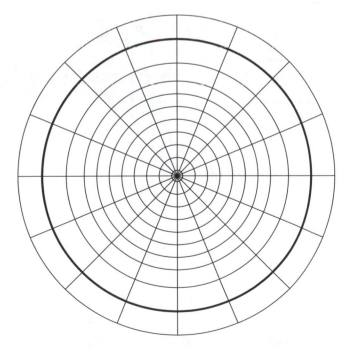

Fig. 1. Example of a blank circular performance profile chart.

top performers in their sport. Profiling can be done individually, or in a team situation. If it is done in groups, it can be useful to brainstorm first, and have the team's top performer lead the session. This can help to reduce any possible resistance from less willing team members. There is of course no reason why individual profiles as well as an overall team profile could not be generated during group sessions. The next step in the profiling process involves getting athletes to consider each of their constructs in turn, and to judge themselves out of ten on each one, in terms of how highly they rate themselves at this moment in time. This provides a graphic representation of the athlete's own view of what is important, and how well they are currently placed in relation to each construct. It immediately throws into relief the areas where things are good, and perhaps more importantly, the areas where improvement is needed. One refinement is to then ask them to rate where they would like to be at some specified time in the future. This can be particularly useful for highlighting training needs. An example of just such a procedure using a linear as opposed to a circular profile is shown in *Fig. 2*.

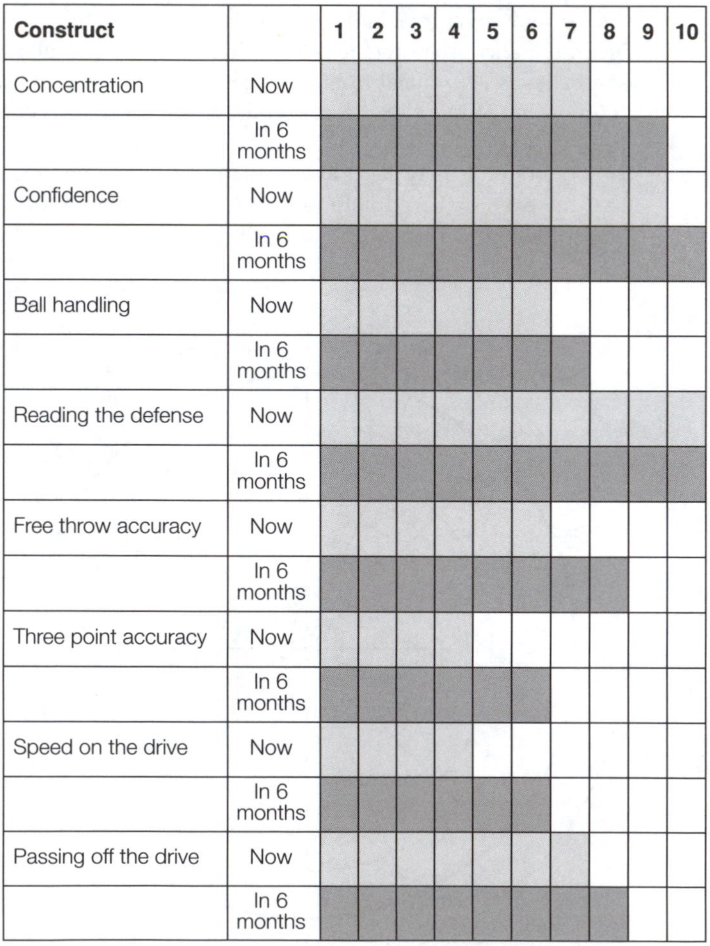

Construct		1	2	3	4	5	6	7	8	9	10
Concentration	Now	▨	▨	▨	▨	▨					
	In 6 months	▨	▨	▨	▨	▨	▨	▨	▨	▨	
Confidence	Now	▨	▨	▨	▨	▨	▨	▨			
	In 6 months	▨	▨	▨	▨	▨	▨	▨	▨	▨	▨
Ball handling	Now	▨	▨	▨	▨	▨	▨				
	In 6 months	▨	▨	▨	▨	▨	▨	▨			
Reading the defense	Now	▨	▨	▨	▨	▨	▨	▨	▨		
	In 6 months	▨	▨	▨	▨	▨	▨	▨	▨	▨	▨
Free throw accuracy	Now	▨	▨	▨	▨	▨	▨				
	In 6 months	▨	▨	▨	▨	▨	▨	▨			
Three point accuracy	Now	▨	▨	▨							
	In 6 months	▨	▨	▨	▨	▨	▨				
Speed on the drive	Now	▨	▨	▨							
	In 6 months	▨	▨	▨	▨	▨	▨				
Passing off the drive	Now	▨	▨	▨	▨	▨	▨	▨			
	In 6 months	▨	▨	▨	▨	▨	▨	▨			

Fig. 2.   Example of a linear performance profile filled out by a basketball point guard, indicating current rating and where they hope to be in 6 months time.

The strength of Butler's method of profiling is that it emphasizes the client's perspective. In terms of coaching style, or consultancy style, this method fits more easily in to the 'joining' as opposed to the 'telling' or 'expert' style of consultancy.

This type of profiling is also useful as a way to open up avenues for coach and athlete/exerciser, or psychologist and athlete/exerciser to communicate, and set goals together. Recent studies have demonstrated the effectiveness of profiling, in terms of a diverse range of benefits, including improved goal setting, better anger management, better communication by getting the athletes and coach 'on the same page', increased commitment to intervention techniques, and of course performance enhancement (Jones, 1993; Dale & Wrisberg, 1996).

L1 ISSUES OF MOTIVATION

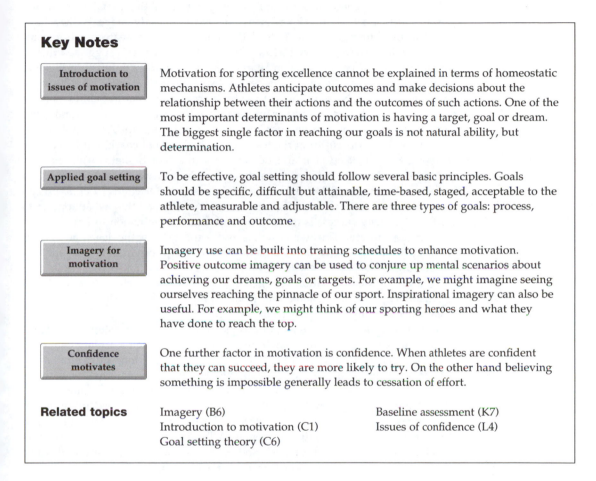

Introduction to issues of motivation

In this section the main psychological problems that athletes face in relation to performance enhancement are discussed, and a set of techniques to deal with each of them is outlined. In Topic C1 we learned that the motivation for sporting excellence is unlikely to be explainable in terms of simple homeostatic mechanisms. Rather, it is more like a kind of 'cognitive calculus' that involves judgments about the value we place on our dreams or targets, and the likelihood of being able to achieve them. Human beings anticipate outcomes and make decisions about the relationship between their actions and the outcomes of such actions.

In terms of performance enhancement, one of the most important determinants of motivation is having a target, **goal** or dream. Consequently, if we want motivated athletes, we have to help them to formulate a dream. Dreams are the fuel that motivates. Some athletes might be daunted by the apparent impossibility of reaching for the stars; however, it is important to realize that the biggest single factor in success is not natural ability, but determination. For example, there do not appear to be differences in simple reaction times or general hand–eye coordination between novices and elite sports performers. In computer terms the difference is not in the 'hardware' but in the 'software', or programming that elite players have. Where the skilled performers have the advantage is in being able to more quickly interpret the visual cues in any given sporting situation. The reason they have this advantage is they have spent a long time getting it! Indeed this notion is encapsulated in Ericsson's **theory of deliberate practice** (Ericsson et al., 1993), where it is suggested that to reach the peak of performance in sports involving complex motor coordination, something akin to a 'ten year rule' exists (equivalent to about 10 000 hours of training/practice). None of this is to suggest that having natural ability is not a good start, but there are many examples of people who were not 'naturals', but who have got to the top because they would not give up. As a sophomore, Michael Jordan was cut from the team by his high-school coach, but he had the determination to keep at it and be, arguably, the best basketball player ever. Interestingly, despite being a fantastic athlete, Jordan was unable, later in his career, to be anything like as successful in baseball. Of course, this is exactly what we would predict from the 'ten year rule'. Given all this, what appears to dictate our likely success is more to do with our determination to practice than our natural ability. This whole ethos was captured by the legendary Vince Lombardi who said that 'many athletes have the will to win, few have the will to prepare'. Even players with Tiger Wood's gifts have taken their skills to a new level by determination and having the will to practice. Indeed, Butch Harman, Tiger's coach, claims that if you want to motivate Tiger to do something, just tell him it is impossible!

Having established the dream, or desired end state, the next step for the sport psychologist is to gauge how far from the dream an athlete currently is. To do this, we need to conduct a needs analysis. This can be done in several ways. The most obvious thing to do is to talk with athletes in an informal way, to get their views on which aspects of their performance require most work. Additionally, we can employ performance profiling as described in Topic K7. Another option is to measure the athlete's current level of mental skills, using one of a number of available mental skills questionnaires (see Topic K7). Having completed a needs analysis and discovered where the work needs to be done, the next step is to do some structured goal setting.

Applied goal setting

In Topic C6 we saw that people who engage in goal setting out-perform those who just try to 'do their best'. There are several different sets of guidelines in the sport psychology literature about how to set goals effectively. These often include catchy acronyms that are designed to make them memorable such as such as SMART, which stands for specific, measurable, adjustable, realistic and time-based. Another widely used acronym is SCAMP, which refers to specific, challenging, acceptable, measurable, personal. These acronyms tend to be similar in terms of their suggestions, reflecting the fact that there are some very basic and important principles that guide effective goal-setting. These guidelines are set out below:

- Firstly, and probably the most crucial of these, is being **specific** about the goal. Failure to be specific is one of the most common errors made by athletes when they engage in goal setting. A non-specific goal such as 'to lose weight' is much less likely to be achieved than the more specific goal of 'to lose seven pounds'.

It is much more motivating to try to lose one pound per fortnight for the next 4 weeks, than to 'lose a bit of weight', because you can always check to see how you are doing, and work harder if just under target, and even be boosted by knowing you are ahead of where you should be.

- A second important goal-setting principle is to make goals **challenging** or **difficult but attainable**. Again this is motivating because when things are too easy, levels of commitment can drop. When there is a challenge this can produce optimum effort.

- A third consideration when goal-setting is to ensure that goals are **time-based**. Again this is designed to ensure optimum motivation because it ties effort to particular times.

- Fourthly, goals should be **stepped or staged**. This means that, although it is good to have an ultimate or dream goal, it is important to have intermediate or sub-goals along the way.

- Fifthly, goals should be **acceptable** to the athlete, rather than having been imposed by coaches. Goals without ownership are not going to be as effective as jointly decided ones.

- Goals need to be **measurable.** The goal of 'being twice the player I am now' might be difficult to demonstrate. It would be better to aim for something more measurable, like 'I will reduce the number of missed passes I make per game by half'.

- Goals should be **adjustable**. By constantly monitoring our sub-goals we can review progress and if necessary adjust them. If events conspire to make a goal unattainable then a new achievable goal must be set. Equally, if we are making better progress than expected, we may wish to make our goals more challenging.

For one piece of dramatic evidence of the effectiveness of these ideas, we need only think back to the John Naber story described in Topic C6. Naber applied these goal-setting principles for his successful gold medal performance in the 1976 Olympics.

In addition to these general principles, sport psychologists suggest the adage 'don't just think it ink it', meaning that it is wise to commit our goals to paper, rather than to keep them in our heads. This ensures that they have an existence outside the mind of the performer.

One other aspect of goal setting relates to the type of goals being set. In Topic C6 we saw that there are three types of goals: process, performance and outcome. Although they are all useful, some psychologists suggest that **process and performance goals** are more useful in goal setting, because they are more within our personal control than outcome goals such as 'to win the race'. However, even if an **outcome goal** is not entirely under our control, it may nevertheless provide an important source of motivation. After all, one of the defining characteristics of sport is competition, and it seems reasonable that we could make use of athlete's desires to beat the other person, or team, to motivate them. Of course, in practice there is no reason why a mix of different types of goal could not be utilized to maximize achievement. The other advantage of a mix of goals is that it may be that different situations are better suited to each type. For example, process goals might be particularly useful for motivation in a day-to-day or training situation. For mid-range time scales, performance goals could be useful, and over the longer term, an outcome goal might motivate better. As yet, however, there is no empirical evidence for these ideas.

Imagery for
motivation

Imagery (see Topic B6) can be used to motivate athletes in a number of ways. For example, we can conjure up mental scenarios about our dreams, goals or targets. This would involve repeatedly imaging positive outcomes, such as seeing ourselves reaching the pinnacle of our sport (or something less demanding if that is not realistic or achievable). For example, we might imagine stepping up to receive a gold medal, or lining up and being presented to a soccer superstar like Pelé, prior to a World Cup final. Inspirational imagery can also be useful. Here we think of our sporting heroes and what they have done to reach the top. This might involve thinking about the hours of pain endured in the saddle by Lance Armstrong, to become a six-time Tour de France winner, or the endless hours of punishing effort on the water that Steven Redgrave put in to win his five consecutive Olympic gold medals for rowing. The technique would be to build into our own training, a way of regularly reminding ourselves of their determination, so that we might find that little bit extra when things get tough.

Confidence
motivates

One further factor in motivation is confidence. When athletes are confident that they can succeed, they are more likely to try. On the other hand believing something is impossible generally leads to cessation of effort. Techniques associated with issues of confidence are dealt with later in Topic L4.

L2 ISSUES OF AROUSAL AND ANXIETY

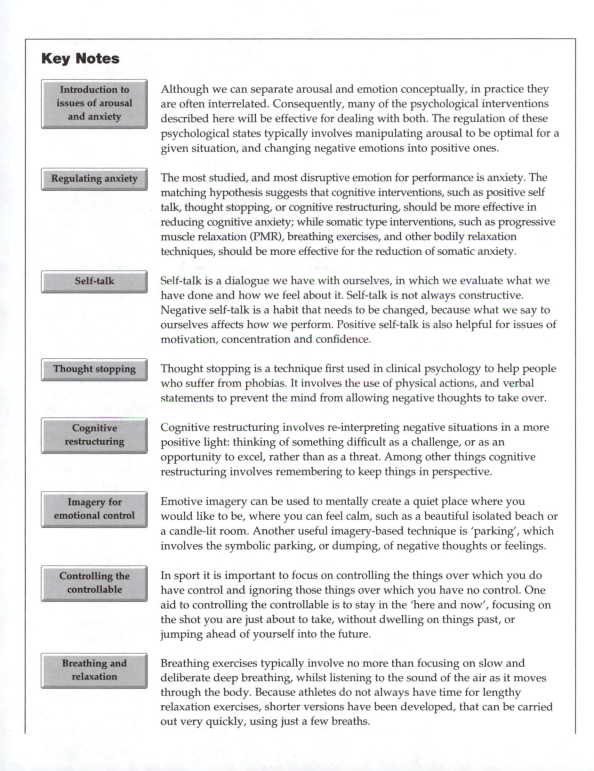

Key Notes

Introduction to issues of arousal and anxiety

Although we can separate arousal and emotion conceptually, in practice they are often interrelated. Consequently, many of the psychological interventions described here will be effective for dealing with both. The regulation of these psychological states typically involves manipulating arousal to be optimal for a given situation, and changing negative emotions into positive ones.

Regulating anxiety

The most studied, and most disruptive emotion for performance is anxiety. The matching hypothesis suggests that cognitive interventions, such as positive self talk, thought stopping, or cognitive restructuring, should be more effective in reducing cognitive anxiety; while somatic type interventions, such as progressive muscle relaxation (PMR), breathing exercises, and other bodily relaxation techniques, should be more effective for the reduction of somatic anxiety.

Self-talk

Self-talk is a dialogue we have with ourselves, in which we evaluate what we have done and how we feel about it. Self-talk is not always constructive. Negative self-talk is a habit that needs to be changed, because what we say to ourselves affects how we perform. Positive self-talk is also helpful for issues of motivation, concentration and confidence.

Thought stopping

Thought stopping is a technique first used in clinical psychology to help people who suffer from phobias. It involves the use of physical actions, and verbal statements to prevent the mind from allowing negative thoughts to take over.

Cognitive restructuring

Cognitive restructuring involves re-interpreting negative situations in a more positive light: thinking of something difficult as a challenge, or as an opportunity to excel, rather than as a threat. Among other things cognitive restructuring involves remembering to keep things in perspective.

Imagery for emotional control

Emotive imagery can be used to mentally create a quiet place where you would like to be, where you can feel calm, such as a beautiful isolated beach or a candle-lit room. Another useful imagery-based technique is 'parking', which involves the symbolic parking, or dumping, of negative thoughts or feelings.

Controlling the controllable

In sport it is important to focus on controlling the things over which you do have control and ignoring those things over which you have no control. One aid to controlling the controllable is to stay in the 'here and now', focusing on the shot you are just about to take, without dwelling on things past, or jumping ahead of yourself into the future.

Breathing and relaxation

Breathing exercises typically involve no more than focusing on slow and deliberate deep breathing, whilst listening to the sound of the air as it moves through the body. Because athletes do not always have time for lengthy relaxation exercises, shorter versions have been developed, that can be carried out very quickly, using just a few breaths.

| Progressive muscle relaxation | With progressive muscle relaxation athletes systematically and deliberately tense every muscle group in the body, and then relax each group, bit by bit, until the whole body is relaxed. Again, with practice, athletes can develop effective short versions of PMR. |

| Under-arousal and lack of emotion | Arousal can be raised by engaging in physical activity or increasing breathing rate. To increase levels of emotion, athletes can employ personalized tapes of inspirational music and use imagery of emotion-provoking events. |

Related topics   Imagery (B6)   Other theories (D7)
                      Multidimensional anxiety theory   Counseling skills (K5)
                         (D4)   Issues of concentration (L3)
                      Reversal theory (D6)

Introduction to issues of arousal and anxiety

In Topic D1 we differentiated between **arousal**, which represents a state of activation ranging from sleep to high alertness, having no emotional component, and **anxiety**, which is a negatively experienced emotion. Although it is easy to separate arousal and emotion conceptually, in practice they are often interrelated. Nevertheless, arousal is not specific to any one emotion. An athlete who is highly aroused may be experiencing the emotion of excitement, distress, anger, anxiety, etc. Although high arousal and high emotion are therefore linked, the link is not straightforward and not, as is sometimes assumed, to anxiety alone. While it is true that high arousal can be a problem for athletes and much is done to try to reduce it, it may be that we want athletes to be highly aroused if the associated emotion is excitement rather than fear. In other words there may be times when what is more crucial to good performance than the level of arousal is how the arousal is emotionally experienced. The task of the applied sport psychologist is to help the athlete to regulate these psychological states so that they are able to perform to their potential. This might involve the manipulation of arousal so that it is optimal for a given situation. Equally, it might involve changing negative emotions into positive ones, or at least shifting them in the positive direction. Despite these considerations, because of the interrelatedness of arousal and emotion, many of the interventions described here will be effective for regulating both.

Regulating anxiety

By far the most studied, and most disruptive emotion for performance is anxiety. Elite sport is full of stories about athletes who had all the requisite skills, but who were beaten by inferior players, because they failed to deal with their anxiety in the crunch situations. Imagine the anxiety that you might feel if you had to sit and wait for ten minutes in a small holding room, with the seven other best swimmers in the world, before being called to the Olympic 100 meter breaststroke final. Imagine the pressure of staring into the faces of your opponents during this period. Think how long that ten minute wait might seem, and how easily anxiety about failure might enter your head.

In Topic D4 on multidimensional anxiety theory the **matching hypothesis** was introduced (see *Fig. 1*). It suggests that since it is generally believed that there are two types of anxiety, cognitive and somatic, caused by two different sets of antecedents, the intervention required to effectively reduce each will be different. In other words, the intervention employed should match the type of

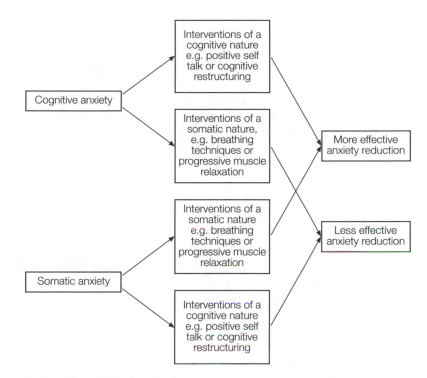

Fig. 1.   The matching hypothesis.

anxiety being treated. If correct, the use of cognitive interventions, such as **positive self-talk, thought stopping** or **cognitive restructuring,** should be more effective in reducing cognitive anxiety; while somatic type interventions, such as **progressive muscle relaxation** (PMR), breathing exercises, and other bodily relaxation techniques, should be more effective for the reduction of somatic anxiety. (These different interventions have also been called 'mind to body' versus 'body to mind' approaches (Williams & Harris, 2001).) With this distinction in mind, we will discuss what might loosely be called cognitive interventions first, and later turn to somatic ones. Although the focus here is on anxiety many of the techniques are equally helpful in relation to other emotions, for example, anger or sorrow.

Self-talk

As the name suggests, self-talk is a dialogue we have with ourselves, sometimes actually spoken, sometimes engaged in internally (Hardy et al., 2001). It usually consists of evaluations about what we have done, how we feel about it, and instructions to ourselves about what we want to do next, in the light of these evaluations. Self-talk is something athletes do naturally, but is not always constructive. Telling yourself that you are an idiot for dropping a catch, or mis-hitting a shot is common. The tendency to engage in negative self-talk is a habit that needs to be changed, because it is not just an irrelevant activity of no consequence. Behavior, thoughts and emotions are interlinked in a chain of causation. One interesting example of this comes from a study in which people either watched cartoons whilst holding a pencil with their lips as if it was a cigarette, or sideways between their teeth (Strack et al., 1988). Both groups then rated how funny they thought the cartoons were. Interestingly, and as the experimenters had predicted, the 'teeth' group thought the cartoons were funnier. The explanation given was that in the 'teeth' group the pencil makes us adopt a smiling position. Having watched the cartoons with a smiling face, participants rated them as funnier. It appears that sometimes we decide what we think and feel, on the basis of what we have done.

Experiments like this provide scientific support for the widely held view that if you want to be confident, you should hold yourself in a confident manner and look smart in your team uniforms, etc. This also fits well with Vealey's (2001) suggestion that physical self-presentation is one of the nine important sources of self-confidence. Dressing smartly and behaving in a confident manner also has the added bonus that it might serve to reduce the confidence of your opponents. From the above, it appears that the effect of saying negative things to yourself is likely to be that you begin to play badly. In contrast, by saying positive things, you can produce a positive attitude in yourself, and this will produce positive behavior.

A systematic approach to self-talk begins with an analysis of our habits. This can be done by thinking back, or by imaging our past behavior in competition, and writing down the kinds of things we say to ourselves. We can ask coaches or friends to observe us, and note what we say, or we can keep a log of self-talk during, if the event permits it, or after competition. If what this demonstrates is the existence of negative self-talk, we need to begin to take control of what we say to ourselves. This can be done in several ways. The most obvious thing to do is to take negative thoughts and turn them into positive ones. For example, a tennis player having identified a habit of saying 'I've messed up again' when they miss a tennis shot, should say 'OK, I won't do that again' or 'I am bound to get the next one'. Instead of thinking 'His serve is just too fast for me' say to yourself 'I will return his next service, if I step back and really focus'. Another simple rule for positive self-talk is to change 'if' to 'when'. Instead of saying to yourself 'If I could score with this free throw', say 'When I score this free throw'.

Although we have introduced self-talk under the topic of anxiety control, self-talk is actually helpful for all of the main psychological issues athletes have to deal with, since it is can serve a motivational function, aid concentration and help to build confidence.

Thought stopping

Another cognitive approach to anxiety reduction is to engage in thought stopping. This is a technique first used in clinical psychology to help people who suffer from phobias. It involves the use of physical actions, and verbal statements to prevent the mind from allowing the phobic thoughts to take over. For example, someone with a fear of spiders would be taught to bang their hand on the table and say 'No!', the moment the thought of spiders came into their consciousness. In a similar way, a tennis player might learn to tap their racquet on the ground and say 'No!', if negative or anxious thoughts began to enter their minds in competition (Zinsser et al., 2001).

Cognitive restructuring

Cognitive restructuring is another 'mind to body' method of reducing anxiety. Here the idea is that we should try to re-interpret any negative situation by seeing 'the silver lining' in the cloud. Thus, the sport psychologist needs to help the athlete to see the competitive situation in a positive light, such as thinking of something difficult as a challenge, or as an opportunity to excel, rather than as a threat. Cognitive restructuring is also linked with rational emotive therapy

(RET) outlined in Topic K5. As with RET the idea is to try to eliminate destructive or irrational thoughts, such as thinking the end of the world will come if we lose a match. Among other things cognitive restructuring involves remembering to keep things in perspective.

Another example of cognitive restructuring is to try to re-interpret a situation of high arousal as exciting, rather than anxiety provoking. This is exactly what reversal theory says we need to do: switching from the telic to the paratelic state (see Topic D6). Cognitive restructuring is also useful to counter the assumption, often made by athletes, that they can be perfect when they play or compete. This only serves to increase pressure, and is certain to be impossible to achieve. Perfectionist thinking is perhaps something to employ as an ideal to aim for as we train, but in competition it can lead to problems. Cognitive restructuring requires the athlete to focus on those aspects of the situation that will help performance, while ignoring those that will be destructive. It requires what coaches often call a bit of 'kidology', except that we have to restructure, to 'kid' ourselves. For example, we have to try and attain the mindset of the basketball player who has missed his last ten shots, yet still pleads with the coach in the final time-out, to be the 'go to' guy for the last shot of a game. His mindset is 'I have missed so much tonight, I cannot possibly miss this one'. In other words, he is focusing on his typical percentages, not his current run of misses. Another example of restructuring and kidding ourselves, is of the golfer who is able to perceive whatever weather conditions she is playing in, as her favorite conditions!

Imagery for emotional control

Imagery is a technique that was described in the topic above, in relation to increasing motivation. However, it is also useful in controlling emotions, and in fact recurs as a technique in all of the main areas of psychological intervention, albeit in different forms (see Topic B6). In relation to anxiety control, we can use **emotive imagery**, in which the images employed will consist of emotional content. For example, a calming imagery script might involve thinking about a quiet place that you like to be, where there is no one to disturb you, and where you can feel calm. It might be a candle-filled room, or an isolated beach, etc. Another imagery-based solution to anxiety problems is to use a technique known as '**parking**' or '**treeing**'. This involves the symbolic parking, or dumping, of negative thoughts or feelings. For example, athletes can be asked to write down the things that are worrying them, and to then put the written list away somewhere, either permanently, as in burning the list, or putting it in the trash. Alternatively, lists can be locked away temporarily, until the competition is over, when the content of the list can be dealt with without disrupting performance. As we shall see in Topic L3 parking or treeing can also be used to aid concentration.

Controlling the controllable

One thing athletes often do, that is really unhelpful to their performance, is to worry about things over which they have no control. There is an instructive story of a Zen monk who was walking along a narrow mountain path, when he slipped and fell over the cliff-edge. He managed to catch hold of a branch halfway down, which saved him from falling to the bottom of the cliff, where several hungry tigers lay in wait. Unfortunately, he was unable to climb up from where he was hanging, and he soon realized that there was actually no hope for him, because he would not be able to hang on indefinitely, and would soon become lunch for the tigers. Just then, he noticed six beautiful strawberries next to his free hand. One by one, he gently and carefully picked the strawberries, and slowly proceeded to eat them, savoring each one, until they had all gone. Shortly after finishing them all, he was unable to hold on any longer and he fell down to be eaten by the tigers! The moral of the story is that despite his terrible predicament, he made sure the enjoyment of the strawberries was not spoiled by something over which he had no control. Athletes need to learn to exercise a similar level of mental control, and to make sure they do not worry about things they cannot change. In contrast, worrying about things they can do something about can be productive, if this leads to problem-solving or increased motivation.

One aid to controlling the controllable is to **stay in the 'here and now'**. In practical terms, this means focusing on the shot you are about to take, or the situation you face right now, without dwelling on things past, or jumping ahead of yourself into the future. Obviously, thinking ahead to plan or make tactical decisions is wise, but thinking ahead to non-task-relevant issues, such as, how bad you will feel if you lose, is counterproductive. One reasonably common experience for competitors is the situation of having been calmly playing well, without expecting to win, and then realizing that the match is nearly over and you are still ahead, and you could just win. In this situation it is hard to avoid thinking ahead to the consequences of winning, thereby failing to stay in the here and now. It is possible that this is what led to the demise of Greg Norman in his unprecedented collapse during the 1996 Masters tournament. Norman was desperate to win the Masters because, great golfer that he was, this particular trophy, and its accompanying famous green jacket, had eluded him throughout his career. Many commentators saw 1996 as one of his last chances to achieve his aim. With the final 18 holes to play, Norman had a huge six-stroke lead over Nick Faldo, however, he eventually finished five strokes behind Faldo, losing eleven shots in the round!

Breathing and relaxation

The other approach to anxiety reduction has been to try to lower arousal by relaxing the body, in the hope that the mind would follow. Bodily relaxation can be achieved in a number of ways, including the use of relaxing imagery, as described earlier. However, the most common approach is achieved by the simple method of controlled breathing. Breathing exercises come in a huge variety of forms, but they typically involve no more than focusing on slow and deliberate deep breathing, whilst listening only to the sound of your breath as you exhale and inhale. Like other techniques, most breathing exercises benefit from practice, and the more we practice, the more relaxed we can become. It also helps to try different types of exercise to see what suits you best. Many breathing techniques require fairly lengthy periods, perhaps 20 or 30 minutes of lying or sitting comfortably in a quiet place. Of course, athletes may not have time for lengthy breathing or relaxation exercises, especially immediately prior to events, so sport psychologists have developed short versions of most exercises that can, with a bit of practice, be carried out very quickly, using just a few breaths. For example, one very quick method involves athletes imagining themselves as a glass statue that fills up with a relaxing or energizing blue liquid, each time they breathe in. Each time they breathe, they bring in more relaxing calm blue liquid until, after a few breaths, the statue is completely full, and they are completely relaxed.

Progressive muscle relaxation

Progressive muscle relaxation (PMR) is another body to mind technique that has been employed to reduce arousal (Hardy et al., 1996). Here athletes systematically and deliberately tense every muscle group in the body, and then relax each group, bit by bit, until the whole body is relaxed. Again, with practice, athletes can develop effective short versions of PMR.

While the use of relaxation techniques to help deal with over-arousal seems sensible enough, and is widely used, some sport psychologists have raised questions about the wisdom and value of relaxation techniques, on the grounds that sporting performance is not usually carried out in a relaxed state, and so we should not induce such a state in athletes prior to competition. This also seems sensible, and perhaps the apparent contradiction is removed if we think of using relaxation to bring an athlete from being over-aroused, to a level where they are back in the zone of optimal functioning, rather than being completely relaxed.

Under-arousal and lack of emotion

Sometimes athletes need to raise their level of arousal, rather than reduce it. Perhaps they are not aroused enough for the demands of their sport and need to 'psych up'.

There are several tried and tested ways to do this. One way is to engage in physical activity itself just prior to competition. Obviously, this should be done at a level which will not tire the athlete too much. One simple variation of this idea is to get athletes to increase their breathing rate, which has the effect of raising arousal.

Just as athletes sometimes need to be encouraged to be more aroused they might need on occasion to be more emotionally pumped up. Imagery can also be a useful way to increase emotion if necessary. Performers can be encouraged to conjure up any number of images that will have the desired effect. For example, athletes might imagine an opponent taunting them, or might imagine something that makes them angry if it was felt that an increase in anger would benefit performance. Self-talk can also be used to increase emotional levels. For example, athletes can repeat inspirational messages to themselves. Another widely used technique is to listen to a previously created, personalized tape of inspirational music. This has the advantage that it can kill two birds with one stone since in addition to raising arousal this is also likely to influence emotions in a positive way.

L3 ISSUES OF CONCENTRATION

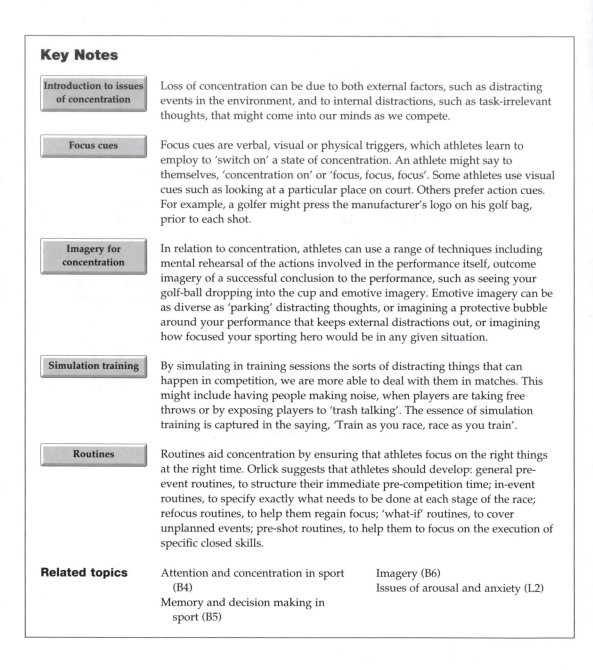

Key Notes

Introduction to issues of concentration	Loss of concentration can be due to both external factors, such as distracting events in the environment, and to internal distractions, such as task-irrelevant thoughts, that might come into our minds as we compete.
Focus cues	Focus cues are verbal, visual or physical triggers, which athletes learn to employ to 'switch on' a state of concentration. An athlete might say to themselves, 'concentration on' or 'focus, focus, focus'. Some athletes use visual cues such as looking at a particular place on court. Others prefer action cues. For example, a golfer might press the manufacturer's logo on his golf bag, prior to each shot.
Imagery for concentration	In relation to concentration, athletes can use a range of techniques including mental rehearsal of the actions involved in the performance itself, outcome imagery of a successful conclusion to the performance, such as seeing your golf-ball dropping into the cup and emotive imagery. Emotive imagery can be as diverse as 'parking' distracting thoughts, or imagining a protective bubble around your performance that keeps external distractions out, or imagining how focused your sporting hero would be in any given situation.
Simulation training	By simulating in training sessions the sorts of distracting things that can happen in competition, we are more able to deal with them in matches. This might include having people making noise, when players are taking free throws or by exposing players to 'trash talking'. The essence of simulation training is captured in the saying, 'Train as you race, race as you train'.
Routines	Routines aid concentration by ensuring that athletes focus on the right things at the right time. Orlick suggests that athletes should develop: general pre-event routines, to structure their immediate pre-competition time; in-event routines, to specify exactly what needs to be done at each stage of the race; refocus routines, to help them regain focus; 'what-if' routines, to cover unplanned events; pre-shot routines, to help them to focus on the execution of specific closed skills.
Related topics	Attention and concentration in sport (B4) Imagery (B6)
	Memory and decision making in sport (B5) Issues of arousal and anxiety (L2)

Introduction to issues of concentration

A third major area of importance in applied sport psychology relates to issues of concentration, and our ability to focus on the crucial aspects of a sporting performance, at any given time. Loss of concentration can obviously be due to both external factors, such as distracting events in the environment, and to internal distractions, such as task-irrelevant thoughts, that might come into our minds as we compete. For example, athletes sometimes allow themselves to ponder mistakes they have just made, or bad calls the referee has made, instead of concentrating on what they have to do now. Thus, they make the mistake of forgetting to 'stay in the present'. Similarly, athletes sometimes allow the importance of an occasion to distract them from the task in hand, forgetting that the importance of the match does not change the demands on them.

To help athletes to be able to maintain focus, or recover from lapses in concentration, applied sport psychologists have developed a number of useful techniques.

Focus cues

Focus cues are verbal, visual or physical triggers, which athletes learn to employ in given situations to 'switch on' a state of concentration. For example, although some golfers do try to concentrate on their game for every minute of each round, most have realized that this is exhausting, and so they relax between shots, and then refocus just prior to their next shot. Focus cues can be used to help them to switch back to concentration mode. Some players have learned to use **verbal cues**, for example, they might say trigger words to themselves such as 'switch' or 'ready again' or 'focus, focus, focus'. Soccer teams might have a cue phrase that players use to remind themselves and each other about the importance of being alert, particularly following a goal. This is a time when teams appear particularly prone to lapses of concentration, allowing their opponents to equalize. The 2003 World-Cup-winning English rugby team used the verbal focus cue, 'hit the beach', to remind the team not to take risks, when they had a narrow lead near the end of a game.

Some athletes use **visual cues** to get them back into a focused state. A squash player might look at the 'T' before each point, or look at the strings of her racquet. Some players write messages to themselves, taped to the back of their hand. Others prefer **action cues** for concentration. For example, a golfer might press the manufacturer's logo on his golf bag, prior to each shot, to signal the start of his focused pre-shot routine, or a tennis player might tap his toe with his racquet before each point, as a way of ensuring that concentration is constantly re-established.

Imagery for concentration

Athletes can use different types of imagery to deal with issues of concentration (Topic B6). Three types of imagery often used are mental rehearsal, outcome imagery and emotive imagery. With **mental rehearsal,** the athlete imagines carrying out the actions involved, immediately prior to executing the actual activity or skill. In this way, players can bring their focus back to the task, and avoid distracting images or thoughts.

Positive **outcome imagery** serves a similar function. Golfers say that the golfer who thinks 'I must avoid the pond' seems magically drawn to it. A more useful strategy is to use positive outcome imagery, as Jack Nicklaus did, to imagine seeing the ball flying from the club-head to the center of the fairway, without any image of ponds! This is not mental rehearsal, because the image is of the ball flying to the target, rather than of the swinging of the club (Taylor & Shaw, 2002).

Emotive imagery involves imagining something that affects emotions, such as thinking calm thoughts. As we saw in Topic L2, it is more often used to regulate arousal, however, it can also serve a concentration function. For example, some athletes find that concentration is improved by imagining being a sporting hero, and imagining how focused this hero would be in this situation. The hero of your imagery need not be restricted to your own sport. Golfer Nick Faldo used tennis ace Bjorn Borg as his role model, whenever he needed to remember to stay focused and disciplined.

Imagery can also be used in the technique known as '**parking**' or '**treeing**'. This involves the symbolic parking, or dumping of negative thoughts or feelings. For example, athletes can be asked to write down the things that are worrying them, and to then put the written list away somewhere, either permanently, as in burning the list, or putting it in the trash. Alternatively, lists can be locked away temporarily, until the competition is over, when it can be dealt with, without disrupting performance. The term 'treeing' comes from an Aboriginal tradition designed to remove people's troubles. This involved tribe members linking hands, with the troubled person at one end of the chain, and with a large tree at the other end. The person with the problem then symbolically passes it to the next person, and so on down the line, until the last person passes the trouble to the tree. One final example of the use of imagery as an aid to concentration is the practice of imagining a protective bubble around the performance. Some golfers imagine a transparent dome that they enter as they step up to play their shot. They think of this bubble as a protective shield that keeps all sorts of external distractions out, such as crowd noise, camera shutters, and even wind and rain. Inside the bubble, all that matters is the shot they are about to play. For example, when Tom Watson enters his bubble he feels as if he has entered a room that is 'dimly lit and quiet' (Rotella, 1995).

As can be seen, the potential of imagery appears only to be limited by the imagination of the performer, or their sport psychologist!

Simulation training

Another approach to the problem of distraction is simulation training. Here, the basic idea is that by simulating in training sessions, the sorts of distracting things that can happen in competition, we are more able to deal with them in matches, and focus on the important aspects of our play (Moran, 2004). For example, coaches often set up drills that involve distractions, such as having people making noise, when players are taking free throws or penalty kicks. Similarly, immunizing players against the 'trash talking' or 'sledging' that goes on in sport is worth doing. Another technique is to expose players, in training sessions, to bad refereeing decisions, or 'bad luck'. Players can occasionally be exposed to old equipment of poor quality, or balls that are not properly inflated. The essence of simulation training is captured in the old adage, 'Train as you race, race as you train'.

Like imagery, simulation training is another of those interventions that is useful for more than one area of performance enhancement. For example, it can help overcome anxiety, in that by simulating every eventuality, we know we can cope with all sorts of setbacks and difficulties when actual competition arrives.

Routines

One absolutely central feature of dealing with concentration is to employ routines. They are crucial because they provide constancy and stability to performance. Apart from the obvious wisdom of planning ahead, the routines serve the useful function of aiding concentration, by ensuring the athlete focuses on the right things at the right time. One of the strongest advocates of routines is Terry Orlick, who has written extensively on the topic (Orlick, 1986, 1990). Orlick suggests we develop the following different routines:

- General **pre-event routines** that structure our immediate pre-competition time, and include all the physical things that need to be done. For example, they might include our warm up; checking the track, court or field; and checking our equipment. They will also include mental preparation, such as time for mental rehearsal, or any emotional control or concentration techniques.
- **In-event routines** that specify exactly what we need to do at each stage of the race or competition. These will be based on decisions about what the crucial moments are in your event, and what your focus should be at each phase of the race. For example, a runner would devise a routine containing the predetermined race plan, with built in reminders or attentional cues for each stage of the race, such as what to do in the early stages, when to consolidate, and when to push, etc. The plan should also include some way of extending personal limits when necessary. Orlick advocates the use of visual representations of the event plan. For example, some might represent their race like a funnel that narrows to the finishing line. A 1500 meter runner might see their race as a spiral, with crucial tactical information, or performance cues written at the relevant points on the 'map'. *Fig. 1* shows an example of an in-event routine for a 100 m breaststroke long course swimmer.
- **Refocus routines** that are designed to help us get back 'on track', following loss of attention or mistakes. These prevent us from dwelling on the errors we have just made. They should consist of at least four components, variously known as the 4 Rs, or Cs, or Fs. For example, the four Rs have been described as:
  - (1) **React:** 'stuff happens' so have your little outburst, but keep it in perspective;
  - (2) **Relax:** perhaps take a couple of deep breaths and say 'cool';
  - (3) **Reflect:** think about what you can do now to put things right (perhaps re-play/rehearse the shot you should have played);
  - (4) **Refocus:** use a refocus cue to get you back to total concentration.
  (The four Cs are Cuss, Calm-down, Correct and Concentrate; and the four Fs are: Cuss! Fix, Forget and Focus).
- **'What-if' routines** to cover most eventualities, such as the competition being delayed, equipment problems, having players sent off, punctures to wheels, etc. In this way performance is less disrupted than it otherwise would have been if such things actually happen.
- **Pre-shot routines** which are very specific sequences of physical and mental activities, that help us to focus on the execution of specific closed skills, such as kicking a goal in football or rugby, taking a penalty in soccer, serving in racquet sports, or hitting a golf shot. Most golfers do have a physical pre-shot routine, however, fewer have routines that incorporate a significant mental component to guard against problems like competitive anxiety, loss of concentration, loss of confidence and so on. *Table 1* shows the stages of a pre-shot routine designed to help a professional golfer who was suffering from distracting thoughts entering his mind as he addressed the ball (Shaw, 2002).

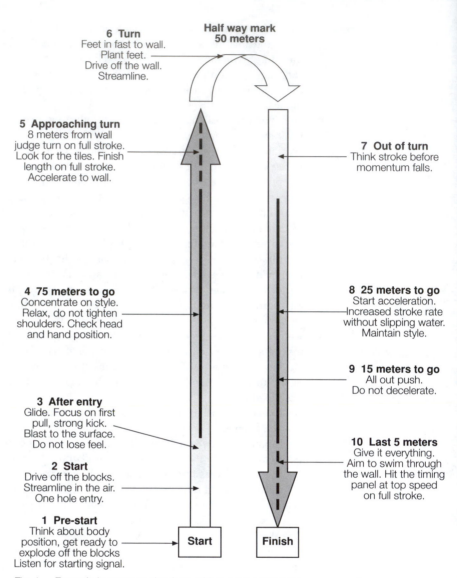

6 Turn
Feet in fast to wall.
Plant feet.
Drive off the wall.
Streamline.

**Half way mark
50 meters**

5 Approaching turn
8 meters from wall
judge turn on full stroke.
Look for the tiles. Finish
length on full stroke.
Accelerate to wall.

7 Out of turn
Think stroke before
momentum falls.

4 75 meters to go
Concentrate on style.
Relax, do not tighten
shoulders. Check head
and hand position.

8 25 meters to go
Start acceleration.
Increased stroke rate
without slipping water.
Maintain style.

9 15 meters to go
All out push.
Do not decelerate.

3 After entry
Glide. Focus on first
pull, strong kick.
Blast to the surface.
Do not lose feel.

2 Start
Drive off the blocks.
Streamline in the air.
One hole entry.

10 Last 5 meters
Give it everything.
Aim to swim through
the wall. Hit the timing
panel at top speed
on full stroke.

1 Pre-start
Think about body
position, get ready to
explode off the blocks
Listen for starting signal.

Start

Finish

Fig. 1.   Example in-event routine for a 100 m breaststroke long course swimmer.

Table 1.   The stages of a pre-shot routine that helped a professional golfer (Mark) to overcome a concentration problem. Mark's specific problem was that just as he stepped up to address the ball, distracting thoughts kept entering his head. These distracting thoughts were not serious nor did they relate to worries about life or anxieties about competing, but rather they were trivial distractions. For example, one recurring theme was that an annoying song would come in to his head as he was about to take his swing. The following describes the mental and physical pre-shot routine that was created to help Mark to overcome this problem. Having assessed distance, wind trajectory and lie, Mark would decided on the 'shot goal' and appropriate club, He then began the following pre-shot routine

Concentration-on time	Look intently at the manufacturer's logo on the golf bag	This served to switch on the concentration routine
	Imagine a protective bubble around yourself into which nothing can penetrate	Here imagery was used to reduce distractions
	Repeat to yourself 'focus, focus, focus'	Here self-talk was used to maintain concentration
Relaxation time	Take four breaths using an image-based breathing exercise	This was designed to create a quiet calmness
Confidence time	Say, one of the following to yourself. 'I have a strong technique, I have hit this shot before, I am a solid striker, I am a good player'	Here self-talk is used to give confidence. The statements were generated by Mark so that he would feel comfortable using them
Target time	Identify a small and precise target to aim for	This maintains the focus on the task
Mental-rehearsal time	Visualize the shot you want to happen	This was designed to prime the swing and help confidence
Auto-pilot time	Execute your normal physical pre-shot routine and hit the shot	
Concentration-off time	Switch off your concentration until you are about to play the next shot	Concentrating for four hours is very demanding, this component ensures concentration is available when needed

Although during the training phase of the routine it takes a while to enact, with practice it soon becomes something that can be carried out very quickly in the normal period before each shot.

L4 ISSUES OF CONFIDENCE

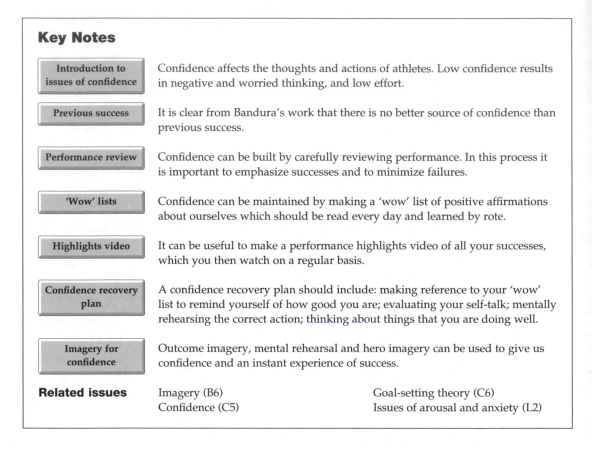

Key Notes

Introduction to issues of confidence	Confidence affects the thoughts and actions of athletes. Low confidence results in negative and worried thinking, and low effort.
Previous success	It is clear from Bandura's work that there is no better source of confidence than previous success.
Performance review	Confidence can be built by carefully reviewing performance. In this process it is important to emphasize successes and to minimize failures.
'Wow' lists	Confidence can be maintained by making a 'wow' list of positive affirmations about ourselves which should be read every day and learned by rote.
Highlights video	It can be useful to make a performance highlights video of all your successes, which you then watch on a regular basis.
Confidence recovery plan	A confidence recovery plan should include: making reference to your 'wow' list to remind yourself of how good you are; evaluating your self-talk; mentally rehearsing the correct action; thinking about things that you are doing well.
Imagery for confidence	Outcome imagery, mental rehearsal and hero imagery can be used to give us confidence and an instant experience of success.
Related issues	Imagery (B6) Goal-setting theory (C6) Confidence (C5) Issues of arousal and anxiety (L2)

Introduction to issues of confidence

Confidence affects the thoughts and actions of athletes. Low confidence results in negative and worried thinking, which can adversely affect performance. Low confidence affects action, by reducing effort and persistence. If athletes believe there is little probability of being successful at something, they are much less likely to try. Sport psychologists and coaches have developed several techniques to help deal with issues of confidence.

Previous success

It is clear from Bandura's work (see Topic C5) that there is no better source of confidence than previous success (Bandura, 1977, 1986, 1997). Coaches and athletes make use of this to boost confidence, by ensuring that training and practice sessions include plenty of positive outcomes, and successful experiences. Another way to help build in success is to set performance or process goals, as opposed to outcome goals (Topic C6), because they are much more in the athlete's control.

Performance review

One useful technique for confidence building is to carry out a performance review, listing all the good things about your last match or race, and then the poorer points (Bull et al., 1996). Next we need to learn from the bad points, in terms of things we can do for next time. Having done this, we should physically get rid of the negative points by cutting them from the bottom of the list, and then trashing them. Finally, we should post the good points somewhere where they can be seen frequently. In this way, we are constantly reminded of what we can do well.

'Wow' lists

Again, based on the notion that we need to remind ourselves what we are capable of, confidence can be boosted by making a list of positive affirmations about ourselves, spelling out just how good we are. This list could contain statements about what we do well, what we have achieved, or our best ever performances. For example, it might say things like, 'I have prepared long and hard'; 'I am capable of this'; 'My goal is realistic, and I can do it'; 'I have won championships'; 'I made the National team on merit'; 'I average 23 points a game', etc. Initially, these 'wow' lists should be read every day and learned by rote, so that they can be called upon on a regular basis to maintain confidence. The information on these lists can be used as the basis for positive **self-talk**, which is also an important technique for confidence maintenance. Self-talk was the subject of Topic L2 above and will not be discussed again here.

Highlights video

Another similar technique to the 'wow' or positive affirmation list, is to make a performance highlights video of all your successes, which you then watch on a regular basis. It might feature your best shots, or fastest runs, or you stepping up to receive trophies and so on. Again, this serves as a regular reminder to yourself of how good you are, and that you can be successful.

Confidence recovery plan

Another useful idea is to develop a confidence recovery plan, which can be implemented when events conspire to make us feel that we will not be able to meet the demands of competition, or attain the performance level we know we are capable of (Bull et al., 1996). The plan should be enacted frequently in training, until it becomes second nature. Among other things it might include:

- making reference to your 'wow' list to remind yourself of how good you are;
- evaluating your self-talk to check that it is not becoming negative;
- mentally rehearsing the correct action, or perfect performance;
- thinking about two or three things that you are doing well;
- thinking about the two or three things you could begin to do right now, that would start a success cycle;
- asking yourself, 'Is the thing that is causing me to lose confidence something over which I have control? If not then take it off your list of concerns;
- checking that your expectations about how well you can perform are realistic.

Imagery for confidence

Just as imagery can be used for issues of motivation, emotional control and concentration, it can also be a useful tool to maintain confidence. For example, outcome imagery combined with mental rehearsal, can be used immediately prior to an event, or at a particularly crucial moment in a competition, to give us an instant experience of success. A tennis player might use the time between games to sit quietly with a towel over his head, and imagine serving four aces in a row, in his upcoming service game.

Another way players use imagery to boost their confidence is to use 'hero imagery', in which they make believe that they are their own hero. If you have a crucial shot to take at the end of a basketball game, why not be Michael Jordan for that moment, because he is not going to miss! In this way, we can derive some confidence in any difficult competitive situation by imagining what our ideal player would do.

M1 STRESS AND COPING

Key notes

Stress	Stress occurs when an outcome is important to a person but they perceive an imbalance between the demands placed upon them and their ability to cope with these demands. The transactional model of stress suggests that the stress process consists of four stages: (1) environmental demand; (2) appraisal/ perception of the environmental demand; (3) physiological and/or psychological response; and (4) behavioral consequences.
Sources of stress	Sources of stress fall into two general categories: situational (e.g., event/ outcome importance and uncertainty) or personal (e.g., trait anxiety and self-esteem).
Coping with stress	Coping strategies, to manage stressful situations, can be learnt. Adaptive strategies facilitate adjustment to the situation, but maladaptive coping strategies lead to under-achievement, dropping out, burnout or poor somatic or mental health. Coping is a complex and dynamic process. Coping strategies can be seen as problem-focused or emotion-focused. Social support and strategies to reduce state anxiety and increase self-esteem are likely to be effective.

Related topics	Anxiety: the basics (D3)	Issues of motivation (L1)
	Multidimensional anxiety theory (D4)	Issues of arousal and anxiety (L2)
		Issues of confidence (L4)
	Mental health (H2)	Injury (M2)
	Consultancy: basic issues (K1)	Burnout and over-training (M3)

Stress

Stress is an integral part of quality of life, it is needed to produce energy and excitement in our lives. However, too much or too little stress is undesirable and in these conditions people may develop symptoms such as anxiety, irritability, sleeplessness or muscle tension. Although many people talk about stress and 'being stressed' it is actually a difficult term to define. In general terms it is a concept meaning something that produces strain. Stress can also be viewed as a complex process where events and individual reactions to events interplay to produce physical and mental responses.

Stress is most often seen to occur when an outcome is important to a person but they perceive an imbalance between the demands placed upon them and their ability to cope with these demands. Taking this view it can be seen that it is not the environment per se that causes stress, rather it is the person's perception of the environment. Stress is manifested in emotional (e.g., changes in mood), physiological (e.g., changes in blood pressure or heart rate), psychological (e.g., anxiety, depression) and behavioral (e.g., restlessness, rate of speech, decreased task performance) responses. The **transactional model** of stress, originally proposed by Lazarus (1966), suggests that the stress process consists of four stages (see *Fig 1*).

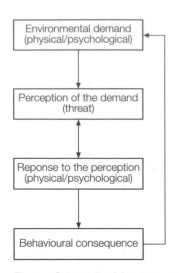

Fig. 1.   Schematic of the stress process.

(1) *Stage 1: Environmental demand.* Some sort of physical or psychological demand is made of an individual.
(2) *Stage 2: Individual's appraisal/perception of the environmental demand.* This could be viewed as the amount of 'threat' the individual perceives. Not all people will see the same demand with the same degree of threat.
(3) *Stage 3: Physiological and/or psychological response.* If an individual perceives the demands to outweigh their resources to cope then they are likely to experience increases in arousal, state anxiety, muscle tension and negative changes in attention. Perceived coping resources are therefore integral to the stress response.
(4) *Stage 4: Behavioral consequences.* This stage refers to the actual behavior the individual exhibits in response to the environmental demand. It may be that an increase in state anxiety causes a decrement in performance, or the individual may have skills for managing the increase in state anxiety and therefore performance remains unchanged or improves.

The process is cyclical with the behavioral outcome feeding back into the situation and the situation appraisal. Likewise if a similar experience in the past has led to stress and a poor outcome, the current situation is likely to be viewed as more stressful. The cognitive appraisal and physiological/psychological response are linked in a reciprocal manner. For example, the initial appraisal may lead to increases in state anxiety, which then lead to re-appraisal of the event as even more stressful. The stress process is influenced by personality and motivational characteristics of the individual (e.g., trait anxiety, self-esteem, achievement goal orientation).

Within sport psychology stress has been most frequently studied in terms of competitive stress, stress and injury, and the role of stress in burnout. In exercise psychology the focus has tended to be on the role of physical activity in stress management.

Sources of stress   There are innumerable sources of stress, that fall into the general categories of **situational** or **personal** sources. The two main situational sources are event/outcome importance and uncertainty. Generally the more important an event the more likely it is to be perceived as stressful. Likewise the greater the uncertainty in a situation the greater the stress. For example, if you are focused on beating your opponent rather than on your own performance, then you have less control of the situation and therefore greater uncertainty.

Trait anxiety and self-esteem are two important personality characteristics that influence the stress experienced. Trait anxiety predisposes a person to view competition or situations of social evaluation as more or less threatening. High trait anxious individuals tend to perceive more situations as threatening compared with low trait anxious individuals. Low self-esteem individuals tend to have less confidence and view competition and situations of self-evaluation as more threatening, and are therefore more likely to perceive the same environmental demand as threatening (stressful).

Coping with stress

Coping is an effort to manage stress. Folkman (1991) defines coping as 'the changing thoughts and acts the individual uses to manage the external and/or internal demands of a specific person–environment transaction that is appraised as stressful' (p. 5). Coping strategies, to manage stressful situations, can be learnt. Within the transactional model of stress coping behaviors are seen as mediating the link between environmental demands and the cognitive appraisal and the physiological/psychological response to this demand. They may alter thought patterns, alter perceptions of personal resources or target a change in typical behavior patterns. Adaptive strategies will facilitate adjustment to the situation, but maladaptive coping strategies might lead to under-achievement, dropping out, burnout, or poor somatic or mental health. Coping is a complex and dynamic process, and the same strategy may not work in all situations. Adaptive coping is more likely to occur when the strategy employed matches either the demands of the situation or deals directly with the physiological/psychological effects of the stress. For example, if someone experiences negative or irrational thoughts as a result of stress, then dealing with these, rather than say teaching a general relaxation strategy is likely to be most effective.

Coping strategies can be seen as problem-focused or emotion-focused. Problem-focused strategies attempt to change the person–environment relationship. For example, an athlete who finds themselves in the situation where they are being outplayed may decide to try another tactic. This alters the person–environment relationship and if successful may reduce the stress being experienced. Emotion-focused coping involves the emotional regulation or reappraisal of the situation. The emotional reaction caused by the stressor may be altered by the individual re-interpreting the event (e.g., using cognitive restructuring to reduce the importance of the event or re-interpreting the event as an exciting chance to meet a challenge).

Seeking social support can be an effective coping strategy. It is argued that social support may buffer the effects of stress because the support helps the individual to either redefine the problem or find a solution to it. Alternatively it has been proposed that social support may have a direct effect on stress by enhancing social integration and well-being.

Because the stress process is affected by trait-anxiety and self-esteem, strategies focused on these aspects are likely to improve the coping resources of individuals. State anxiety may be reduced by both cognitive and somatic relaxation control and task-oriented goal setting. Self-esteem may be maintained or enhanced through the use of cognitive restructuring and positive self-talk. At times of general life stress physical activity can be used to help manage stress by reducing stress reactivity (see Topic H2).

M2 Injury

Key notes

Psychology and injury	Psychological factors play a role in the incidence of injuries, athletes' responses to injury and in rehabilitation from injury.
Psychosocial factors and incidence of injury	There is evidence that psychosocial factors such as state anxiety, life stress and daily hassles, may predispose individuals to injury. The relationship is complex and may be mediated by the perceived social support and coping resources of the athlete. This relationship is represented in the model of injury antecedents proposed by Andersen and Williams (1988; Williams & Andersen, 1998).
Responses to injury	Grief response models to injury have had limited empirical support. Stress reaction models suggest that response to injury is a function of the reciprocal interaction between the cognitive appraisal of, and emotional reaction to, the injury. These reactions then influence the behavior of the individual. The stress response is influenced by characteristics of the individual and the context in which the injury occurred. This relationship is represented in the model of injury response (Wiese-Bjornstal et al., 1998).
Facilitating recovery from injury	Good communication between doctors, physiotherapists, athletes and coaches is critical. Goal-setting, relaxation and imagery techniques, and positive self-talk training may also be helpful in providing direction and motivation to the athlete. Social support for the injured person is also important. More research is needed to examine the effectiveness of such strategies.
Related topics	Consultancy: basic issues (K1) Issues of confidence (L4) Motivational issues (L1) Stress and coping (M1) Issues of arousal and anxiety (L2)

Psychology and injury

Injury is a stressful event for anyone who is committed to their sport or physical activity, whether they are a novice or an international representative. It is also important in exercise adherence as it is one of the reasons people drop out or don't even start participating. Psychological factors play a role in the incidence of injuries, athletes' responses to injury and in rehabilitation from injury.

Psychosocial factors and incidence of injury

Most factors which contribute to injury are physical in nature, but despite alterations in rules, and changes in safety equipment, coaching, and training, injuries continue to happen. There is evidence that psychosocial factors may predispose individuals to injury. Much of this work has been centered on the stress model of injury proposed by Andersen and Williams (1988; Williams & Andersen, 1998). This model has at its core the transactional model of stress (see Topic M1). Added to this, as mediators of the stress response are three psychosocial factors (history of stressors, personality, and coping resources) and two categories of interventions (cognitive appraisal and attentional aspects) aimed at reducing injury risk. The psychosocial factors influence each other, as well as influencing the stress response.

History of stressors include life change events, daily hassles and previous injury. Support is strongest for the negative effects of major life events. For example, footballers who report more negative events are more likely to get injured (Passer and Seese, 1983). There is limited support for the role of daily hassles (e.g., minor daily irritations) but this may be due to methodological problems (e.g., assessing daily hassles retrospectively). A prospective study has shown significant increases in daily hassles in the week prior to injury (Fawkner et al., 1999). Injury history has not been examined extensively but it is logical that an athlete who is still concerned about a previous injury may experience heightened stress and therefore greater risk of further injury. This assumption should be investigated further.

Personal characteristics may influence individuals' perceptions of the environment and its stressors. There have been mixed results for both locus of control and trait anxiety. When sport-specific measurement tools are used, athletes scoring higher on either locus of control or trait anxiety experienced more injuries (e.g., Petrie, 1993). There is some evidence that mood states influence the risk of injury. For example, Lavallee and Flint (1996) demonstrated that higher levels of tension/anxiety were related to higher rates of injury.

Coping resources show more consistent results. The stronger an athlete's coping resources, particularly social support, the less stress created by negative life events and therefore the injury-stress relationship is ameliorated.

Within the Andersen and Williams model two intervention approaches are proposed. One targets the cognitive appraisal of stressful events so that they are viewed more positively. This may be done through techniques such as cognitive restructuring. The second approach targets the physiological/attentional aspects of the stress response, proposing techniques such as progressive muscle relaxation, meditation, breathing exercises and attentional control training. These intervention ideas are rooted in two possible explanations for the effect of anxiety and stress on injury risk. The first is that stress and anxiety cause attentional focus to narrow resulting in the athlete or exerciser missing vital environmental cues. Attention may also be impaired because stress and anxiety may cause distraction and irrelevant thoughts. The second explanation is that stress and anxiety cause an increase in muscle tension that interferes with coordination and increases the risk of musculoskeletal injuries.

Responses to injury

How individuals react and deal with injury will influence their rate of recovery and the confidence with which they approach rehabilitation and return to their sport. Athletes perceive injury in different ways. For some it may be a welcome relief from a poor season, others may see it as an opportunity to show how strong and brave they are and for others it may be seen as a disaster.

Initially, psychological reactions to injury were modeled on the grief-reaction response (Kubler-Ross, 1969), suggesting that responses to injury follow a five-stage process: (1) denial, (2) anger, (3) bargaining, (4) depression and (5) acceptance and reorganization. The idea was that most injured people moved through these stages but the speed of progress through them would vary. It has now been shown that there is little consistent empirical support for grief models of reaction to injury.

Responses to injury may be better viewed as stress reactions. The work of Wiese-Bjornstal and colleagues (Wiese-Bjornstal & Smith 1993; Wiese-Bjornstal et al., 1995, 1998) in developing the model of injury response is important in this area and extends the Andersen and Williams model. As with the Andersen and Williams model stress reactions are seen as involving cognitive appraisal of, and physiological/psychological reaction to, a stressor. These reactions then influence the behavior of the individual (Topic M1). Note that cognitive appraisal and emotional reaction influence each other. This stress reaction is influenced by characteristics of the individual and the context in which the injury occurred. As examples, an individual's self-esteem, trait-anxiety, psychological investment in the sport, self-motivation and injury history may all influence each part of the stress reaction. Psychological reactions may be greater if the athlete perceives it resulted from a cheap shot compared to an accidental collision, or if the injury is likely to prevent participation in a long-awaited and important competition.

The cognitive appraisal of the injury, or how the individual interprets the injury, can be positive or negative. The more positively it is appraised the less the emotional reaction. An intervention based on an accurate diagnosis may have a strong effect on influencing cognitions. Cognitive appraisal may be influenced by athletic identity (the degree to which an individual identifies themselves as an athlete). Those with a stronger athletic identity may be more prone to anxiety, depression or hopelessness, or they may be more motivated to return to action too soon. The emotional response may be influenced by situational factors such as injury prognosis, recovery progress, social support, impairment of daily activities and life stress. Emotional responses may have an effect on the actual injury, by, for example, increasing muscle tension at the site of the injury. The behavioral response to the injury is usually reflected in the degree of adherence to the rehabilitation program, and this ultimately determines whether the athlete recovers from the injury.

Facilitating recovery from injury

Many factors and strategies (e.g., stress inoculation training) have the potential to facilitate recovery from injury and ensure that the athlete is both physically and psychologically ready to return. However, relatively few studies have examined the efficacy of these strategies. Strategies that have been proposed include:

- **Good communication** between doctors, physiotherapists, athletes and coaches is critical. It is important that athletes understand the exact nature of their injury, its severity, and the rationale for any treatment.
- Rehabilitation programs will not be effective unless the athlete sticks to them, therefore it is important that motivation issues are addressed, this can be assisted by proper **goal-setting**, with realistic targets and strategies for achieving the goals.
- **Relaxation and stress management techniques** can be employed to help cope with anxiety, reduce pain and assist goal attainment. For example, in a study with athletes who had just had a knee operation Cupal and Brewer (2001) showed that athletes who received a multifaceted intervention that included imagery and relaxation training reported less re-injury anxiety, greater control over recovery and a faster return to desired levels of activity. In another study, Ross & Berger (1996) used stress inoculation training (SIT) to reduce post-surgery distress in injured athletes. Results showed that

injured athletes who received SIT reported lower levels of post-surgical anxiety and pain and took a shorter time to recover knee strength.

- Imagery can be used in a variety of ways. There is some evidence that imagery of the healing going on during treatment can accentuate treatment effects, however, more work is required in this area. For this to be effective athletes must have a detailed explanation of the injury and the healing process. During treatment the athlete is then asked to image the healing process that is occurring. Imagery can be used to practice skills and tactics mentally while physical practice is prevented. Imagery of the return to competition may also be useful.

- Often injured athletes have a tendency to dwell on negative and/or irrational thoughts, therefore using **positive self-talk strategies** (Topic L4) can help provide direction and motivation to the athlete.

- **Social support** for the injured person is also important. Peer-modeling, whereby an injured athlete is linked with those who have successfully recovered from the same injury can be useful. Regular meetings with all those involved in the rehabilitation process to discuss progress, problems, etc., may also be useful. Injured athletes may feel isolated from their teammates which for some can become a source of frustration and stress. This can be overcome by continuing to involve the injured athlete as much as possible in the team.

M3 BURNOUT AND OVER-TRAINING

Key notes

Defining burnout and over-training	Burnout is typically defined as a psychological, emotional and at times physical withdrawal from a previously enjoyed activity in response to excessive chronic stress (Smith, 1986). Over-training occurs when training loads are too high for individuals to adapt to, resulting in decreases in performance. Burnout is generally viewed as a psychological construct and over-training as a physiological construct.
Models of burnout	Several models of burnout have been proposed: the cognitive–affective stress model (Smith, 1986), the negative training stress response model (Silva, 1990), the investment model based on sport commitment (Schmidt & Stein, 1991; developed further by Raedeke, 1997) and the unidimensional identity development and external control model (Coakley, 1992). There has been limited research employing any of these models.
Factors causing burnout	There is limited research on burnout in athletes and coaches and that which exists is largely cross-sectional or retrospective. Physical, psychological, social and situational factors are all likely to influence the occurrence of burnout.
Preventing burnout	An essential step in preventing burnout is ensuring that coaches and athletes understand and can recognize the early warning signs. Many of the contributing factors to burnout can be eliminated or reduced through the design of coaching programs and education of athletes, coaches and parents.
Related topics	Anxiety: the basics (D3) Stress and coping (M1) Consultancy issues (K1)

Defining burnout and over-training

There is confusion about the differences between over-training, staleness and burnout. Over-training occurs when training loads are too high for individuals to adapt to, resulting in decreases in performance. It is not the same as over-load, which is part of a normal periodized program and designed to maximize physiological adaptation and ultimately performance. The end product of over-training is staleness, or a state in which the athlete struggles to maintain previous training and performance levels. Staleness is often seen as a warning sign for burnout.

Burnout is typically defined as a psychological, emotional and at times physical withdrawal from a previously enjoyed activity in response to excessive chronic stress (Smith, 1986). According to Maslach and Jackson (1981) burnout is characterized by feelings of emotional exhaustion, a sense of detachment (depersonalization) and reduced feelings of accomplishment. Emotional exhaustion describes how the individual begins to feel that they are no longer able to give themselves at a psychological level, and is manifested as feelings of extreme fatigue. Depersonalization involves the development of negative attitudes towards others and cynicism that may be linked to the experience of emotional exhaustion. The third dimension of reduced sense of performance accomplishment concerns evaluating oneself negatively, individuals are unhappy and dissatisfied with themselves.

Burnout is thought to be caused by a variety of personal and situational factors, and as such, not all people experiencing the same level of chronic stress will experience burnout.

Models of burnout

Stress-based models have dominated the burnout literature. The most widely cited model of burnout is Smith's (1986) cognitive-affective stress model, based on a general model of stress (see Topic M1). According to Smith's model burnout occurs via a four-stage process:

(1) Environmental demand. Some physical (e.g., training overload) or psychological (e.g., high expectations from parents/coaches) demand is made of the athlete.

(2) Athlete perception or cognitive appraisal of this demand. Athletes perceive or appraise this demand differently. For some it is a challenge and for others it is threatening.

(3) Physiological/psychological response. If the demand is perceived negatively the athlete has a negative response such as anxiety or fatigue.

(4) Behavioral consequences. As a result of 2 and 3 there is a behavioral response to deal with the situation (e.g., decreased performance, interpersonal conflict, reduction of effort, withdrawal from the activity).

It is assumed that all four phases of Smith's model will be influenced by individual differences in motivation and personality, for example, self-esteem or trait anxiety. It is hypothesized that there are reciprocal links between all four phases, so for example, the cognitive appraisal affects the physiological response, but this physiological response in turn affects further appraisals of the situation. The model is also considered to be circular and continuous with the effect of the behavioral consequences feeding back into the environmental demand phase.

Another conceptualization of burnout is the negative training stress response model (Silva, 1990). Although not ignoring psychological factors this model focuses more attention on responses to physical training. It is proposed that physical training physically and psychologically stresses the athlete resulting in positive or negative effects. Positive effects include physiological adaptation and therefore increased performance. Negative effects result initially in staleness and ultimately in burnout.

Non-stress perspectives on burnout have been proposed based on a rationale that everyone can experience stress but not everyone who experiences stress experiences burnout. Schmidt and Stein's (1991) sport commitment model of burnout (further developed by Raedeke, 1997) suggests that there are three primary determinants that influence athlete commitment, and that athletes who experience burnout are committed to sport for reasons that differ from those who do not experience burnout. The determinants of athlete commitment are: satisfaction based on rewards and costs associated with sport, attractiveness of alternative options, and resources athletes have invested in sport. Schmidt and Stein explain that burnout is likely to occur in athletes who display an entrapment profile, where they are participating in the sport because they have to rather than want to. This occurs when the athlete experiences high costs and low rewards but remains in the sport because they feel that they have invested a lot in terms of resources, and perceive a lack of attractive alternatives (high investment and low alternatives). This contrasts with the dropout athlete who is not committed to the sport. Results of Raedeke (1997) showed that swimmers with higher sport entrapment scores also had higher burnout scores.

Another alternative to stress-based models is the unidimensional identity development and external control model (Coakley, 1992), which focuses on how the social environment of sport affects identity development and personal control in young athletes. While not ignoring the role of stress in burnout Coakley proposes that stress is a symptom and not a cause of burnout. Coakley suggests that burnout occurs because the structure of sport prevents the young athlete from developing a normal multifaceted identity. When injury, performance failure or a performance plateau occurs the unidimensional identity means the individual's whole sense of self is threatened which causes stress and may lead to burnout. It is also proposed that the structure of elite sport prevents young people from taking personal control and decision-making with respect to their careers (e.g., elite sport administrators often decide where and when an athlete will compete, and funding structures may require athletes to participate in a certain number of competitions to remain funded). This lack of control ultimately leads to stress and potentially burnout.

There has been limited research work investigating the efficacy of any of these theories. Because of the complex and individual nature of burnout it is likely that each theory will offer something to the explanation of burnout and all should be further explored.

Factors causing burnout

There is limited research on burnout in athletes and coaches and that which exists is largely cross-sectional or retrospective. There is a need for multidisciplinary, prospective longitudinal studies to examine how burnout develops over time.

The most comprehensive set of studies on athletes to date has been conducted by Gould and colleagues with elite junior tennis players (Gould et al., 1996a, 1996b, 1997). They found situational, personality and coping strategy differences between burned out and non-burned out players. For example, burned out players perceived they had less input to their training, were higher in amotivation, were higher on some perfectionism subscales (e.g., perceived parental criticism) and were less likely to use planning strategies to cope. Further work revealed two major categories of burnout symptoms: mental (e.g., lacking motivation, concentration problems) and physical (e.g., illness, lacking energy).

There are little empirical data on the factors believed to lead to burnout in athletes. Some factors which may be associated with burnout are:

- physical factors (e.g., injury, over-training, lack of physical development, erratic performance, feeling tired all the time);
- logistical factors (e.g., travel grind, time performing, having little time for anything else);
- social and interpersonal factors (e.g., dissatisfaction with social life, negative parental/team/coach influences, dissatisfaction within the sporting world, cheating by competitors);
- situational factors (e.g., coach relationship, low social support, high competitive demands, time and energy demands, insufficient skills, boredom, regimentation and lack of autonomy);

- psychological factors (e.g., unfulfilled or inappropriate expectations, over-emphasis on rankings, realization that a professional career was unlikely, lack of enjoyment, coach and parental pressure to practice and win, pressure to win or maintain scholarships, self pressure and motivational concerns such as wanting to try other sports and non-sport activities or simply being tired of playing the same sport).

Similar characteristics have been found when burnout has been examined in coaches, athletic trainers, athletic directors and officials. In addition, role conflict, role ambiguity, marital status (single), gender (female), age (younger), and experience (less) have been associated with burnout in these groups.

Preventing burnout

An essential step in preventing burnout is ensuring that coaches and athletes understand and can recognize the early signs of staleness. Physiological warning signs are often hard to detect, but at the psychological level changes in mood, self-confidence, and sleep disturbances may indicate the onset of over-training and staleness, which may lead to burnout. For example, Morgan and colleagues (1987) showed that with increasing training levels the iceberg profile (Topic D2) disappeared and an overall negative mood appeared. These mood disturbances fell to 'normal' levels when training was reduced. It is obvious that a number of factors contribute to staleness and burnout, many of which can be eliminated or reduced through the design of coaching programs and education of athletes, coaches and parents. Programs directed at modifying problematic coaching and parent behaviors should be useful in reducing stress from these sources. Other strategies to help prevent staleness and burnout include the effective use of goal setting, developing programs to increase social support, scheduling time outs, allowing athletes to make some decisions, using mental practice periods to reduce physical training, and teaching problem-solving skills and effective stress management strategies. Maintaining an environment which the athletes perceive as fun and enjoyable while still working hard should also help prevent staleness and burnout.

M4 DRUGS IN SPORT

Key notes

Evidence for drug use in sports and exercise

It is difficult to get an accurate estimate of the extent of drug use in sport. Anecdotal evidence suggests drug use is widespread. Scientific evidence suggests drug use rates from 2–64% but such work is limited due to under-reporting.

Categories of drugs

Drugs used in sport and exercise fall into two categories: performance-enhancing and recreational or social. Performance-enhancing drugs include *anabolic steroids, stimulants, narcotic analgesics, beta-adrenergic blockers, diuretics, peptide hormones*. Although not a drug *blood doping* is also a banned performance-enhancing strategy. Recreational or social drugs include drugs such as marijuana and cocaine.

Why do athletes take drugs?

There are many physical, psychological and social reasons why individuals take drugs, and the reason will influence the drug used. Physical reasons include performance enhancement, physical appearance, weight control, coping with pain and injury and to avoid missing training or a competition. Psychological causes include coping with stress and anxiety, boredom, personal problems, low self-confidence, perfectionistic tendencies or a sense of being impervious to any side effects of drugs. Social reasons include peer pressure, gaining peer acceptance, modeling and to gain social support.

Interventions to prevent drug use

Strategies may be cognitive or behavioral. Cognitive strategies include education, coaches communicating their feelings about and awareness of drug use and the development of team/squad guidelines for acceptable behavior. Behavioral strategies include drug testing, goal-setting and behavioral contracting.

Related topics

Consultancy: basic issues (K1)
Issues of arousal and anxiety (L2)

Issues of confidence (L4)

Evidence for drug use in sports and exercise

In sport, the need to stand apart and demonstrate one's superiority is encouraged and great praise is given for sporting success. The need to be the best has led some to the use of drugs to enhance performance or cope with the pressures of success. There is also evidence for increasing drug use in other environments such as gyms, the security services and male modeling.

Due to the illicit nature of much drug use it is difficult to get an accurate estimate of the extent of drug use in sport. Anecdotal evidence from athletes, based on their own experiences or perceptions, suggests drug use is widespread, and that in some cases coaches sanction drug use. However, anecdotal evidence is limited because it provides no concrete evidence for the extent of drug use. Scientific evidence is also limited because the illicit nature of drug use promotes under-reporting. Where scientific research exists it has mostly examined anabolic steroids. Figures from scientific research on steroid use vary from 2% to 64% depending on sport investigated and the data collection methods employed (Anshel, 2001).

Categories of drugs

Drugs used in sport and exercise fall into two categories: performance-enhancing and recreational or social. Performance-enhancing drugs include:

- *Anabolic steroids*, which are derived from testosterone and are used to increase strength and endurance, improve mental attitude, and increase training and recovery rates. Would be of most potential use in sports where strength is important, such as throwing events or weight lifting.
- *Stimulants* (e.g., amphetamines, ephedrine), which are used to decrease fatigue, and increase alertness, endurance and aggression. Would be of most potential use in endurance sports, such as road cycling.
- *Narcotic analgesics* (anti-inflammatories), which are used to reduce pain, to slow or stop inflammation and to reduce fever. Would be of most potential use by athletes recovering from injury or dealing with a chronic injury. These may also be used by someone wishing to continue playing with an injury.
- *Beta-adrenergic blockers*, which are used to slow the heart rate, reduce anxiety and steady natural body tremors. Would be of most potential use in sports requiring fine motor skills and precision such as snooker, shooting events and golf.
- *Diuretics* are used to increase the loss of urine, which may help mask other drugs and also to gain temporary weight loss. Aside from masking other drug use diuretics may be useful to athletes in sports that compete in weight categories as they could be used to help an athlete 'make weight'.
- *Peptide hormones* (e.g., human growth hormone), which are used to increase strength and endurance, and muscle growth. Would be of most potential use in sports where strength and power is important, such as throwing events or weight lifting.
- *Blood doping*, which involves the removal of an athlete's blood that is then stored and re-infused prior to competition to increase oxygen-carrying capacity and thereby increase endurance. Potentially most useful in endurance events, such as the marathon or cycling.

Despite the reported benefits of these different classes of drugs all of them have negative consequences for the user. Drug use can lead to long-term health (e.g., cancers, premature heart disease) and psychological problems (e.g., heightened aggression, self-injury) and in some cases death.

Recreational or social drugs such as marijuana and cocaine tend to slow response and decision-making time and are not therefore used to enhance performance. They are drugs that people use for personal pleasure, to escape from pressures, to fit in, or for thrills and excitement. Recreational drugs are illegal in most countries.

Why do athletes take drugs?

Understanding why athletes or exercisers take drugs is important for the development and delivery of drug use prevention programs and to those who provide counseling to athletes. There are many physical, psychological and social reasons why individuals take drugs and the reason will influence the drug used (Anshel, 1991).

The most common physical cause is performance enhancement. Depending on the perceived need of the athlete they may take drugs to increase strength, power, endurance, alertness or aggression, or to decrease reaction time, fatigue, anxiety and muscle tremor. Non-athletes may take drugs to improve physical appearance. Athletes and exercisers may take drugs to assist with weight control. Another physical cause is to assist athletes to cope with pain and injury and to perhaps hasten rehabilitation. Athletes may take drugs to mask pain so that they don't miss training or risk losing their place on a team.

Psychological causes are usually associated with the use of recreational drugs. Such drugs may be used as a means of coping with stress and anxiety, boredom, personal problems, low self-confidence, perfectionistic tendencies or a sense of being impervious to any side effects of drugs.

Social reasons are potentially very powerful causes of drug use. Individuals may start drug use in response to peer pressure or to gain peer acceptance. Young athletes may model their behavior on older more experienced athletes whom they believe to take drugs. Finally athletes may take drugs to gain social support through recognition of their improved appearance or performances.

Interventions to prevent drug use

The strategies to prevent or inhibit drug use vary according to the athlete's perceived need for drugs, the type of drug usage, the physical demands of the sport and the situational demands upon the athlete. The actual strategies may be cognitive or behavioral.

Cognitive strategies focus on influencing the athlete's behaviors and attitudes intellectually and psychologically. The most widely used cognitive strategy is education about the negative consequences of drug use. However, the effectiveness of this approach has been less than optimum, probably because it assumes that drug users make rational judgments on drug use, having weighed up the advantages and disadvantages. Other cognitive approaches include coaches communicating their feelings about and awareness of drug use, the development of team/squad guidelines for acceptable behavior, the teaching of coping skills to deal with stress and anxiety, and providing an environment in which athletes have a sense of autonomy.

The objective of behavioral strategies is to create an environment that controls or influences behavior. The main behavioral strategy is drug testing. This needs to be associated with a consistent application of sanctions. As one of the main reasons for drug use is performance enhancement, coaches should structure a training program to keep developing skills and make sure the athlete is aware of these skill improvements. This may be assisted by the use of proper goal setting. Behavioral contracting is an agreement between the player and the coach on what is acceptable behavior on both parts. The contract would include specified reinforcements or sanctions for behavior. For elite athletes, structuring some of the free time between training sessions may help to prevent boredom. The development of a support group of peers, in which athletes can discuss any concerns, may create a self-regulating influence on individual behavior.

FURTHER READING

Section A

Cox, R.H. (2002). *Sport Psychology: Concepts and applications*, 5th edn. Dubuque, Iowa: Brown and Benchmark.

Hill, K. (2001) *Frameworks for Sport Psychologists: Enhancing Sport Performance*. Champaign, IL: Human Kinetics.

Lavellee, D, Kremer, J, Moran, A and Williams, M (2003) *Sport Psychology: Contemporary Themes*. Basingstoke: Palgrave MacMillan.

Singer, R.N., Hausenblas, H.A. and Jannelle, C. (2001) *Handbook of Sport Psychology*, 2nd edn. New York: John Wiley.

Thomas, J. & Nelson, J. (2001) *Research Methods in Physical Activity*, 4th edn. Champaign, IL: Human Kinetics.

Section B

Hall, C. (2001). Imagery in Sport and Exercise. In R.N. Singer, H.A. Hausenblaus & C.M. Janelle (eds) *Handbook of Sport Psychology*, 2nd edn. New York: John Wiley.

Moran, A.P. (1996). *The Psychology of Concentration in Sport Performers: A Cognitive Analysis*. Hove, UK: Psychology Press.

Temprado, J.J. & Laurent, M. (1999). Perceptuo-motor coordination in sport: Current trends and controversies. *International Journal of Sport Psychology*, 30, 417–436.

Williams. A.M., Davids, K. and Williams, J.G. (1999). *Visual Perception and Action in Sport*. London: E & FN Spon.

Section C

Biddle, S.J.H., Hanrahan, S.J. & Sellars, C.N. (2001) Attributions: Past, present and future. In R.N. Singer, H.A. Hausenblas, and C. Jannelle (eds) *Handbook of Sport Psychology*, 2nd edn. New York: John Wiley.

Duda, J. L. (1992) Motivation in sport settings: A goal perspective approach. In *Motivation in Sport and Exercise*, G.C. Roberts (ed.). Champaign, IL: Human Kinetics.

Duda, J.L. & Hall, H. (2001) Achievement goal theory in sport: Recent extensions and future directions. In R.N. Singer, H.A. Hausenblas, and C. Jannelle (eds) *Handbook of Sport Psychology*, 2nd edn. New York: John Wiley.

Feltz, D.L. and Lirgg, C.D. (2001) Self-efficacy beliefs of athletes, teams and coaches. In R.N. Singer, H.A. Hausenblas, and C. Jannelle (eds) *Handbook of Sport Psychology*, 2nd edn. New York: John Wiley.

Roberts, G. (2001) *Advances in Motivation in Sport and Exercise*. Champaign, IL: Human Kinetics.

Vealey, R. S. (2001) Understanding and enhancing self-confidence in athletes. In R.N. Singer, H.A. Hausenblas and C. Jannelle (eds) *Handbook of Sport Psychology*, 2nd edn. New York: John Wiley.

Section D

Burton, D., Naylor, S. & Holliday, B. (2001) Goal setting in sport: Investigating the goal effectiveness paradox.

In R.N. Singer, H.A. Hausenblas and C. Jannelle (eds) *Handbook of Sport Psychology*, 2nd edn. New York: John Wiley.

Hanin, Y.L. (2000) *Emotions in Sport*. Human Kinetics, Champaign, IL.

Hardy, L., Jones, G. & Gould, D. (1996). *Understanding Psychological Preparation For Sport: Theory and Practice of Elite Performers*. Chichester: Wiley.

Jones, J.G. and Hardy, L. (1990) *Stress and Performance in Sport*. Chichester: John Wiley and Sons.

Kerr, J.H. (1999). *Experiencing Sport: Reversal Theory*. Chichester: Wiley.

Section E

Auweele, Y.V., Nys, K., Rzewnicki, R. & Van Mele, V. (2001) Personality and the athlete. In R.N. Singer, H.A. Hausenblas, and C. Jannelle (eds) *Handbook of Sport Psychology*, 2nd edn. New York: John Wiley.

Cox, R.H. (2002). *Sport Psychology: Concepts and Applications*, 5th edn. Dubuque, Iowa: Brown and Benchmark.

Kremer, J.M.D. & Scully, D.M. (1994) *Psychology in Sport*. Bristol: Taylor & Francis.

Section F

Baron, R.A., & Byrne, D. (2003) *Social Psychology*, 10th edn. New York: Allyn & Bacon.

Fiske, S.T. (2004) *Social Beings: Core Motives in Social Psychology*. New York: Wiley.

Russel, G.W. (1993) *The Social Psychology of Sport*. New York: Springer-Verlag.

Section G

Brown, R. (2000) *Group Processes* 2nd Ed. Oxford: Blackwell.

Moran, A.P. (2004) *Sport and Exercise Psychology: A Critical Introduction*. London: Routledge.

Paskevich, D.M., Estabrooks, P.A. Brawley, L.R. & Carron, A.V., (2001) Group cohesion in sport and exercise. In R.N. Singer, H.A. Hausenblas and C. Jannelle (eds) *Handbook of Sport Psychology*, 2nd edn. New York: Macmillan.

Section H

Biddle, S. (2000). Emotion, mood and physical activity. In Biddle, S., Fox, K. & Boutcher, S. (eds) *Physical Activity and Psychological Well-being*. New York: Routledge.

Boutcher, S. (2000). Cognitive performance, fitness and aging. In Biddle, S., Fox, K. & Boutcher, S. (eds) *Physical Activity and Psychological Well-being*. New York: Routledge.

Fox, K. (2000). The effects of exercise on self-percep-tions and self-esteem. In Biddle, S., Fox, K. & Boutcher, S. (eds). *Physical Activity and Psychological Well-being*. New York: Routledge.

Hausenblas, H. & Symons Downs, D. (2002). Exercise dependence: a systematic review. *Psychology of Sport and Exercise* 3, 89–123.

Mutrie, N. (2000). Emotion, mood and physical activity. In Biddle, S., Fox, K. & Boutcher, S. (eds) *Physical Activity and Psychological Well-being.* New York: Routledge.

Szabo, A. (2000). Physical activity as a source of psychological dysfunction. In Biddle, S., Fox, K. & Boutcher, S. (eds) *Physical Activity and Psychological Well-being.* New York: Routledge.

Taylor, A. (2000). The effects of exercise on self-perceptions and self-esteem. In Biddle, S., Fox, K. & Boutcher, S. (eds) *Physical Activity and Psychological Well-being.* New York: Routledge.

Section I

Biddle, S. & Mutrie, N. (2001). *Psychology of Physical Activity: Determinants, Well-being and Interventions.* London: Routledge.

Gill, D. (2000). *Psychological Dynamics of Sport and Exercise,* 2nd edn. Champaign, IL: Human Kinetics.

Sallis, J. F., Prochaska, J. J., & Taylor, W. C. (2000). A review of correlates of physical activity of children and adolescents. *Medicine and Science in Sports and Exercise* 32, 963–975.

Trost, S., Owen, N., Bauman, A., Sallis, J. & Brown, W. (2002). Correlates of adults' participation in physical activity: Review and update. *Medicine and Science in Sports and Exercise* 34, 1996–2001.

Section J

Biddle, S. & Mutrie, N. (2001). *Psychology of Physical Activity: Determinants, Well-being and Interventions.* London: Routledge.

Culos-Reed, S., Gyurcsik, N., & Brawley, L. (2001). Using theories of motivated behavior to understand physical activity: Perspectives on their influence. In Singer, R., Hausenblas, H. & Janelle, C. (eds) *Handbook of Sport Psychology,* 2nd edn. New York: John Wiley.

Prochaska, J. & Marcus, B. (1994). The transtheoretical model: Applications to exercise. In Dishman, R. (ed.) *Advances in Exercise Adherence.* Champaign, IL: Human Kinetics.

Sallis, J., & Owen, N. (2002). Ecological models of health behavior. In K. Glanz, B. Rimer & F. Lewis (eds) *Health Behavior and Health Education: Theory, Research and Practice,* 3rd edn. San Francisco, CA: Jossey Bass.

Section K

Andersen, M. (2000) *Doing Sport Psychology.* Champaign, IL: Human Kinetics.

Butler, R.J. (1996). *Sport Psychology in Action.* Oxford: Butterworth Heinemann.

Cockerill I.M. (ed.) (2002) *Solutions in Sport Psychology.* London: Thompson Publishers.

Section L

Bull, S. Albinson, J. & Shambrook, C. (1996) *The Mental Game Plan.* Eastbourne: Sport Dynamics.

Butler, R.J. (1997). *Sport Psychology in Performance.* Butterworth Heinemann.

Cockerill I.M. (ed.) (2002) *Solutions in Sport Psychology.* London: Thompson Publishers

Hardy, L., Jones, G., & Gould, D. (1996). *Understanding Psychological Preparation For Sport: Theory and Practice of Elite Performers.* Chichester: Wiley.

Orlick, T (1986) *Psyching for Sport.* Champaign, IL: Leisure Press, Human Kinetics.

Williams, J.M. (2001) *Applied Sport Psychology: Personal Growth to Peak Performance,* 4th edn. Palo Alto, CA: Mayfield.

Section M

Anshel, M. (2001). Drug abuse in sport: Causes and cures. In Williams, J. (ed) *Applied Sport Psychology: Personal Growth to Peak Performance,* 4th edn. Mountain View, CA: Mayfield.

Brewer, B. (2001). Psychology of sport injury rehabilitation. In Singer, R., Hausenblas, H. & Janelle, C. (eds) *Handbook of Sport Psychology,* 2nd edn. New York: John Wiley.

Gould, D. (1996). Personal motivation gone awry: Burnout in competitive athletes. *Quest* 48, 275–289.

Hardy, L., Jones, G. & Gould, D. (1996). *Understanding Psychological Preparation for Sport: Theory and Practice of Elite Performers.* Chichester: John Wiley

Henschen, K. (2001). Athletic staleness and burnout: Diagnosis, prevention and treatment. In J. Williams (ed.) *Applied Sport Psychology: Personal Growth to Peak Peformance,* 4th edn. Mountain View, CA: Mayfield Publishing Company.

Madden, C. (1995). Ways of coping. In Morris, T. & Summers, J. (eds) *Sport Psychology: Theory, Applications and Issues.* Milton, QLD: John Wiley.

Udry, E. & Andersen, M. (2002). Athletic injury and sport behavior. In T. Horn (ed.) *Advances in Sport Psychology,* 2nd edn. Champaign, IL: Human Kinetics.

Williams, J. (2001). Psychology of injury risk and prevention. In Singer, R., Hausenblas, H. & Janelle, C. (eds) *Handbook of Sport Psychology,* 2nd edn. New York: John Wiley.

REFERENCES

Abernethy, B. (2001). Attention. In R.N. Singer, H.A. Hausenblas, C.M. Janelle (eds.) *Handbook of Sport Psychology*, 2nd edn. New York: John Wiley and Sons.

Abernethy, B. & Wood, J.M. (2001). Do generalized visual training programes for sport really work? An experimental investigation. *Journal of Sports Sciences* **19**, 203–222.

Agnew, G.A. & Carron, A.V. (1994). Crowd effects and the home advantage. *International Journal of Sport Psychology* **25**, 53–62.

Ajzen, I. (1991). The theory of planned behavior. *Organizational Behavior and Human Decision Processes* **50**, 179–211.

Andersen, M. & Williams, J. (1988). A model of stress and athletic injury: Prediction and prevention. *Journal of Sport and Exercise Psychology* **10**, 168–173.

Anderson, A.G., Miles, A., Mahoney, C. & Robinson, P. (2002). Evaluating the effectiveness of applied sport psychology practice: Making the case for a case study approach. *Sport Psychologist* **16**, 432–453.

Annesi, J.J. (1997). Three-dimensional state anxiety recall: Implications for individual zone of optimal functioning research and application. *Sport Psychologist* **11**, 43–52.

Anshel, M. (1991). Causes for drug abuse in sport: A survey of intercollegiate athletes. *Journal of Sport Behavior* **14**, 283–307.

Anshel, M. (2001). Drug abuse in sport: Causes and cures. In Williams, J. (ed.) *Applied Sport Psychology: Personal Growth to Peak Performance*, 4th edn. Mountain View, CA: Mayfield.

Asch, S.E. (1956) Studies of independence and conformity: A minority of one against a unanimous majority. *Psychological Monographs* **70**(416).

Bales, R.F., & Cohen, S.P. (1979). *SYMLOG: A System for the Multiple Level Observation of Groups*. New York: Free Press.

Bandura A. (1997). *Self-efficacy: The Exercise of Control.* New York: W.H. Freeman and Company.

Bandura, A. (1977). Self-efficacy: Toward a unifying theory of behavioral change. *Psychological Review* **84**, 191–215.

Bandura, A. (1977). *Social Learning Theory.* New York: General Learning Press.

Bandura, A. (1986) *Social Foundation of Thought and Action.* Prentice Hall, Englewood Cliffs, NJ.

Bandura, A., Ross, D. & Ross, S.A. (1961) Transmission of aggression through imitation of aggressive models *Journal of Abnormal and Social Psychology* **63**, 575–582.

Baron, R.A. & Byrne, D. (2003) *Social Psychology*, 10th edn. New York: Allyn & Bacon.

Becker, M., & Maiman, L. (1975). Socio-behavioral determinants of compliance with health and medical care recommendations. *Medical Care* **13**, 10–24.

Beedie, C.J., Terry, P.C. & Lane, A.M. (2000) The profile of mood states and athletic performance. Two meta-analyses. *Journal of Applied Sport Psychology* **12**(1): 49–68.

Belbin, R.M. (2003) *Management Teams: Why they Succeed or Fail*, 2nd edn. Oxford: Butterworth Heinemann.

Berger, B. & Motl, (2001). Physical activity and quality of life. In R. Singer, H. Hausenblas, & C. Janelle (eds) *Handbook of Sport Psychology*, 2nd edn. New York: John Wiley and Sons.

Biddle, S. (2000) Exercise emotions and mental health. In Y.L. Hanin (ed.) *Emotions in Sport*. Champaign, IL: Human Kinetics.

Biddle, S. (2000). Emotion, mood and physical activity. In Biddle, S., Fox, K. & Boutcher, S. (eds) *Physical Activity and Psychological Well-being*. New York: Routledge.

Biddle, S. & Mutrie, N. (2001). *Psychology of Physical Activity: Determinants, Well-being and Interventions.* London: Routledge.

Biddle, S.J.H., Markland, D., Gilbourne, D., Chatzisarantis, N.L.D. & Sparkes, A.C. (2001) Research methods in sport and exercise psychology: quantitative and qualitative issues. *Journal of Sports Sciences* **19**, 777–809.

Boutcher, S. (2000). Cognitive performance, fitness and aging. In Biddle, S., Fox, K. & Boutcher, S. (eds) *Physical Activity and Psychological Well-being*. New York: Routledge.

Brewer, B. (2001). Psychology of sport injury rehabilitation. In Singer, R., Hausenblas, H. & Janelle, C. (eds). *Handbook of Sport Psychology*, 2nd edn. New York: John Wiley.

Brown, R. (2000) *Group Processes*, 2nd edn. Oxford: Blackwell.

Bryan, J., & Test, M. (1967). Models and helping: Naturalistic studies in aiding behavior. *Journal of Personality and Social Psychology* **6**, 400–407.

Bryman, A. (1988) *Quality and Quantity in Social Research*. London: Unwin Hyman.

Buckworth, J. & Dishman, R.K. (2002) *Exercise Psychology*. Champaign, IL: Human Kinetics.

Bull, S.J. (1997) The Immersion Approach. In R.J. Butler (ed.) *Sports Psychology in Performance*. Oxford: Butterworth Heinemann.

Bull, S.J., Albinson, J.G. & Shambrook C.J. (1996) *The Mental Game Plan*. Sports Dynamics: Eastbourne.

Burton, D. (1988) Do anxious swimmers swim slower? Re-examining the elusive anxiety-performance relationship. *Journal of Sport and Exercise Psychology* **10**, 45–61.

Burton, D., & Naylor, S. (1997). Is anxiety really facilitative? Reaction to the myth that cognitive anxiety always impairs sport performance. *Journal of Applied Sport Psychology* **9**(2), 295–302.

Butler, R.J. (1996). *Sport Psychology in Action*. Oxford: Butterworth Heinemann.

Carron, A.V., Brawley, L.R. & Widmeyer, W.N. (1998). The measurement of cohesiveness in sport groups. In J.L. Duda (ed.) *Advances in Sport and Exercise Psychology Measurement*. Morgantown, WV: Fitness Information Technology.

Carron, A.V., Colman, M.M., Wheeler, J. & Stevens, D. (2002). Cohesion and performance in sport: A meta analysis. *Journal of Sport and Exercise Psychology* **24**, 168–188.

Carron, A.V., Widmeyer, W.N. & Brawley, L.R. (1985). The development of an instrument to assess cohesion in sport teams: The group environment questionnaire. *Journal of Sport Psychology* **7**, 244–266.

Cerin, E., Szabo, A., Hunt, N. & Williams, C. (2000). Temporal patterning of competitive emotions: a critical review. *Journal of Sports Sciences* **18**(8), 605–626.

Chelladurai, P. (1990). Leadership in sports – a review. *International Journal of Sport Psychology* **21**, 328–354.

Cialdini, R.B., Kenrick, D.T. & Baumann, D.J. (1982). Effects of mood on prosocial behavior in children and adults. In N. Eisenberg (ed.) *The Development of Prosocial Behavior*. New York: Academic Press.

Coakley, J. & White, A. (1992). Making decisions: gender and sport participation among British adolescents. *Sociology of Sport Journal* **9**, 20–35.

Coakley, J. (1992). Burnout among adolescent athletes: A personal failure or a social problem? *Sociology of Sport Journal* **9**, 271–285.

Costa, P.T., Jr., & McCrae, R.R. (1992). Normal personality assessment in clinical practice: The NEO Personality Inventory. *Psychological Assessment* **4**, 5–13.

Cottrell, N.B., Wack, D.L., Sekerak, G.J., & Rittle, R.H. (1968). Social facilitation of dominant responses by the presence of an audience and the mere presence of others. *Journal of Personality and Social Psychology* **9**, 245–250.

Courneya, K.S. & Carron, A.V. (1992). The home advantage in sport competitions: A literature review. *Journal of Sport and Exercise Psychology* **14**, 13–27.

Cox, R.H., Russell, W.D. & Robb, M. (1998). Development of a CSAI-2 short-form for assessing competitive state anxiety during and immediately prior to competition. *Journal of Sport Behavior* **21**, 30–40.

Craft, L. & Landers, D. (1998). The effect of exercise on clinical depression and depression resulting from mental illness: A meta-analysis. *Journal of Sport and Exercise Psychology* **20**, 339–357.

Craft. L.L., Magyar, T.M., Becker, B.J. & Feltz, D.L. (2003). The relationship between the Competitive State Anxiety Inventory-2 and sport performance: A meta-analysis. *Journal of Sport and Exercise Psychology* **25**, 44–65.

Crocker, P.R.E. (1997) A confirmatory factor analysis of the positive affect negative affect schedule (PANAS) with a youth sport sample. *Journal of Sport & Exercise Psychology* **19**, 91–97.

Culos-Reed, S., Gyurcsik, N., & Brawley, L. (2001). Using theories of motivated behavior to understand physical activity: Perspectives on their influence. In Singer, R., Hausenblas, H. & Janelle, C. (eds) *Handbook of Sport Psychology*, 2nd edn. New York: John Wiley.

Cupal, D. & Brewer, B. (2001). Effects of relaxation and guided imagery on knee strength, reinjury anxiety, and pain following anterior cruciate ligament reconstruction. *Rehabilitation Psychology* **46**, 28–43.

Dale, G.A. & Wrisberg, C.A. (1996). The use of a performance profiling technique in a team setting –

getting the athletes and coach on the same page. *Sport Psychologist* **10**, 261–277.

Dale, G.A. (1996) Existential phenomenology – emphasizing the experience of the athlete in sport psychology research. *Sport Psychologist* **10**, 307–321.

Deci, E.L. & Ryan, R.M. (1980). The empirical exploration of intrinsic motivational processes, In L. Berkowitz (ed.) *Advances in Experimental Social Psychology*, vol. 13. New York: Pergamon, pp. 38–80.

Deci, E.L. (1975) *Intrinsic Motivation*. New York: Plenum.

Deci, E.L., & Ryan, R.M. (1985). *Intrinsic Motivation and Self-determination in Human Behavior*. New York: Plenum.

Dishman R.K. (1988) *Exercise Adherence: Its Impact on Mental Health*. Champaign, IL: Human Kinetics.

Dishman, R. & Dunn, A. (1988). Exercise adherence in children and youth: Implications for adulthood. In R.K. Dishman (ed.) *Exercise Adherence: Its Impact on Public Health*. Champaign, IL: Human Kinetics.

Dishman, R. & Gettman, L. (1980). Psychobiologic influences on exercise adherence. *Journal of Sport Psychology* **2**, 295–310.

Dishman, R. (1990). Determinants of participation in physical activity. In C. Bouchard, R. Shephard, T. Stephens, J. Sutton, & B. McPherson (eds) *Exercise, Fitness, and Health*. Champaign, IL: Human Kinetics.

Dollard, J. Doob, L.W. Miller, N.E., Mowrer, O.H. & Sears, R.R. (1939) *Frustration and Aggression*. New Haven: Yale University Freer.

Duda, J.L. (1987). Toward a developmental theory of children's motivation in sport. *Journal of Sport Psychology* **9**, 130–145.

Duda, J.L. (1989) Relationship between task and ego orientation and the perceived purpose of sport among high school athletes. *Journal of Sport and Exercise Psychology* **11**(3), 318–335.

Duda, J. L. (1992) Motivation in sport settings: A goal perspective approach. In G.C. Roberts (ed.) *Motivation in Sport and Exercise*. Champaign, IL: Human Kinetics.

Duda, J.L. (1997) Perpetuating myths: A response to Hardy's 1996 Coleman Griffith Address. *Journal of Applied Sport Psychology* **9**(2), 303–309.

Duda, J.L., Likang, C., Newton, M.L., Walling, M.D. & Catley, D. (1995) Task and ego orientations and intrinsic motivation in sport. *International Journal of Sport Psychology* **26**, 40–63.

Duda, J.L., Olson, L.K. & Templin, T.J. (1991) The relationship of task and ego orientation to sportsmanship attitudes and the perceived legitimacy of injurious acts. *Research Quarterly for Exercise and Sport* **62**, 79–87.

Duda, J.L. & Nichols, J. (1992) Dimensions of achievement motivation in schoolwork and sport. *Journal of Educational Psychology* **84**, 290–299.

Duda, J.L., & Hall, H. (2001) Achievement goal theory in sport. In R.N. Singer, H.A. Hausenblas, and C. Jannelle (eds) *Handbook of Sport Psychology*, 2nd edn. New York: John Wiley and Sons.

Duda, J.L., Chi, L., Newton, M.L., Walling, M.D. & Catley, D. (1995) Task and ego orientation and intrinsic motivation in sport. *International Journal of Sport Psychology* **26**(1), 40–63.

Dunn, J.G.H. (1994). Toward the combined use of nomothetic and idiographic methodologies in sport psychology: An empirical example. *The Sport Psychologist* **8**, 376–393.

Easterbrook, J.A. (1959). The effect of emotion on cue utilisation and the organisation of behaviour. *Psychological Review* **66**, 183–201.

Ericsson, K.A., Krampe, R.Th. & Tesch-Roemer, C. (1993). The role of deliberate practice in the acquisition of expert performance. *Psychological Review* 100, 363–406.

Etnier, J., Salazar, W., Landers, D., Petruzello, S., Han, M. & Nowell, P. (1997). The influence of physical fitness and exercise upon cognitive functioning: A meta-analysis. *Journal of Sport and Exercise Psychology* **19**, 249–277.

Eysenck M.W. & Calvo M.G. (1992) Anxiety & performance: The processing efficiency theory. *Cognition and Emotion* 6(6), 409–434

Fawkner, H., McMurray, N. & Summers, J. (1999). Athletic injury and minor life events: A prospective study. *Journal of Science and Medicine in Sports* **2**, 117–124.

Feltz, D. & Landers, D. (1983). The effects of mental practice on mental skill learning and performance: a meta-analysis. *Journal of Sport Psychology* **5**, 25–57.

Feltz, D.L., and Lirgg, C.D. (2001) Self-efficacy beliefs of athletes, teams and coaches. In R.N. Singer, H.A. Hausenblas, and C. Jannelle (eds) *Handbook of Sport Psychology*, 2nd ed. New York: John Wiley and Sons.

Fiedler, F.E. (1967) *A Theory of Leadership Effectiveness*. New York: McGraw-Hill.

Fishbein, M., & Ajzen, I. (1975). *Belief, Attitude, Intention, and Behavior: An Introduction to Theory and Research*. Reading, MA: Addison-Wesley.

Fiske, S.T. (2004) *Social Beings: Core Motives in Social Psychology*. New York: Wiley.

Fitts, P.M., and Posner, M.I. (1967). *Human Performance*. Belmont CA, Brooks-Cole.

Folkman, S. (1991). Coping across the lifespan: Theoretical issues. In E.M. Cummings, A.L. Greene & K.H. Karraker (eds) *Lifespan Developmental Psychology: Perspectives on Stress and Coping*. Hillsdale, NJ: Lawrence Erlbaum.

Fox, K. (2000). The effects of exercise on self-perceptions and self-esteem. In Biddle, S., Fox, K. & Boutcher, S. (eds) *Physical Activity and Psychological Well-being*. New York: Routledge.

French, J.P.R. Jr., and Raven, B. (1960). The bases of social power. In D. Cartwright and A. Zander (eds) *Group Dynamics*. New York: Harper and Row.

George, T.R. & Feltz, D.L. (1995). Motivation in sport from a collective efficacy perspective. *International Journal of Sport Psychology* **26**, 98–116.

Gergen, K.J., Gergen, M. & Barton, W. (1973) Deviance in the dark. *Psychology Today* **7**, 129–130.

Gibson, J.J. (1979). *An Ecological Approach to Visual Perception*. Boston MA, Houghton-Mifflin.

Gill, D. (2000). *Psychological Dynamics of Sport and Exercise*, 2nd edn. Champaign, IL: Human Kinetics.

Gill, D.L. & Deeter, T.E. (1988). Development of the SOQ. *Research Quarterly for Exercise and Sport* **59**, 191–202.

Glass, G.V. (1976) Primary, secondary, and meta-analysis research. *Educational Researcher* **5**, 3–8.

Gould, D. (1996). Personal motivation gone awry: Burnout in competitive athletes. *Quest* **48**, 275–289.

Gould, D., Jackson, S., & Finch, L. (1993) Sources of stress in national champion figure skaters. *Journal of Sport and Exercise Psychology* **15**, 134–159.

Gould, D., Tuffey, S., Udry, E., & Loehr, J. (1996a). Burnout in competitive junior tennis players: I. A quantitative psychological assessment. *The Sport Psychologist* **10**, 322–340.

Gould, D., Tuffey, S., Udry, E., & Loehr, J. (1996b). Burnout in competitive junior tennis players: II. Qualitative analysis. *The Sport Psychologist* **10**, 340–366.

Gould, D., Tuffey, S., Udry, E., & Loehr, J. (1997). Burnout in competitive junior tennis players: III. Individual differences in the burnout experience. *The Sport Psychologist* **11**, 257–276.

Groff, B.D., Baron, R.S. & Moore, D.L. (1983). Distraction, attentional conflict, and drivelike behavior. *Journal of Experimental Social Psychology* **19**, 359–380.

Hall, C. (2001). Imagery in Sport and Exercise. In R.N. Singer, H.A. Hausenblas, C.M. Janelle (eds) *Handbook of Sport Psychology*, 2nd edn. New York: John Wiley and Sons.

Hanin, Y.L. (2000) *Emotions in Sport*. Champaign, IL: Human Kinetics.

Hanton, S. & Jones, G. (1995) Antecedents of multi-dimensional state anxiety in elite competitive swimmers. *International Journal of Sport Psychology* **26**, 512–523.

Hardy, J., Gammage, K., & Hall, C. (2001). A descriptive study of athlete self-talk. *Sport Psychologist* **15**, 306–318.

Hardy, L. & Parfitt, G. (1991). A catastrophe model of anxiety and performance, *British Journal of Psychology* **82**, 163–178.

Hardy, L. & Parfitt, G. (1994). The development of a model for the provision of psychological support to a national squad. *The Sport Psychologist* **8**, 126–142.

Hardy, L. (1996). Testing the predictions of the cusp catastrophe model of anxiety and performance. *Sport Psychologist* **10**, 140–156.

Hardy, L. 1997, The Coleman Roberts Griffith Address: Three myths about applied consultancy work. *Journal of Applied Sport Psychology* **9**(2), 277–294.

Hardy, L., Jones, G., & Gould, D. (1996). *Understanding Psychological Preparation for Sport: Theory and Practice of Elite Performers*. Chichester: John Wiley.

Hardy, L., Parfitt, G. & Pates, J. (1994). Performance catastrophes in sport: A test of the hysteresis hypothesis. *Journal of Sports Sciences* **12**, 327–334.

Harkins, S.G. & Szymanski, K. (1989) Social loafing and group evaluation. *Journal of Personality and Social Psychology* **56**: 934–941.

Harrison, J., Mullen, P. & Green, L. (1992). A meta-analysis of studies of the Health Belief Model with adults. *Health Education Research: Theory and Practice* **7**, 107–116.

Harter, S. (1978) Effectance motivation reconsidered: Towards a developmental model. *Human Development* **21**: 34–64.

Hausenblas, H. & Symons Downs, D. (2002). Exercise dependence: a systematic review. *Psychology of Sport and Exercise* **3**, 89–123.

Hausenblas, H., Carron, A. & Mack, D. (1997). Application of the theories of reasoned action and planned behavior: A meta-analysis. *Journal of Sport and Exercise Psychology* **19**, 36–51.

Hayes, N. (1997) *Doing Qualitative Analysis in Psychology*. London: Taylor & Francis.

Hill, A. (1965). The environment and disease: Association or causation? *Proceedings of the Royal Society of Medicine* **58**, 295–300.

Holt, J.H. (1987) *The social laboring effect: A study of the effects of social identity on group productivity in real and notional groups using Ringelmann's method*. Unpublished manuscript. University of Kent.

Hooke, R. (1972) Statistics sports and some other things. In Tanur et al (eds) *Statistics: A Guide to the Unknown*. San Francisco: Holden-Day.

Houlston, D.R. and Lowes, R. (1993). Anticipatory cue-utilisation processes amongst expert and non-expert wicketkeepers in cricket. *International Journal of Sport Psychology* **24**, 59–73.

House, R. J. (1971). A path-goal theory of leader effectiveness. *Administrative Science Leadership Review* **16**, 321–339.

Ingham, A. G., Levinger, G., Graves, J. & Peckham, V. (1974). The Ringelmann effect: Studies of group size and group performance. *Journal of Experimental Social Psychology* **10**, 371–384.

Isen, A.M. & Levin, P.A. (1972). Effect of feeling good on helping: Cookies and kindness. *Journal of Personality and Social Psychology* **21**, 384–388.

Jackson, J.M. & Padgett, V.R. (1982). With a little help from my friend: Social loafing and the Lennon–McCartney songs. *Personality and Social Psychology Bulletin* **8**, 672–677.

Jackson, S., & Roberts, G.C. (1992). Positive performance states of athletes: Toward a conceptual understanding of peak performance. *The Sport Psychologist* **6**, 156–171.

James W. (1890) *Principles of Psychology*. New York: Holt.

Janis, I. (1982). *Groupthink: Psychological Studies of Policy Decisions and Fiascoes*. Boston MA: Houghton Mifflin.

Janz, N. & Becker, M. (1984). The Health Belief Model: A decade later. *Health Education Quarterly* **11**, 1–47.

Johnson, R.D. & Downing, L.L. (1979). Deindividuation and valence of cues: Effects on prosocial and anti-social behavior. *Journal of Personality and Social Psychology* **37**, 1532–1538.

Johnston, L.H., Corban, R.M. & Clarke P (1999). Multimethod Approaches to the investigation of adherence issues within sport and Exercise: Qualitative and quantitative techniques. In S. Bull (ed.), *Adherence Issues in Exercise & Sport*. Chichester, Wiley & Sons.

Jokela, M. & Hanin Y.L. (1999) Does the individual zone of optimal functioning model discriminate between successful and less successful athletes? A meta-analysis. *Journal of Sports Sciences* **17**, 873–887

Jones, G. (1993). The role of performance profiling in cognitive behavioral interventions in sport. *The Sport Psychologist* **7**, 160–172.

Jones, G., Swain, A. & Hardy, L. (1993) Intensity and direction dimensions of competitive state anxiety and relationships with performance. *Journal of Sports Sciences* **11**, 523–532.

Kahneman, D. (1973). *Attention and Effort*. Englewood Cliffs NJ: Prentice Hall.

Kelly, G.A. (1955) *The Psychology of Personal Constructs*. New York: Norton.

Kerr, J.H. (1985) The experience of arousal: A new basis for studying arousal effects in sport. *Journal of Sports Sciences* **3**, 169–179.

Kerr, J.H. (1999). *Experiencing Sport: Reversal Theory*. Chichester: Wiley.

Kleiber, D.A., & Roberts, G.C. (1981). The effects of sport experience in the development of social character: An exploratory investigation. *Journal of Sport Psychology* **3**, 114–122.

Krane, V. (1994) The mental readiness form as a measure of competitive state anxiety. *The Sport Psychologist* **8**(2), 176–189.

Kubler-Ross, E. (1969). *On Death and Dying*. New York: Macmillan.

Landin, D. & Hebert, E.P. (1999). The influence of self-talk on the performance of skilled female tennis players. *Journal of Applied Sport Psychology* **11**, 263–282.

Lane, A.M., Sewell, D.F., Terry, P.C., Bartram, D. & Nesti, M.S. (1999). Confirmatory factor analysis of the CSAI-2. *Journal of Sports Sciences* **17**, 505–512.

Latané, B. and Darley, J.M. (1970) *The Unresponsive Bystander: Why Doesn't he Help?* Englewood Cliffs, NJ: Prentice Hall.

Latané, B., Williams, K., & Harkins, S., (1979). Many hands make light the work: The causes and consequences of social loafing. *Journal of Personality and Social Psychology* **37**, 822–832.

Latham, G.P. & Locke, E.A. (1979). Goal-setting: A motivational technique that works. *Organizational Dynamics* **8**, 68–80.

Lavallee, L. & Flint, F. (1996). The relationship of stress competitive anxiety, mood state, and social support to athletic injury. *Journal of Athletic Training* **31**, 296–299.

Lazarus, R. (1966). *Psychological Stress and Coping Process*. New York: McGraw-Hill.

Lehman, D.R. & Reifman, A. (1987). Spectator influence on basketball officiating. *Journal of Social Psychology* **127**, 663–675.

Lepper, M.R., Greene, D., & Nisbett, R.E. (1973) Undermining children's intrinsic interest with extrinsic rewards: A test of the overjustification hypothesis. *Journal of Personality and Social Psychology* **28**, 129–137.

LeUnes A. Hayward S.A. & Daiss S. (1988) Annotated bibliography on the profile of mood states in sport, 1975–1988. *Journal of Sport Behavior* **11**(3), 213–240.

Locke, E.A. (1991) Problems with goal-setting research in sports-and their solution. *Journal of Sport and Exercise Psychology* **8**, 311–316.

Loy, J.W. (1968) The nature of sport: A definitional effect. *Quest* **10**, 1–15.

Madden, C. (1995). Ways of coping. In Morris, T. & Summers, J. (eds) *Sport Psychology: Theory, Applications and Issues*. Milton, QLD: John Wiley.

Magill, R.A. (2001). *Motor Learning: Concepts and Applications*, 6th edn. Singapore, McGraw Hill.

Mahoney, M.J., Gabriel, T.J. & Perkins, T.S. (1987). Psychological skills and exceptional athletic performance. *The Sport Psychologist* 1, 181–199.

Marcus, B.H., Selby, V.C., Niaura, R.S. & Rossi, J.S (1992) Self-efficacy and the stages of exercise behavior change. *Research Quarterly for Exercise and Sport* 63, 60–66.

Marcus, B., Emmons, K., Simkin-Silverman, L., Linnan, L., Taylor, E., Bock, B., Roberts, M., Rossi, J., & Abrams, D. (1998). Evaluation of motivationally tailored vs. standard self-help physical activity interventions at the workplace. *American Journal of Health Promotion* 12, 246–253.

Marcus, B., Rossi, J., Selby, V., Niaura, R. & Abrams, D. (1992). The stages and processes of exercise adoption and maintenance in a worksite sample. *Health Psychology* 11, 386–395.

Marsh, P.E., Rosser, E. & Harré, R. (1978) *The Rules of Disorder*. London, Boston: Routledge and K. Paul.

Marshall, S. & Biddle, S. (2001). The transtheoretical model of behavior change: A meta-analysis of applications to physical activity and exercise. *Annals of Behavioral Medicine* 23, 229–246.

Martens, R., Burton, D., Vealey, R.S., Bump, L.A., & Smith, D. (1990). Development and validation of the competitive state anxiety inventory-2. In R. Martens, R.S. Vealey, & D. Burton (eds.) *Competitive Anxiety in Sport*. Champaign, IL: Human Kinetics Books.

Martens, R., Vealey, R.S. & Burton, D. (1990) *Competitive Anxiety in Sport*. Human Kinetics, Champaign, IL.

Martin, R.A., Kuiper, N.A., Olinger, L.J. & Dobbin, J. (1987). Is stress always bad – telic versus paratelic dominance as a stress-moderating variable. *Journal of Personality and Social Psychology* 53, 970–982.

Maslach, C. & Jackson, S.E. (1981). The measurement of experienced burnout. *Journal of Occupational Behaviour*, 2, 99–113.

Maslow, A.H, (1954) *Motivation and Personality*. New York: Harper and Row

Masters, R.S.W. (2000). Theoretical aspects of implicit learning in sport. *International Journal of Sport Psychology* 31, 530–541.

Maynard, I.W. & Cotton, P.C.J. (1993) An investigation of two stress-management techniques in a field setting. *The Sport Psychologist* 7(4), 375–388.

Maynard, I.W., Hemmings, B. & Warwick-Evans, L. (1995) The effects of a somatic intervention strategy on competitive state anxiety and performance in semiprofessional soccer players. *The Sport Psychologist* 9, 51–64.

Maynard, I.W., & Cotton, P.C.J. (1993). An investigation of two stress-management techniques in a field setting. *The Sport Psychologist* 7, 375–388.

Maynard, I.W., Hemmings, B., & Warwick-Evans, L. (1995). The effects of a somatic intervention strategy on competitive state anxiety and performance in semiprofessional soccer players. *The Sport Psychologist* 9, 51–64.

Mayo, E. (1933) *The Human Problems of an Industrial Civilization*. London: Macmillan.

McAuley, E. & Tammin, V.V. (1989) The effects of subjective and objective competitive outcomes on intrinsic motivation. *Journal of Sport and Exercise Psychology* 11, 84–93.

McAuley, E., Duncan, T.E. & Russell, D.W. (1992) Measuring causal attributions – the revised causal dimension scale (CDSII). *Personality and Social Psychology Bulletin* 18(5), 566–573.

McClelland, D.C., Atkinson, J.W., Clark, R.A. & Lowell, E.C. (1953). *The Achievement Motive*. New York: Appleton-Century-Crofts.

McGrath, J.E., & Altman, J. (1966). *Small Group Research: A Synthesis and Critique of the Field*. New York: Holt, Rinehard & Winston.

McLeroy, K., Bibeau, D., Steckler, A., & Glanz, K. (1988). An ecological perspective on health promotion programs. *Health Education Quarterly* 15, 351–377.

McNair, D.M., Lorr, M., & Droppleman, L.F. (1992), *Profile of Mood States*. EdITS, San Diego, California.

Mcpherson, S.L., French, K.E. (1991). Changes in cognitive strategies and motor skill in tennis. *Journal of Sport and Exercise Psychology* 13(1), 26–41.

Medvec, V.H., Madey, S.F., & Gilovich, T. (1995). When less is more: Counterfactual thinking and satisfaction among Olympic medalists. *Journal of Personality and Social Psychology* 69, 603–610.

Michaels, J.W., Blommel, J.M., Brocato, R.M., Linkous, R.A. and Rowe, J.S. (1982). Social facilitation and inhibition in a natural setting, *Replications in Social Psychology* 2, 21–24

Milgram, S. (1963). Behavioral study of obedience. *Journal of Abnormal and Social Psychology* 67, 371–378.

Milgram, S. (1983). *Obedience to Authority: An Experimental View*. New York: Harper Collins.

Moran, A.P. (2004). *Sport and Exercise Psychology: A Critical Introduction*. London: Routledge.

Moreno, J.L. (1960). *The Sociometry Reader*. Glencoe, Illinois: The Free Press.

Morgan, W., Brown, D., Raglin, J., O'Connor, P. & Ellickson, K. (1987). Psychological monitoring of overtraining and staleness. *British Journal of Sports Medicine* 21, 107–114.

Mullen, B. & Copper, C. (1994). The relation between group cohesiveness and performance – An integration. *Psychological Bulletin* 115, 210–227.

Mulvihill, C., Rivers, K. & Aggleton, P. (2000). *Physical Activity 'at our time': Qualitative Research Among Young People Aged 5 to 15 Years and Parents*. London: Health Education Authority.

Murgatroyd, S., Rushton, C., Apter, M.J., & Ray, C. (1978). The development of the telic dominance scale. *Journal of Personality Assessment* 12, 519–528.

Mutrie, N. (2000). Emotion, mood and physical activity. In Biddle, S., Fox, K. & Boutcher, S. (eds) *Physical Activity and Psychological Well-being*. New York: Routledge.

Neisser, U. (1976). *Cognition and Reality*. New York: W.H. Freeman & Co.

Nevill, A.M. & Holder, R.L. (1999). Home advantage in sport – An overview of studies on the advantage of playing at home. *Sports Medicine* 28, 221–236.

Nevill, A.M., Balmer, N.J. & Williams, A.M. (2002). The influence of crowd noise and experience upon refereeing decisions in football. *Psychology of Sport and Exercise* 3, 261–272.

Nevill, A.M., Newell, S.M. & Gale, S. (1996). Factors associated with home advantage in English and Scottish soccer matches. *Journal of Sports Sciences* 14, 181–186.

Nichols, J.G. (1984) Achievement motivation: Conceptions of ability, subjective experience, task choice and performance. *Psychological Review* **91**, 328–346.

Nisbett, R.E., & Wilson, T.D. (1977). Telling more than we can know: Verbal reports on mental processes. *Psychological Review* **84**, 231–259.

Norris, R., Carroll, D. & Cochrane, R. (1992). The effects of physical activity and exercise training on psychological stress and well-being in an adolescent population. *Journal of Psychosomatic Research* **36**, 55–65.

Northouse, P.G. (2001). *Leadership Theory and Practice*, 2nd edn. Thousand Oaks, CA: Sage Publications, Inc.

Oakes, P.J. & Turner, J.C. (1980). Social categorization and intergroup behaviour: Does minimal intergroup discrimination make social identity more positive? *European Journal of Social Psychology* **10**, 295–301.

Orlick, T. (1986). *Psyching for Sport: Mental Training for Athletes*. Champaign, IL: Leisure Press.

Orlick, T. (1990). *In Pursuit of Excellence: How to Win in Sport and Life Through Mental Training*. Champaign, IL: Leisure Press.

Orne, M.T. (1962). On the social psychology of the psychological experiment: With particular reference to demand characteristics and their implications. *American Psychologist* **17**, 776–783.

Paulus, P.B. (1989) *Psychology of Group Influence*, 2nd edn. Hillsdale, NJ: Erlbaum.

Paffenbarger, R., Lee, I., & Leung, R. (1994). Physical activity and personal characteristics associated with depression and suicide in American college men. *Acta Psychiatrica Scandinavia* **89**, 16–22.

Paskevich, D.M., Estabrooks, P.A. Brawley, L.R. & Carron, A.V., (2001) Group Cohesion in Sport and Exercise. In R.N. Singer, H.A. Hausenblas, and C. Jannelle (eds) *Handbook of Sport Psychology*, 2nd edn. New York: John Wiley and Sons.

Passer, M. and Sesse, M. (1983). Life stress and athletic injury: examination of positive versus negative events and three moderator variables. *Journal of Human Stress* **9**, 11–16.

Perkins Wilson & Kerr (2001). The effects of elevated arousal and mood on maximal strength performance in athletes. *Journal of Applied Sport Psychology* **13**, 239–259.

Petrie, T. (1993). Coping skills, competitive trait anxiety, and playing status: Moderating effects of the life stress injury relationship. *Journal of Sport and Exercise Psychology* **15**, 261–274.

Petty, R. & Cacciopo, J. (1986). *Communication and Persuasion: The Central and Peripheral Routes to Attitude Change*. New York: Springer-Verlag.

Poczwardowski, A., Sherman, C.P., & Henschen, K.P. (1998). A sport psychology service delivery heuristic: Building on theory and practice. *Sport Psychologist* **12**, 191–207.

Pollard, R. (1986). Home advantage in soccer: A retrospective analysis. *Journal of Sports Sciences* **4**, 237–248.

Pollard, R. (2002). Evidence of a reduced home advantage when a team moves to a new stadium. *Journal of Sports Sciences* **20**, 969–973.

Popper, K. (1959) *The Logic of Scientific Discoveries*. London: Hutchinson.

Porter, L.W. & Lawler, E.E. (1968) *Managerial Attitudes and Performance*. New York: Irwin Dorsey.

Prentice-Dunn, S. Rogers, R. (1982). Effects of Public and Private Self-Awareness on Deindividuation and Aggression. *Journal of Personality and Social Psychology*, **39** 104–113.

Prochaska, J. & DiClemente, C. (1983). Stages and processes of self-change of smoking: Toward an integrative model of change. *Journal of Consulting and Clinical Psychology* **51**, 390–395.

Prochaska, J. & Marcus, B. (1994). The Transtheoretical Model: Applications to exercise. In Dishman, R. (Ed.). *Advances in Exercise Adherence*. Champaign, IL: Human Kinetics.

Raedeke, T. (1997) Is athlete burnout more than just stress? A sport commitment perspective. *Journal of Sport and Exercise Psychology* **19**, 396–417.

Reicher, S. (1984). Social influence in the crowd: Attitudinal and behavioral effects of deindividuation in conditions of high and low group salience. *British Journal of Social Psychology* **23**, 341–350.

Renger, R. (1993) A review of the profile of mood states (POMS) in the prediction of athletic success. *Journal of Applied Sport Psychology* **5**, 78–84

Richardson, A. (1969). *Mental Imagery*. London: Routledge & Kegan Paul.

Ringelmann, M. (1913) Research on animate sources of power: The work of man. *Annales de l'Institut National Agronomique*, 2e seriotome XII, 1–40.

Rogers, C.R. (1951) *Client-centered Therapy*. Boston: Houghton Mifflin.

Rogers, R. (1983). Cognitive and physiological processes in fear appeals and attitude change: A revised theory of protection motivation. In J. Cacioppo & R. Petty (eds) *Social Psychology: A Sourcebook*. New York: Guildford Press.

Ross, M. & Berger, R. (1996). Effects of stress inoculation training on athletes' postsurgical pain and rehabilitation after orthopedic injury. *Journal of Consulting and Clinical Psychology* **64**, 406–410.

Rotella, R. (1995) *Golf is Not a Game of Perfect*. New York: Simon & Schuster

Sallis, J. & Hovell, M. (1990). Determinants of exercise behavior. *Exercise and Sport Sciences Reviews* **18**, 307–330.

Sallis, J.F., Prochaska, J.J. & Taylor, W.C. (2000). A review of correlates of physical activity of children and adolescents. *Medicine and Science in Sports and Exercise* **32**, 963–975.

Sallis, J., & Owen, N. (2002). Ecological models of health behavior. In K. Glanz, B. Rimer & F. Lewis (eds) *Health Behavior and Health Education: Theory, Research and Practice*, 3rd edn. San Francisco, CA: Jossey Bass.

Sanders, G.S., Baron, R.S. and Moore, D.L. (1978). Distraction and social comparison as mediators of social facilitation effects. *Journal of Experimental Social Psychology* **14**, 291–303.

Savelsbergh, G.J.P. and Bootsma, R.J. (1994). Perception-action coupling in hitting and catching. *International Journal of Sport Psychology* **25**, 331–343.

Schmidt, G. & Stein, G. (1991). Sport commitment: A model integrating enjoyment, dropout, and burnout. *Journal of Sport and Exercise Psychology* **13**, 254–265.

Schmidt, R.A. (1988). Motor and action perspectives on motor behavior. In O.G. Meijer & K. Roth (eds) *Complex Motor Behavior: The Motor-Action Controversy*. Amsterdam, Elsevier.

Schmidt, R.A. (1991). *Motor Learning and Performance: From Principles to Practice*. Champaign, Human Kinetics.

Schwartz, B. & Barsky, S.F. (1977). The home advantage. *Social Forces* **55**, 641–661.

Shaw, D.F. (2002). Confidence and the pre-shot routine in golf. In I.M. Cockerill (Ed.) *Solutions in Sport Psychology*. London: Thompson Publishing.

Sherif, C.W. (1936). *Orientation in Social Psychology*. New York: Harper & Row.

Sherif, M. (1956) *The Psychology of Social Norms*. New York: Harper.

Sherif, M., Harvey, O.J., White, J., Hood, William, & Sherif, C.W. (1961). *Intergroup Conflict and Cooperation: The Robbers Cave Experiment*. Norman, OK: Institute of Group Relations.

Sherman, C.P. & Poczwardowski, A. (2000) Relax!... It Ain't Easy (Or Is It?). In M.B. Anderson (ed.) *Doing Sport Psychology*. Champaign, IL: Human Kinetics.

Silva, J. (1990). An analysis of the training stress syndrome in competitive athletics. *The Journal of Applied Sport Psychology* **8**, 36–50.

Singer, R.N., Hausenblas, H.A. & Jannelle, C. (2001) *Handbook of Sport Psychology*, 2nd edn. New York: John Wiley and Sons.

Skinner, B.F. (1938) *The Behavior of Organisms. An Experimental Analysis*. New York: Appleton-Century.

Slater, M.R., & Sewell, D.F. (1994). An examination of the cohesion-performance relationship in university hockey teams. *Journal of Sports Sciences* **12**, 423–431.

Smith, R. (1986). Toward a cognitive-affective model of athletic burnout. *Journal of Sport Psychology* **8**, 36–50.

Smith, R.E., Schutz, R.W., Smoll, F.L. & Ptacek, J.T. (1995). Development and validation of a multidimensional measure of sport-specific psychological skills – the athletic coping skills inventory – 28. *Journal of Sport and Exercise Psychology* **17**, 379–398.

Smoll, F.L. & Smith, R.E. (1989). Leadership behaviors in sport: A theoretical model and research paradigm. *Journal of Applied Social Psychology* **19**, 1522–1551.

Snyder, E.E. & Purdy, D.A. (1985). The home advantage in collegiate basketball. *Sociology of Sport Journal* **2**, 352–356.

Spielberger, C.D., Gorsuch, R.L. & Lushene, R.L. (1970) *Manual for the State-Trait Anxiety Inventory*. Consulting Psychologists, Palo Alto, CA.

Stokols, D. (1992). Establishing and maintaining healthy environments: Towards a social ecology of health promotion. *American Psychologist* **47**, 6–22.

Strack, F., Martin, L. & Stepper, S. (1988). Inhibiting and facilitating conditions of the human smile: A nonobtrusive test of the facial feedback hypothesis. *Journal of Personality and Social Psychology* **54**, 768–777.

Strauss, B. (2002). The impact of supportive spectator behavior on performance in team sports. *International Journal of Sport Psychology* **33**, 372–390.

Svebak, S. & Murgatroyd, S. (1985) Metamotivational dominance: A multimethod validation of reversal theory constructs. *Journal of Personality and Social Psychology* **48**(1), 107–116.

Szabo, A. (2000). Physical activity as a source of psychological dysfunction. In Biddle, S., Fox, K. & Boutcher, S. (eds) *Physical Activity and Psychological Well-being*. New York: Routledge.

Tajfel, H. & Turner, J.C. (1986). The social identity theory of intergroup behavior. In S. Worchel & W. Austin (eds) *Psychology of Intergroup Relations*. Chicago: Nelson-Hall.

Tajfel, H., Billig, M., Bundy. R. & Flament, C. (1971). Social categorization and intergroup behaviour. *European Journal of Social Psychology* **1**, 149–178.

Taylor, A. (2000). The effects of exercise on self-perceptions and self-esteem. In Biddle, S., Fox, K. & Boutcher, S. (eds) *Physical Activity and Psychological Well-being*. New York: Routledge.

Taylor, J.A. and Shaw D.F. (2002). The effects of outcome imagery on golf-putting performance. *Journal of Sport Sciences* **20**, 607–613.

Taylor, S.E. (1989). *Positive Illusions: Creative Self-deception and the Healthy Mind*. New York: Basic Books.

Terry P. (1995) The efficacy of mood state profiling with elite performers: A review and synthesis. *The Sport Psychologist* **9**, 309–324.

The Sports Council and Health Education Authority (1992). *Allied Dunbar National Fitness Survey: Main Findings*. London: Sports Council and Health Education Authority.

Thibaut, J.W. and Kelley, H.H. (1959) *The Social Psychology of Groups*. New York: Wiley.

Thomas, J. & Nelson, J. (2001) *Research Methods in Physical Activity*, 4th edn. Champaign, IL: Human Kinetics.

Thomas, P.R., Murphy, S.M. & Hardy, L. (1999). Test of performance strategies: Development and preliminary validation of a comprehensive measure of athletes' psychological skills. *Journal of Sport Sciences* **17**, 697–711.

Triplett, N. (1897). The dynamogenic factors in pacemaking and competition. *American Journal of Psychology* **9**, 507–553.

Trost, S., Owen, N., Bauman, A., Sallis, J. & Brown, W. (2002). Correlates of adults' participation in physical activity: review and update. *Medicine and Science in Sports and Exercise* **34**, 1996–2001.

Tuckman, B.W. (1965) Developmental sequences in small groups. *Psychological Bulletin* **63**(6), 384–399.

Udry, E. & Andersen, M. (2002). Athletic injury and sport behavior. In T. Horn (ed.) *Advances in Sport Psychology*, 2nd edn. Champaign, IL: Human Kinetics.

Vallerand, R.J. (1983) Effect of differential amounts of positive feedback on the intrinsic motivation of male hockey players. *Journal of Sport Psychology* **6**, 94–102.

Vallerand, R.J. & Reid, G. (1984) On the causal effects of perceived competence on intrinsic motivation: A test of cognitive evaluation theory. *Journal of Sport Psychology* **6**, 94–102.

Vallerand, R.J., & Blanchard, C.M. (2000) The study of emotion in sport and exercise: Historical, definitional and conceptual perspectives. In Y.L. Hanin (ed.) *Emotions in Sport*. Champaign, IL: Human Kinetics.

Vanderswaag, H. (1972) *Towards a Philosophy of Sport*. Addison & Wesley.

Vealey, R.S. (1986). Conceptualization of sport-confidence and competitive orientation: Preliminary investigation and instrument development. *Journal of Sport Psychology* **8**, 221–246.

Vealey, R.S. (2001) Understanding and enhancing self-confidence in athletes. In R.N. Singer, H.A. Hausenblas, and C. Jannelle (eds) *Handbook of Sport Psychology*, 2nd edn. New York: John Wiley and Sons.

Vroom, V.H. (1964) *Work and Motivation*. New York: Wiley.

Wankel, L. & Kriesel, P. (1985). Factors underlying enjoyment of youth sports: Sport and age group comparisons. *Journal of Sport Psychology* **7**, 51–74.

Ward, P., and Williams, A.M. (2003). Perceptual and cognitive skill development in soccer. The multidimensional nature of expert performance. *Journal of Sport and Exercise Psychology* **25**(1), 93–111.

Watson, D., Clark, L.A. & Tellegen, A. (1988). Development and validation of brief measures of positive and negative affect: The PANAS scales. *Journal of Personality and Social Psychology* **54**: 1063–1070.

Watson, J.B. (1913) Psychology as the behaviorist views it. *Psychological Review* **20**, 158–177.

Watson, R.I. (1973). Investigation into deindividuation using a cross-cultural survey technique. *Journal of Personality and Social Psychology* **25**, 342–345.

Weinberg, R.S. and Gould, D. (2003). *Foundations of Sport and Exercise Psychology*, 3rd edn. Champaign, IL: Human Kinetics.

Weiner, B. (1985). An attributional theory of achievement motivation and emotion. *Psychological Review* **92**, 548–573.

Wiese-Bjornstal, D. & Smith, A. (1993). Counseling strategies for enhanced recovery of injured athletes within a team approach. In D. Pargman (Ed.), *Psychological Bases of Sport Injuries*. Morgantown, WV: Fitness Information Technology.

Wiese-Bjornstal, D., Smith, A., & LaMott, E. (1995). A model of psychologic response to athletic injury and rehabilitation. *Athletic Training* **1**, 17–30.

Wiese-Bjornstal, D., Smith, A., & Shaffer, S. & Morrey, M. (1998). An integrated model of response to sport injury: Psychological and sociological dynamics. *Journal of Applied Sport Psychology* **10**, 5–25.

Williams, J. & Andersen, M. (1998). Psychosocial antecedents of sport injury: Review and critique of the stress and injury model. *Journal of Applied Sport Psychology* **10**, 5–25.

Williams, J. (2001). Psychology of injury risk and prevention. In Singer, R., Hausenblas, H. & Janelle, C. (eds) *Handbook of Sport Psychology*, 2nd edn. New York: John Wiley.

Williams, J.M. & Harris, D.V. (2001) Relaxation and energizing techniques for regulation of arousal. In J.M. Williams (ed.) *Applied Sport Psychology: Personal Growth to Peak Performance*, 4th edn. Palo Alto, CA: Mayfield.

Williams, K.D., Nida, S.A., Baca, L.D. & Latané, B. (1989). Social loafing and swimming: Effects of identifiability on individual and relay performance of intercollegiate swimmers. *Basic & Applied Social Psychology* **10**(1), 73–81.

Williams. A.M., Davids, K. and Williams, J.G. (1999). *Visual Perception and Action in Sport*. London, E & FN Spon.

Williamson, D., Netemeyer, R., Jackman, L., Anderson, D., Funsch, C. & Rabalais, J. (1995). Structural equation modeling of risk factors for the development of eating disorders symptoms in female athletes. *International Journal of Eating Disorders* **17**, 387–393.

Wulf, G., McConnel. N., Gärtner, M., Schwarz, A. (2002). Enhancing the learning of sport skills through external-focus feedback. *Journal of Motor Behavior* **34**(2), 171–182.

Yukelson, D., Weinberg, R., & Jackson, A. (1984). A multidimensional group cohesion instrument for intercollegiate basketball. *Journal of Sport Psychology* **6**, 103–117.

Zajonc, R.B. (1965) Social facilitation. *Science* **149**, 269–274.

Zajonc, R.B., Heingartner, A. and Herman, E.M. (1969) Social enhancement and impairment of performance in the cockroach. *Journal of Personality and Social Psychology* **13**, 83–92.

Zeller, R. and Jurkovac, T. (1988). Doming the stadium: the case for baseball. *Sport Place International* **3**, 35–38.

Zimbardo, P.G. (1969) The human choice: Individuation, reason, and order versus deindividuation, impulse, and chaos. In W.T. Arnold & D. Levine (eds) *Nebraska Symposium on Motiviation*, Vol 17, 237–307.

Zinsser, N., Bunker, L. & Williams, J.M. (2001) Cognitive techniques for building confidence and enhancing performance. In J.M. Williams (ed.) *Applied Sport Psychology: Personal Growth to Peak Performance*, 4th edn. Palo Alto, CA: Mayfield.

INDEX